MULTIMEDIA DATABASE SYSTEMS
Design and Implementation Strategies

MULTIMEDIA DATABASE SYSTEMS
Design and Implementation Strategies

Edited by

Kingsley C. Nwosu
AT&T Bell Laboratories
Whippany, New Jersey, USA

■

Bhavani Thuraisingham
The MITRE Corporation
Bedford, Massachusetts, USA

■

P. Bruce Berra
CASE Center, Syracuse University
Syracuse, New York, USA

KLUWER ACADEMIC PUBLISHERS
Boston/London/Dordrecht

Distributors for North America:
Kluwer Academic Publishers
101 Philip Drive
Assinippi Park
Norwell, Massachusetts 02061 USA

Distributors for all other countries:
Kluwer Academic Publishers Group
Distribution Centre
Post Office Box 322
3300 AH Dordrecht, THE NETHERLANDS

Library of Congress Cataloging-in-Publication Data

A C.I.P. Catalogue record for this book is available
from the Library of Congress.

Printed on acid-free paper.

Printed in the United States of America

CONTENTS

v

PREFACE

It is unarguably evident that the advent of Multi-Media Information Processing (MMIP) has profoundly and irreversible changed our technological landscape. MMIP encompasses the integrated generation, representation, storage, retrieval, processing, transmission, and presentation of dependent and independent data that are expressed in multifarious time dependent and independent media. Over the years, several technological approaches have been utilized to realize some form of Multi-Media systems. However, past and present experience indicate that in order to adequately, sufficiently, and meaningfully address the capabilities of MMIP, Multi-Media Data Base Systems (MMDBS) have to be designed and developed. For conventional text-based information processing, activities like data storage, access, manipulation, etc., have advanced considerably; however, for systems that incorporate multifarious data such as continuous media data, those activities pose novel problems. The main issues which multimedia database researchers/designers need to face include, but not limited to:

- development of sophisticated multimedia database conceptual models,
- design of multimedia database query and retrieval languages,
- design of powerful indexing and organization techniques,
- development of efficient storage layout models to manage real-time multimedia data,
- development of efficient and reliable retrieval and delivery strategies, and
- development of flexible, adaptive, and reliable presentation techniques.

In this edition of **Multimedia Database Systems**, we concentrate on the issues related to storage, query language design, presentation, search and retrieval (including indexing), and the object-oriented paradigm for designing MMDBS.

We are very grateful to the authors for their cooperation and timely delivery of the Chapters. We are also thankful to Alex Greene of Kluwer Academic Publishers for his dedication towards the publication of this book.

Kingsley C. Nwosu
Bhavani Thuraisingham
P. Bruce Berra

CONTRIBUTORS

Cyril Orji
School of Computer Science
Florida International University
Miami, FL 33199, USA.

Scott T. Campbell
Technology & Development
AT&T Global Information Solutions
Dayton, Ohio 45479, USA

Soon M. Chung
Dept. of Computer Science and Engr.
Wright State University
Dayton, Ohio 45435, USA

Brigitte Simonnot and Malik Smail
CRIN/CNRS, Batiment LORIA B.P 239
F54506 Vandoeuvre-les-Nancy, France

Qi Yan and Son K. Dao
Hughes Research Laboratory
3011 Malibu Canyon Rd.
Malibu, CA 90265

Asha Vellaika
Hughes Research Laboratory
3011 Malibu Canyon Rd.
Malibu, CA 90265

Rune Hjelsvold, Roger Midstraum and Olav Sandstaa
Dept. of Comp. Systems & Telematics
Norwegian Inst. of Tech.,
N-7034 Trondheim, Norway

Stacie Hibino and Elke A. Rudensteine
Dept. of EECS, Univ. of Michigan
1301 Beal Avenue, Ann Arbor,
MI 48109-2122

Nael Hirzalla and Ahmed Karmouch
Dept. of Electrical Engineering,
University of Ottawa,
Ottawa, Ont. K1N 6N5 Canada

Taeck-Geun Kwon and Sukho Lee
Dept. Comp. Engr., Seoul Nat'l Univ.,
Seoul 151-742, Korea

Michael Vazirgiannis
Dept. of Informatics,
Univ. of Athens, Ktiria Typa
Panepistimiopolis, 15771 Ilisia,
Athens, Greece

Donald A. Adjeroh and Moon C. Lee
Dept. of Computer Science,
The Chinese Univ. of Hong Kong
Shatin N-7, Hong Kong

Heiko Thimm and Wolfgang Klas
GMD-IPSI, DolivostraBe 15, D-64293,
Darmstadt, Germany

Michel Adiba
IMAG-LGI, Grenoble University,
BP 53, 38041
Grenoble Cedex 9 France

1

MULTIMEDIA DBMS – REALITY OR HYPE?

Cyril Orji

School of Computer Science
Florida International Univ.
Miami, Florida, USA

1 INTRODUCTION

A Database Management System (DBMS) is "... the software that allows one or many persons to use and/or modify ... data [stored in a database]..."[1]. A major role of the DBMS is to allow the user to deal with the data in abstract terms, rather than as the computer stores the data. This book is devoted to the discussion of issues relevant to multimedia database management. In succeeding chapters, attempts are made to question and provide answers to important issues. What really is the role of a DBMS in multimedia data presentation? How feasible is it? Assuming that a multimedia DBMS is feasible, is it necessary, or do we need to build presentation routines for multimedia applications and use them together with existing DBMSs?

In this introductory chapter, we recap some of the views expressed on this issue during the 1995 International Workshop on Multimedia DBMS. Although questions arose that helped the participants gain a better understanding of the issues involved, it is safe to say that a majority of the workshop participants agreed to the need for a multimedia DBMS. In fact, this is reflected in the themes addressed in the workshop papers. Some of those issues form the central themes of this book. These issues include proper and accurate characterization of multimedia data, multimedia data integration, and multimedia query language and processing. Others include multimedia data management and storage issues, and multimedia retrieval and indexing.

2   VIDEO SERVICES

Video delivery systems are a very important class of multimedia application and have attracted a lot of attention from the research community. We first present a brief overview of types of video services, their characteristics and delivery properties before discussing the more general issues of multimedia DBMS.

2.1   Types of Video Services

The classification of video services is primarily based on the flexibility of control by which a user can obtain specific video entities or sessions; and the temporal implications. We account for the services that are currently available to users and the services that should be available with the advent of improved digital information processing technologies. Currently, users can generally obtain their video services through Community Antenna Television (CATV) or simply Cable Television, Pay-Per-View (PPV), or Video Repository Center (VRC). Furthermore, users want to be able to obtain their video services through Video On Demand (VOD) service. A summary of their distinguishing characteristics is presented in Table 1.

Type of Service	Characteristics		
	Program Availability	FF/ Reverse	Cost of Service
CATV	Only at designated times; Once a day	No	Flat rate, independent of programs viewed.
PPV	Only at designated times; More than once a day	No	Sliding rate based Per program viewed.
VCR	Always, if program is on tape	Yes	Rental cost
VOD	Any time	Yes	Not clearly defined. Possibly based on amount of video data.

Table 1   Video Services and Major Characteristics

CATV Service

Subscribers to CATV services obtain their video information by channel selection through a TV at specified times. The services are broadcast to the subscribers from a video source and special devices may be required to block unauthorized access. The services are multicast to the users and the users must tune to the appropriate channel and at designated times in order to view a specific program. Users can tune to a particular program during its transmission, but they will be unable to view the program after its transmission unless it is being re-broadcast at another time. The re-broadcast for CATV is infrequent or seldom, consequently, as a distinguishing characteristic, we will assume, without loss of generality, that CATV programs are broadcast once a day. The CATV service customers are usually charged flat rates. So, whether the customer viewed any programs or not, he/she must pay for the service.

PPV Service

Subscribers to PPV services have more viewing opportunities than the CATV customers because programs are broadcast more than once a day. Similar to CATV service, PPV programs are broadcast at specific times. Due to the frequent re-broadcast, the PPV service gives its customers viewing time flexibility to view a particular program from its scheduled times. Unlike the CATV customers, the PPV customers are charged per program viewed. After a customer has been given access to view a program, whether he/she actually viewed the program, is inconsequential - he/she must pay for it.

VRC Service

Besides satisfying one's viewing desire through the CATV or PPV service, one can obtain desired video tapes from video rental centers at per tape charge. A video rental center stores a number of recorded events (such as movies, sports, and music videos) and rents them to the public. Usually, a customer needs a tape playing device interface to a TV (such as a VCR) to view the video tapes. We assume that there is no limit to the number of tapes that a customer may rent. However, as a business policy, a video rental center may prefer to impose a limit on the number of tapes that may be rented at a given time. A disadvantage of the VRC service is that not all programs or movies are available for rental. Furthermore, viewing recorded versions of some events may take away the element of realism, suspense, or simultaneity.

VOD Service

In a VOD service, a customer has full control of what to see, when to see, and how to see any video program. It offers a customer all the services available in

CATV, PPV, and VRC services with much more flexibility. Under the VOD service, a user has the capability to request for any available program, real time or not, at any time, and starting at any specified duration of the event (in the case of recorded events). Like the VCR, one can fast-forward or reverse any video program and can jump to any part of a video with minimal delay. Customers can also terminate a video program they are viewing at any time. Since there is a control and management site that extracts the required video segments for the customers, the customers can be billed based on the amount of video data viewed (this is possible, but may not be feasible); not a flat rate or per program. One of the major limiting constraints on VOD is the ability to satisfy the huge bandwidth and capacity requirements of VOD. Currently, arrays of inexpensive disks (RAID) [17] and high performance servers with large switching capacity to instantly connect data from disks to I/O channels are used to address these problems.

2.2   Video Delivery Properties

There are certain requirements and expectations about a video program that customers may not be willing to compromise. With respect to viewing video programs, users are particularly cognizant of the quality of the video image and the response time.

Quality of Image

The quality of the image is very important to a user. Usually, video customers can afford to make some sacrifices provided that the quality of the image does not become unbearably degraded. With respect to digital video, there are a number of characteristics that greatly affect image quality. Prominent among them is the digital video coding rate. For digitally encoded videos with 1.5 $Mbps$, the quality is close to that of videos from a VHS-VCR. At 3 $Mbps$ digital coding, image quality comparable to the NTSC Entertainment video is obtained while at 6 $Mbps$ image quality comparable to the NTSC Studio video is obtained. Obviously, increasing the bit coding rate for digital video increases the image quality which invariably increases the amount of data that must be handled and transported. The amount of data that must be available at a display site or location is one of the problems of continuous media since this volume of data is inherently large and the transport media were not originally designed to solve these kinds of problems. However, intelligent utilization and advancement of current technologies have mitigated the problems.

Response Time

Another important issue to video customers is the timing delay between requesting for a particular video program and getting the requested video scenes. For all practical purposes, a customer's expected or real response time depends largely on the type of service requested. In the case of the CATV, the customer has absolutely no option on program availability since programs are usually scheduled for specific number of times (usually once per day) at inflexible times. A customer can only view a program at the scheduled time. Once a CATV program is being broadcast, the response time becomes equivalent to the delay necessary for changing from one channel to another.

For PPV, on the other hand, a given program is scheduled more frequently over a 24-hour period than a CATV program. In that case, given the static and pre-knowledge of the showing times of PPV programs, the response time is usually minimal relative to the scheduled time. A time delay, in the magnitude of one to a couple minutes, is usually permissible.

For VOD, due to its complexity and technological requirements, the response time is greatly affected by a number of factors. However, the response time should be in the range of the CATV and PPV response times. In other words, it is expected that the response time may be greater than CATV response time, but should be less than the PPV response time. Since different customers may be requesting the same or different programs at any given time, the response time is greatly affected by the technology of the storage and delivery system. As an example, consider a local multimedia server serving a neighborhood. For this example adapted from [7] (See Figure 1), due to disk I/O bandwidth limitation, only 120 out of the 1000 households can simultaneously receive movies-on-demand. The number of concurrent subscribers can be increased by using one of the following techniques:

- Increasing the number of disks which will increase the I/O throughput.

- Transmitting video that have a lower data rate demand. For example, instead of transmitting 16-Mbps HDTV movies, 3- to 6-Mbps MPEG-2 movies can be transmitted.

- Using techniques that increase the capacity of VOD systems such as segmentation and multicasting.

The response time for VRC requests is very different from its counterparts. For one, the customer has to make a trip to the video center, and secondly, he/she

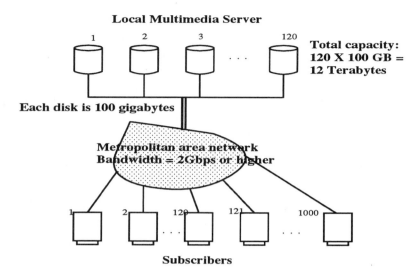

Figure 1 A local multimedia server serving a neighborhood of 1,000 households. Server provides HDTV-type movies-on-demand; only 120 users can receive movies-on-demand simultaneously. (Adapted from [7].)

has to contend with other customers by either waiting in line or waiting for some time for a tape availability. In other words, considerable amount of time may elapse from the time one got a desire to view a given program and the time that he/she is actually able to bring the tape home. Sometimes, a customer may have to visit more than one VRC in order to obtain a frequently requested tape. Therefore, an implicit assumption with obtaining videos from VRC is that a customer is willing to expend the possible considerable time-delay involved.

3 MULTIMEDIA DATABASE MANAGEMENT

Is multimedia DBMS a reality or is it a hype by database researchers? Participants at the 1995 International Workshop on Multimedia DBMS battled with this question. As noted earlier, although a majority of the workshop participants felt very strongly about the need for a multimedia DBMS, there were some strong arguments to the contrary by other participants. These participants were of the view that there was really no need to define or build a multimedia DBMS. They believe that current DBMSs are able to handle storage and computational issues of data – be they traditional or multimedia. What is needed, they assert, is a strong front end or back end presentation manager, external to the DBMS which can be called upon to present multimedia data when required. This argument is based on the notion that presentation has always been, and must remain external to the DBMS. It is important though to note that proponents of this view are not opposed to the use of a DBMS in a multimedia environment - they believe that there is a strong need to manage multimedia meta-data with a DBMS.

A counter opinion is that presentation is a very important part of multimedia data processing. The argument was advanced that with traditional data processing, early designers of DBMSs saw no need for presentation because in a sense there was nothing to present. However, with the advent of multimedia data processing, there is a strong need to build a database management system that can handle multimedia data seamlessly from input to output (presentation). Presentation, they argued, is the key to multimedia data processing and for efficiency, the presentation manager must be a part of the multimedia DBMS.

There was also an argument for the formal development of a data model for multimedia data. A data model is a collection of tools for describing data, data relationships, data semantics and constraints on data [2]. A clearly defined data model would facilitate the construction of a multimedia DBMS. Such a new data model must capture the storage and delivery properties of multimedia data.

Some of the key strengths of the relational data model [3] is that it is well understood with a strong based mathematical foundation. Incidentally, newer data models like the Object-Oriented data model and even multimedia data are less well understood. The result is that a good portion of the DBMS research community have more confidence with the relational model and use it as a basis for exploring new models. A typical example would be the Postgres database management system [4], which is clearly an extension of the Ingres relational database management system [18]. However, Postgres is, in a sense, a completely different system, supporting both the relational model and a host of functionalities typical of object-oriented systems.

In Chapter 2, Campbell & Chung, provide a characterization of multimedia data management. They survey four techniques that have been used in multimedia data management. These include the use of local storage, media server, binary large objects, and Object-Oriented methodologies. The use of local storage in the management of multimedia data is analogous to the use of traditional file processing before the advent of database management system. In this technique, multimedia data management is directly supported by a conventional operating system just like early file processing systems. Permanent multimedia records are stored in various files, and a number of application programs are written to extract records from and add records to the appropriate files.

Because multimedia data are usually large, it is becoming commonplace to use hierarchical storage scheme to store them. At the lowest level of such a storage scheme would be optical tapes or disks. Although these storage media have very high latency, their storage cost per byte is usually small. To compensate for the high latency of these tertiary media, frequently accessed multimedia data would be kept in magnetic disks which have a relatively low access latency when compared with tertiary media. Although the use of local storage has the attraction of simplicity, ease of implementation and ease of delivery, it has associated with it most of the disadvantages of a traditional file processing system – which were resolved by the use of database management system. Such problems include the difficulty of having the application program maintain the multimedia data. This is likely to result in possible concurrency control problems and very high overhead in the development of application programs. These concurrency control and update problems are made even more severe in a network environment.

A media server can help improve performance in a network environment. A media server is essentially a shared resource capable of delivering multimedia data. The problem with a media server is that to a large extent it is just a resource manager; it is unable on its own to determine the best access method for data delivery. This is still the responsibility of the application program.

Binary Large Objects (BLOBs) have been used to integrate multimedia data with traditional data. In this technique, a traditional relational database management system can "process" both traditional and multimedia data. As the name suggests, the multimedia data is treated as a binary large object pointed to by an untyped variable (attribute) in a relational table. When requested, the BLOBs are simply delivered to an application program as blocks of data. The application program is responsible for processing them intelligently. An advantage to this scheme is that it provides some level of associative access and minimally integrates multimedia with traditional data managed by a relational DBMS. There are, however, some obvious problems associated with this approach. The key factor here is that the DBMS is unaware of the structure of the BLOB and cannot apply delivery and processing optimizations techniques to a BLOB.

Object-oriented techniques have been used to overcome some of the problems associated with BLOBs. In [5], object-oriented techniques are applied to multimedia data. The object-oriented techniques of class definitions, encapsulation, and inheritance provide the database management system a richer understanding of the multimedia data. These can be exploited by the system for efficient delivery and presentation. More work, however, needs to be done before object-oriented techniques can be considered as an adequate solution for all storage, indexing, retrieval and updating issues associated with multimedia data.

One of the challenges for the evolution of future DBMS is their ability to handle multimedia data in an integrated and efficient way. Several approaches have addressed the topic of multimedia data management and many commercially available DBMS already allow storage of texts, images and sound. However, most of these systems do not offer integrated capabilities for building, updating and querying presentations which combine and synchronize different kinds of data [19].

The STORM project discussed in Chapter 3 is an attempt to address some of these issues. In particular two issues are addressed: (1) modeling and management of time-based data, and (2) capabilities, languages and interfaces for building, querying and updating multimedia data. STORM is a prototype under development at Grenoble University, France. It is built on top of the O_2 DBMS and provides facilities for describing and storing time-based objects, and for building sequential or parallel presentations of multimedia data.

The STORM DBMS integrates structural and temporal aspects for building different presentations of multimedia objects and integrates structural operators and temporal relationships for defining multimedia presentations. The approach in STORM provides sequential and parallel presentations synchronizing different objects. These presentations are themselves stored as database objects and can be derived automatically from the schema, updated and queried.

4   MULTIMEDIA INTEGRATION

Three chapters discuss issues related to multimedia integration. In Chapter 9, Adjeroh & Lee present a predictive synchronization approach to distributed multimedia presentation. Their scheme is premised on predicting the optimal retrieval schedule based on the desired presentation time and network characteristics. This schedule is used to construct a presentation graph representing the multimedia objects, their intervals and their temporal relations as a timed Petri net. Using the Petri net approach, they develop models to capture network delays and limited bandwidth. These are then used to derive a retrieval schedule for the multimedia objects and the amount of buffer required to ensure that a stated Quality of Service (QoS) is maintained. On the issue of synchronization for special effects such as *skip, pause, resume, reverse, etc.*, it is suggested that local secondary storage can be used to temporarily keep the retrieved objects after they have been presented.

In Chapter 12 , Thimm & Klas argue that Playout Management must be an integrated service of a multimedia DBMS. Reporting on their experience at GMD-IPSI where they are developing the distributed multimedia database management system AMOS (**A**ctive **M**edia **O**bject **S**tore), they argue that the integration makes the handling of multimedia database management system more efficient since the storage, retrieval, buffering, and playout management is performed by one consistent system. Playout management, Thimm & Klas point out, consists of four distinct tasks:

- *Device Management*: to effect control of possibly multiple devices involved in the presentation.

- *Data Stream Management*: to ensure that for continuous data, playout deadlines are met.

- *Synchronization Enforcement*: to ensure a global enforcement of synthetic, natural (intermedia), and intramedia synchronization.

- *Support of Interactivity*: to ensure that user interactions are appropriately responded to, for example, in interactive on-demand environments.

This chapter also presents an excellent overview of issues related to playout management and the need to integrate the services within a multimedia DBMS. It suggests alternative solutions and discusses the solution strategy adopted in AMOS.

In Chapter 8, Vazirgiannis proposes a new object-oriented model for a complete representation of multimedia objects and applications. The application representation is based on composition (spatial and temporal) modeling and scenario modeling. An important feature of their model is that there is an integrated modeling of the multimedia objects as well as of the applications that utilize them.

5 QUERY LANGUAGE AND PROCESSING

Multimedia applications involve very huge amount of data. There is, therefore, need to develop novel techniques for data processing. Since multimedia data contains a mixture of video, image, audio, text and graphics data, it becomes very imperative that an appropriate query language is designed to accurately specify these components of video data. A few chapters address these issues in this volume.

In Chapter 6, Hirzalla & Karmouch propose a specification language for multimedia query. Although query mechanisms have been proposed for specific types of multimedia documents (example, documents having only text and image content [15]), enough attention has not been given to the problem of query mechanisms for a wide range of multimedia documents. The technique proposed by Hirzalla & Karmouch will allow for the retrieval of relevant multisegments from a multimedia database. For example, using their query language specification, a user can pose a query to retrieve a multisegment consisting of text, video, and audio segments.

Hibino & Rundensteiner discuss a query language for identifying temporal trends in video data in Chapter 5. The work reported here focused on the need to support video analysis by developing a user-friendly interactive visualization environment to query video data using spatio-temporal characteristics and to review results for trend analysis. A temporal visual query language for specifying relative temporal queries between sets of annotations is also presented. The query language uses the notion of dynamic query filters and extends them with temporal query support.

In Chapter 4, Hjelsvold et. al provide a brief overview of the the VideoSTAR storage architecture and report on some results with their proposed technique. VideoSTAR (Video STorage And Retrieval) is an experimental system under construction at the Department of Computer Science and Telematics at the Norwegian Institute of Technology. To facilitate video querying and browsing, a technique that allows a user to control the degree of meta-data sharing is being implemented on top of VideoSTAR. The Chapter provides a brief overview of the VideoSTAR storage architecture and reports on some results with this technique.

6   MULTIMEDIA STORAGE ISSUES

Recent advances in high speed networks such as Asynchronous Transfer Mode (ATM) [16, 6] have made possible the concurrent transmission and delivery of independent compressed video streams. These high performance networks will facilitate a wide range of new state-of-the-art multimedia services like Video-On-Demand (VOD), home shopping and distance learning among others. Furht et. al [7] have discussed a number of design issues and proposed a hierarchical configuration of multimedia servers and network switches for interactive on-demand TV services. Gemmell et. al [8] surveyed multimedia storage servers and discussed efficient algorithms for continuous media (CM) playback. Berson and Ghandeharizadeh [9] have proposed a staggered striping technique for multimedia information systems. Design and data placement issues were also discussed in [10, 12, 11].

Some of these issues are also discussed elsewhere in this volume. In Chapter 7, Kwon & Lee discuss data placement for continuous media in multimedia DBMS, and the effect of using multiple disks to provide natural retrieval of different portions of video concurrently. Kwon & Lee have proposed the prime round-robin (PRR) placement scheme which provides uniform load-balance of disks unlike the classical round-robin (RR) which shows a hot spot behavior when multimedia objects are accessed in a non-uniform manner. The focus in this Chapter is on the need to guarantee load balancing across all the disks even during fast and non-uniform data retrievals from the server.

The PRR uses arbitrary number of disks (N) with uniform load balance for fast retrievals as well as display and slow retrievals, but the rounding distance is the biggest prime number $N_p(\leq N)$ instead of N. Using their model, the jth segment of the ith object would be stored in disk k of N where k is given by

$$k = \begin{cases} ((N - N_p + 1)i + j mod(N - N_p + 1))mod N & \text{if } j = cN_p \\ ((N - N_p + 1)i + N - N_p + (j mod N_p))mod N & \text{otherwise} \end{cases}$$

An excellent additional treatment of the topic of data storage, playout and synchronization is [13] by Buddhikot and Parulkar. This paper which focuses on the Massively-parallel And Real-time Storage (MARS) project at Washington University, St. Louis, Missouri has a number of interesting results especially with respect to scheduling and playout control operations in an Interactive video On-Demand (IVOD) environment.

One of the major issues of research interest in IVOD applications is the need to support *fast forward (ff), rewind (rw), slow play, slow rewind, frame ad-*

vance, pause and *stop-and-return* operations on a media stream. Two ways of implementing stream control for some of these operations are:

- **Rate Variation Scheme (RVS)**: In this technique, the rate of display at the client and hence the rate of data retrieval at the server is changed. For *ff* the data retrieval at the server is increased. A performance study of this type of scheme is presented in [14].

- **Sequence Variation Scheme (SVS)**: In this technique, the sequence of frame display and hence the sequence of data retrieval and transmission from the server is varied. The display rate at the client side is unaltered.

Buddhikot and Parulkar noted three disadvantages of the RVS implementation for *ff* and *rw*. These include (1) Increased network and storage bandwidth requirement since the data rate is increased;(2) Inappropriate for real-time decoders, since the decoders may be unable to handle the increased throughput they now face; and (3) Increased buffer requirement at the buffer since the arrival rate of data has increased. For their MARS project, it was reported that the SVS implementation was chosen for *ff* and *rw* operations. Scheduling and data placement algorithms were also developed to ensure a balanced load at all times without regard to the operation being performed.

7 MULTIMEDIA RETRIEVAL AND INDEXING

Two chapters are devoted to multimedia retrieval and indexing. In Chapter 10, Simonnot and Smail discuss a Model for Interactive Retrieval of Videos and Still Images. The chapter presents a flexible model for the information retrieval process which provides relevance feedback facilities and embodies a mechanism to exploit a typology of information needs. This model integrates various alternatives for information retrieval primitives into a single framework and the adequacy of the model is studied with respect to the retrieval of multimedia documents – namely pictures and videos.

In Chapter 11, Yang et. al. propose a new data structure – the MB$^+$-Tree. This new indexing structure for multimedia databases is designed to assist content-based retrieval in image and video databases. The MB$^+$-Tree is particularly effective for nearest neighbor query based on a weighted Euclidean-distance similarity measure and the range query, both in a multidimensional space. The indexing structure can support queries which retrieve a large number of approximate matches as well as those which retrieve a small number of close matches. This data structure is based on linear order in the multidimensional space and has several features of the standard B^+-tree.

8 CONCLUSION

The role of a DBMS in multimedia data processing cannot be overstated. While it is possible to build presentation front-ends to multimedia applications, a seamless integration of the presentation manager with the rest of the DBMS will clearly improve performance.

Various chapters in this book discuss and present solutions to some of the many problems in multimedia DBMS. Here, we have used the video service as a special class of multimedia application and discussed the various types of video services available to the user. We then presented a high level overview of the other chapters in the book.

It is clear that there are many unsolved problems in multimedia data processing and presentation and the debate over the need for a multimedia DBMS will probably continue. However, we believe that this book will be a very useful and invaluable resource to everyone involved in multimedia data and information processing.

REFERENCES

[1] Ullman, J. Principles of Database Systems, Second Edition. Computer Science Press, Rockville, Maryland.

[2] Korth, H. and Silberschatz, A. Database System Concepts. McGraw Hill, New York, 1991.

[3] Codd, E. A Relational Model for Large Shared Data Banks. *Communications of the ACM*, 13:6, pp. 377-387.

[4] Stonebraker, M. and Rowe, L. The Design of POSTGRES. *Proceedings of the International Conference of the ACM SIGMOD*, Washington, D. C., May 1986.

[5] Kim, W., Garza, J., and Ballou, N. and Woelk, D. Architecture of the ORION Next-Generation Database System. *IEEE Transactions on Knowledge and Data Engineering*, Vol. 2, No. 1, March 1990, pp. 109-124.

[6] Asynchronous Transfer Mode: Solution for B-ISDN, Ellis Horwood Ltd., 1991.

[7] Furht, B., Kaira, D., Kitson, F., Rodriguez, A. and Wall, W. Design Issues for Interactive Television Systems. *IEEE Computer*, May 1995, pp. 25-38.

[8] Gemmell, D., Vin, H., Kandlur, D., Rangan, P. and Rowe, L. Multimedia Storage Servers: A Tutorial. *IEEE Computer*, May 1995, pp. 40-49.

[9] Berson, S. and Ghandeharizadeh, S. Staggered Striping in Multimedia Information Systems. *Proceedings of the 1994 ACM SIGMOD*, Minneapolis, Minnesota, May 24-27, 1994.

[10] Orji, C., Bobbie, P. and Nwosu, K. Decomposing Multimedia Data Objects for Parallel Storage Allocation and Retrieval. Submitted to *Journal of Intelligent Information Systems (JIIS)*.

[11] Orji, C., Bobbie, P. and Nwosu, K. Design and Configuration Rationales for Digital Video Storage and Delivery. Submitted to *Journal of Multimedia Tools and Applications (JMTA)*.

[12] Orji, C., Bobbie, P. and Nwosu, K. Spatio-Temporal Effects of Multimedia Objects Storage and Delivery for Video-On-Demand Systems. To appear in *Multimedia Systems Journal (MSJ)*.

[13] Buddhikot, M. and Parulkar, G. Distributed Data Layout, Scheduling and Playout Control in a Large Scale Multimedia Storage Server. *Technical Report WUCS-94-33*, Department of Computer Science, Washington University, St. Louis, MO 63130.

[14] Dey-Sircar, J., Salehi, J., Kurose, J. and Towsley, D. Providing VCR Capabilities in Large-Scale Video Servers. *Proceedings of ACM Multimedia International Conference*, San Francisco, October 1994, pp. 25-32.

[15] Cakmakov, D. and Davcev, D. Experiments in Retrieval of Mineral Information. *Proceedings of ACM Multimedia International Conference*, Anaheim, CA., October 1993, pp. 57-64.

[16] Maier, D., Walpole, J. and Staehli, R. Storage System Architectures for Continuous Media Data. *Proceedings of Fourth International Conference on Foundations of Data Organization and Algorithms*, October 1993, pp. 1-18.

[17] Patterson, D., Chen, P., Gibson, G. and Katz, R. A Case for Redundant Arrays of Inexpensive Disks (RAID). *Proceedings of the International Conference of the ACM SIGMOD*, Chicago, Illinois, June 1988, pp. 109-116.

[18] Stonebraker, M. The INGRES Papers: Anatomy of a Relational Database System. *Addison-Wesley*, Reading, Massachusetts, 1985.

[19] Adiba, M. STORM: Structural and Temporal Object-Oriented Multimedia Database System. *Proceedings 1995 International Workshop on Multi-Media Database Management Systems*, Blue Mountain Lake, New York, August 1995, pp. 12-19.

DATABASE APPROACH FOR THE MANAGEMENT OF MULTIMEDIA INFORMATION

Scott T. Campbell and Soon M. Chung*

Technology & Development
AT&T Global Information Solutions
Dayton, Ohio 45479, USA

* Dept. of Computer Science and Engineering
Wright State University
Dayton, Ohio 45435, USA

ABSTRACT

Today we are in an information flood as computing and communication makes more information available than ever before. Hypermedia, multimedia and database technologies are powerful tools that facilitate information access and management. In this paper we examine the role of database systems in managing multimedia data. Database systems need to do more than providing a document model or binary large objects to implement multimedia database systems. They need to incorporate the role of media servers which are extensions of traditional file servers with isochronous multimedia data delivery capabilities. To support this we propose a novel temporal query script methodology to provide the database system with information about future requests. The database system can use this information to optimize the retrieval and delivery of multimedia streams.

1 INTRODUCTION

As multimedia data proliferates, we need to look at the role of database systems in the emerging multimedia information environment. It is true that database systems are a traditional enterprise data management tool. As multimedia moves from a local storage environment to an enterprise level, how can we apply database technology? What capabilities should a multimedia database system provide? We feel that multimedia specific database storage and management needs have not been clearly articulated even though several existing research and prototype systems support multimedia data. One specific need is for a clear and distinct separation between the database system's data model and the application's data model. This separation helps shift the work and role of managing multimedia information from the application to the database system, and hence allows easier application development and more reuse of multimedia information. This in turn makes the multimedia information more globally available, provides a central and consistent data model, and expands the use of multimedia information. We envision multimedia information having a profound and positive impact on computing and on the way people interact with computers, since the richer information types that multimedia provides enable computer systems to deal with people-oriented information rather than making people deal with computer-oriented information.

Today multimedia data access is mainly a local affair. Most data delivery is from CD-ROM or other local storage media due to the size and difficulty of delivering the data in real-time. There are many efforts underway to utilize higher bandwidth networking techniques coupled with advanced storage server methodologies to enable real-time access to multimedia data in a network and distributed environment. The next step is to provide the ability to relate, correlate, link, and package individual pieces of multimedia data.

In our view the database system has two major roles, one is in the management of the high-level information models. The second role is in the active management of the storage and delivery of the multimedia information. Using the database system's knowledge of the structure of the data and the relationships between the data we can optimize the retrieval and delivery of the multimedia streams to clients. This is possible since the database system maintains data composition structures, associative access structures, and uses queries that enable it to schedule deliveries rather than simply reacting to client requests. Our research focus is on a query script that is a tool to enable this optimization. The query script creates a novel client-database interface that allows the database system to better manage system resources through multimedia data delivery scheduling. Query script's temporal modeling ability also helps database systems maintain the separation between the database system's data model and the application's data model.

2   MULTIMEDIA DATA MANAGEMENT

The first question really is should we integrate multimedia information management and database systems? The basic level of multimedia data management simply requires data storage and isochronous delivery capabilities and all systems that provide these functions are not database systems. Database systems typically focus more on the advanced data management functions such as data modeling, linking multimedia elements, searching and locating multimedia data. To better look at the role of database systems in managing multimedia information we start by understanding the basic functions necessary to enable computing systems to manage, store, manipulate and retrieve multimedia information.

Multimedia information consists of new classes of data types. These new data types represent information with temporal and synchronization characteristics and require that the data be delivered or displayed as time continuous streams. These new data types include video, audio, graphics, and animation. Multimedia information's time continuous nature is due to its presentational and representational characteristics. It is during the presentation process that people experience and utilize these new data types.

Multimedia objects are large, a 30 second MPEG-1 multimedia video segment with CD quality audio can consume 5 megabytes of disk storage and requires a 1.5 Mbps channel for delivery, and few systems can deal with objects measured in tens or hundreds of megabytes. Today it requires optical storage systems to cost-effectively store multimedia data, but the slow speed and difficulty in updating the information make traditional magnetic storage more desirable. Even traditional disk-based storage needs new techniques to store, organize and deliver multimedia streams measured in the hundreds of kilobytes per second. Existing networks simply can not handle hundreds of simultaneous requests for large multimedia objects. While the emerging ATM networks and other higher speed and isochronous networks are suitable for multimedia, we need more research on issues like dynamic bandwidth management and quality of service management.

Efficient temporal management is also important since multimedia information exhibits jerky motion or dropouts if data underrun occurs. The most popular solutions are buffering and isochronous delivery. Buffering multimedia requires massive storage requirements to overcome network delivery variations, and can lead to large startup latencies as the presentation waits for the buffers to fill. Hence many multimedia solutions require isochronous delivery mechanisms. Isochronous delivery guarantees tightly bounded delivery timing and ensures that there will always be information ready for presentation. Another major problem is media synchronization such as synchronizing the sound track with the video track or getting the voice to correspond with the motion of the speaker's lips. Other basic management functions include maintaining the content's structure, updating multimedia streams, backup and recovery of the large streams, reusing pieces of content and real-time editing problems.

Once we can handle the basic management functions there exists a need to support multimedia data operations such as access and media control. Access methods need to be concerned with finding, starting and stopping collections of multimedia data as well as individual multimedia streams. One typical method of providing access control is through the use of scripts. A script is a sequence of commands that depict how, where, and in what order individual pieces of multimedia information appear. The script controls the presentation of the multimedia streams and acts as a high-level modeling tool.

Another problem is in providing users with interactive controls like start, stop, pause, fast forward, reverse, and jump. These controls cause real-time manipulations of the stream and affect its presentation. These manipulations are difficult to manage since many system components, including the disk, network, and client application, must act in a coordinated fashion. This further highlights the presentational nature of multimedia information and the difficulty of managing multimedia information.

One way of integrating multimedia data and database systems is to use hypermedia models. In this case the database system manages the hypermedia document models. This creates a layered architecture, such as the one we propose in Figure 1. Here hypermedia document modeling adds user navigable semantics that link multimedia content elements together [14], offers to make multimedia data types even more useful and typically separates the presentation aspects from the storage and management concerns.

While there are multiple hypermedia models, we first present a generic model that cleanly shows the hypermedia layering methodology and then present two standard hypermedia models. The generic Dexter Hypermedia Model defines a three-layer model, shown in Figure 2, for hypermedia document structuring. The layers are the runtime, storage and within-component layers [5]. The runtime layer deals with presentation and user input issues. The storage layer provides an encapsulation mechanism for creating a content container object and also defines models for specifying links and composite entities. The within-component layer stores the physical realization of the multimedia content and is application and tool specific. Within-component entities are designed to be managed by their respective tools while the storage layer entities are managed by the hypermedia document tools. There are too many different media formats

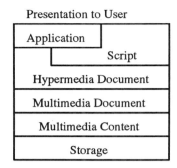

Figure 1 Multimedia Data Access Hierarchy

to completely standardize the internal structure of multimedia content and the within-component structure allows the use of internal formats while the system manages the object [16]. The concept of containers and links allows specialized and appropriate tools and techniques to be used in providing specific customized solutions.

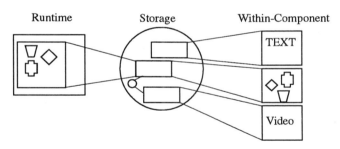

Figure 2 Dexter Hypermedia Model

The HyTime standard provides a method for representing multimedia content's temporal and spatial relationships as well as linking information [12]. HyTime is an ISO standard and creates architectural document forms that are extensions of the Standard Generalized Markup Language (SGML). These architectural forms implement hypermedia links, a finite coordinate presentation space, temporal synchronization, and add information about document semantics [6]. A HyTime engine has six modules: base, measurement, scheduling, hyperlinks, rendition and address location modules that control and define its operations. HyTime grew out of efforts to create a standard music description language and provides strong semantics for the encoding of temporal and spatial synchronization. HyTime is a collaborative development tool for creating, editing and presenting hypermedia documents, and as such can require significant processing to decode.

Another hypermedia model was developed with the goal of creating a final form presentation environment without significant processing for presentation. The Multimedia Hypermedia Expert Group (MHEG) standard defines representation and encoding of multimedia and hypermedia objects as interchange definitions between applications or services. MHEG provides abstractions suited to real-time presentation and interchange and works with final form representations. MHEG defines multiple object classes for content encoding, managing objects, creating hyperlinks between objects, creating scripts for the temporal presentation of objects, defining composition and aggregation services, and defining user selectable or modifiable objects. MHEG is a set of encoding rules that are interpreted by an MHEG engine within the end user's application [13].

This paper is not about hypermedia modeling but rather about trying to understand the role of database systems in the direct management of multimedia data. There is a clear role for database systems in managing hypermedia documents. Given multimedia's lack of a computational nature and the need for hypermedia document models, is there a direct role for database systems to play in the basic management of multimedia data? The lack of a computational nature implies that systems can treat multimedia data storage and delivery as simple, isochronous events. This allows the use of extended file servers or media servers rather than database systems to manage the storage and delivery. In this scenario, the application manages the presentation of the information while the media server manages the storage and delivery of the information. Then what is the role for database systems?

Traditionally, database systems provide advantages over file based storage and application based data modeling by providing logical and physical data independence, common data model access, security, backup, and recovery. They also provide consistent data models across organizational and application boundaries [1]. These are important goals for multimedia data management. One way to accomplish this is to provide separation between the application's logical view of data organization and the physical organization of the stored data. This is a natural role for the database system and can be easily realized by keeping a central repository of information about the structure of the data. However today's multimedia database systems are like early database systems which were difficult to use and inefficient due to primitive interfaces between the application and database system. The user or the application had to manage the access paths and sequentially search the records to locate pertinent information [17].

Today's multimedia data management systems seem to have many problems, particularly the close connection between the application and storage data model and the difficulty in creating access paths. Applications use their own individual form of managing multimedia information. There are few widely accepted storage structures and technologies that offer a common framework. The application and the data storage system require significant amounts of time to update when new tools or techniques are included. Given these problems we feel that properly adapted database solutions are the keys to solving the management problems of multimedia information, much as they solved earlier data management problems.

2.1   Today's Multimedia Data Management

Local Storage

Today, many applications use files to store multimedia data. The application and operating system directly manage both the multimedia data and associated data models. The multimedia data is stored in one or more files on the local system drive, typically on CD-ROM, which provides the ability to store 680 megabytes of data and deliver two or more video streams.

The advantages of this approach are simplicity, ease of implementation and no serious delivery problems. There are few resource contentions since only a single system is attempting to access the data. The application is able to totally monitor and manage system resource utilization and can predict system loads. Another advantage is that there is no network or enterprise system delays imposed on the delivery of the multimedia data.

However, since the application directly maintains the data model, as new storage formats and data models evolve, the applications must be updated to access the multimedia data. There is no possibility of using techniques, like views, to map the internal structure into a format that older programs can understand. This leads to lots of replicated data in an enterprise since there may be no sharing of data storage locations. As a result, available data is limited to what can be locally stored in CD-ROM, disks, etc. This type of data is difficult to update since every machine must be individually sent updates. These updates must be manually transmitted or mailed and this process creates its own management problems.

When the data is actually located in a network file server then the problems
of updating, replicated data and limited data are reduced. However now there
are serious problems in managing the isochronous nature of the data delivery.
Traditional network file systems are not capable of supporting multiple applications requesting multimedia data due to the high bandwidth requirements.
Buffering and other techniques, while necessary, are not sufficient. A network
environment requires a media server.

Media Server

A media server is a shared storage facility that is analogous to a network file
server with the added capability of delivering multimedia data. An application
makes a request to receive multimedia data file and the media server responds
by opening the multimedia data file and delivering the multimedia content in
an isochronous fashion. The media server can use techniques like the ones
proposed in [2, 15, 25] for data retrieval.

The first problem with a media server is that the application's document model
is fixed to that physically stored on the media server. Changes to multimedia
data storage formats force changes to all applications that access the data.

The second problem is that the application still determines access methods.
The media server simply performs resource management, usually by applying
admission tests then only offering a best-effort delivery guarantee. Additionally
the media server has problems in providing advanced synchronization capabilities since there is no higher level data model associated with the data.

Binary Large Objects

Another method of managing multimedia data is to use binary large objects
(BLOBs) to integrate multimedia data into database systems. A BLOB is an
untyped, typically long, variable length field that the database system uses
to store multimedia data. The database system stores the multimedia data
as untyped data and simply delivers blocks of data to the application upon
request.

A relational database stores multimedia data as an attribute of its relations.
This provides some level of associative access and minimally integrates the
multimedia data into the database schema. Including the BLOB in the schema
allows associations to be maintained between the multimedia data and other

data. All the power of relational or extended relational database systems can be applied to managing the data and its relations, as long as the multimedia content is treated as a single large object.

The problem with this approach is that the database system does not have any information about the data it can use for resource optimization. The data is untyped and there is no method of working with or modifying its structure. The database system, being unaware of the structure and associations like composition, can not apply delivery optimization techniques.

Object-Oriented Methodologies

One popular method of overcoming the problems with BLOBs is to use object-oriented methodologies. Object-oriented methodologies provide a framework for defining extensible user defined data types and the ability to support complex relationships in the object-oriented database. The Orion project [8] uses the object-oriented methodology to manage multimedia data. Object-oriented techniques of encapsulation, inheritance and nested classes allow a standard set of functionality to be defined and then extended for different specific instances of multimedia data. These features allow applications to introduce, include and manage multimedia data [8]. However, the object-oriented paradigm does not adequately solve all problems associated with multimedia management, specifically problems associated with storage, indexing, updating, retrieving, querying, and concurrency control [8].

The advantage of the object-oriented approach is that now the database system has a better understanding of the multimedia data and its operations and behavior (through well-designed classes). Unlike BLOBs, the database system now has richer definitions of the format and semantics of the media that it can exploit in storing, managing and delivering the content. This allows the database system to better manage and optimize the delivery and management of the multimedia data. The application's document model and the database schema can be clearly separated and decoupled through the use of well-defined classes. The storage of class data types and operations define an interface that provides this separation.

The problem is that the use of object-oriented systems begs the questions of how to provide better management of multimedia data in a database system environment. The object-oriented system does not inherently provide the new techniques and methods for the basic storage and management of multimedia data. Storage and retrieval methods still need to be developed and integrated into the database system. Also it is very difficult to create class definitions that truly separate the application's document model and the storage data model. In several systems the storage is simply a persistent instance of the application's document model. If this is true then we are effectively back to using local storage models but now with more powerful tools.

2.2 Multimedia Document Model

Specifying a common data model is important in defining a database system's functionality. Researchers utilize a variety of models for their multimedia database system research, but many focus on a document model structure rather than more generic data models [21, 22, 23]. A document model attempts to capture the structure and relationships of information, typically memos, folders, or other existing office like examples. However we feel that focusing on this high-level structure has not placed sufficient focus on the basic needs of managing multimedia data.

The MCC Orion prototype uses a document structuring system and was an early system utilizing object-oriented database technology for creating and managing document oriented multimedia information as part of their MUSE system [8, 23, 24]. Another approach to storing multimedia data is exemplified in the Multimedia Medical Database [21] which couples multimedia storage to a relational database system for storing X-ray and voice data with patient medical records. They store multimedia content in UNIX files with pointers maintained by an Oracle DBMS. This technique allows simple connection of multimedia data types to existing information structures.

The inclusion of multimedia in a database has a profound impact on its design, features and functions. If a database is only storing multimedia for delivery, then a multimedia capable file server coupled with the ability to store pointers, filenames or object identifiers in the database is sufficient. Utilizing deeper semantic knowledge about the media such as the ability to index, search and relate information is truly a database system's value added function.

3 MULTIMEDIA DATABASES

The system environment in Figure 3 shows a view of applications accessing multimedia content from a database system. The client application's MHEG document defines the multimedia content's presentational and relationship information, and makes a request to the multimedia database management system (MMDBMS). The MMDBMS then locates the content and, in conjunction with the client interface, initiates and performs a stream delivery. The stream delivery is a server-push methodology in which the database incrementally delivers content. This approach works better than the typical data-pull methodology where the application keeps requesting the next piece of data, since this can result in excessive network traffic and delays. In this fashion the MMDBMS can also use its knowledge about the content structure for optimal delivery. This minimizes the application's concern with delivery issues and allows the application to focus on presentation and user interaction issues. Other applications can use the same multimedia data since the database system, not the local applications, is responsible for maintaining the multimedia content.

The database system basically offers a consistent data model, a consistent user interface, and a set of tools for managing the storage and retrieval of the multimedia data.

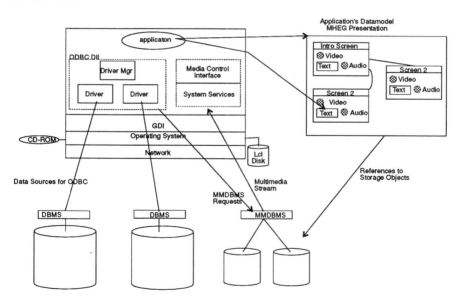

Figure 3 Multimedia Environment

3.1 Data Model

The multimedia database system's data model captures the multimedia content's objects, attributes, relationships and possibly the semantics. Having a common data model allows multiple applications to share the data and creates a common and consistent repository of knowledge about the multimedia content stored in the database. Hence the selection of the data model is an important consideration in deciding how to integrate multimedia information and database systems. Another part of the multimedia database system design is defining the storage and delivery models. When the database system is responsible for storage management, it also makes delivery management an implicit requirement. As such, the database system is responsible for operations such as start, stop, jumping, synchronization, and temporal linking. Coupling storage and delivery capabilities with the database system's enhanced access capabilities makes a more efficient system. It also better supports separation between the application and the database.

Multimedia data modeling should support creating a model of the real world, its relationships and abstractions. It needs to provide support for a range of existing and future data types, and needs to include support for both temporal and spatial modeling while supporting these features in a fashion that maximizes data abstraction. The abstraction and independence allow the database system to control redundancy by sharing data and minimizing duplication of data that saves required storage space.

The ability to separate the application's document model and the storage data model is the central concept of program-data independence. The presentational aspect of multimedia makes it inherently more difficult to separate those models. The application needs to manage the rendering and presentation of the multimedia content at the workstation. Satisfying this need does not require that the application's document model and the database schema are the same. Rather the database system simply needs to deliver the multimedia content in forms that satisfy the application's document model structure. This frees the database system to optimize its internal storage structures.

Given a common repository of shared information, integrity constraints become important. Traditional integrity constrains, such as updates and type consistency, are necessary. However it is interesting to contemplate additional constraints such as semantic content linking, scene continuity, audio filtering continuity, and others that are media specific. Semantic content integrity helps ensure that the basic semantic information people are utilizing does not change as media changes. An example is when people use a single picture to represent multiple messages. Take a class photograph. Author A might utilize the photograph to represent the class membership. Author B might use this picture to represent the color coordination of shirts between a random group of individuals. If the picture is updated with a more current class picture, a totally different set of shirts will be worn. In this case the semantic information desired by author B is lost. The database system should preserve the original picture and maintain links to the old picture for author B while updating the links for author A. The same type of update problems occur as the authors change media. Suppose that author A now wants to use a video segment of the class. In this case author B is definitely in trouble since his/her applications are expecting images.

Another difficulty is how to maintain consistency of data as the native formats and encoding standards change. What if the multimedia content changes coding standards as it's updated. One technique is to provide a view of the data. Then newer applications can access the data directly while older applications are provided a view of the data in the old format. Multimedia views are difficult to implement given the high performance requirements necessary to perform real-time conversion. Advanced views along with composition techniques could dynamically alter stored multimedia objects to create new objects. An example would be to zoom in on a portion of a video to provide enlargement services. Providing multimedia views mean changing properties and allowing the system to store data separately from its presentational requirements. This is a step in providing workable separation between the application and the database.

3.2   User Interface

Stored data is not quite useful unless there are simple, efficient methods of gaining access to it. Today the major interface to relational database systems is the SQL language, but there are several custom interfaces at both the user and programming level. A well-defined and standard interface allows multiple programs to access the data and can also migrate the workload from the application to the database.

A multimedia query language requires a rich set of features to support multimedia content specification and retrieval. A powerful query language greatly helps to maintain the desired independence between the database and the application. There are multiple levels of query languages ranging from simple object identifier based retrieval queries to complex content understanding searches. The simplest query is a request to access and deliver a specific piece of multimedia content. More complex queries offer applications the ability to search based upon attributes and synchronization relationships of the multimedia content.

An example is a search that finds all AVI formatted videos with keywords "President Clinton" and "golf." Additionally we could ask logical questions like find all videos of President Clinton related to audio clip "jazz_1." This last request combines the database system's knowledge of the synchronization primitives between audio and video.

More advanced searches start getting into content understanding. In [20] they discuss the ability to search pictures using a "like" function. They discuss using spatial attributes and return all images meeting the search. Another content understanding approach is introduced in [7] where they work at recognizing facial features and using this information to match pictures or drawings of people to their records in the database system.

Standards like SQL3 provide many object-oriented features and enable a wide range of database systems to directly support semantically rich multimedia content through the use of abstract data types, user defined functions and new basic data types [18]. In addition to SQL3, the emerging SQL/MM [19] is a user community defined set of multimedia specific abstract data types that offers to bring rich commonality to the creation of native multimedia content support. The problem with SQL/MM is that it is still emerging and focuses on providing a core set of basic multimedia content types rather than addressing larger data modeling issues.

3.3   Databases or Media Servers?

Multimedia data management support in enterprise environments requires more than just media servers. There are more features and functions required than simply the ability to store and deliver multimedia information. As we have just shown there are many features that the database system can provide. Prior to database systems, the file system was the common component. Database systems actually utilize file systems and add additional functionality. Database system structures like indexes, catalogs, dictionaries are stored using file systems. The database system extends the file system's management capability. We feel that a similar architectural hierarchy exists between multimedia database systems and media servers as shown in Figure 4. The media server provides basic level storage and delivery control. The database system adds features and functions described in the previous sections to these basic capabilities.

Multimedia database systems need to support a variety of features:

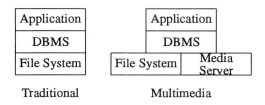

Traditional   Multimedia

Figure 4   Database System Environment

- Native support of multimedia data types

- Ability to create a model of real world

- Temporal and spatial modeling

- Presentation ability

- Multimedia transactions

- Hierarchical storage management

- Storage, retrieval, and delivery

One advantage that database systems hold over media servers is that they can store a richer model of the multimedia content. This allows them to optimize the delivery of sets of multimedia content. Media servers, by definition, manage multimedia content under application control. Database systems have the ability to use complex interfaces and then optimize the delivery of the selected content. Through richer modeling techniques, the database system can create composites and hierarchical content entities. The multimedia database system then can optimize their delivery and presentation.

4   INTRODUCTION OF QUERY SCRIPT

Clients use queries as their main interface for manipulating data in a database system. The query interface defines a criterion for selecting a subset of information found in the database system. This interface plays a major role in maintaining independence between the client's view of the logical data model and the physical organization of the data. Due to this independence, the database system can physically organize the data for best performance without worrying about influencing the client's view of the data [1]. Historically a major part of database system research has been in creating efficient access paths for satisfying queries.

Query scripts extend the database system's interface by providing the ability to define, select, and manage objects for retrieval and delivery. Our query script enables the database system to schedule both current and near-future object retrievals. A query script captures the client's selection and temporal ordering information, and provides the database system with additional information about content requests, as depicted in Figure 5. This information allows the database system to generate an optimized access plan to meet the client's requests.

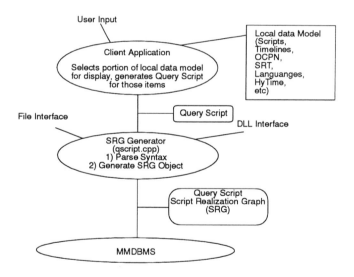

Figure 5   Query Script as Interface to MMDBMS

For example, using the following query script language we could instruct the database system to retrieve and deliver a series of multimedia content objects.

Declaration

```
Define A Video="Scott's Introduction";
Define B Video="New Building Proposal";
Define C Audio="Bach";
Define D Animation="Building Growing";
```

Temporal Ordering

```
A, when A then B and C, when B then D, when D then stop all.
```

This script might mean:

1. Deliver a video clip

2. When done, simultaneously deliver a video clip and an audio clip

3. When the video clip is done, deliver animation

4. When animation is done, stop the audio

In this example the database system anticipates that a new video will start at the end of the first video. The database system can start early pre-fetching of the second video to minimize startup latency. Then the database system can anticipate that the audio will end with the animation, and can stop fetching the audio when the animation ends.

In a single user environment these functions are fairly simple to implement. The client pre-optimizes the data accesses to guarantee that the animation is presented when the video completes. In a multi-client environment, clients can not perform complete optimization since each client is unaware of other client's requests. Only techniques like query scripts can examine all user requests and globally optimize them to ensure the best access plan to meet the set of deadlines.

Using a query script has several attractive features. It can decrease the latency between object accesses (latency reduction), reduce the waste of system resources due to staggered endpoints (stop excess problem), and provide better information for delivery scheduling.

Latency reduction minimizes the time between the client's request and the corresponding delivery. Latency is reduced by providing the database system with a priori knowledge of future accesses via the query script. This allows the database system to pre-deliver multimedia content objects. In the example shown in Figure 6, the client requests a video object followed by a picture. Figure 6.(b) shows the latency resulting from the client's request for the picture at the conclusion of the video. The latency is reduced in Figure 6.(c) since the database system knows that the picture is needed at the conclusion of the video. The database system pre-delivers the picture so that it is at the client in time. Note that the delivery time remains the same. The database system simply started the delivery earlier.

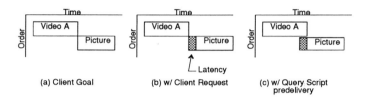

Figure 6   Startup Latency Reduction

Query scripts can also help reduce the waste of system resources by intelligently stopping the delivery of multimedia content to prevent the stop-excess problem. Let's consider a situation the client needs two pieces of multimedia content of different lengths. The objects shown in Figure 7.(a) are an audio clip of length 40 seconds and a video clip of length 20 seconds. The client wants to stop the audio clip when the video clip ends. With the traditional request model, the client sends a stop command to the database when the video ends. However due to the latency of the request, the database system will keep delivering data for the latency period. This needlessly consumes resources, as shown in Figure 7.(b). With a query script the database system stops the audio delivery when the video ends, as in Figure 7.(c), and avoids the waste of system resources.

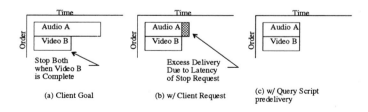

Figure 7   Minimization of Stop Excess

Query scripts furnish database systems the ability to better balance resource utilization using pre-delivery techniques. The database system has limited resources available to meet client requests. Better information enables the database system to pre-deliver content to balance the load. For example, Figure 8.(a) shows two clients requesting delivery of a video followed by a picture. Figure 8.(b) shows the associated latency when the clients make individual requests. If the clients perform their own optimization the resulting requests can still collide, as shown in Figure 8.(c). Optimal scheduling is not accomplished since the clients are unaware of each other's requests. Query scripts allow the database system to schedule the two picture deliveries at separate times, as shown in Figure 8.(d), thus better utilizing the resources.

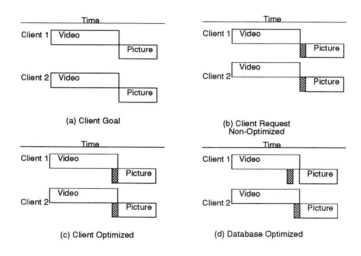

Figure 8   Global Optimization Using Pre-Delivery

Offsetting these benefits of query scripts are the higher complexity of the system and the loss of flexibility in user interaction. Complexity is increased since there is a complex set of interactions between the client and database system. The database system and the client need to closely work together to manage the data. In traditional multimedia database system solutions, the database system delivers the data while the client handles the physical display of the video, audio and pictures. Query scripts add additional client workload since the client must generate the script and then handle more management tasks associated with pre-delivery. Pre-delivery in the above example requires the client to buffer the picture while simultaneously receiving and presenting the video stream.

Query scripts can lead to a loss of flexibility in user interaction. Interactive multimedia implies unpredictable user input. When the client issues single requests, the impact of client input is minimized. At most a single request needs to be canceled or changed. However, interactive user operations can affect the processing of query scripts to a large degree, because query scripts can be overruled by user input. To minimize this problem, the query script should extend minimally into the future, but for maximum optimization it should extend as far as possible. The issue of these two conflicting goals is currently being investigated.

We feel that the query script offers a useful additional tool for the management of multimedia information. Query scripts provide the database system a priori knowledge about requests allowing the database system to optimize access and delivery. This methodology also provides enhanced logical/physical independence since now the database system has more management information separate from the client's tools and systems. The database system can subsume some level of timing and synchronization control while working in close conjunction with the client.

Temporal modeling as found in [4, 9, 11] focuses on the conceptual modeling of time and on providing complete specification for temporal relationships between multimedia objects. Object Composition Petri Nets (OCPN) for the specification and modeling of temporal relationships is proposed in [10]. Their work initially defined 13 binary relationships that capture all possible temporal semantics between two objects. This work was later extended to include n-ary relationships and coupled with the concept of temporal intervals [11] allowing them to create scheduling algorithms for presentation of objects. This work allows authoring and presentation systems to store and define temporal orchestration of the associated multimedia objects. The application can use the OCPN model to determine which objects to play in what order. Li's time-flow graph model [9] utilizes graph theory for the temporal ordering of sets of objects and their relationships. Gibbs defines temporal modeling in terms of active objects [3] rather than as separate data structures. Active objects define rules and methods on multimedia objects and define their own synchronization and relationship requirements. This approach makes the objects responsible for modeling the relationships between each other.

5   QUERY SCRIPT PROCESSING

Query scripts provide the database system a sequence of requests. This allows the database system to create a time-based access plan for the retrieval of the requested content objects. The client workstation converts the query script into a Script Realization Graph (SRG). Figure 9 shows the separation between the query script, parser and the database system's major modules for processing the SRG.

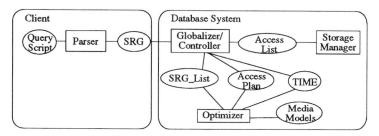

Figure 9   Query Script Processing

5.1   Query Script Language

There are many possible types of query scripts. We have created a simple query script language for our research. We are investigating existing script languages and may adopt some of their features as our research progresses.

The query script has two sections, declaration and temporal ordering. The declaration section of the script defines the involved multimedia content objects (MMCOs) by specifying object identifiers or multimedia content keywords. The temporal ordering section defines the timing relationships between the identified MMCOs. There are three possible temporal ordering actions: initiate a stream, wait for streams to complete, and terminate streams.

The query script declaration section uses MMCOs as its primary objects. A MMCO is the basic storage unit that encapsulates single multimedia content for database system storage. This entity encapsulates content elements like a video or a sound sequence. It acts as a basis for more complex passages or sequences to be created via aggregation using query scripts. Each MMCO is associated with a specific media type.

Separating the declaration and temporal ordering is mainly for simplicity but also introduces variables that can be used in the query script's *when* and *stop* commands, which are used to control the delivery and temporal relationships between the content objects.

5.2   Script Realization Graph (SRG)

The script realization graph is the data structure transmitted to the database system and is a concise representation of the query script. The SRG is a graph structure that defines the temporal ordering via initiator arcs, defines how streams are combined via the uniter nodes, and then defines stop semantics for the uniter. The SRG is similar to Li's time-flow graph proposed in [9].

The initiators define the delivery of MMCOs and can be either in sequential or parallel. They are combined in hierarchical fashion to realize the temporal ordering defined in the query script.

The uniter brings together multiple streams. The uniter has several variants due to the set of semantics available for synchronizing MMCOs of different length. We now describe the uniters with Wait All, Wait Set, and Wait Any commands, shown in Figure 10.

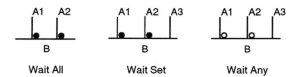

Figure 10   Wait Commands

1. Wait All – Wait for all named streams to complete and then continue with another stream.

2. Wait Set – Similar to Wait All but wait only for explicitly named streams to complete. These named streams are graphically identified with a bullet by their arc.

3. Wait Any – Wait for any indicated stream, identified with a circle, to complete.

These wait commands define the methods of collapsing multiple streams into a single stream.

Stop commands define the methods of stopping active streams when a uniter successfully collapses streams. There are several options for stopping streams as shown in Figure 11.

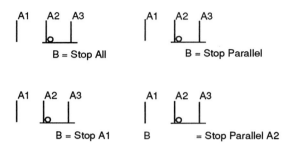

Figure 11 Stop Commands

1. Stop All – Stop any streams currently being delivered as part of this script. Here assume that A1 plays longer than A2. The uniter specifies that B is started when A2 ends. Then the Stop All command will stop both A1 and A3.

2. Stop Parallel – Stop any streams started at the same time. In this example B will stop only A3 when A2 ends since A3 was started in parallel with A2. A1 will continue to operate until its normal termination point.

3. Stop Specific – Identify a specific stream to stop. Here that stream is A1, and A1 is stopped when A2 ends.

4. Stop Parallel Specific – Stop a specific object and all streams started with it. In this example, B specifies that stopping of A2 occurs when A1 terminates. A3 is also stopped since it was initiated in parallel with A2.

An example query script requiring the initiator, uniter and stop semantics is as follows and the corresponding SRG is shown in Figure 12.

Declaration

```
Define A Video Stream="Scott's Video";
Define B Video Stream="Bill's Video";
Define C Audio Stream="Vivaldi";
```

.
.

```
Temporal Ordering

A then B and C,
when B then D and E,
when C and E then F and G and H,
when G then X,
when D and H then Z, when X and Z stop all.
```

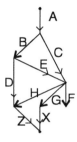

Figure 12   Example SRG

6   QUERY SCRIPT SCHEDULING

Up to this point in the paper we have focused on optimizing the processing of individual query script. Now the focus shifts to scheduling a set of query scripts. Decisions involving the delivery of multimedia information have long reaching temporal consequences. Once a multimedia stream is initiated the database system is committed to delivering that stream until the stream completes. The database system must make intelligent and wise decisions to avoid overcommitting system resources and causing one or more stream interruptions.

Global scheduling optimization also offers the ability to balance system load. Good scheduling decisions will minimize instantaneous system resource requirements. This makes more resources available for other requests and also provides more opportunities for scheduling additional query scripts.

The MMDBMS performs several layers of optimization and traditionally optimization cost is a serious factor. If the optimal plan takes 1 second to generate and 0.2 seconds to execute while a sub-optimal plan takes 0.2 seconds to generate and 0.5 seconds to execute, then it is better not to fully optimize and have a total execution time of 0.7 seconds. Optimal scheduling of query scripts is different because the results of the optimization are long-lived, typically in the length of seconds or minutes. Optimization times on the order of 200 ms are acceptable since query scripts specify lengthy temporal operations.

Once a query script is admitted and is in the database system's queue, it must be scheduled for delivery. The MMDBMS performs optimization as it selects query scripts for initiation and schedules query scripts for delivery. In addition, the scheduling policy must be fair, avoid starvation, should not unduly increase the initiation latency, and should provide some level of performance improvement.

Our current scheduler, the Scan/Accept scheduling algorithm, takes scripts in sequential order and integrates the query script into the system schedule. A realizable schedule is guaranteed since the query script must pass the admission criteria, and one of the criteria is that the query script's resource needs do not exceed those available. In the worst case this may simply require a query script to be scheduled when all existing query scripts are complete. This approach is sequential in that it considers one query script at a time.

Scheduling the candidate query script for initiation at the end of all existing query scripts leads to a very inefficient system as only one query script is executed at a time. A better approach is to schedule the query script to begin at the earliest time possible so that multiple query scripts can be executed concurrently. The goal of this optimization is to find this initiation time efficiently.

Scheduling begins by identifying the start and end points of each segment of multimedia content. These start and end points form an interval and all the intervals of the query script are combined to make up the resource utilization vector (RUV). The RUV also captures the bandwidth requirement for each interval, and thus contains the necessary information to optimize system resource utilization. The scheduler performs this optimization by varying the query script's start time, which determines the multimedia database system's resource utilization.

The scheduler needs an efficient algorithm to select the start time of each query script. A brute force approach is shifting the candidate query script's start time by a single time unit and evaluating the resultant resource utilization. This approach is expensive and wasteful since resource utilization does not change until the start or end points of content intervals meet together.

In Figure 13.(a) we see an existing query script on the top and a new query script below it. The later figures all show different possible start times for the new query script. Each new start time is a result of aligning the start or end points of intervals. Calculating resource utilization at these potential start times reduces the scheduler's search set and greatly reduces the optimization process.

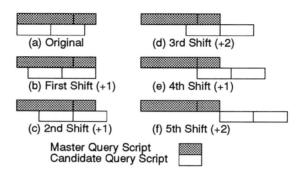

Figure 13   Interval Calculations

In the example in Figure 13, the master query script has two intervals of length 5 and 2. The start and end points are encoded into a RUV as (0:600, 5:150, 7). The first interval starts at time 0, ends at time 5, and requires 600 KB/sec bandwidth. The second interval starts at time 5, ends at time 7, and requires 150 KB/sec bandwidth. Since two consecutive intervals must always meet in time, they share the common start/end time.

To find the start time for the new query script with two intervals of length 3 and 3, the algorithm first finds the minimum time slip necessary in order to align start or end points of two intervals, one from each query script. The first slip is found to be one time unit, which causes the two query scripts' second intervals to end together. This slip results in a new query script's candidate RUV of (1:600, 4:300, 7), assuming that the two intervals' bandwidth requirements are 600 KB/sec and 300 KB/sec, respectively. The algorithm then computes the next candidate slip, which again is one time unit. The resulting candidate RUV is (2:600, 5:300, 8), which aligns the end times of the two first intervals. This process continues until the master query script's last interval ends at the same time as the new query script's first interval begins, shown in Figure 13.(f). No further shifting is needed after this point as the resource utilization will not change.

Once the potential set of RUVs is known for the new query script, the next step is to calculate the total system resource utilization by merging the two RUVs into a single RUV. For example, the combined RUV for the case of Figure 13.(a) is (0:1200, 3:900, 5:450, 6:150, 7). Figure 14 shows the resulting intervals and combined resource utilization for the different cases in Figure 13.

Now the task is to select one start time for the new query script from this set. This selection process can be as simple as selecting the earliest start time where the combined resource utilization is achievable. Other possible optimization goals are: lowest average utilization, lowest standard deviation of the utilization, etc. For the current prototype and evaluation work, we select the first combined script whose requirement falls at or below the available system resource level.

Interval:	0		3	5		6	7
Utilization		1200	900	450		150	

(a) Original

Interval:	0		4	5	7		10
Utilization		600	1200	750	300		

(d) 3rd Shift

Interval:	0	1		4	5	7
Utilization		600	1200	900	450	

(b) 1st Shift

Interval:	0		5	7	8		11
Utilization		600	750	600	300		

(e) 4th Shift

Interval:	0	2		5	7	8
Utilization		600	1200	450	300	

(c) 2nd Shift

Interval:	0		5	7	10		13
Utilization		600	150	600	300		

(f) 5th Shift

Figure 14 Combined RUV

7 CONCLUSION

Multimedia Information in a distributed network environment requires new tools and techniques to facilitate access and presentation methodologies. A multimedia database system needs to extend the traditional query response role and provide multimedia specific data modeling, delivery modeling, access modeling and storage modeling, while storage technology needs to deal with the multi-megabyte multimedia content. This paper examines the combination of media servers and database management systems and focuses on the storage and management of multimedia data in a database environment.

The database system extends the delivery functions of media servers by providing richer modeling tools. These tools allow users to develop and maintain separation between the application and the database. The richer data models also provide the framework for our optimization work using query scripts.

Query scripts provide database system with a priori information about access requests that allows the database systems to generate efficient schedules for delivering multimedia content. Efficient delivery of multimedia content is necessary to make systems, like digital libraries, work. Distributed environment requires the multimedia database to take an active role in delivering the multimedia content. Using the query script to specify the delivery timing allows the database system to schedule the query script's start time and thus manage overall system utilization. Thus, query scripts can perform a vital role in the management of multimedia information.

New information systems are making use of multimedia information and the resulting layered architecture needs the services of database systems to create a common and consistent information repository. Database technology makes the information more globally available, provides a central and consistent data model, and supports timely multimedia data access.

Acknowledgements

This work was supported in part by AT&T Global Information Solutions.

REFERENCES

[1] Elmarsi, R. and Navathe, S., *Fundamentals of Database Systems, 2nd ed.,* Benjamin/Cummings, 1994.

[2] Gemmel, J. and Christodoulakis, S., "Principles of Delay-Sensitive Multimedia Data Storage and Retrieval," ACM Transactions on Information Systems, Vol. 10, No. 1, 1992, pp. 51–90.

[3] Gibbs, S., "Composite Multimedia and Active Objects," Proceedings of OOPSLA, 1991, pp. 97–112.

[4] Gibbs, S., "Data Modeling of Time Based Media," Proceedings of ACM SIGMOD Conference, 1994, pp. 91–102.

[5] Gronbaek, K. and Trigg, R. H., "Design Issues for a Dexter-Based Hypermedia System," CACM, Vol. 37, No. 2, 1994, pp. 41–49.

[6] ISO 10744, "Information Processing – Hypermedia/Time-based Structuring Language (HyTime)," 1993, Photocopied.

[7] Jain, R., "Multimedia Databases," Tutorial Notes from ACM Multimedia Conference, 1993.

[8] Kim, W., Garza, J. F., Ballou, N., and Woelk, D., "Architecture of the ORION Next-Generation Database System," IEEE Transactions on Knowledge and Data Engineering, Vol. 2, No. 1, 1990, pp. 109–124.

[9] Li, L., Karmouch, A., and Georganas, N. D., "Multimedia Teleorchestra with Independent Sources: Part 1 – Temporal Modeling of Collaborative Multimedia Scenarios," Multimedia Systems, Vol. 1, No. 4, February 1994, pp. 143–153.

[10] Little, T. and Ghafoor, A., "Spatio-Temporal Composition of Distributed Multimedia Objects for Value-added Networks," IEEE Computer, October 1991, pp. 42–50.

[11] Little, T. and Ghafoor, A., "Interval-Based Conceptual Models for Time-Dependent Multimedia Data," IEEE Transactions on Knowledge and Data Engineering, Vol. 5, No. 4, 1993, pp. 551–563.

[12] Markey, B. D., "Emerging Hypermedia Standards," Proceedings of the USENIX Conference, June 1991.

[13] Meyer-Boudnik, T. and Effelsberg, W., "MHEG Explained," IEEE Multimedia, Spring 1995, pp. 26–38.

[14] Newcomb, S. R., Kipp, N. A., and Newcomb, V. T., "The "HyTime" Hypermedia/Time-Based Document Structuring Language," CACM, Vol. 34, No. 11, 1991, pp. 67–83.

[15] Rangan, P. V. and Vin, H. M., "Designing File Systems for Digital Video and Audio," Operating Systems Review, Vol. 25, No. 5, 1991, pp. 81–94.

[16] Shepherd, B., "Multimedia Hypermedia Model and Framework," Tutorial Notes from ACM Multimedia Conference, 1993.

[17] Silberschatz, A., Stonebraker, M. and Ullman, J., "Database Systems: Achievements and Opportunities," CACM, Vol. 34, No. 10, 1991, pp. 110–120.

[18] Working Draft of SQL3, 1992, Photocopied.

[19] Working Draft of SQL/Multimedia, 1992, Photocopied.

[20] Stonebraker, M. and Olson, M., "Large Object Support in POSTGRES," Proceedings of International Conference on Data Engineering, 1993, pp. 355–362.

[21] Sudhakar, G. N. M., Karmouch, A. and Georganas, N. D., "Design and Performance Evaluation Considerations of a Multimedia Medical Database," IEEE Transactions on Knowledge and Data Engineering, Vol. 5, No. 5, 1993, pp. 888–894.

[22] Thomas, R. H. et al., "Diamond: A Multimedia Message System Built on a Distributed Architecture," IEEE Computer, December 1985, pp. 65–78.

[23] Woelk, D., Kim, W., and Luther, W., "An Object-oriented Approach to Multimedia Databases," Proceedings of ACM SIGMOD Conference, 1986, pp. 311–325.

[24] Woelk, D. and Kim, W., "Multimedia Information Management in an Object-Oriented Database System," Proceedings of the 13th VLDB Conference, 1987, pp. 319–329.

[25] Yu, P. S., Chen, M. S., and Kandlur, D. D., "Grouped Sweeping Scheduling for DASD-Based Multimedia Storage Management," Multimedia Systems, Vol. 1, No. 3, 1993, pp. 99–109.

3

STORM: AN OBJECT-ORIENTED MULTIMEDIA DBMS

Michel ADIBA

IMAG, Grenoble University
BP 53, 38041 Grenoble Cedex 9, France
e-mail: Michel.Adiba@imag.fr

ABSTRACT

Based upon the Object-Oriented approach, the STORM[1] DBMS integrates structural and temporal aspects for managing different **presentations of multimedia objects** (i.e. Text, Audio, Image, Video). We provide a mapping between structural operators (e.g. **tuple, list, set**) and temporal relationships (e.g. **before, after, equal**) involved in presentations. Temporal aspects are modeled through the notion of **Temporal Shadow** which incorporates **free** or **bound** durations and/or delays. We extend the **type system** of an Object-Oriented data model for expressing and controlling synchronization between objects in order to provide **sequential** and **parallel** presentations. These presentations are themselves stored as database objects and can be derived automatically from the schema, updated and queried. We describe also several extensions to an object **query language** in order to deal with specific temporal and synchronization aspects of multimedia presentations. Our approach shows how current object-oriented DBMS architectures and functions should be revisited in order to provide an integrated environment to handle time-based multimedia data.

1 MULTIMEDIA OBJECTS AND TEMPORAL ASPECTS

One of the challenges for the evolution of future DBMS is their ability to handle multimedia data in an integrated and efficient way (i.e. text, images, audio and digitized full-motion video). Several approaches address the topic of

---

[1]STORM stands for "Structural and Temporal Object-oRiented Multimedia"

multimedia data management [20], [13], [3] and commercially available DBMS already allow storage of texts, images and sounds. Some of them are able to store video data. However, almost none of them offers integrated capabilities for building, updating and querying presentations which combine and synchronize different kinds of data. There are several reasons to such a situation. First, multimedia data require large amount of storage space. Texts and images are of the size of several MB, one hour of digitized (compressed) video requires 1GB. Second, multimedia data need specific input and output devices but also high speed and bandwidth communication facilities [19]. Finally, audio and video data have specific temporal characteristics which are not easily modelled by current database models [23].

In fact, temporal issues are essential for managing multimedia data. Time and several related aspects have also been a domain of intense work in the area of databases and information systems [46]. There are also several studies about real-time [44] or active databases [15]. Although these activities were done independently, we believe that they should be adapted and integrated in future (multimedia) DBMS.

Several standards exist and concern multimedia and hypermedia data. Among them we find: HyTime, MPEG JPEG, MHEG. For instance, HyTime is an international standard for storing and interchanging multimedia, hypermedia, time-based documents [38]. It is included in SGML and provides a collection of abstract semantic constructs associated with syntactic conventions. Structured multimedia documents are often stored in file systems. We believe that OODBMS technology [18] can bring a lot of benefit to future multimedia document management: modelling concepts, concurrency control, high level query facilities, etc. There are several approaches in this area [29], [14].

To participate to the development of future Multimedia DBMS (or MDBMS in short) we address the following problems: (1) modelling and management of time-based data and (2) capabilities, languages and interfaces for building, querying and updating multimedia data (Text, Image, Audio, Video). We address such problems in the framework of a MDBMS prototype under development on top of the O_2 DBMS [8], [4]. This prototype, called STORM, provides facilities for describing and storing time-based objects, and for building sequential or parallel presentations of multimedia data [5]. The database system allows to store and retrieve data and our extension provides a way to build multimedia presentations expressing temporal and synchronizations constraints between objects. From one database object it is possible to define different presentations. For instance, the same image can be presented alone two minutes in one presentation, while it can be associated (and synchronized) with an audio comment in another presentation. Finally, presentations are themselves considered as database objects and can be stored, updated and retrieved (*e.g.* *give me all the presentations with a picture of Paris displayed three minutes, followed by a picture of Grenoble, with the Beethoven's ninth symphony as a background music*).

The paper is organized as follows: Section 2 describes the STORM multimedia DBMS. We show how our approach is based upon an extension of the O_2 DBMS for integrating temporal and structural aspects. Section 3 describes how to extend a type system in order to handle time-based data both at schema and instance levels. We establish the mapping between structural constructors and temporal (and synchronization) aspects. We describe several classes and persistent roots which are used in the query language extensions proposed in Section 4. Finally, Section 5 concludes with a brief comparison with similar works and gives directions of future work.

2 THE STORM MULTIMEDIA OBJECT-ORIENTED DBMS

2.1 Functional architecture

Figure 1 is the functional architecture of a multimedia database system. The STORM level corresponds to an extension of an object server. The user interface controls user interaction through a multimedia workstation, and provides specific media editors to build, to manipulate and to compose different (database) objects. The result of such an editing process is considered as a STORM object and contains structural and temporal descriptions which can also be stored into the database.

Our approach is strongly influenced by the fact that a multimedia presentation is manipulated by a human operator through a workstation. At this level, we assume the existence of several physical channels being able to handle specific data. For instance, a Bitmap screen for displaying still images or video sequences, loud-speakers for audio data. In order to treat in a uniform way, objects from integers to video sequences, we assume, without any loss of generality, that each (multimedia) object presentation can be controlled by the human operator through a window on the screen. Even though an audio signal is directed through loud-speakers, we have a corresponding window on the screen for controlling, for instance, the volume.

Here we concentrate on database aspects and this functional architecture is mapped to an existing object-oriented DBMS. We choose the O_2 system which provides several facilities for storing and manipulating objects. The O_2 DBMS provides a database programming language O_2C, a query language OQL and a standard interface with the C++ language [39]. At the interface level, the facilities of O_2 Look, built on top of X-Window, provides primitives to present objects on the screen and to handle spatial aspects [8]. We emphasize that the prototyping on top of O_2 is intended to show the feasibility of our approach. Our ultimate goal is to define the necessary extensions for building a complete multimedia DBMS. These extensions concern not only the data model (and the associated DDL and DML) which should integrate structural and temporal aspects, but also specific data structures to store and retrieve in an efficient way multimedia data (e.g. BLOBs and associated specific access methods). In future multimedia object servers, these extensions should be added at the different levels of the physical architecture. Notice that the use of an object-oriented DBMS does not exclude that some data are stored in traditional files or by specific media servers [7], [30].

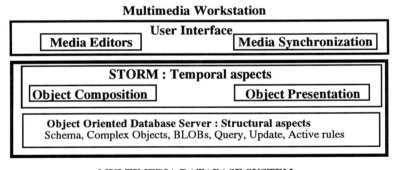

MULTIMEDIA DATABASE SYSTEM

Figure 1   Functional architecture of a Multimedia DBMS.

2.2 Modeling multimedia data and presentations

For modeling multimedia data, and for the sake of simplicity, we consider text (strings of arbitrary length) and images (e.g. Bitmap pictures) as **static** multimedia data. Digitized audio and full-motion video are considered as **dynamic** or ephemeral data. Static means that there is no specific time associated with an image. It can be displayed ten minutes or ten seconds. Dynamic data are explicitly time-dependent. A video display lasts for a specific amount of time at a usual rate (25 or 30 frames per second). Going forward or backward will take the same time unless we change the rate (fast forward or backward). The duration of a video or audio sequence can be either stored with the object or computed in some way (for instance on the basis of the number of frames), but it can be considered as an inherent property of the object.

We model the notion of **presentation** which includes the time during which an image (or a video) is observable by the user[2], but also which expresses the fact that the image display should be synchronized with another piece of data, either in sequence or in parallel. A classical example of such a presentation is a slides show.

In the O_2 DBMS, a class is defined by a type and a set of methods. Each object is a class instance and is a pair of (oid, value), where the value can be complex using constructors like tuple, list, set. Persistency is achieved through the notion of names and persistent roots for objects and values. Besides the basic types as **integer** or **string**, the O_2 system provides a library of predefined classes (types) such as **Text**, **Bitmap** (X-window), **Image** (Gif format) and **Sound**. For specific applications it is possible to define and implement Video classes as well (e.g. a MPEG class [31], [9]). Here we assume the existence of four basic monomedia classes, **Text, Image, Audio and Video**[3].

In an application, classes, types, methods and names constitute the database schema. Objects are created and stored into the database independently of any presentation. For instance we may have an image database where each image is described by specific attributes. The following O_2 description is the definition of a class and a name (i.e. a persistent root) for a set of pictures [39].

Class Mypicture

---

[2] From a database point of view, the time required to display an image is irrelevant.

[3] These classes provide physical independance and we make no particular assumption about media servers.

```
type tuple (title :   string,
            pdate :   Date,
            subject :   string,
            content :   Image)
method ...
end ;
name Mypictures :   set(Mypicture) ;
```

So, it is possible to define and store a set of images into the database. To each image, several descriptive external attributes such as title, date, subject, are associated with the image content. In the O_2 system, associations between objects can be expressed using structural constructors and object references (i.e. oid). For instance, if i1, i2, i3 are instances of **Mypicture** and a1, a2, a3 instances of the **Audio** class, the following value is a list of pairs (image, sound):

```
list (tuple(picture:i1, comment:a1),
      tuple(picture:i2, comment:a2),
      tuple(picture:i3, comment:a3))
```

Traditional object models are not able to take into account temporal aspects for combining and synchronizing different objects when we want to present them to the user. We propose to add a temporal dimension to such a structural and static description. For instance, allocate to each picture an amount of time, and, assuming that audio comments are associated with images, present each pair (sound, image) in parallel immediately followed by the next pair, etc. We define the **presentation** of several pictures as a STORM object where a specific amount of time is allocated to each object to be presented and where we indicate how objects should be synchronized (e.g. one after the other, or all you can show in the screen, etc.). We express sequential or parallel synchronizations between objects. In the example above, the list constructor can be interpreted as a sequence, while the tuple is viewed as a parallel arrangement of two (heterogeneous) objects. The result is an integration of structural and temporal aspects into presentations derived from static descriptions or explicitly composed of existing database objects.

2.3   Temporal aspects

Simple types like **Time** (e.g. GMT) and **Date** are now part of the SQL and ODMG standards. In the ODMG we also find **Timestamp** (Time and Date) and **Interval** which represents a duration of time.

We choose a temporal model based upon widely accepted notions and using interval operators [6], [2], [32], [33]. Basically, we need to express durations and delays for objects to be presented. We use also the concept of time interval as the set of instants when each object is presented [20]. An interval is defined in the following way: given a set S partially ordered ($\leq$) and two elements a and b belonging to S, the set $\{x|\ a\leq x\leq b\}$ is an interval of S (denoted by [a,b]).

To relate intervals to time-dependant data it is necessary to map S on a set of instants, and then speak of temporal interval. However, in this paper *each interval corresponds to the presentation of one object* (e.g. an image or a music selection). In that sense, the beginning and the end of an interval are **logical times** which will really correspond to physical time during the effective presentation to the user. For an interval [a,b], a and b corresponds to specific events which are either system or user driven. We choose a time granularity of a second and the length of our intervals correspond to a duration expressed in seconds (and managed by C functions). For a given interval x, duration(x) is a number of type **Duration**. Although the word "span" might be more adequate than interval [28], several other works on multimedia databases use also temporal interval based models [47].

Several relationships have been defined on time intervals: before, meet, equal, overlap, during, start, finish[6]. Usually, they are binary relationships but can be easily extended to n-ary ones [33]. **Sequential** relationships combine intervals which share the same timeline (mutual exclusion), occurring one after the other with (**before**) or without delay (**meet**) between them. **Parallel** relationships relate intervals which have their own timeline. In our model these relations are used for composing and synchronizing multimedia objects in presentations.

Temporal aspects are also discussed in standards like HyTime where the concept of finite coordinate system is used to define a set of axes of finite dimensions. The system designer defines both the number of axes and the units of dimension used along each of them. Hence, an x-y-time coordinate system can be used to model spatial as well as temporal relationships. Here, we are not dealing with spatial relationships and we only want to model temporal aspects for database objects belonging to presentations. In MHEG [43], time is introduced by a temporal axis (from 0 to ∞) with the notion of GTU (Generic Time Unit) which is the unit of the axis, and GTR (Generic Time Ratio) which is the number of consecutive intervals of one GTU in a second. For video (European), GTU=40 msec and GTR=25. Here, we consider times expressed in seconds as the unit of our logical time scale and consecutive intervals are modelled by the meet relationship.

2.4   Temporal shadow

Let us now explain why we use the term **Temporal Shadow** for each object
appearing in a presentation. For an object x, and a presentation p of x, the
notion of Temporal Shadow expresses the fact that in p, x is associated with
specific temporal values. In another presentation p' of x, it is possible to
associate different temporal values with x. For instance, if x is an image, it
can be presented 3 minutes in p and 30 seconds in p'. Intuitively, the notion
of Temporal Shadow (TS) is a way to model and to store specific temporal
information for multimedia data. Thus, depending on the point of view, it
is possible to associate several different TS with a given (database) object
resulting in different presentations. The Temporal Shadow is composed of two
elements a duration and a delay, as it is explained below.

In each presentation, we associate with each data item a **duration** attribute.
For any object x, duration(x) is the time (in seconds) during which the object
will be perceived by a human operator. For instance, the duration of an image
(or an integer) is the time during which the image (or the integer) is displayed
on the screen, while for an audio object, it is the time during which the sound
is played.

A **duration** is either a **free** (i.e. unlimited) value if the corresponding item is
static (e.g. an integer, a text, an image), or a **bound** (i.e. limited) value in the
case of **dynamic** or ephemeral data such as audio or video. This means that
the duration associated with a given integer, a text or an image is unlimited
by default. Once an image is displayed, it is the user's responsibility to erase
it. Of course, it is possible to allocate a fixed amount of time (e.g. 5 minutes)
during which the image is displayed and then automatically erased. For audio
and video, there is, inherent to the nature of this kind of data, a fixed (bound)
duration which corresponds to a correct (i.e. without distortion) presentation
of the information.

Specific operations are allowed to modify the duration associated with an object. First, it is possible to transform a free duration into a bound one by
allocating a fixed amount of time. Second, for a given bound duration it is possible to **stretch** it or to **shrink** it. For instance, stretching a video sequence,
results in a slow motion. Third, the **repeat** operation can be used to play the
same object either several times or indefinitely. The last case corresponds to
the conversion of a bound duration into a free one. Observe that the repeat
operation is meaningless for static (free duration) data.

In a presentation, we also associate with each data item a **delay.** For any object x, delay(x) is the time (e.g. in seconds) before observing x. In other words, it is the waiting time before presenting (i.e. playing) the object at the interface level. For instance, wait ten seconds before playing an audio comment. Here again we have either **bound** or **free delays.** A bound delay has an obvious meaning and has just been exemplified. The notion of free delay needs however some explanations. By definition, a free delay is an unlimited duration which means that we are waiting "forever"! We propose to use this concept in order to express the fact that the system is ready for presenting an object, but is waiting until some event occurs, typically a user action. For instance, the system displays an icon showing that a video object is ready to be played (e.g. a small TV) together with specific buttons such as "play", "stop", "backward", "forward" and waits until the user chooses the "play" button. In our model this object will have a free delay. Note that the waiting time can also be interrupted due to some specific synchronization constraints.

To summarize, we propose to associate with each object appearing in a presentation, a pair of temporal elements, **duration** and **delay** each of them being either **free** or **bound** and constituting the **Temporal Shadow TS** of the object. For object x, TS(x) = tuple(duration: Duration, delay: Duration) is a tuple of two durations, one is the presentation time allocated to the object and the other is the waiting time before observing it.

Any object (from integer to video) has at least one Temporal Shadow which is defined by default. We have (1) for static data, a bound delay to zero and a free duration; and (2) for dynamic objects, a bound duration and a free delay (see Section 3). For any given object x, there are four ways to combine its delay and duration: (Free, Free), (Free, Bound), (Bound, Free), (Bound, Bound). Of course a Free delay should be interpreted as "until an event occurs" and corresponds to an arbitrary large value of time.

2.5   The STORM Object Model

A STORM Object (or SO in short) is a **quadruplet (i, d, δ, c)** where **i** is the object identifier. The duration **d** and the delay δ constitute the **Temporal Shadow.** They can be either free or bound. The data to be presented is the **content c** which can be either monomedia (or atomic) or composed of several objects using sequential and parallel operators.

We consider the following basic (static) types which objects are supposed atomic ones: `integer, real, boolean, bits, char, string, Date, Time, Duration`. We denote by `Atomic` the union of all these types. Although it should be possible to present an integer or a character string during a specific amount of time, we give a special attention to the following pre-defined monomedia types: `Image, Text, Audio, Video`. As we said before, images and texts (but also `Atomic` elements) are considered as static, audio and video objects as dynamic, having a specific duration.

The following rules state the definition of STORM objects (i denotes an object identifier):

- **Rule 0**: **(i, d, δ, nil)** is a SO[4]

- **Rule 1**: **(i, d, δ, c)** is a SO where c is an instance of `Atomic, Image, Text, Audio, Video`.

Two main (generic) temporal operators, namely sequence (`seq`) and parallel (`par`) can be used for building presentations. They do not affect the structural definition of objects but express temporal and synchronization constraints for presenting them. Interval relationships (see Rule 4) allow to define several kinds of synchronization which can cover a wide range of multimedia applications.

If $s_1, s_2, \dots s_n$ (n$\geq$1) are SO, then

- **Rule 2**: **(i, d, δ, seq(s_1, s_2,...s_n))** is a SO (a sequential presentation)

- **Rule 3**: **(i, d, δ, par(s_1, s_2,...s_n))** is a SO (a parallel presentation)

Note that in a sequential or parallel presentation each s_i has its own Temporal Shadow. So, we consider that two lists are associated to the presentation: a list of durations d_i and a list of delays δ_i. For each sequential or parallel presentation, the delay δ is the time before starting the whole presentation, while the duration **d** depends on the respective durations and delays d_i and δ_i.

Notice that these notions of sequential and parallel presentations are logical, in the sense that we do not take into account the existence of physical channels for the corresponding objects. For instance, in parallel presentations, the

---

[4] We associate to nil a temporal shadow which can change depending of the context where nil is used.

existence of separate physical channels can provide true parallelism. We think that our approach provides a good level of independence because it concentrates on temporal and synchronization aspects between objects. The mapping between a STORM presentation and physical channels should be made at the user interface level (cf. Figure 1).

Another important remark is that presentations refer to multimedia objects through their oids and they do not "contain" them. This is important because these objects are large and should not be replicated. Here, using oid, several different presentations can share the same multimedia object (e.g. a video).

- **Rule 4: Qualifying presentations**

To express synchronization between objects, qualifiers can be applied to the generic **seq** and **par** temporal operators. They are denoted by **seq-α** (where α is **meet** or **before**) and **par-β** (where β is **equal, start, finish, during, overlap**) and they are briefly discussed below. Most of the time we consider a two objects presentation but this case can easily be extended to n-ary ones.

Sequential presentations

The **seq** operator builds a sequential presentation of objects which are mutually exclusive. However, they may share the same physical channel. For instance, if **m1, m2** are (SO) musical selections and **p1, p2** (SO) pictures, we can have: (i) **seq(m1,m2)** for a sequence of musical selections; (ii) **seq(m1,p1)** where the display of **m1** will precede **p1**; (iii) two sequences of **p1** and **p2** with different TS, **s1= seq(p1,p2)** with TS1=$((d_{11}:10, \delta_{11}:F),(d_{21}:20, \delta_{21}:F))$, and **s2= seq(p1,p2)** with TS2=$((d_{12}:F, \delta_{12}:30),(d_{22}:F, \delta_{22}:40))$. *Durations are given in seconds and F denotes Free.*

- **Seq-meet(o_1, o_2)**

The meet relationship imposes that there is no delay between the objects and they should be played one after the other. If all the durations are free, there are two cases:
- present o_1 and then wait for an external event (e.g. the user), then process o_2, etc.;
- bind d_i for each o_i. Each duration can be different or not, one can also be computed from the other (e.g. $d_{i+1} = f(d_i)$);

If we have bound durations, then each item has its own fixed duration and will be presented accordingly. In all cases[5], the total duration for a sequence s is:

$$duration(s) = \sum_{i=1,n}^{n} d_i$$

For example, assume a1 through a5 are of type Audio. If we want to play them in sequence without delay, we build the following SO: seq-meet (a1, a2, a3, a4, a5).

In a presentation, it is possible to repeat a given object. Consider, for instance, the following sequence seq-meet (m12*,v10) where m12 is an audio object (musical selection) and v10 a video. Both objects have bound durations, but we repeat m12 "forever" resulting in a free duration for the first operand (see Section 2.6 for the definition of the repeat operation). The musical selection should be stopped in order to start the video presentation. This is not the same as seq-meet(m12,v10).

- Seq-before(o_1,o_2)

The **before** relationship introduces a non zero delay between every item. This delay can be the same for all the elements or it can be different. After a delay of δ_1, item o_1 is presented during d_1 and erased. Then we wait for a delay δ_2 before presenting item o_2, etc. The discussion about the duration list is very similar to the previous case. The difference here is that the delay list can be free, partially bound or bound. A bound delay is directly handled by the system. A free delay means that the system waits before playing the next item, so it is necessary to process specific (user) event.

Parallel presentations

In a parallel presentation, several objects can be observed simultaneously, each object having its own timeline. In the general case, there is no specific predefined synchronization constraints between the objects. Objects may or may not share the same physical channel resulting, for the end-user, into true or false parallelism. To impose synchronization constraints between objects, the **par** operator should be qualified: **par-equal, par-during, par-start, par-finish, par-overlap**. Some qualifiers requires that delays are bound to

---

[5] Finally, we assume that nothing will really last forever!

zero (e.g. `par-start`), while for others, they should be non zero values (e.g. `par-overlap`).

- Par-equal(o_1,o_2)

This relationship imposes that all the durations d_i are the same and that all delays are bound to zero. The duration list may contain zero, one or several bound values. There are three possibilities[6]for (d_1, d_2):

- (Free, Free): o_1 and o_2 start simultaneously and as soon as one is stopped, the other one is also stopped accordingly;
- (Free, Bound): in this case we consider that the bound duration of o_2 is assigned to o_1 and hence, the resulting presentation will be Bound. Note that we allow the user to stop either o_2 or o_1 at any time. However, stopping one of them will automatically trigger the end of the other one;
- (Bound, Bound): this case is only allowed if $d_1=d_2$ otherwise this results in a temporally inconsistent SO (see Section 2.7). Note that it is possible to stretch or shrink o_1 or o_2 in order to make d_1 and d_2 equal (see Section 2.6).

For instance, consider an object identified by `music1` (type `Audio`) that we want to play as a background music when we show a sequence of (three) images `p1`, `p2`, `p3`, each of them associated with an audio comment `a1`, `a2`, `a3`[7]. The following SO content expresses the desired synchronization:

```
par-equal(music1*,
        seq-meet(par-equal(p1,a1),
                par-equal(p2,a2),
                par-equal(p3,a3)))
```

The external `par-equal` has two parameters: a musical selection which is played "forever" (Free duration) and a sequence (without delay) of parallel streams which are of the kind (Free, Bound). Each picture is displayed (Free) with its associated comment (Bound). Equality is achieved by allocating the duration of each audio object to the corresponding picture. The sequence results in a Bound duration so the external `par-equal` is of type (Free, Bound) and the background music will be stopped as soon as the picture show is finished (see Section 2.7).

- Par-during(o_1,o_2)

---

[6] In this case, `par-equal`(o_1, o_2) = `par-equal`(o_2, o_1).

[7] We assume that the user workstation has the capabilities for handling two audio channels.

We make the convention that the **during** relationship imposes that $d_1 > d_2$ or in other words that o_{i-1} cannot be stopped if o_i is still active. This is expressed by constraints associated to the **par-during** operator applied to objects. In **par-during**(o_1, o_2) we assume that o_1 starts first and then after a delay δ_2, o_2 starts. However, duration d_2 associated to o_2 should be such that $d_2 + \delta_2 < d_1$. This should hold for all the objects.

When d_1 and d_2 are bound, it might be interesting to "temporally" center the occurring of o_2 in the middle of o_1. This is similar to the work described in [26] where the notion of delay is called "temporal glue" by analogy with the T_EX formatter. Here, we obtain the same effect by modifying the delay of o_2 in the Temporal Shadow: $\delta_2 = (d_1 - d_2)/2$

- **Par-start**(o_1, o_2), **Par-finish**(o_1, o_2)

The **start** relationship imposes only that all the o_i are displayed in parallel without constraint about their respective durations. Observe that **par-start** imposes only that several objects start simultaneously while **par-equal** corresponds to objects which start and finish together.

The **finish** relation however should consider the respective durations of the data items but also the possible delays between the beginning of o_1 and the beginning of o_2, for instance. The constraint which should be ensured is that once o_i is stopped (because of time-out or by a user action), all the others should stop as well. Consider **par-finish**(o_1, o_2) and assume d_1 is free and d_2 is bound. In this case d_1 will be bound to $\delta_2 + d_2$.

- **Par-overlap**(o_1, o_2)

Such a presentation means that o_1 starts first, followed after a (non zero) delay by o_2, etc. The constraint is that the end of o_i should occur before the end of o_{i+1}. Let us analyze the cases where some durations may be Free (F) or Bound (B). Consider two objects o_1 and o_2, and their respective durations d_1 and d_2. There are four cases (1) : (F, F), (2) : (F, B), (3): (B, F), (4) (B, B). The constraint is easy to enforce for cases (1) and (4). We forbid case (2) because it may result into a during relationship. Case (3) is allowed but o_2 cannot be stopped before the end of o_1.

Concerning overlap, there is another interesting case where one want to build a transition between two object presentations p_1 and p_2. This supposes that before the end of p_1, p_2 starts and that they overlap for the time of the transition. In the case of bound durations without user interaction, it is easy to compute δ_2 in order to start p_2 accordingly.

2.6 The STORM Meta-schema

In the previous sections we have presented the basic elements of the STORM data model. In this section, we describe how this model is implemented using the O_2 Object-Oriented DBMS. We claim that the mapping between the STORM model and O_2 is general enough to be applied to any other Object-Oriented DBMS including extended relational systems.

Figure 2 sketches the hierarchy of O_2 classes which constitutes the meta-schema of our extension. The root called SO (for Storm Object) is associated with specific methods (e.g. **present**). At this level, the Temporal Shadow is represented by two methods **delay** and **duration**. The delay is an attribute defined in SO, and is inherited by every other STORM object. The **rep** attribute indicates how many times the presentation should be repeated. The duration is either stored in the presentation of each static objects (class **Static**) or computed from the description of a dynamic object.

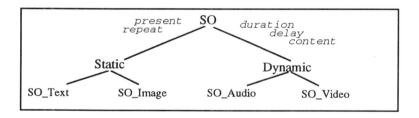

Figure 2   Meta-schema of the STORM extension.

```
Class SO
      type tuple (delay :  Duration, rep :  integer)
      method present ,
      method delay :  Duration,
      method duration :  Duration,
      method allocdelay (d:Duration) :  SO,
      method repeat (n:integer) :  SO
      method content :  ANY
 ....  end;
```

The method **present** has an obvious meaning: present the object to the user.
Allocdelay allocates a delay to an object. **Repeat** is used to repeat the presentation of the object n times or an unlimited number of times (for simplicity, this is denoted in the paper by x*, i.e. repeat x indefinitely). The **content** method is used to access the object content to be presented. At that level, it is only a signature (it returns **ANY**, the top of all the class hierarchy) and the method is redefined at each level of the inheritance graph, depending upon the type of object to be presented (e.g. return the bitmap associated with an **Image** or the signal of an **Audio** object).

STORM objects are then subdivided into **Static** and **Dynamic**. A static object is a presentation of a monomedia element such as a **Text** or an **Image**. Dynamic objects are presentations of **Audio** or **Video** objects. Classes like **SO_C** where C is either **Text**, **Image**, **Video** or **Audio** are used to associate with a database object one or several presentations. An **SO_Image**, for instance, is a presentation of an **Image**. This approach establishes a clear distinction between database objects and presentations of them[8]. The use of oid allows several presentations with different Temporal Shadows to share the same object. The definitions of **Static** and **Dynamic** classes are given below (for simplicity, we do not describe all the methods). Notice that **Dynamic** has an empty type but specific methods. They are explained below.

```
Class Static inherit SO
      type tuple (duration :  Duration)
      method allocduration :  SO
 ....  end;
Class Dynamic inherit SO
      method stretch (n:integer) :  SO
      method shrink (n:integer) :  SO
      method extract (b:integer, d:Duration) :  SO
 ....  end;
Class SO_Image inherit Static type tuple (content :  Image) ....
Class SO_Text inherit Static  type tuple (content :  Text) ....
Class SO_Audio inherit Dynamic type tuple (content :  Audio) ....
Class SO_Video inherit Dynamic type tuple (content :  Video) ....
```

For static objects the operation **allocduration** allocates a specific amount of time or assigns a free duration. For dynamic objects it is possible to change

---

[8] It is possible to define other classes SO_C where C can be **string** or any other user-defined class, for instance SO_Mypicture.

their (bound) duration by using the **stretch** and **shrink** operations (using a factor n). Note, that these last two operations are irrelevant for free duration objects[9].

Consider a dynamic object x with its bound duration d. If we allocate d' to x with d' < d this results in an incomplete presentation of x (i.e. the first d' seconds). We think that this is too restrictive and instead, we propose an operation for extracting a subpart of x (e.g. extract the last five minutes of video v). The operation **extract** has two parameters for defining the sub-part extracted from the object. For instance, for video v, b is a frame number and d a duration. The method call **v.extract(b,d)** gives the sub-part of video v starting at frame b and lasting d seconds[10]. There is no duplication of information, since extract means *access* to a sub-part of a continuous object.

2.7   Temporal consistency

Each STORM object is intented to be presented to a human user during a time interval. According to the notion of Temporal Shadow, two intervals are associated with each object. The first one is the delay and the second one, the duration. Both intervals can be open on the right in case of a free delay or duration. For object x, the beginning of the first interval corresponds to the invocation of the **present** operation applied to x (denoted here by **present(x)**). The beginning of the second interval is **present(x)+delay(x)**, denoted by **begin(x)**. The end of the presentation occurs at **present(x)+delay(x)+duration(x)**, which is denoted by **end(x)** (see Figure 3).

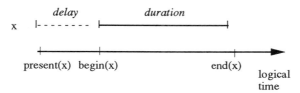

Figure 3   Presentation of object x as two temporal intervals.

The two events **begin(x)** and **end(x)** are considered as atomic (i.e. zero duration) and can be either system or user driven. For instance, suppose that a sequence of images is started by the user. Once the first image is presented,

---

[9] For audio and video data it might be interesting to define reverse playout [33]. So, it is possible to add a method **reverse**. However, we do not develop this point here.

[10] It is also possible to define the interval by two frame numbers.

it will be automatically erased in case of time-out, and the following picture will be presented. On the contrary, if an unlimited (free) duration is associated with each image, a user action is required to stop each image in order to obtain the following one. Due to some synchronization constraints it might be possible that the user action will be ignored or will trigger other actions (for instance, stopping automatically an audio comment synchronized with the image display).

Let us now compute the temporal shadow for sequential and parallel presentations. Suppose $\Theta(o_1, o_2)$ is a temporal presentation where Θ can be one of the seven operators (two sequential and five parallel). The respective durations of o_1 and o_2 are d_1, and d_2 (free and bound are denoted respectively by F and B). For all operators, two free or two bound durations result respectively into free or bound durations. However, when we have one free and one bound duration, the result depends of the operator. Due to their particular semantic, **par-equal** and **par-finish** result in an object with a bound duration. For all the others, the result has a free duration (Table 1).

Object consistency is defined in terms of structural and temporal consistency. Structural refers to object composition without any temporal or synchronization consideration. For instance define an object value as a tuple with two attributes of type string. Temporal consistency expresses that objects should obey specific constraints with respect to time. There are two kinds of such constraints, static and dynamic. Static temporal constraints express consistency at creation time, while dynamic constraints should be enforced at presentation time through active rules [15].

duration d1 d2	F	B
F	F	par-equal or par-finish: B other: F
B	par-equal or par-finish: B other: F	B

Table 1   Combining Free (F) and Bound (B) durations.

Let us take an example. Assume we have two audio objects a1 and a2 with respective (bound) durations d1 and d2 (and bound delays $\delta1$ and $\delta2$), and suppose we want to build the following SO: **par-overlap(a1,a2)**. At creation time we have to check that $d2 + \delta2 > d1$, otherwise the object is inconsistent. Notice that this constraint can be verified because we have here bound durations. At presentation time, we should enforce the following constraint: $end(a2) > end(a1)$[11] which means that the user is not allowed to stop a2 if a1 is active.

STORM object	d1	d2	$\delta1$	$\delta2$	Constraints
seq (o1, o2)	F ,B	F ,B	F,B	F,B	$begin(o2) \geq end(o1)$
seq-meet (o1, o2)	F,B	F,B	0	0	$begin(o2)=end(o1)$
seq-before (o1, o2)	F,B	F,B	F,B ($\neq 0$)	F,B ($\neq 0$)	$begin(o2)=end(o1)+\delta2$
par (o1, o2)	F,B	F,B	F,B	F,B	
par-equal (o1, o2)	F,B	F,B	0	0	$d1 = d2$ $\wedge\ begin(o1)=begin(o2)$ $\wedge\ end(o2)=end(o2)$
par-overlap (o1, o2)	F B B	F F B	F,B ($\neq 0$)	F,B ($\neq 0$)	$d2 + \delta2 > d1$ $\wedge\ begin(o2)=begin(o1)+\delta2$ $\wedge\ end(o2)> end(o1)$ $\wedge\ begin(o2) < end(o1)$
par-during (o1, o2)	F,B	F,B	F,B ($\neq 0$)	F,B ($\neq 0$)	$d1 > d2$ $\wedge\ begin(o2)=begin(o1)+\delta2$ $\wedge\ end(o2) < end(o1)$
par-start (o1, o2)	F,B	F,B	0	0	$begin(o2)=begin(o1)$
par-finish (o1, o2)	F,B	F,B	F,B ($\neq 0$)	F,B ($\neq 0$)	$d1 = d2 + \delta2$ $\wedge\ begin(o2)=begin(o1)+\delta2$ $\wedge\ end(o2)=end(o1)$

Table 2 Consistent STORM Objects.

Giving more details on this notion is out the scope of this text but Table 2 is a summary for sequential presentations and parallel presentations (considering only two objects) with durations, delays and associated constraints. In this table, the first column indicate the kind of presentation. Delays and durations are shown for each operand. The notation F,B means that both types are allowed. Refer to Figure 3 for the definition of begin and end. Some constraints may seem redundant but one has to remember that durations may be free or bound. For instance, the `equal` qualifier imposes that the two objects have the same duration. However, if both durations are free, the static constraint is not violated but it is necessary, at presentation time, to start the two objects at the same time and, as soon as one is stopped, to stop the other one accordingly.

---

[11]We should have a strict greater than, otherwise we have `finish(a1, a2)`

3   TYPING AND BUILDING MULTIMEDIA PRESENTATIONS

STORM objects are presentations of other objects with specific temporal and synchronization constraints. We address now two problems: (1) at the **schema** level, how is it possible to define types (or classes) for creating STORM objects? (2) for any existing (database) non STORM object, how is it possible to define a default presentation?

3.1   Typing sequential and parallel presentations

For solving problem (1) we have to define type constructors which provide the semantic of the **seq** and **par** operators. We claim that it is not necessary to define a completely new data model but only to extend an object model in the following way. First, we observe that the **list** constructor has a behaviour similar to **seq**: lists are ordered collections of objects while **sets** (or **bags**) are not ordered which suggest a mapping with the **par** operator. Second, we observe that we are interested of gathering **homogeneous** or **heterogeneous** objects. Lists and sets are homogeneous collections of objects, while **tuples** (or **struct**) can be used to gather objects of different types. So, the idea is to have **sequential and parallel tuples** and this is why we define two kinds of tuples, one called **tuple** which attribute values are not ordered, and the second one called **stuple** where attribute values are considered as ordered.

Finally, we observe that lists and sets are collections of an **unlimited** number of objects, while tuples (or stuples) are **limited** by the number of attributes. So, the **union** type is introduced to model unlimited heterogeneous collections of objects (see Table 3).

	unlimited homogeneous	limited heterogeneous or homogeneous	unlimited heterogeneous
seq	list (T)	stuple (a1:T1, ... an:Tn)	list (union (a1:T1,.... an:Tn))
par	set (T)	tuple (a1:T1, ... an:Tn)	set (union (a1:T1,.... an:Tn))

Table 3   Combining structural and temporal aspects.

The underlying type system of our extension is based on the O_2 model [8] and also on other propositions [17], [14].

- Let A be a set of attribute names, I a set of object identifiers called oids and C a set of class names[12]. An object is a pair (oid, value) where the value is of a given type. First we define values and then types.

i) **nil** is the undefined value;

ii) each element of **Atomic** (2.5) or each oid of I is a value;

iii) if v_1, $\ldots v_n$ are values and a_1, $\ldots a_n$ distinct attribute names, then
- **set(v_1, $\ldots v_n$)**, **list(v_1, $\ldots v_n$)**, are set and list values;
- **tuple(a_1:v_1, $\ldots a_n$:v_n)**, **stuple(a_1:v_1, $\ldots a_n$:v_n)**, are tuple values.
For each permutation **i1**, $\ldots$ **in** of **1**, $\ldots$ **n** which is not the identity, we have: **stuple(a_1:v_1, $\ldots a_n$:v_n)** $\neq$ **stuple(a_{i1}:v_{i1}, $\ldots$, a_{in}:v_{in})**.

- Types over a set C of classes are defined in the following way:

a) **integer, real, boolean, bits, char, string, Date, Time, Duration** are types;
b) class names in C (including **Image, Text, Audio, Video**) are types;
ANY (the top of the class hierarchy) is a type;
c) if **T** is a type then **set(T)** , **list(T)** are set and list types;
d) if T_1, $\ldots T_n$ are types and a_1, $\ldots a_n$ distinct attribute names, then :
- **tuple(a_1:T_1, $\ldots a_n$:T_n)**, **stuple(a_1:T_1, $\ldots a_n$:T_n)**, are tuple and ordered tuple types.
- **union(a_1:T_1, $\ldots a_n$:T_n)** is the union type

Sub-typing rules are defined like in O_2 with the necessary extensions due to the introduction of sequential tuples and union types. Following [14] we consider that a stuple is a special case of heterogeneous list. If the sub-typing relationship is denoted by $\leq$ we have: **stuple(a_1:T_1, $\ldots a_n$:T_n)** $\leq$ **list(union(a_1:T_1, $\ldots a_n$:T_n))**

---

[12] A class is considered here as a typing notion and should not be confused with the class extension.

3.2   Default Presentations for Database Objects

Now we address problem (2) for presenting existing (database) objects. These objects are created, stored (i.e. made persistent) and updated according to application requirements. Using structural constructors as list, tuple and set it is possible to define arbitrary complex values for them. Then, what happens if we want to present a complex value (e.g. a set of images)?

For this we recall that object values can be either atomic or complex. Also we remember that we distinguish between static and dynamic objects. Finally we have indicated that in the O_2 DBMS, there are only three structural constructors, namely list, set and tuple. In this discussion it is worth noting that the database objects do not have a predefined Temporal Shadow stored according to the meta-schema given in Section 2.6. So, the behavior that we are describing here is only relevant at presentation time. In other words, the main idea is to present any existing (O_2) object (or value) as a STORM object even though it is not an instance of a STORM class (see next section).

The following rules are used in order to define a standard presentation for given objects and values.

Let $o = (i, v)$ be an object with oid i and value v.

(i) If o has an **atomic** value, then we associate to it a Temporal Shadow (d, δ) in the following way:
- for static types (i.e. `integer`, `real`, `boolean`, `bits`, `char`, `string`, `Date`, `Time`, `Duration`, `Time_Interval`, `Text`, `Image`): (F, 0), that is a Free duration and a zero delay;
- for dynamic types (`Audio`, `Video`): (B, F), that is a Bound duration and a Free delay. For instance, the presentation of a string, say "Paris" will be done without delay with a Free duration.

(ii) For any **oid** from a user defined class, we associate a Free delay to the referenced object. For instance, consider an object p with a tuple value of the type: `tuple(name :string, country :   Country)` and suppose we want to present `p.country` which is a reference to an instance of a user defined class named `Country`. This instance will be presented with a Free delay.

(iii) If v is a **list** value, $v = \text{list}(o_1, o_2, \ldots o_n)$, then it corresponds to a **sequential** presentation : $\text{seq}(o_1, o_2, \ldots \ldots o_n)$. Depending upon the

Temporal Shadow associated to each o_i, the sequence can be interpreted either with the **meet** or **before** qualifier. For instance if we consider a list of images, having all a zero delay, we will have a **seq-meet**.

In O_2, there exist a conversion function called **listoset** in order to transform a list into a set. This is useful in our context if we want to present the elements of a given list in parallel: first, transform the list into a set and then use the following rule.

(iv) If v is a **set** value, v = **set**(o_1, o_2, ...o_n). then it corresponds to a **parallel** presentation : **par**(o_1, o_2, ...o_n). Depending upon the Temporal Shadow associated to each o_i, the parallel presentation can be interpreted with one of the parallel qualifiers **equal, start, finish, during, overlap** provided that the result is a consistent presentation.

In a set there is no specific order for the elements, and in order to interpret a set as a sequence it is necessary to transform it into a list (O_2 operation **setolist**).

(v) If v is a **tuple** value, v = **tuple**(a_1:o_1, ..., a_n:o_n) then by default we consider it as a **parallel** presentation : **par**(o_1, o_2, ...o_n). However, it should be possible to present it as a **sequence**, this is why we provide conversion functions similar to the ones discussed above. The **tostuple** or **totuple** functions respectively transform a tuple into a stuple or a stuple to a tuple. Depending upon the Temporal Shadow associated to each o_i, the parallel presentation can be interpreted with one of the parallel qualifiers **equal, start, finish, during, overlap** provided that the result is a consistent presentation. For instance the **tuple(m:m12,v:v10)** can be interpreted as **par-start(m12,v10)** or as **seq-meet(m12,v10)**

The complete language for building presentations is still part of our future work. Here, we only sketch through several examples, the process of defining presentations. A browser is used to extract objects to be presented. By default, each structural constructor is mapped to a sequential presentation or parallel presentation according to the rules given above. Each component of the object has an associated Temporal Shadow which can be modified. So, it is possible to override the **par** or **seq** operators in order to define the desired synchronization (for instance, transform a **seq-meet** into a **par-start**). For all this process we propose to adapt and to apply the ideas of [10]. Indeed, the main idea here is to view each structured object through a temporal filter and to apply specific transformations on its structural/temporal attributes. These transformations are either explicit by the application of operations (e.g. **repeat, stretch**) or implicit through synchronization constraints between objects (e.g. **par-equal**).

At each stage it is necessary to check the consistency of the defined presentation (2.7).

Consider the following list of tuples given in Section 2.2:

```
list(tuple(picture:i1, comment:a1),
     tuple(picture:i2, comment:a2),
     tuple(picture:i3, comment:a3))
```

Suppose this is an object value that we want to present as a STORM object. We show this value in the first row of Table 4, but for simplicity, we do not mention attribute names which are respectively picture (type **Image**) and comment (type **Audio**). Remember that an image has a free duration and an audio object a bound one. Then Table 4 shows three possible presentations (1/, 2/ and 3/) associated to this object:

In the first one, each pair (image, sound) is presented in turn, where the image and the sound start in parallel. In the second presentation,[13] we interpret the tuple as a stuple with **seq-before** which supposes that a non zero delay is associated to each image and sound. In this case, the image is presented after the delay, stay there for a while and is erased. Then the sound is processed in the same way. The third presentation supposes also a delay but before each pair and not "inside" them. The tuple is interpreted as a **par-equal** meaning that image and sound are presented in parallel but the image duration is bound to the duration of the sound.

list(	tuple(i1, a1)	tuple(i2, a2)	tuple(i3, a3))
1/ seq-meet	par-start	par-start	par-start
2/ seq-meet	seq-before	seq-before	seq-before
3/ seq-before	par-equal	par-equal	par-equal

Table 4   Different presentations for one object value.

As another example, assume **france, mexico, italy** are video presentations of their respective countries. The following value results into a presentation where a menu is presented, and the user can ask for the presentation (s) he/she wants:

---

[13] According to the semantic of the temporal relations [6], the second presentation is equivalent to: `seq-before(i1,a1,i2,a2,i3,a3)`

```
set(tuple(name :"France", vidclip :france),
    tuple(name :"Mexico", vidclip :mexico),
    tuple(name :"Italy",  vidclip :italy))
par(par("France",france),
    par("Mexico",mexico),
    par("Italy",italy))
```

Query result

It is also possible to define a presentation for a query result. For instance, the following statement builds a sequential presentation for a set of pictures extracted from the database (see Section 2.2 for the definition of the database objects). By default, each picture will have a free duration and a bound delay equal to zero.

```
show = setolist
    (select p.content from Mypictures p where p.subject=''Paris'')
```

3.3   Defining classes for presentations

In this section we indicate how it is possible to use the STORM type system in order to create sequential or parallel presentations as objects. In the discussion, we have two dimensions to consider for the **content** attribute of a multimedia presentation: (1) homogeneous vs. heterogeneous and (2) sequential vs. parallel presentations. We consider also constrained presentations by using a specific clause at the schema level.

In an application schema, the STORM Meta-Schema given in 2.6 can be imported. So, it is possible to combine application dependent classes with those defining presentations. Remember that the **content** attribute plays a key role in such a combination. Through this attribute, and its associated method, we express either monomedia object presentation or sequential and parallel ones.

For instance, given the class **Mypicture** (2.2), we define the class **SO_Mypicture** (and associated persistent root) where each instance can be linked to an existing picture.

```
Class SO_Mypicture inherit Static
      type tuple(content :Mypicture))
  ...     end;
```

```
name SO_Mypictures :   set(SO_Mypicture)
```

For illustration purpose we create also two classes, one for Audio objects called
Music with an associated STORM class **SO_Music** and a class **Movie** which
inherits directly from the **Dynamic** class. Notice the differences between these
definitions, showing the flexibility of our approach.

```
Class Music type tuple(            Class Movie inherit Dynamic
title :  string,                   type tuple(title :  string,
opus :  string,                    director :  string,
composer :  string,                year:  integer,
duration :  Duration,              duration :  Duration,
content :  Audio)                  content :  Video)
...                                ...
end                                end
Class SO_Music inherit Dynamic
type tuple(content :  Music)       name Movies :  set(Movie)
...
end;
```

More generally, Table 5 shows the mapping between database objects and
STORM presentations. A given class C is intended to define database objects
with specific attributes and methods. We denote by Cs the extension of class
C, called a (named) persistent root in O_2. Presentation of each instance of C
can be defined through the class SO_C which is a subclass of SO. Each instance
of SO_C is a presentation of an instance of C with temporal and synchronisation
constraints. Then, it is possible to build and to store several presentations
under the persistent root SO_Cs. A given C instance may be shared by several
presentations. Note however that designing database and STORM classes are
application dependent and therefore many choices are possible.

	DB Objects	STORM presentations
Persistent roots	Cs	SO_Cs
Class names	C	SO_C

Table 5   Mapping between database and STORM classes.

We give several examples by making variations on the notion of slides show. We
assume that the database contains several pictures and music selections which
can be associated to them. The following class definition allows the creation
of objects which have a sequence of images as their content (homogeneous
sequential presentation):

```
Class Show1 inherit SO
```

```
type tuple(content :  list(SO_Mypicture))
```

Assuming that i1, i2, i3, i4 are existing database instances of **Image**, we create corresponding instances of **SO_Mypicture** (si1, si2, si3, si4) each with its specific Temporal Shadow. This can be done interactively or by an application program. Then, we create an instance of **Show1**, say s and we relate it to the objects to be presented. The following is an example of O_2C code to present a sequence s where each image will be displayed 20 seconds. The dot notation "." is uniformly used to denote method call or attribute access.

```
{......
s = new Show1; {create a new instance}
s.content += list(si1, si2, si3, si4) ;   {update SO content}
for x in s.content x.allocduration(20); {establish the TS}
s.present ;
.........}
```

By default, each image has a zero delay which means that the list in this example behaves as a **seq-meet**. As it is shown in the example, it is possible to arrange the Temporal Shadow of the objects in such a way that they obey the constraint (e.g. allocate zero to delays, make several durations equal, etc.).

As it was said in 2.7, static temporal constraints should be enforced at creation time. So, when we build a list, a stuple, a set or a tuple value of **SOs** it is necessary to express and/or to enforce specific constraints (e.g. **meet** or **equal**). However, we propose also to express such a constraint at the schema level. Because we may have several level of nesting, it is necessary to qualify each level. This is done through a constraint clause (called **qualify**) added to the DDL which is applied on the **content** attribute of a STORM object. For instance, Table 6 illustrates the definition of two **content** attributes and associated constraints. It indicates the resulting type of synchronization. The syntax of the **qualify** clause is explained below.

When creating and composing STORM objects, these constraints are verified. This is done by using active rules (Event-Condition-Action) that we have implemented as an extension to the O_2 system [16]. One consequence of such an approach is that in each list, set, tuple or stuple, the same synchronization constraint is applied to all the elements. In other words, if we qualify, it is not possible in a set to have two objects synchronized by a **par-equal** while the others are overlapping. Of course it is not mandatory to use this clause if we want more freedom.

Ex1/ content:	list(T)
constraint	qualify(content, meet)
synchro	seq-meet(T)
Ex2/ content:	list(tuple(a1:T1, a2: tuple(a21:T21, a22:T22)))

constraints	for x in content:
	qualify(content, meet);
	qualify(x, start);
	qualify(x.a2, equal)

synchro	seq-meet(par-start(a1:T1,a2:par-equal(a21:T21,a22:T22)))

Table 6   Synchronization constraints at schema level.

The general format of the qualify clause is `qualify($\pi$, $\tau$)` where π is a path expression starting from the `content` attribute and $\tau \in$ {`before, meet, start, equal, finish, overlap, during`}. In a qualify constraint, `before` and `meet` are associated with `list` and `stuple`, and the other qualifiers are associated with `set` and `tuple`. Each path expression uses the dot notation to express navigation through attributes (`content.a1.a2...`). In order to refer to list or set elements which are structured (see example 2 of Table 6) it is necessary to use a `for` clause similar to the `from` clause used in OQL for defining query variables [40]. If needed, this clause is used before qualifying the desired level. For instance:

```
content :  list(set(tuple(a1:T1, a2:T2)))
for x in content, y in x :
qualify(content, meet), qualify(x, start), qualify(y, equal);
```

Table 7 shows several classes which are all SO sub-classes. We only give the definition of the attribute `content` and, eventually, some constraint using the `qualify` clause. The example of class `Show1` defined above illustrates an homogeneous sequential presentation for several images. The class `Show2` corresponds to a sequence of only two elements, a music and an image.

Using the set constructor, the class `Show3` illustrates a parallel arrangement of objects. An instance `s3` of this class is a set of pictures which are presented in parallel with a kind of "all you can show" behaviour. In other words, `s3.present` results in displaying all the set content on the screen. If, by default each picture has a free duration, it will be displayed until the user decides to erase it. Otherwise, each picture is displayed according to its Temporal Shadow. There is no specific constraint on the parallel arrangement of these pictures.

Class	Attribute content
Show1	list(SO_Mypicture)
Show2	stuple(a1:SO_Music, a2:SO_Mypicture)
Show3	set(SO_Mypicture)
Show4	tuple(a1:SO_Music, a2:SO_Mypicture) qualify(content,equal)
Show5	list(tuple(a1:SO_Music, a2:SO_Mypicture))) for x in content : qualify(x,equal)
Show6	tuple(back:SO_Music, picom:list(tuple(pic:SO_Mypicture, com:SO_Audio)))) for x in content.picom : qualify(content,equal) qualify(content.picom,meet) qualify(x,equal)

Table 7   Classes for presentations.

We consider now heterogeneous presentations, and the class **Show4** which is a parallel presentation for only one music and one picture. The constraint means that the picture should be displayed during the same temporal interval as the music. In contrast, **Show5** corresponds to a sequence of pairs (music, picture).

The example of **Show6** is a combination of sequential and parallel presentations : a pair of a background music with a sequence of pairs (picture, comment) and associated constraints.

3.4   Temporally homogeneous list

From a structural point of view, an interesting use of the list concept is to gather elements of the same type. From a temporal point of view, if each element has the same durations and (or) delays then we have a temporally homogeneous list. For instance, a list of images, displayed with a ten seconds delay and sixty seconds each. Note that we can consider a video object as atomic but also as a list of frames (still images) occurring at a rate of 1/30 second each (1/25 in Europe) without delay between them (**seq-meet** constraint).

For modeling such kind of multimedia data, we define the notion of Temporally Homogeneous List (or THL in short) as a list of STORM objects having the same Temporal Shadow, that is:

l = list(s_1, s_2, ...s_n) is a THL iff, s_i is a SO $\land$ $\delta_i = \delta_j$ $\land$ $d_i = d_j$ $\forall$ i, j=1,n

From this definition, the content of `Audio` and `Video` classes can be considered as THL.

3.5 Correlated lists

The list constructor corresponds to a partial function from integer to any other object types (atomic, complex), that is a function `f : integer → ANY`. Considering continuous multimedia objects like `Audio` and `Video`, we propose to model them by several associated correlated lists, each one representing specific information. This approach shares some analogy with data models dedicated to sequences of data [45], [21].

For instance, consider a list of pictures `LI:list(Image)` with `D:list(Duration)` and Δ`:list(Delay)` its duration and delay lists. We can associate to `LI`, several other lists, for example
`English_st:list(string), French_st:list(string)`
(for subtitles in different languages), `LB:list(Boolean)` which indicates if Yes or No a given subject is present in the corresponding image, etc.

More generally we define correlated lists as a tuple of the type:
`tuple(`a_1`:list(`T_1`), `a_2`:list(`T_2`), ....  `a_n`:list(`T_n`))`
with the following properties:

a) all the lists are of the same length[14]$\forall$ i, j , i $\neq$ j, $\text{length}(a_i) = \text{length}(a_j)$

b) a_1 is considered as the master list for specific operations.

c) For two lists a_k and a_l, there exists a semantic relationship between $a_k[i]$ and $a_l[i]$.

Indexing video data can be done using the concept of correlated lists. By considering a_1 as the list of frames, we use other lists for describing information appearing in the corresponding frame(s): a subject, a person, any other criteria. We indicate in Section 4.4 the directions that we are taken to address this open problem and which needs further investigations.

---

[14] This is a modeling point of view and not an implementation choice. It is necessary to find efficient data structures to store lists where several consecutive elements are identical.

4 QUERYING TEMPORAL PRESENTATIONS

This section gives the main extensions in order to manipulate time-based multimedia data. Our approach extends the query facilities of the O_2 DBMS which provides the O_2SQL language (similar to the OQL language of the ODMG [40]). The extensions concern principally:
- query on temporal attributes, (i.e. the Temporal Shadow);
- query on collections of time-based objects with specific synchronization;
- query on correlated lists for continuous time-based data.

4.1 Database entry points

Classes (types and methods) are intentional data in the O_2 system. Persistent objects are linked to persistent roots which are the database entry points. In Section 3.3 we took a convention in order to associate to a class C its extent named Cs. A persistent root names a collection (i.e. a set or a list) of instances or an individual object (or value). Let us define the following database entry points:

```
Mypictures :  set(Mypictures) {objects without Temporal Shadow}
SO_Mypictures :  set(SO_Mypicture) {presentations}
Musics :  set(Music)  {music database}
SO_Musics :  set(SO_Music) {musics as SO}
OneShow1 :  Show1    {named object, a sequence}
Show1s :  set(Show1)  {a collection of Show1}
Oneshow3 :  Show3 {named object, a parallel presentation}
Show6s :  set(Show6)  {collection of Show6}
Movies :  set(Movie)  {collection of movies}
```

These entry points are used to express different kinds of queries. Describing the facilities of the O_2SQL language is obviously out the scope of this paper, but we show the main extensions that we provide through several examples.

4.2   Querying the Temporal Shadow

The first query shows the `select-from-where` filter, the use of a variable over a collection and the manipulation of the Temporal Shadow of a dynamic object. This illustrates how to combine selections on several attributes.

Q1: Select titles of musics which last less than 10 minutes and which are composed by Beethoven:

```
Select    m.title
from      m in Musics
where     m.duration < 600 and m.composer=''Beethoven''
```

Q2: Play the 30 first seconds of each music composed by Debussy:

```
Select    m.extract(1,30).present
from      m in Musics
where     m.composer=''Debussy''
```

The Temporal Shadow is composed of two elements, the duration and the delay. We already showed in Q1 the manipulation of the duration which was compared to a constant. We provide also a specific predicate to check if a duration or a delay is (not) free. For instance,

Q3: Select the title of each picture which has a free duration:

```
Select    p.content.title
from      p in SO_Mypictures
where     p.duration is FREE
```

Q4: Select each picture of Paris which has a bound duration in one show:

```
Select    p
from      p in Mypictures, s in Show1s, sp in s.content
where     p.subject=''Paris'' and sp.duration is NOT FREE
and       sp.content=p
```

To understand Q4 it is necessary to remember that each element in the set `Show1s` is an instance of `Show1` and therefore has a content which is a list of `SO_Mypicture`. Also each `SO_Mypicture` refers to an instance of `Mypicture`!

4.3 Query on synchronization

Sequential and parallel synchronizations are expressed by the constructors list, set, tuple and stuple, where qualifiers provide specific constraints. At the query language level, these qualifiers correspond to (temporal) predicates (τ) defined in the following manner:

τ : SO x SO $\rightarrow$ Boolean with
$\tau \in$ {before, meet, start, equal, finish, overlap, during}

Given two SO, s_1 and s_2, the notation $s_1 \tau s_2$ checks if s_1 and s_2 verify the constraint τ.

Q5: In Oneshow1, select each picture of Grenoble which is followed by a picture of Paris:

```
Select    pg
from      (pg, pp) in Oneshow1.content
where     pg.subject=''Grenoble'' and pp.subject=''Paris''
and       pg meet pp
```

Q6: In Oneshow3, select any pair of pictures having the same subject which overlap:

```
Select    tuple(pic1:p1, pic2:p2)
from      (p1, p2) in Oneshow3.content
where     p1.subject=p2.subject and p1 overlap p2
```

4.4 Querying Lists

Several operators on lists are available in O_2. For instance, if l is a list, l[i] denotes the ith element, while l[i:j] is the sublist starting at i and ending at j. first(l) and last(l) denotes respectively the first and last element, and count(l) is the number of elements of the list. The empty list is denoted by list(), and if m is another list, l+m is the concatenation of the two lists. There are also functions like min(l), max(l), avg(l), sum(l) with their obvious meaning and listoset(l) which convert a list into a set (setolist exists also). Finally the operator flatten is used to eliminate nesting.

Now, let us discuss some extensions which concerns lists applied to time-based data. Let L be a list of elements of type T (L:list(T)). To filter data in such a list, O_2SQL allows to define only one variable of type T which successively takes the value of each element in the list. However, these elements are ordered and can be directly accessed given the index. We propose to define indexed variables (e.g. x[i]) in order to manipulate not only the element value but also its position in the list, and therefore its chronological order. Using several indexed variables on the same list is a way to compare the respective positions of the corresponding elements. This may also help for extracting sublists. In example Q7, two variables are defined in the where clause, p is a picture and i is an integer. The selection results into a list of tuples, one for each picture of Grenoble.

Q7: In Oneshow1, select each picture of Grenoble with its position and its associated duration:

```
Select     tuple(pos:i, pic:p, dur:p.duration)
from       p[i] in Oneshow1.content
where      p[i].subject=''Grenoble''
```

In the following example, the from clause defines four variables, p1, p2, i, j. The list is scanned by the two indexed variables in embedded loops. Note the test on i,j. Several other tests can be done, for instance it is possible to check if p1 and p2 correspond to consecutive elements (i.e. j=i+1). Compare with Q5.

Q8: In Oneshow1, select each picture of Grenoble which is followed by a picture of Paris if the duration of the first one is greater than the duration of the second one:

```
Select     p1
from       (p1[i], p2[j]) in Oneshow1.content
where      p1[i].subject=''Grenoble'' and p2[j].subject= ''Paris''
and        p1[i].duration > p2[j].duration and  i < j
```

For extracting a sublist, it is necessary to express the two ends. For instance,

Q9: In Oneshow1, select the sublist starting with picture entitled "Gr003" and ending at picture "Pr001". We assume that the title is unique by picture. If j>i the empty list is returned:

```
Select     p1[i:j]
from       (p1[i], p2[j]) in Oneshow1.content
where      p1[i].title=''Gr003'' and p2[j].title= ''Pr001''
```

Finally, let us express a query which combines list and tuple manipulation.

Q10: In Show6s, what are the audio comments in parallel with pictures of Versailles, having the Beethoven's ninth symphony as a background music? We use the define facility provided by O_2SQL for expressing the query in a clear way:

```
define S9 as
        element(Select m
                from    m in Musics
                where   m.title=''Ninth Symphony'
                and     m.composer=''Beethoven'');
Select  pc.com
from    s in Show6s, pc in s.content.picom
where   pc.pic.subject=''Versailles'' and s.content.back = S9
```

• Correlated lists

These lists have been introduced in Section 3.5 and are a family of partial functions from integer to any type of objects. The idea is to model continuous time-based data by several associated lists which can be combined by specific operations. We first consider a generalized **selection** which concerns operations on boolean lists (i.e. $\neg l, l \wedge m, l \vee m$). Suppose we have a correlated list defined as: `tuple(lp:list(Image), cr1:list(Boolean), cr2:list(Boolean))`

We assume that `lenght(lp) = lenght(cr1) = lenght(cr2)`. `lp` is a sequence of pictures, `cr1` and `cr2` correspond to a respective criteria, for instance `cr1[i]` is true if `lp[i]` is a picture where there is a bird (otherwise it is false), while `cr2[i]` is true if `lp[i]` represents a mammal (otherwise it is false).

The generalized selection consists of applying pairwise one boolean list `b` on a given list `l`. We denote this operation as: `l` σ `b`. The result is a list where `l[i]` is replaced by `nil` if the coresponding element in the boolean list `b[i]` is false. For instance, `lp` σ `cr1` generates a list, say `result` (of type `list(Image)`) where: `result[i] = lp[i]` if `cr1[i]` else `result[i] = nil`.

Of course we can have also expressions like: `lp` σ `(cr1` $\wedge$ `cr2)`.

By combining these operations with specific ones called "pointwise splicing" in [21] it is possible to provide very powerful facilities to manipulate (create, query) this kind of data. This is why we are currently extending the operations on lists. We consider shifting operations (either right or left) of a specified number of positions. For instance, let l = list(s1, s2, s3, s4, s5, s6), then, l.shift_right(2) results in: list(nil, nil, s1, s2, s3, s4). Stretch and shrink can also be defined on lists. For example, l.shrink(2) gives list(s1, s3, s5). Other operations are binary ones and compare elements of two lists pairwise. A more detailed discussion of this aspect is out the scope of this chapter and part of our future work.

4.5 Presentation for query results

If we query a collection of SO, the result is also a collection of SO and therefore it can be presented accordingly. For instance Q11 corresponds to the presentation of a sequence of movies.

Q11: Build a sequence of movie fragments (60 first seconds):

```
setolist(Select    m.extract(1, 60)
         from      m in Movies
         where     m.year = 1994)
```

Because we query a set, the result is also a set and therefore we need to apply the setolist function in order to get the desired sequence.

5 CONCLUSIONS

We have described how to extend an object-oriented database system in order to build a Multimedia DBMS. Our extension concerns not only the data model (and its type system) but also the data definition and query languages. Although we did not give a complete description of such languages, we gave the main concepts of our approach which combine structural and temporal aspects of multimedia data. We are aware of the fact that we left aside some important problems concerning real-time constraints for proper presentation of audio or video data. We believe that future object servers and low level components of (future) operating systems will provide specific mechanisms to efficiently handle these constraints.

Several other works on temporal (multimedia) database has also been used to define the STORM model and system. In [47] one can find an interesting study of different concepts to represent time in multimedia systems. First, point-based and interval-based frameworks are compared and translations between them are discussed. Then, an evaluation of multimedia time models is provided together with an interval based model.

Concerning multimedia databases, several works inspired the genesis of STORM and its associated language. For instance, our approach bears some similarities with the approach developed in [32], [33]. As them we adopted an interval-based model for time-dependent data, but we use object-oriented database technology to handle them instead of relational one. More recently, in [27] an object-oriented model is proposed for spatio-temporal description and synchronization of multimedia data. Although an object-oriented model is considered, it is still not clear how this proposition can take advantage of the existing object-oriented database technology. The extensions that we propose for the query language are similar to the propositions of [14], [45]. However, they do not take into account time aspects and synchronizations for multimedia data.

The work in [1] is a proposition for a model and a language for expressing temporal aspects of multimedia database objects. The notions of schedule and event (associated with a kind of extended active rules) are used to express object synchronization. Examples of different kinds of synchronizations including parallel and sequential streams are given and discussed. An implementation framework is also described.

One can find in [22] a discussion on the problem of managing audio and video data, where synchronization aspects and temporal constraints are also described. In [23], three kinds of structuring mechanisms for multimedia objects are proposed. First *interpretation* is used to extract multimedia objects from BLOBs. Second, *derivation* is defined as the process which computes objects from other objects and several kinds of derivations are possible. Third, *composition* (close to the concept of STORM presentation) can be used to combine and assemble various elements by specifying temporal and spatial relationships.

The work in [11], [42], [25], [26] can also be compared with our approach but in most of these articles, the database issue is left aside. Several other related works on specific problems for handling video data can be found in [48], [34], [41]. Interface aspects and query languages are treated by [12], [24], [37], [36].

For the future, we are trying to map our data modeling concepts to the ones proposed in standards like Hytime [38] and ODMG [40]. A special interest is dedicated to MHEG [43] which is intended for the interchange of sets of multimedia and hypermedia objects, because we believe that future multimedia DBMS should be open to this kind of standards.

A first version of the STORM DBMS is running on top of O_2 [5]. We want to implement a second version of STORM using an extended version of the O_2 system which incorporates active rules [16] and parallel facilities [35]. Indeed, if for prototyping, we build a specific layer on top of the O_2 system, it should be clear that the implementation of an integrated multimedia DBMS requires several extensions and particularly at the level of the object manager. Dynamic, continuous media such as audio and video require not only new modeling concepts, but also specific data structures to efficiently handle temporal and synchronization aspects.

Acknowledgements

I am very grateful to several people who helped me in various ways with this work. Many thanks to Ofélia Cervantes for many helpful discussions and for her interest in STORMs. Thanks also to Christine Collet, Christian Esculier and Hervé Martin for several (very) alive and stimulating brain STORMing! I am also grateful to Pierre-Claude Scholl and Don Chamberlin for their careful reading of previous versions of this text, and to Françoise Mocellin for her effort in implementing version 1 of the prototype and to Marie-Christine Fauvet for her help in Latex.

REFERENCES

[1] K.Aberer, W.Klas, Supporting Temporal multimedia Operations in Object-Oriented Database System, International Conference on Multimedia Computing and Systems, Boston, May 1994

[2] M.Adiba, Bui Quang Ngoc, Historical multimedia databases, VLDB 1986, Kyoto (Japan)

[3] M.Adiba, Management of multimedia complex objects in the '90s, Lecture Notes in Computer Science N.466, Database systems of the 90s, Springer Verlag, 1990

[4] M.Adiba, C.Collet, Objets et Bases de Données : le SGBD O_2, Hermès, 1993 (book in french)

[5] M.Adiba, STORM: Structural and Temporal Object-oRiented Multimedia database system. IEEE International Workshop on Multimedia DBMS, Minnowbrook Conference Center, Blue Mountain lake, NY, USA, August 1995

[6] J.F.Allen, Maintaining knowledge about temporal intervals, CACM, Vol.26, N. 11, 1983

[7] D.P.Anderson, G.Homsy, A continuous media I/O server and its synchronization mechanism, Computer, October 1991

[8] F.Bancilhon, C.Delobel, P.Kanellakis (Editeurs), Building an Object Oriented Database System: The story of O_2, Morgan Kaufmann, 1992

[9] F.Bancilhon, Private communication, April 1994

[10] E.Bier, M.Stone, K.Pier, W.Buxton, T.DeRose, Toolglass and magic lenses: the see-through interface, ACM SIGRAPH 93, Anaheim, August 1993

[11] M.C. Buchanan, P.Zellweger, Automatic temporal layout mechanisms, First International Conference on Multimedia, Anaheim, California, August 1993

[12] A.Cardenas, et al., The knowledge-based object-oriented PICQUERY+ language, IEEE Transactions on Knowledge and Data Engineering, Vol.5, N.4, August 93

[13] S.Christodoulakis, Multimedia Information Systems, Tutorial notes, EDBT Conference, Cambridge, March 1994

[14] V.Christophides, S.Abiteboul, S.Cluet, M.Scholl, From Structured Documents to Novel Query Facilities, SIGMOD 1994

[15] C.Collet, P.Habraken, T.Coupaye, M.Adiba, Active rules for the software engineering platform Goodstep, 2nd International Workshop on Database and Software Engineering, 16th Int. Conference on Software Engineering, Sorrento, Italy, May 94

[16] C.Collet, T.Coupaye, T.Svensen, NAOS: Efficient and modular reactive capabilities in an object-oriented Database System, VLDB Conference, Chili, September 1994

[17] P.Dechamboux, M.Adiba, Combining safety, flexibility and efficiency through an Object-Oriented DBPL: PEPLOM. Ingénierie des Systèmes d'Information, Vol.2, N.5, 1994.

[18] K.Dittrich, U.Dayal, A.P.Buchman (Editors), On Object-Oriented Database Systems, Topics in Information Systems, Springer Verlag, 1991

[19] E.A. Fox, Advances in interactive digital multimedia systems, Computer, October 1991

[20] A.Ghafoor, Multimedia Database Systems, Tutorial notes, Data Engineering Conference, 1994

[21] SM.Gandhi, E.L.Robertson, A Data Model for Audio-Video Data, COMAD, Bangalore, India, December 1994

[22] S.Gibbs, C.Breiteneder, D.Tsichritzis, Modelling of audio/video data, 11th Conf. on the Entity Relationship approach, Karlsruhe, October 1992

[23] S.Gibbs, C.Breiteneder, D.Tsichritzis, Data modelling of time-based media, SIGMOD 1994

[24] J.Griffioen, R.Mehrotra, R.Yavatkar, An object-oriented model for image information representation, CIKM 1993

[25] R.Hamakawa, J.Rekimoto, Object composition and playback models for handling multimedia data, First International Conference on Multimedia, Anaheim, California, August 1993

[26] R.Hamakawa, H.Sakagami, J. Rekimoto, Mbuild- Multimedia data builder with box and glue, International Conference on Multimedia Computing and Systems, Boston, Mass., May 1994

[27] M.Iino, Y.F.Day, A.Ghafoor, An Object-Oriented model for spatio-temporal synchronization of multimedia information, International Conference on Multimedia Computing and Systems, Boston, Mass., May 1994

[28] C.Jensen, J.Clifford, R.Elmasri, S.Gadia, P.Hayes, S.Jajodia (Editors), A consensus glossary of temporal database concepts, SIGMOD Record, Vol. 23, N.1

[29] J.F.Koegel, L.W.Rutledge, J.L.Rutledge, C.Keskin, HyOctane: a HyTime engine for an MMIS, First ACM International Conference on Multimedia, Anaheim, Ca., August 1993

[30] A.Laursen, J.Olkin, M.Porter, Oracle Media Server: providing consumer interactive access to Multimedia data, SIGMOD 1994

[31] D.Le Gall, MPEG: A video compression standard for multimedia applications, CACM, April 1991

[32] T.D.Little, A.Ghafoor, Spatio-Temporal composition of distributed multi-media objects for value-added networks, Computer, October 91

[33] T.D.Little, A.Ghafoor, Interval-based conceptual models for time-dependent multimedia data, IEEE Transactions on knowledge and data engineering, Vol.5, N.4, August 93

[34] T.D.Little, G.Ahanger, R.J.Folz, J.F.Gibbon et al, A digital on-demand video service supporting content-based queries, First ACM International Conference on Multimedia, Anaheim, Ca., August 1993

[35] J.Machado, C.Collet, B.Defude, P.Dechamboux, M.Adiba, The parallel PEPLOM execution model, 31st ACM Southeast Conference, Birmingham, USA, April 1993

[36] S.R.L.Meira, A.E.L.Moura, A scripting language for multimedia presentation International Conference on Multimedia Computing and Systems, Boston, Mass., May 1994

[37] J.G.Neal, S.C.Shapiro, Intelligent multi-media interface technology, ACM Press Intelligent user interfaces, J.W.Sullivan and S.W.Tyler editors, 1991

[38] S.R.Newcomb, N.A.Xipp, V.T.Newcomb, The Hytime Hypermedia Time-based Document structuring language, CACM Vol.34, N.11, November 1991

[39] The O_2 User Manual (Version 4.2.), O_2 Technology, Versailles, France, 1993

[40] R.Cattel (Editor), Object Databases: the ODMG93 Standard, Morgan-Kaufmann, 1993

[41] E.Oomoto, K.Tanaka, OVID: design and implementation of a video-object database system, IEEE Transactions on Knowledge and Data Engineering, Vol.5, N.4, August 93

[42] B.Prabhakaran, S.V.Raghavan, Synchronization models for multimedia presentations with user participation, First ACM International Conference on Multimedia, Anaheim, Ca., August 1993

[43] R.Price, MHEG: an introduction to the future International Standard for Hypermedia Object Interchange, First ACM International Conference on Multimedia, Anaheim, Ca., August 1993

[44] K.Ramamritham, Real-time databases, Distributed and parallel databases, Vol.1, 1993

[45] P.Seshadri, M.Livny, R.Ramakrishnan, Sequence Query Processing, SIG-
     MOD 1994

[46] A.U.Tansel, J.Clifford, S.Gadia, S.Jajodia, A.Segev, R.Snodgrass, Tempo-
     ral Databases, The Benjamin/Cummings Publishing Company, 1993

[47] T.Wahl, K.Rothermel, Representing time in multimedia systems Interna-
     tional Conference on Multimedia Computing and Systems, Boston, Mass.,
     May 1994. Also extended version from Stuttgart University, 1994.

[48] R.Weiss, A.Duda, D.K.Gifford, Content-based access to algebraic video,
     International Conference on Multimedia Computing and Systems, Boston,
     Mass., May 1994

4

SEARCHING AND BROWSING
A SHARED VIDEO DATABASE

Rune Hjelsvold, Roger Midtstraum, and Olav Sandstå

Department of Computer Systems and Telematics
The Norwegian Institute of Technology
Trondheim, Norway

In this chapter we will discuss issues related to searching and browsing a shared video database. The discussion will be founded on a review of characteristics of video information and video database applications, and we will discuss requirements to be fulfilled by video databases in shared environments. The issues that will be discussed include video database architectures, video algebra operations, video querying, and video browsing . We have developed an experimental environment called *VideoSTAR (Video STorage And Retrieval)* that will be used to illustrate the issues being discussed.

1   INTRODUCTION

There is a strong technology push behind the development of video databases, but there is also a real end-user demand for video database technology. Such end-user demands should be taken into considerations when developing video database systems. There is a variety of users and types of applications and this makes it difficult to put up one set of requirements that can be unanimously agreed upon. Thus, if video database functionality for searching and browsing is based on requirements from one specific application only - e.g., video-on-demand - one may end up with a video database system that does not fulfill the needs for other users.

Television archives can serve as an example where video information sharing is important. The primary purpose of a television archive is helping reporters and directors in finding pieces of video with a specific image content - e.g., pieces of video showing a specific person, object, or location. The television archive is also used by reporters for programme research - i.e., when they are searching for background information that might shed light on a specific issue.

A television archive may also have users outside the television company. Historians and media researchers have started going to the television archives because these archives are a rich source of documentary information from the last half of the 20th century. The television company might also make use of digital video technology to overcome some of the limitations with the broadcasting concept: Television programmes might be stored on video-on-demand servers so that the viewers can decide *when* to watch a given programme, or more interactive services might be provided - e.g., news-on-demand.

2   VIDEO INFORMATION IN A SHARED ENVIRONMENT

Databases are especially developed for managing data in shared environments. By shared environment we mean an environment where data are to be shared between different users. Also, in a shared environment different computer tools - e.g., planning tools, editors, and query tools - may access a common data repository for sharing and exchanging data. To develop video databases for shared environments, therefore, one should consider characteristics of video information and video database applications.

2.1   Video Information

Video information is not a very stringently defined term. To make the following discussion on video information sharing clearer, we will define our interpretation more precisely. We will use *video document* as the term denoting video compositions, such as movies and television programmes. A video document is often composed of still images, audio, and other types of media in addition to video data. We will use *video information* as a collective term that includes both *media data* and *meta-data* to be associated with the media data. The types of data that may be present in a video database include:

- *Media Data.* This category includes audio and video data *as recorded*, audio and video data generated during editing (e.g., when effects such as wipes and dissolves are applied to video data), and other media data.

- *Media-specific Data.* Some meta-data is required to control playback and rendering of media data - e.g., video format, frame rate, and size of the video window.

- *Compositional Data.* A composition defines the relations between a video document and the media data that are used. Today, compositional data are often used to generate complete copies of the document on video tape. The resulting video plays a dual role: It can be considered as one contiguous audio and video segment, and, at the same time, it represents a possibly complex video document.

- *Bibliographic Data.* This category describes the video document as a whole and includes information such as title, date of issue, production team, and actors/reporters contributing in the video document.

- *Structural Data.* Video documents are often well-structured into a structure hierarchy in similar ways as books are organized into chapters, sections, and subsections.

- *Content Annotations.* Content annotations are textual descriptions of the sensory content in a video. These annotations are manually entered by users and serves as indexes to the content of a piece of video.

- *Content Feature Data.* This category includes features that are automatically extracted from video and audio data. Such features can be used instead of - or in addition to - content annotations to provide content-based retrieval.

- *Topic Annotations.* The topics that are presented or elucidated in a video document are determined by the contents of the individual pieces of audio and video used in the document *and* by the way the individual pieces are combined. Content annotations can be used to describe or classify the issues being raised in video documents.

- *Supplementary Information.* Content and topic annotations serve as indexes to the content and topics in video. The user may want to associate other types of information to a piece of audio/video - e.g., for making personal remarks.

One important question for the users of a video database is how to acquire meta-data. There are several approaches that can be taken. The most ambitious one, *feature extraction*, assumes that characteristic features can be automatically extracted from media data. A less ambitious approach, *in-production capturing*, assumes that the tools used for recording and/or video editing (semi)

Meta-data	Feature extraction	In-production	Post-production
Compositional	Cut-detection [10, 30]	Yes	Yes
Bibliographic	No	Some	Yes
Structural	Simple structures	Yes [12]	Yes
Sensory content	Limited domains	Little	Yes
Topic content	Hardly	Some	Yes
Supplementary	No	Yes	Yes

Table 1   Usability of Different Meta-data Capturing Methods

automatically collects meta-data - e.g., when recording tools automatically register date and time for recording, or when compositional data are generated by authoring tools. The approach that is chosen by most users today (though this is a time-consuming task), *post-production capturing*, assumes that users - e.g., librarians - manually enters meta-data when the production process is completed. Table 1 indicates how the different methods apply to different types of meta-data.

2.2   A Variety of Video Applications

A shared video database should support different types of applications in sharing of video information. In this section we will take a closer look at some classes of applications that might use video databases. The purpose of this presentation is to illustrate that a shared video database must give consideration to the needs of more than one specific application. For this purpose, we have chosen five different classes of applications:

■   *Video-On-Demand services.* VOD services allow users to search for videos and movies stored on a digital video server [6, 19, 20, 27]. A typical VOD service is aimed at offering the user flexibility in choosing movies from a large set of available titles. The entire movie is presumed to be the unit of interest and, thus, selection is mainly based on bibliographic data such as title, genre, or director. When a video has been selected, it is assumed that the movie will be viewed from beginning to end with little user interaction: Users may start, stop, pause, or playback a part of the video, but they do not need functionality to skip parts of the video, change the sequence of scenes, or search for parts of the video having a specific content.

- *Interactive video applications.* Most videos and movies on VOD servers can be classified as *linear* [21]. As opposite to linear video, interactive video assumes that the users may access scenes in any order. An interactive *News-on-demand* service [24] is an example of an interactive video application. The users of a news-on-demand service may want to select news items based on topic - and possibly on image contents - and may request the ability to decide in which sequence the news items should be played. Structural and compositional data are a prerequisite for offering this kind of functionality.

- *Shot-stock applications* are applications that access information related to recorded audio and video. A *shot* is a film theoretical term for a piece of film or video that has been recorded continuously. Shot-stock applications are especially used by film [33] or television directors and television reporters to retrieve video with a certain image content - e.g., to find video shots showing a specific person or object.

- *Programme research applications* are applications that assist users - e.g., television reporters, mass media researchers, or historians - in finding video documents related to a specific, but not necessarily precisely defined, topic. "People's Century" is considered to be the biggest and most ambitious historical documentation series that BBC has ever undertaken [35]. During the work on the series BBC has gained substantial experience with this kind of research: Topic data are needed to retrieve a collection of television programmes that can serve as the starting point for the research. A comprehensive breakdown of the individual programmes, identifying each shot *and* its source, is needed because BBC has to acquire permission from owners and authors in order to reuse archival material. In such a large project, it is also necessary to add personal remarks to interesting shots in the archive for use in later stages of the process [35].

- *Video documentation applications* support users in using video to document aspects of the real-world. This includes, for instance, anthropology [29], hand craft documentation [22], and user requirements analysis [18]. The main difference between this class of application and the others is the strong emphasis on supplementary data; users want to attach their detailed remarks and analysis to the video data.

Table 2 summarizes the importance of different types of meta-data for these classes of applications.

Meta-data	VOD	I-video	Shot-stock	Research	Docum.
Compositional	No	High	No	High	Low
Bibliographic	High	High	Medium	High	Medium
Structural	Low	High	No	High	Med./high
Sensory content	No	Medium	High	High	High
Topic content	Low	High	Medium	High	High
Supplementary	No	Medium	Low	Medium	High

Table 2   Importance of Meta-data in Different Applications

2.3   Temporal Aspects of Video Information

Video data are inherently temporal in the sense that the content of a video display is dynamically changing during playback. Technically, video data can be considered as a stream of images (called *frames*) displayed to the user at a constant frame rate. Video information is, however, more complex than just a stream of images: The way a user interprets individual pieces of video is influenced by the surrounding parts (i.e., the context into which the piece of video is used). This was evidently shown in a series of experiments by Soviet film makers in the last half of the 1920s [7].

These film makers noticed that temporal composition (in film theory called *montage*) was at least as important as spatial composition - i.e., how the scene space is organized (in film theory called *mise en scène*):

> *Pudovkin offers a sort of formula: Film creation equals (1) what is shown in the shots, (2) the order in which they appear, and (3) how long each is held on the screen. [7]*

Temporal composition gives the director a means for creating contexts that give the user the ability to correctly interpret the contents of a video document.

Video documents and audio/video recordings define their own, discrete time systems because of their temporal characteristics. A specific part of a video defines a *temporal interval* within the time system of this video. This means that audio/video data and related meta-data, in contrast to traditional data types, may have temporal relationships to each other. During composition, the audio/video recordings are bound to the time system of the video document.

Thus, video document and video recording time systems may be related to each other.

2.4   Sharing Video Information

In a shared video environment, the same pieces of media data may be part of several different video documents. Different documents define different contexts and, since the interpretation of video data is strongly dependent on its context, context handling is an important feature of a shared video database. A key question for context handling is how meta-data, especially structural and content data, can be shared in a consistent way when media data are shared or parts of video documents are reused in other documents.

Some researchers [26, 34] have proposed to support reuse of video information by allowing parts of a video document to be a component of other video documents and, thus, introducing an unconstrained hierarchy of video documents. We recommend to have only two levels in a video database: media recordings and video documents. This allows us to organize meta-data into three different classes with different relevance for a given document:

- The *primary context* contains meta-data that are specifically valid for the given document. If a part of the video document is reused in another video document, primary context meta-data may no longer be valid.

- The basic context for a piece of video contains meta-data that are valid independent of which primary context it is being used in - e.g., the name of a person shown on the video and the time and location for the recording.

- The *secondary context* for a given video document exists if the video document uses media data that are also being used in other video documents. These other document's primary contexts comprise the secondary context.

Figure 1 illustrates these concepts using a sample database consisting of two video documents (*I* and *II*) and three video recordings (*III, IV,* and *V*). The two documents share an interval from recording *IV*. The database also contains six image content annotations (*a1* through *a6*) and five topic content annotations (*a7* through *a11*). (The annotations have the format *(AnnotationID, Title, StreamInterval)* where *StreamInterval* is an interval from a video document or video recording having the format *(StreamID, StartTime, EndTime).*)

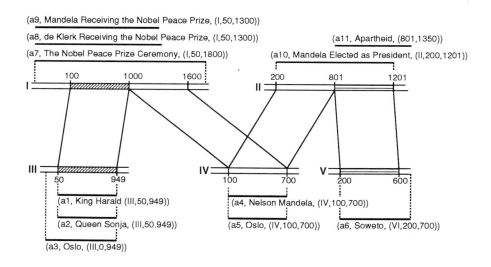

Figure 1   Example Video Data and Meta-data

Take the stream interval *(I, 1000, 1600)* as an example. The *primary context* for this piece of video consists of video document *I* and three annotations (*a7* through *a9*) which say that the topic of the news item is the Nobel Peace Prize Ceremony for Mandela and de Klerk. The basic context consists of video recording *IV* and two sensory content annotations *a4* and *a5* which say that this video was recorded in Oslo, Norway, and that it shows Mr. Nelson Mandela. The *secondary context* for the stream interval, in the current state of the database, consists of video document *II* and one topic annotation, *a10*, associated with it. It is important to note that the secondary context is a virtual concept which identifies a collection of (other) primary contexts sharing a piece of video.

The reason we have defined the basic, primary and secondary contexts is to provide better control of sharing and visibility of the descriptive data. Annotations related to an audio/video recording that will be valid in any context, are represented in the basic context and can be "seen" and shared by all video documents using the recording. Annotations that are specific to a video document are represented in the primary context of the document and will not be intermixed with annotations specific to other documents, even when the two documents share some piece of video. When needed, the secondary context

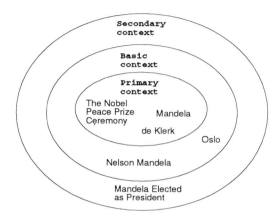

Figure 2   Annotations Grouped by Context

can be searched to find other video documents using the same piece of video and the annotations defined in this context. Figure 2 illustrates the relation between different contexts for the example discussed above.

2.5   Querying Browsing

In this paper we will focus on querying and browsing features that allow the user to retrieve media or meta-data from a video database. For querying, we will focus on how to retrieve pieces of video from video documents or from recordings by specifying meta-data properties. For browsing, we will discuss operations that allow the user to either browse meta-data or to browse the media data by using structural data. From the discussion in the previous subsections, we conclude that a video database supporting video information sharing should include the following features:

- *Generic architecture/data model.* Users and applications that need to share video information must share a common interpretation and understanding of video and meta-data. A generic video database architecture, including a generic data model, would reduce the effort needed to obtain such a common view of video and meta-data. This is further discussed in Section 3.

- *Content indexing.* Content-based retrieval is an important task for most video databases. This can be done by using advanced feature extraction/matching tools or by providing tools and methods that can enhance manual indexing (see Section 5). Feature extraction/matching is a challenging research area but will not be further discussed in this chapter.

- *Temporal relations.* It should be possible for users to exploit the temporal nature of video information in video querying - e.g., by specifying temporal relationships between pieces of video.

- *Controlling scope of interest.* It should be possible for users to control the degree of sharing and, thereby, the scope of interest. Temporal and search scope operations are further discussed in Section 4 and their use in querying and browsing are discussed in Sections 6 and 7, respectively.

3   FRAMEWORKS FOR VIDEO DATABASES

As discussed in the Section 2, video databases might be rather complex with a number of different types of media and meta-data. To ease development of video database applications, one may develop video database frameworks that can hide some of this complexity from the applications.

3.1   Architecture

The framework presented here, VideoSTAR, provides an overall architecture for storing and management of media *and* meta-data from which video database applications can be developed. Other researchers have proposed generic multimedia information system architectures [9] and multimedia processing architectures [3]. The three-level VideoSTAR architecture, which is shown in Figure 3, is richer than existing architectures in supporting video information management:

- *Specialized repositories.* Four specialized repositories are defined: *Stored Media Segment DB* stores uninterpreted media data together with media-specific and bibliographic data, *Video Document DB* stores compositional and bibliographic data, *Video Structure DB* stores structural data, while

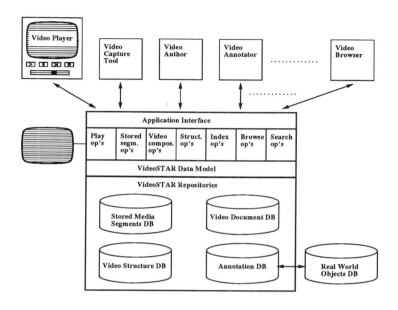

Figure 3 The VideoSTAR Architecture

Annotation DB can be used for any type of content or supplementary data that links real world concepts to a specific piece of video.

- *Generic data model.* The framework includes a generic data model which is further discussed in Section 3.2

- *Video database API.* An application's programming interface offers operations for managing the contents of the repositories, for allowing applications to control video replay, and for querying and browsing.

3.2   Data Models

If video information is to be shared by different applications and users, these applications and users have to share a common understanding of how the video data and meta-data are to be interpreted. The generic VideoSTAR data model is specially designed to represent relations between the contents of the four repositories. The data model is discussed in detail elsewhere [16] while Figure 4 highlights the dominant characteristics of the model.

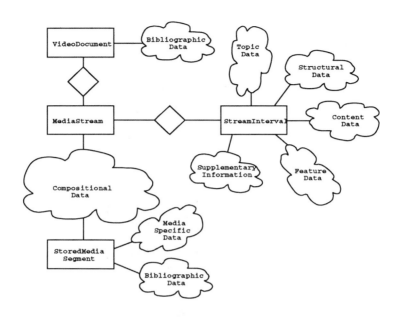

Figure 4   Overview of the Generic VideoSTAR Data Model

The model is a refined successor of earlier models [13, 15]. The core of the model is the **MediaStream**, which capture the most important characteristics of continuous media data like audio and video, and which provides the play operations offered in the API. Each video document is associated with a **MediaStream** that represents the document's video stream. Compositional data represents relations between video documents and **StoredMediaSegment**s - i.e., media data - which, in turn, are specializations of **MediaStream**s. Bibliographic data are associated with video documents and media data.

A **StreamInterval** is an arbitrary (temporal) interval from a **MediaStream**. **StreamIntervals** is the means for relating meta-data to specific pieces of a video document or a media segment, as illustrated in the figure. The structure part of our model is inspired from film theory [25] and defines a structural hierarchy consisting of *shots*, *scenes*, *sequences*, and (possibly recursive) *compound units*.

We do not claim that the proposed model is ideal for every application and user. It is rather a kernel model that can be tailored to the needs of specific application domains by giving structural components an application domain specific interpretation, by refining meta-data definitions, and by linking meta-data to a specific real-world model.

4 FUNDAMENTAL QUERYING AND BROWSING OPERATIONS

In [11] Hampapur, Jain and Weymouth write: *"The nature of indexing video is dependent on the problem of modeling video which in turn depends on the nature of the application of the database."* Querying and browsing are different ways to make use of the results from the indexing efforts, and thus are equally dependent of the model of the video data.

Meta-data models are used in many parts of computer science, such as databases [32], information retrieval [28], knowledge representation [31], and image processing [8, 11]. Models from different domains tend to focus on different types of information and solve different aspects of the problem of modelling and retrieving information.

Considering the different types of data in a shared video database as defined in Section 2.1, database type models are most suited for modelling of *media data, media specific data, compositional data, bibliographic data* and *structural data*. Information retrieval models are most suitable for modelling of *content annotations* and *topic annotations*, image processing models are most suitable for *content feature data*, and knowledge representation models are most suitable for the representation of *supplementary information*.

When used in a video database system, browsing and querying of the different types of meta-models are done by the standard techniques used for that type of model. What is novel in video databases is that some of the descriptive data are related to pieces of video data – stream intervals in the VideoSTAR model – and that it may be necessary to consider both the temporal and the compositional aspects of the video information to provide the necessary functionality.

Take the situation in Figure 1 as an example and consider a media researcher studying the television news related to the last president election in South Africa. She could for instance want to investigate how video related to apartheid was used. One possible query could be to find video data related both to the election of Nelson Mandela and to apartheid. It is straightforward to find the set of stream intervals related to Mandela and the set of stream intervals related to apartheid, but in order to combine these two sets into the wanted result, temporal operations have to be applied.

In the work with VideoSTAR we have developed a video query algebra [17] that allows us to formulate complex queries based on temporal relationships between stream intervals. This algebra allows the user to define the contexts to be searched. The algebra is defined over a special type of sets that are called *Mapped video object sets.* Mapped video object sets contain tupples *(ObjRef, StreamInt)* where *ObjRef* is the object identifier of one of the objects in a VideoSTAR repository (see Figure 3) while *StreamInt* is the stream interval that the object is mapped onto.

The video algebra operations will be briefly described in this section and their use in querying and will be further discussed in Section 6 and Section 7.

4.1   Temporal operations

In order to be able to express the necessary relations between sets of mapped video objects we have to extend the standard set operators. The new operators take into account the temporal nature of the mapped video objects.

Normal Set Operations: Normal set operations – i.e., intersection (AND), union (OR), and difference (NOT^1) where two elements are defined to be identical if they refer to the same object over the same stream interval. Assuming that A and B are sets of person annotations, A AND B will contain elements from A where an element from B is referring the same person annotation over the same interval.

Temporal Set Operations: As noted by Clifford and Crocker [4], normal set-theoretic operations of union, intersection and difference produce counter-intuitive results when applied to temporal data. Therefore, temporal variants called *tAND*, *tOR*, and *tNOT* are defined. The elements of the result set contain the stream intervals resulting from intersecting, merging and subtracting stream intervals from the input sets as illustrated in Figure 5. Assuming that A is a set of annotations related to the election of Nelson Mandela as president and B is a set of annotations related to apartheid, A *tAND* B will have elements

---

[1] *NOT* is used to denote the difference between two sets – i.e., A *NOT* $B \equiv A$ *AND (NOT B)*.

identifying the stream intervals which can be associated with *both* Mr. Mandela and apartheid.

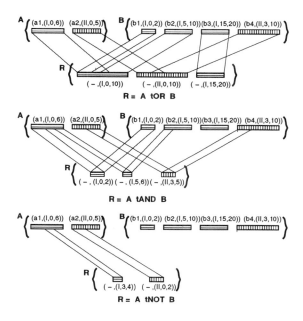

Figure 5   Example Showing the Interval Set Operators

Filter Operations: Allen has shown that there are 13 possible (distinct) relationships that can exist between two temporal intervals [1] – e.g., *before*, *overlaps* and *equals*[2]. Filter functions compare two stream intervals to check whether a given temporal relationship exists. We have defined the *tREDUCE* operator to take two input sets and one filter function as arguments. It returns the elements from the first input set that have the given relationship to at least one element from the second input set. Assuming that A is a set of scenes and B is a set of annotations related to Nelson Mandela, *tREDUCE(A, B, intersects)* will return the scenes from A that can be related to Nelson Mandela.

Macro operations: To ease the specification of two common tasks we have defined two (macro) operators – *ANNOT* and *STRUCT*. The *ANNOT* operator takes one input set and one annotation type parameter as arguments and retrieves all annotations of the given type that intersects any of the elements

---

[2]By combining these one may also define other operations such as *intersects*.

in the input set. The *STRUCT* operator takes one input set and one structure type parameter as arguments and retrieves all structural components of the given type that intersects any of the elements in the input set.

4.2   Compositional operations

In the example where a researcher wanted to find video related both to the election of Mr. Mandela as president and to apartheid, we could use a temporal *tAND* operator because the annotations were made in the same (primary) context. If the researcher instead had wanted to find video recordings from the Soweto area used in relation to the election of Mr. Mandela as president, a *tAND* operator would not have given the wanted result because the annotations are made in different contexts. In order to process such queries, which require temporal operations on annotations from (possibly) different contexts, one will have to apply compositional operations.

The compositional operations map objects from one time coordinate system onto another time coordinate system. A mapping operation does not affect the *ObjRef* part of a mapped video object, while the *Interval* part after the operation gives the stream interval onto which the object is mapped.

The *Decompose* operator which is illustrated in Figure 6 maps the objects in the input set onto the basic context. If an element in the input set is already related to a part of a basic context, the element will be copied without changes to the output set. If an element in the input set is related to a primary context, the element will be mapped onto the basic context(s) from which the corresponding stream interval is composed. The left part of figure 6 shows an example where the annotation *a10* made in the primary context of video document *II* is decomposed onto the basic contexts of stored media segments *IV* and *V*.

The *MapToComposition* operator maps objects in the opposite direction – i.e., from the time coordinate systems of a basic context to the related primary contexts. If an element in the input set is related to a primary context, the element will be copied without changes to the output set. If, on the other hand, the element is related to a basic context, the element will be mapped onto all primary contexts which uses parts of the basic context in its composition. The right part of figure 6 shows an example where the annotation *a6* made in the basic context *V* is mapped onto the (in this example single) primary context *II*.

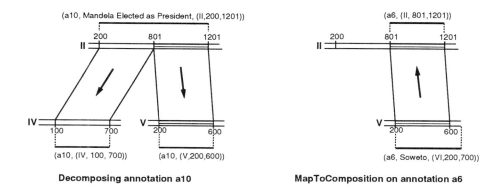

Figure 6   Compositional Operations

This operator can be used to find the result for the query on Mandela and Soweto. Assume that A contains the elements related to the election of Nelson Mandela, $A = \{(a10, (II,200,1201))\}$. Assume further that B contains the elements related to Soweto, $B = \{(a6, (V,200,700))\}$. The video related to both Soweto and Mandela can then be obtained by use of *A tAND MapToComposition(B)*. This will give the result $\{(-, (II,801,1201))\}$.

5   AN EXPERIMENTAL VIDEO ARCHIVE ENVIRONMENT

The previous sections have given a general introduction to the main aspects of searching and browsing in a shared video database. In this and the following sections we will focus on how searching and browsing are supported in the VideoSTAR framework, and how the VideoSTAR applications use this functionality to allow users to search and browse the contents of the video database.

During the VideoSTAR project we have developed several experimental video archive tools. The main reasons for developing these video tools have been to create an experimental environment for working with digital video databases, and to test out the usability of the VideoSTAR framework. The tools have also been used to get feedback from potential users of digital video databases – e.g., librarians working in television news archives.

The VideoSTAR tools are combined into an *integrated video tool environment* [14] which we is presented in this section. Tools for searching and browsing are presented in the following sections.

5.1   Tool Integration

The VideoSTAR integrated video tool environment consists of a video player, a tool manager, and tools for searching, browsing, and registration of meta-data.

A key feature for video archive tools is to provide interactive access to the video database including stored video documents and recordings. In providing such functionality, the video tools will need the capability to instruct the video player, for instance to load a specific video document and to jump to a specific point within the document. The VideoSTAR video player has the functionality that can be expected from a video player. In addition, it has a programming interface which allows the archive tools to control the playback by sending commands to the video player.

For some operations, the video tools do also need status information from the video player – e.g., to get the identity of the video that it is currently playing and the identity of the current frame – to allow the tools to operate synchronously with the video player. The VideoSTAR player can be instructed to report such status information regularly and the video tools can update their user interfaces according to the new state.

The integrated tool environment has been developed to make it possible for users to have different video archive tools interoperating simultaneously. The *Tool Manager* facilitates such synchronous interoperability: From the Tool Manager interface the user can choose which of the tools he/she needs for doing the work. The tool manager acts as a *broadcast message server* between the video tools and the video player. It broadcasts control commands from every video tool to every other active tools and distributes status information from the video player to every active tools.

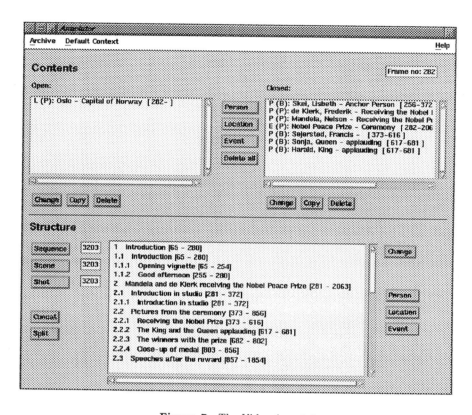

Figure 7　The Video Annotator

5.2　The Video Annotator

In Section 3 the VideoSTAR architecture was presented. In addition to storing the media-data, we must be able to register meta-data related to the video data. For this purpose we have developed a registration tool which is used to register both content annotations and structure information. The user interface is shown in Figure 7.

Registration of annotations is done by using the registration tool together with the video player. The user starts the registration process by playing the video document of interest – e.g., an evening news which among other things cover the Nobel Peace Prize Ceremony. Assume the user want to register information about the location of the Nobel Peace Prize Ceremony. When the user has found the start of the part of the video related to the Nobel Peace Prize Ceremony, he/she pauses the video player and presses the "Location" button. The video player informs the annotator about the current frame number. This frame number[3] is used as the *start time* for the annotation, and the user can register Oslo as the location together with an optional explanatory text. The user then continues the playback until Oslo no longer is the location, pauses the player, position the player on the last frame where Oslo is the location, and register the *end time* of the location annotation.

Structure information is registered in much the same way as content annotations. The structure part of the registration tool is seen in the lower part of the figure.

Registration of meta-data is an important, but time consuming task. Our registration tool has mainly been developed to show how registration tools can benefit from having direct access to the video data and from having control over the video player. Different users need to have registration tools tailored to their particular way of doing registrations.

6   QUERYING

VideoSTAR contains a video query module that implements the algebra presented in Section 4. In this section we will describe how the algebra operations can be used to formulate video queries with a focus on context handling. The examples used in this section are taken from television news archives. The structure of a news report is represented as a ordered set of *sequences* where each sequence corresponds to one news item. The *primary* context of the news represents the issues being covered in the news items.

6.1   Query Processing

Query processing usually involves parsing a query, breaking it into basic (often algebra-based) operations, determining - and possibly optimizing - a query plan defining the sequence of basic operations, and performing this plan. The current version of VideoSTAR offers a pure video query algebra interface that allows us to test the usefulness of the algebra discussed in Section 4 without having

---

[3] In our implementation we use frame numbers as a simplification of time codes.

to implement a complete query processor. Figure 8 gives an overview of the four steps that an application has to go through when requesting VideoSTAR to process video queries.

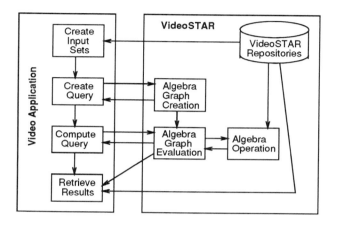

Figure 8   Query Processing Steps

Step 1: The application retrieves objects from the VideoSTAR repositories and inserts them into appropriate input sets for the query processing.

Step 2: The application instructs VideoSTAR to create the query graph with the corresponding operations. VideoSTAR will return a reference to each node that can be used by the application to access the node – e.g., for modifying the operation or for retrieving its result set.

Step 3: The application instructs VideoSTAR to perform the computation. The VideoSTAR *Algebra Operation* module computes the operations one-by-one in the sequence defined by the user application. The intermediate results are explicitly stored in each node and are used as input sets to other operations.

Step 4: The application accesses the appropriate node in the query graph and retrieves the corresponding result set.

The VideoSTAR repositories are used in the first step for selecting input sets, they are accessed by the *Algebra Operation* module to perform annotation, structure, and mapping operations, and they are accessed in the last step when the application retrieves the resulting objects themselves.

6.2   Experimental Video Query Tool

There are several ways to formulate queries – e.g., graphically such as QBIC
[2], by using icons [5], or textually such as SQL [23]. The video query tool
shown in Figure 9 offers the VideoSTAR query algebra directly to the user. It
is not a query interface that can be offered most (at least infrequent) users but
it provides us with an experimental environment for testing the video query
algebra.

The user interface of the query tool is divided into three main parts. In the
upper part the user can select from the set of content annotations contained in
the database. In our implementation we have so far restricted these to be either
persons, events, or locations. The middle part is used to create and compute
the query, while the lower part is used to present the query results. Each item
in the result list can be selected for replay by the video player.

When the user selects a person, event, or location, the query tool creates a
mapped video object set which contains one mapped video object for each
annotation related to the selected item. A tag is assigned to the set and the
user can refer to the input set by using this tag.

The user creates a query step-by-step by selecting one of the operations offered
in a list of commands. In addition to the operations defined in Section 4, the
user may select an *INPUT* operation that connects input sets to the query. For
convenience, most of the operations are also provided in versions that maps
the input sets to the context of the operation before performing the operation
– e.g., *tmAND* performs a temporal intersection operation after mapping the
input set onto primary contexts. Each operation is tagged and these tags can
be used to define the the result of one operation as an input argument to other
operations.

When the query has been constructed, the user can select the *Compute* button
to process the query. The sizes of all intermediate result sets are displayed
next to each operation, and the items of the final result set are displayed in the
result list.

6.3   Searching Primary Context

Assume that the user is searching for news items discussing the relations between Nelson Mandela and Frederik Willem de Klerk – i.e., the user is searching

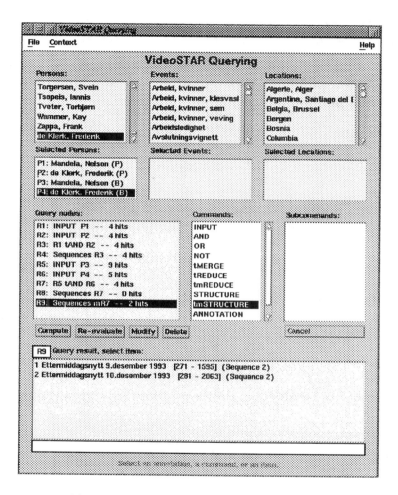

Figure 9 The VideoSTAR Experimental Query Tool

for pieces of video from the primary context which can be associated with both persons. If we let P1 be the set of annotations from the *primary* context related to Mr. Mandela and P2 the set of annotations related to the Mr. de Klerk, the query can be expressed as:

```
R1 = INPUT P1        // Retrieves Mandela from primary context
R2 = INPUT P2        // Retrieves de Klerk from primary context
```

```
R3 = R1 tAND R2      // Finds intersecting stream interval
R4 = Sequences R3    // Finds the corresponding sequences
```

R1 and R2 contain the annotations from the primary context that are related to Mr. Mandela and Mr. de Klerk, respectively. As can be seen from Figure 9, R1 and R2 each contains four annotations. R3 determines the four stream intervals which can be associated with both persons, while R4[4] retrieves the corresponding four news items (sequences).

6.4   Searching Basic Context

Assume that a news reporter is searching for one piece of video *showing* Mr. Mandela together with Mr. de Klerk. One solution would be to watch the news items resulting from the previous query to check whether such pieces exist. The user would then have to spend some time watching video to identify the relevant pieces. Even worse, the user may not get all pieces of video fulfilling the condition. For instance, assume that a news item related to economical reforms in South-Africa contains a shot from the Parliament showing Mr. Mandela and Mr. de Klerk together. Neither of the two are within the primary context of this news item, so this item would not be retrieved by the query.

The user should explicitly search the basic contexts because sensory information is registered in basic contexts. If P3 the set of annotations from the *basic* context related to Mr. Mandela and P4 is the set of annotations related to Mr. de Klerk, the query can be expressed as:

```
R5 = INPUT P3        // Retrieves Mandela from basic context
R6 = INPUT P4        // Retrieves de Klerk from basic context
R7 = R5 tAND R6      // Finds intersecting stream interval
```

As seen from Figure 9, there are four such pieces in the current database. If the user wants to retrieve the news items into which these stream intervals have been used, he/she should retrieve the corresponding news items (sequences):

```
R8 = Sequences R7    // Tries to find corresponding sequences
R9 = Sequences mR7   // Maps to primary context, finds sequences
```

As could be expected the set R8 is empty since R7 contains objects mapped to the basic context. By definition, basic context does not have structure and the

---

[4] Sequences R3 is a more readable form of the operation $STRUCT(R3, sequence)$

objects have to be mapped to the primary contexts – i.e., onto news documents – before news items can be retrieved. The `mR7` denotes that `R7` is mapped to the primary context before applying the `Sequences` operation. This makes `R9` return the two news items containing the stream intervals held by `R7`.

7 BROWSING AND PRESENTATION OF VIDEO INFORMATION

A user of a video database who are watching or working with a video document may wish to get more information about the video material than can actually be seen in the pictures and heard from the sound. The user may, for instance, want to know the names of the persons shown, the name of the locations where the video was recorded, and the time of recording. The user may also wish to get an overview of the video without having to watch the video, or to navigate within the video document without having to use fast forward or fast backward. To address this kind of needs, the database system should support browsing of structure information and presentation of content indexes related to a video document.

In this section we show how the structure and content meta-data can be used for browsing a video document and we present the VideoSTAR document browser.

7.1 Contents Browsing

In VideoSTAR, content browsing allows the user to retrieve annotations from the database intersecting a given interval of a video stream. By specifying what kind of annotations the user is interested in, he/she can restrict the browsing along two dimensions; by specifying *context(s)* for browsing and by specifying *conditions* on the annotations.

The different contexts a video document can be interpreted in, were introduced in Section 2.4. These contexts are the primary means for allowing the user to specify the scope of the browsing. VideoSTAR offers three different browsing functions: By browsing the *primary* context, the user gets all annotations related to the topic of a video document – i.e., all annotations related specificly to that document. By browsing the *basic* context, the user gets all annotations related to the stored media segments used in the document's composition - e.g., annotations related to persons, objects or locations seen in the video recording.

By browsing the secondary context, the user gets annotations related to other video documents using some intersecting parts of the video document's stored media segments. The user can also specify that he/she wants information from two of the contexts or from all three contexts.

These browsing functions are implemented by using the fundamental operations defined in Section 4 [17]. To retrieve the annotations valid for the primary context the *ANNOT* operation is used. To retrieve the annotations from the basic (or secondary) context, the video stream interval has to be mapped to the basic (or secondary) contexts before the annotations can be retrieved.

The second dimension a user can restrict the information in, is to specify predicates on the content annotations. Such predicates can be that the user is only interested in person annotations, that he/she is not interested in the name of the photographer, or only want to get annotations registered by a certain user – e.g. the news archive department.

7.2   Structure Browsing

Assume that a user of a television news archive wants to browse through a collection of television news to have a quick impression of their contents. Fast forward replay has been the traditional way to do this kind of browsing. In a video database containing structural data, these data can be used for browsing. The purpose of structure browsing of a video document is to give the user an overview of the structure of the video document, and to let the user navigate within the document. The structure information can also be used to give the user a description of the context into which a piece of video has been used – e.g., when pieces of video have been retrieved in content-based queries.

Structure information differs from content annotations. In VideoSTAR, the structural components are organized as a hierarchy consisting of compound units, sequences, scenes and shots. To get structure information for a video document or an interval from a video document, the *STRUCT* operation defined in Section 4 is used. The VideoSTAR API provides operations that can be used to navigate in this hierarchical structure.

By using the structure information, a *table of contents* for the video document can be created. This can be used to give the user information about which part of the document that is currently being shown in the video player. It also provides an easy way for the user to move within the document. It allows, for

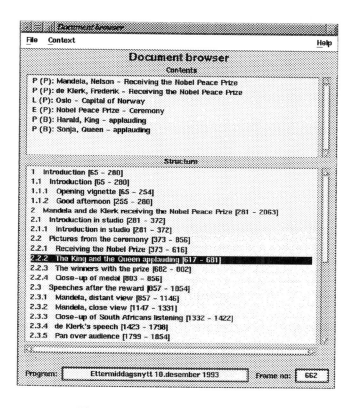

Figure 10   The Video Document Browser

instance, the user to directly jump to one given news item or to one specific scene within a news item.

7.3   The VideoSTAR Document Browser

The main task for the video document browser is to present to the user the meta-data related to the video as the video is played back. The temporal aspect of video information requires that the document browser is synchronized with the video playback, and there is a need for a close cooperation between the video player and the browser. The Tool Manager is responsible for keeping the browser synchronized with the video player.

The user interface of the browser is shown in Figure 10. As the figure shows, the browser is divided into two main parts, the upper part shows content annotations while the lower part shows structure information.

Content Annotations

In our experimental database we have chosen to group content annotations into the categories *persons, locations,* and *events.* Figure 10 shows a snapshot of a video document containing the evening news from December 10th, 1993. From the figure we can see that four different people are related to the current part of this video document. The event (preceded by an E) is the Nobel Peace Prize Ceremony, and the location (preceded by an L) is Oslo. The browser distinguishes between annotations related to the topic in question (primary context – marked with "P"), and annotations describing what is actually seen on the video (basic context – marked with "B").

The browse window is updated each time the browser gets a new frame number from the video player. This frame number is used for finding the content annotations which are valid for that frame. Content annotations that are no longer valid are removed from the window and new annotations are added.

Structure Information

The structure window of the video document browser is organized in the same way as the table of contents in a book. The highlighted line shows which part of the video document that is currently being played. As the document is being played back, the highlighted line scrolls down the "table of contents".

The structure window can also be used for interacting with the video player. By selecting a line in the structure window, the browser causes the video player to jump to this part of the video document and continue playing from that position. This makes it easy for the user to navigate within the video document.

8   EXPERIENCES AND DISCUSSION

To gain experience with VideoSTAR environment and the video tools we have digitized and annotated 15 television news programs from The Norwegian Broadcasting Company (NRK), 15 news programs from TV 2 Norway, and

5 ethnographic films from the collections of The Norwegian Folk Museum. Besides our own experiences with this database, and casual demonstrations, we have arranged extensive demonstrations and discussions with archivists from the two national broadcasting companies, as well as with conservators from museums.

8.1   User Responses

The professional users have consistently given a very positive response to the philosophy behind the video tools. Of course, they would like a mini-world model tailored to their own needs and traditions, and they would like to change parts of the user interfaces, to bring them in accordance with personal preferences and practice. The Norwegian Folk Museum has, for instance, expressed the need for six different types of content annotations and supplementary information, in addition to the three types we have defined.

Still, altogether users acclaim to the power and flexibility of the underlying video data model which provides means for both structuring and free annotating of video material. They also appreciate the tool support of the registration process and are especially pleased with the direct connection to the video material during this process.

The query facility, which gives content based access to the video data, is seen as a very productive tool. It will, when used in real archives, do away with a lot of transport of video cassettes between magazines and users, and will significantly reduce the considerable amount of time spent on tedious sequential searching in today's archives.

More experiences related to the integrated video archive environment can be found in [14].

8.2   Context Handling

The clear definition of, and distinction between, primary and basic contexts supports sharing of meta-data, in two ways:

- When users classify meta-data as basic context data, they clearly indicate that this information is always relevant to the video. Since the basic context related to a piece of video is common to all video documents using this piece, basic contexts preserve meta-data in well-structured ways. From the cooperation with television companies, we have learned that much sensory content data which have been registered in relation to a specific video document in their systems today - e.g., name of persons shown in the video - are not "inherited" to or visible from other documents reusing the video.

- By classifying some meta-data as part of the primary context of a piece of video, the user indicates that this information should be interpreted in relation to the specific video document, and may not be relevant for contexts. When shared video databases become common, we expect that it will be important to separate such context specific meta-data but in such ways that they are still available for users - e.g., media researchers - that need the possibility to search across several contexts. Librarians that have tested the VideoSTAR tools have responded positively to this possibility of determining the query scope.

By using the VideoSTAR tools, we have seen how useful the context handling is to establish a context for interpreting small fragments of video that are returned by a query. The following example may illustrate this: If we are using the query tool to retrieve all pieces of video showing the Norwegian King from the database, we will, as one of the resulting items, get a very short video fragment showing the King and Queen applauding. The user will have no idea what the occasion is, and why the King and Queen are applauding, by only watching the small fragment. If, however, the browser is active, the browser will provide the primary context for this shot as shown in Figure 10. The user will then immediately see that the royalties are applauding for Nelson Mandela and Frederik de Klerk, and that the occasion is the Nobel Peace Prize Ceremony.

No tools for video editing have been included into the video database environment yet, and, thus, we have not had the opportunity to experiment with secondary contexts. One of the the experiences made by BBC in the "People's Century" project [35], was that specific video documents were the starting point for a comprehensive browsing of the related documents. The explicit support for browsing secondary contexts can play a significant role in simplifying this kind of research.

8.3 Querying Temporal Relationships

The most valuable effect of giving the user the opportunity to specify temporal relations in a video query, is that this reduces the size of the result and the effort needed to get an overview of it: First, because it allows the user to formulate more precise queries which will result in fewer, but more relevant, result items; second, because the items themselves may be smaller because irrelevant parts have been removed; third, small fragments of video that intersects can be merged into fewer and larger result items and, thus, it will be easier to examine the result. The price one has to pay is a more complex query language and a more complex query processor. To fully exploit temporal relationships, one also has to spend a lot of effort on indexing the video to ensure that meta-data have a proper accuracy.

Though less complex mechanisms may be sufficient for many applications - especially when sharing of meta-data is not required - we think that temporal operations are necessary to achieve acceptable accuracy when meta-data are shared. Assume, for instance, that each shot is described as one complete entity [33], and that one specific shot shows a pan over a crowd of people ending up with a zoom on Nelson Mandela. This shot would have Nelson Mandela as part of its basic context. Assume now that the first part of this shot which shows the crowd only, is used in another document. Since Nelson Mandela was part of the basic context, Nelson Mandela will implicitly be related to the sensory contents of the second document even though he is not shown on the part of the video that is actually used in this document. This will reduce the quality of the meta-data and result in highly undesirable effects that may confuse the user.

Acknowledgements

We are especially grateful to researcher Stein Langørgen who has turned our ideas into running software and to the LAVA project (funded by the Norwegian Research Council, UNINETT and Telenor) for the financial support of our research. We would like to thank all master students at NTH who have contributed to our research on digital video applications and video database environments. We will also thank the Norwegian Broadcasting Corporation, TV2 Norway, and the Norwegian Folk Museum for participating in the work.

REFERENCES

[1] J.F. Allen. Maintaining Knowledge about Temporal Intervals. *Communications of the ACM*, November 1983.

[2] J. Ashley et al. Automatic and Semi-Automatic Image Retrieval Methods in QBIC. In *Proceedings of Storage and Retrieval for Image and Video Databases III - part of IS&T/SPIE's Symposium on Electronic Imaging: Science and Technology*, San Jose, CA, February 1995.

[3] J.F.K. Buford. Architectures and Issues for Distributed Multimedia Systems. In J.F.K. Buford, editor, *Multimedia Systems*, chapter 3, pages 45–64. Addison-Wesley Publishing Company, Inc., 1994.

[4] J. Clifford and A. Crocker. The Historical Relational Data Model (HRDM) Revisited. In A.U. Tansel et al., editors, *Temporal Databases: Theory, Design, and Implementation*, chapter 1. The Benjamin/Cummings Publishing Company, Inc., 1993.

[5] M. Davis. Media Streams: An Iconic Language for Video Annotation. In *Proceedings of 1993 IEEE Symposium on Visual Languages*, Bergen, Norway, 1993.

[6] D. Deloddere, W. Verbiest, and H. Verhille. Interactive Video On Demand. *IEEE Communications Magazine*, 32(5):82–88, May 1994.

[7] J.C. Ellis. *A History of Film*. Prentice Hall, 3rd edition, 1990.

[8] R.C. Gonzales and R.C. Woods. *Digital Image Processing*. Addison-Wesley Publishing Company, 1992.

[9] W.I. Grosky. Multimedia Information Systems. *IEEE Multimedia*, Spring 1994.

[10] A. Hampapur, R. Jain, and T. Weymouth. Digital Video Segmentation. In *Proceedings of ACM Multimedia '94*, pages 357–364, San Francisco, USA, October 1994.

[11] A. Hampapur, R. Jain, and T. Weymouth. Indexing in Video Databases. In *Proceedings of the IS&T/SPIE Symposium on Electronic Imaging Science and Technology, Conference on Storage and Retrieval for Image and Video Databases III*, pages 292–306, San Jose, CA, February 1995.

[12] L. Hardman, G. van Rossum, and D.C.A. Bulterman. Structured Multimedia Authoring. In *Proceedings of ACM Multimedia 93*, pages 283–290, Anaheim, CA, August 1993.

[13] R. Hjelsvold. Video Information Contents and Architecture. In *Proceedings of the 4th International Conference on Extending Database Technology*, pages 259–272, Cambridge, UK, March 1994.

[14] R. Hjelsvold, S. Langørgen, R. Midtstraum, and O. Sandstå. Integrated Video Archive Tools. In *Proceedings of the ACM Multimedia'95*, San Francisco, California, November 1995.

[15] R. Hjelsvold and R. Midtstraum. Modelling and Querying Video Data. In *Proceedings of the 20th VLDB Conference*, pages 686–694, Santiago, Chile, September 1994.

[16] R. Hjelsvold and R. Midtstraum. Databases for Video Information Sharing. In *Proceedings of the IS&T/SPIE Symposium on Electronic Imaging Science and Technology, Conference on Storage and Retrieval for Image and Video Databases III*, pages 268–279, San Jose, CA, February 1995.

[17] R. Hjelsvold, R. Midtstraum, and O. Sandstå. A Temporal Foundation of Video Databases. In *Proceedings of the International Workshop on Temporal Databases*, Zürich, Switzerland, September 1995.

[18] M.E. Hodges and R.M. Sasnett. *Multimedia Computing. Case Studies from MIT Project Athena*. Addison-Wesley Publishing Company, Inc., 1990.

[19] T.D.C. Little et al. A Digital On-Demand Video Service Supporting Content-Based Queries. In *Proceedings of ACM Multimedia 93*, pages 427–436, Anaheim, USA, August 1993.

[20] T.D.C. Little and D. Venkatesh. Prospects for Interactive Video-on-Demand. *IEEE Multimedia*, 1(3):14–24, Fall 1994.

[21] C. Locatis, J. Charuhas, and R. Banvard. Hypervideo. *Educational Technology, Research and Development*, 38(2), 1990.

[22] A.O. Martinussen. Håndverksregistrering på S-VHS. In *Fra idé til virkelighet*. Norske Kunst- og Kulturhistoriske Museer, 1994.

[23] J. Melton and R. Simon. *Understanding the New SQL: A Complete Guide*. Morgan Kaufmann Publishers, 1993.

[24] G. Miller, G. Baber, and M. Gilliland. News On-Demand for Multimedia Networks. In *Proceedings of ACM Multimedia 93*, pages 383–392, Anaheim, CA, August 1993.

[25] J. Monaco. *How to Read a Film. The Art, Technology, Language, History and Theory of Film and Media*. Oxford University Press, 1981.

[26] E. Oomoto and K. Tanaka. OVID: Design and Implementation of a Video-Object Database System. *IEEE Transactions on Knowledge and Data Engineering*, 5(4):629–643, 1993.

[27] L.A. Rowe, J.S. Boreczky, and C.A. Eads. Indexes for User Access to Large Video Databases. In *Proceedings of the IS&T/SPIE Symposium on Electronic Imaging Science and Technology, Conference on Storage and Retrieval for Image and Video Databases II*, San Jose, CA, February 1994.

[28] G. Salton. *Automatic Text Processing - The Transformation Analysis, and Retrieval of Information by Computer*. Addison-Wesley Publishing Company, 1988.

[29] T.G.A. Smith. If You Could See What I Mean... Descriptions of Video in an Anthropologist's Notebook. Master's thesis, MIT, 1992.

[30] S.W. Smoliar and H. Zhang. Content-Based Video Indexing and Retrieval. *IEEE Multimedia*, 1(2):62–72, Summer 1994.

[31] J. Sowa, editor. *Principles of Semantic Networks*. Morgan Kaufmann, 1991.

[32] D.C. Tsichitzis and F.H. Lochovsky. *Data Models*. Prentice-Hall, 1982.

[33] J. Turner. Representing and accessing information in the shotstock database at the National Film Board of Canada. *The Canadian Journal of Information Science*, 15(4), December 1990.

[34] R. Weiss, A. Duda, and D.K. Gifford. Composition and Search with a Video Algebra. *IEEE Multimedia*, 2(1):12–25, Spring 1995.

[35] C. Whittaker. People's Century - Through the Archives. In *FIAT/IASA Internationaler Kongress 1994*, pages 123–129, Bogensee, Germany, September 1994. Battert Verlag, Baden.

5

A VISUAL MULTIMEDIA QUERY LANGUAGE FOR TEMPORAL ANALYSIS OF VIDEO DATA

Stacie Hibino, Elke A. Rundensteiner

Electrical Engr. and Computer Sc. Dept.
Software Systems Research Laboratory
University of Michigan, Ann Arbor

ABSTRACT

The storage of various media in multimedia databases poses new challenges to query techniques — challenges that exceed the expressive power of traditional text-based query languages. New query interfaces should take advantage of characteristics *inherent* in multimedia data, such as the dynamic temporal nature of video, the visual and spatial characteristics of images, the pitch of audio, etc. The focus of our research is to exploit the temporal *continuity* and combined *spatio-temporal* characteristics of video data for the purpose of video analysis. We do so by integrating a visual query paradigm with a dynamic visual presentation of results into a user-friendly interactive visualization environment. In this chapter, we present our overall approach for identifying trends in video data via querying for *relationships* between video annotations. Our approach allows users to analyze the video in terms of *temporal* relationships between events (e.g., events of type A frequently follow events of type B). We present a temporal visual query language (TVQL) for specifying relative temporal queries between sets of annotations. This query language builds on the notion of dynamic query filters and significantly extends them. It is tailored for temporal analysis — allowing users to pose queries, as well as to *browse* the data in a *temporally continuous* manner, thereby aiding them in the discovery of temporal trends. The TVQL is augmented with complementary temporal diagrams, which provide intuitive visual feedback for quickly and qualitatively verifying the temporal query specified. This chapter includes the complete specification of our TVQL, a transformation function for generating corresponding temporal diagrams, and the process for mapping TVQL queries to system queries.

1 INTRODUCTION

1.1 Motivation

Multimedia databases are becoming more and more common, allowing users to store and retrieve various media for different purposes. Medical researchers are storing x-rays in medical image databases, art historians are archiving and documenting artwork, geographers are creating geographical information systems, and digital libraries are becoming more popular. Video data is also becoming more common, being collected by educational researchers for classroom studies, by software evaluators during usability testing, by scientists for evaluating the behavior of microscopic entities, etc. An advantage of video data is that it preserves detailed information which would be difficult to capture by other means of data collection. The challenge of analyzing video data is to abstract and conclude quantitative results from such a rich, qualitative medium.

The ability to store various media thus poses new challenges to query techniques, moving beyond traditional text-based query languages. This is due to the fact that media such as audio, images and video have basic characteristics which are different from text. For example, video has temporal and visual characteristics, audio has basic characteristics such as pitch and timbre, images have features of hue and saturation, etc. Query interfaces to multimedia databases should thus take advantage of such inherent characteristics in order to properly allow the exploitation of the richness of information captured in the media.

Recent work in image and video databases illustrate the use of query techniques which exploit inherent visual and spatial characteristics [20, 26]. For example, Ueda, et al [26] have developed techniques to find images based on the user's selection of an area in an existing image. Their technique works for simple queries equivalent to "find all images with blue sky" to more sophisticated queries such as object extraction, including the location of video segments containing a specific person. The same techniques for locating segments containing complex objects such as people can also be used to determine situations such as whether a person is standing in a doorway. While these techniques do take advantage of the inherent characteristics of the media, they typically focus more on "low-level" bit analysis and typically have high computation costs. In order to support a higher level of analysis — and video analysis in particular, we need to move up to an *object* level of abstraction. In this way, once we can characterize media according to the objects they contain, we can then more efficiently query the media database based on inherent *relationships* between these objects. In the case of video analysis, we can then examine temporal and/or spatial relationships between objects and events.

While some work in video databases and analysis[1] [19, 21, 27, 13] has used the temporal characteristics of video, little work in temporal query techniques of dynamic media has been done to take advantage of the temporal *continuity* and/or the combined *spatio-temporal* characteristics of the medium. Even when users may only be interested in temporal analysis, the use of spatial context may provide visual clues aiding in the analysis process. As video data becomes more and more a common form of data collection, such techniques will become a more critical need for analysis. Our work is designed to address issues related to these needs.

1.2 Introduction to Our Approach

In order to support temporal analysis of video data, using spatio-temporal characteristics and exploiting the temporal continuity of the medium, we have identified three primary needs to address: 1) the need to abstract and store spatio-temporal (and semantic) information from the video data directly, 2) the need to query for temporal relationships within the data in a continuous manner, and 3) the need to present the results in a spatio-temporal visualization.

Similar to previous work in video analysis [13, 19, 22], we are also using annotations for abstracting information and coding the video data. The advantages of using annotations are that 1) they allow users to abstract both *temporal and spatial* information from the data, 2) they simplify analysis by reducing the amount of information to be processed, and 3) when layered on top of the original data, they allow users to preserve context without corrupting the original data. In contrast to previous work, however, we are not using annotations to *pre-code* relationships, but we restrict them to only abstracting information about *atomic* objects and events. Coding only the atomic content requires less storage space and less time than coding every relationship between each atom, especially when users are interested in several different types of relationships. In addition, it provides more flexibility in the analysis process, aiding users in *discovering relationships* rather than requiring them to predefine or pre-code all possible relationships. Our annotation model is described in Section 2.

---

[1] As suggested in the previous paragraph, we use the term *video analysis* to refer to the process of identifying trends and relationships between events in the video data. This is in contrast to bit-level video analysis such as that used for object extraction.

Once we have stored video annotations in a database, we can then query the annotation collection in search of data trends. In order to support the trend searching process and exploit the temporal continuity and combined spatio-temporal characteristics of the underlying medium, we are designing a user-friendly interactive visualization environment. This environment integrates a visual query paradigm with a dynamic visual presentation of results. The visualization is *dynamically* updated as users incrementally adjust query parameters via direct manipulation of buttons and sliders. This chapter describes our over-all environment (Section 3) and then presents the details of our *temporal* visual query language (TVQL — see Section 5). Our TVQL can be used to spec-ify *relative* temporal queries between sets of annotations. This query language builds on the notion of dynamic query filters [2] and significantly extends them. It is tailored for temporal analysis — allowing users to pose queries, as well as to *browse* the data in a *temporally continuous* manner, thereby aiding them in the discovery of temporal trends. The TVQL is augmented with complemen-tary temporal diagrams, which provide intuitive visual feedback for quickly and qualitatively verifying the temporal query specified (Section 6).

1.3   Sample Scenario

Consider the case where educational researchers collect and analyze classroom video data to study social interactions in the classroom. The researchers could use annotations to code (i.e., describe and interpret) the video data, abstracting information such as when the teacher is speaking, when the student is speaking, etc. That is, they can create annotations such as text labels to identify objects and people, circles to highlight interesting situations, etc. Once the annota-tions have been stored in a database, the researchers can begin exploring the relationships between different types of classroom events. For example, they can create one subset of "student speaking" events and one subset of "teacher speaking" events. They could then search for temporal trends in the video data by specifying queries to locate occurrences of, and relationships between subsets of annotations. In this way, the researchers can use our TVQL to de-termine temporal relationships such as which students frequently speak after the teacher speaks. They might first search for temporal relationships where a student starts talking at least ten seconds *after* the teacher stops speaking. By incrementally adjusting this query to locate those students who begin speaking *before* the teacher finishes, researchers can identify situations where a student might be interrupting the teacher or talking out of turn. This ability to incre-mentally adjust queries allows users to temporally browse the data in a new and powerful way.

1.4 Relationship to Previous Work

Preliminary descriptions of this work have been presented elsewhere [14, 16]. This chapter expands this previous work, providing a more refined and complete description and derivation of our temporal visual query language (TVQL). More specifically, in this chapter, we present the full specification of the TVQL, including the derivation of the temporal duration component and more technical details regarding the underlying relationships between the four relative temporal position filters. In addition, we also include a complete description of the annotation model, as well as an outline of the process for mapping TVQL queries to system queries.

1.5 Overview

This chapter is organized into nine additional sections. Section 2 describes our annotation model. Section 3 presents an overview of our interactive visualization approach and Section 4 describes how we specify *relative* queries within our framework. Section 5 describes our temporal visual query language for specifying relative temporal queries and Section 6 presents our visual enhancements to our TVQL, including the derivation of our complementary temporal diagrams. Section 7 describes the process of mapping TVQL queries to system queries and Section 8 presents some preliminary evaluation of the query language. Section 9 discusses related work and finally, Section 10 presents our current status along with a summary of contributions.

2   ANNOTATION MODEL

Section 1.2 introduced the use of annotations for abstracting spatio-temporal and semantic information from video data. The use of annotations simplifies the analysis process by allowing us to evaluate and manipulate the data at an object and event level rather than at the bit-level. Recall that we restrict annotations to coding *atomic* objects and events rather than for *pre-coding* relationships within the video data. In this way, users can *explore* the data *in search of* relationships rather than predefining a subset of relationships to evaluate. This section provides an overview of the annotation model we assume by defining the terms video, video segment, event, and video annotation as they are used in the context of this chapter.

Video. In this chapter, a *video* object v has the following temporal characteristics: a start time, $v.t.start\_time$ (defined as time 0); an end time, $v.t.end\_time$, defining the finite (maximum) length of the video in seconds (up to two decimal points); a start frame, $v.t.start\_frame$, indicating the physical video frame number corresponding to the start time of the video; a corresponding end frame $v.t.end\_frame$. We assume for simplicity that the frames are numbered consecutively, starting from 0. We define a function $VF(Vtime)$ which maps a given video time (in seconds) to the corresponding frame: $VF(Vtime) = round((Vtime * fps) + f\_offset)$, where fps = the number of frames per second of the video and f_offset = the frame number corresponding to time 0 of the video. Similarly, we define a function $VT(frameNum) \longrightarrow time$: $VT(frameNum) = (frameNum - f\_offset)/fps$.

A video object v also has some spatial characteristics including position ($v.sp.x$, $v.sp.y$), width ($v.sp.width$), and height ($v.sp.height$) of the video in screen pixel units. We assume that a video object is one *continuous* medium, including the start and end frames as well as *every* frame between them. In other words, v is a complex object decomposed of an ordered sequence F of frame objects, $F = [f_0, f_1, \ldots, f_z].^2$

Video segment. A *video segment* vs is a continuous subset of frames of the video object (i.e., vs is defined over frames $[f_i, \ldots, f_j]$, where $0 \leq i \leq j \leq z$). Similar to the video object v, a video segment vs of v has a start frame ($vs.start\_frame \geq v.start\_frame$) and an end frame ($vs.end\_frame \leq v.end\_frame$) as well as starting and ending times. In addition, the length of a video segment must be less than or equal to that of the video (i.e., $vs.end\_frame - vs.start\_frame \leq v.end\_frame - v.start\_frame$).

Video annotations. A *video annotation* va is used to indicate real-world situations within the video, also referred to as *events*. It is visually represented by a media object (e.g., text, audio, graphic, etc.) that is temporally linked to a video segment and spatially linked to a position on top of the video. That is, the video annotation specifies spatial information for displaying the media object relative to the video window, so that $v.sp.x \leq va.sp.x \leq v.sp.x + v.sp.width$ and $v.sp.y \leq va.sp.y \leq v.sp.y + v.sp.height$. The video annotation references the media object through a reference to a content-based descriptive object. In addition to spatial, temporal and content-based characteristics, each annotation also has space for user-specified comments.

---

[2] We assume that we are dealing with uncompressed video, so that (unlike MPEG files) every frame is complete and independent of its predecessors. As a consequence each frame is directly accessed without the need for additional calculations.

More formally, for a given video v_p, we denote the set of annotations $Ann(v_p) = \{va_1, va_2, \ldots, va_n\}$. Each annotation va_i (where $1 \leq i \leq n$) has four components: temporal information $va_i.t$, spatial information $va_i.sp$, a reference to a descriptive object $va_i.d$ and space for users' comments $va_i.comments$ (see Figure 1).

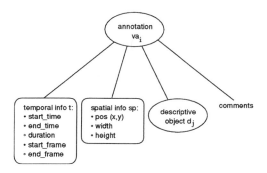

Figure 1   Characteristics of a video annotation object.

The reference from an annotation va_i to a descriptive object d_j is denoted by $description(va_i) = d_j$. Given $D = \{d_1, d_2, \ldots, d_m\}$ as the set of all descriptive objects, then each descriptive object d_j (where $1 \leq j \leq m$) has four components: content information $d_j.content$, history information $d_j.history$, default spatial information $d_j.sp$, and a reference to a media object $d_j.md$. The characteristics of the descriptive object are presented in Figure 2.

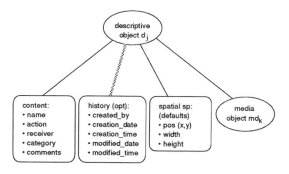

Figure 2   Characteristics of a descriptive object.

The descriptive object *content* is used to store semantic information about the event being annotated. *Content.name* is the name of the object or person that d_j represents. *Content.action* is the action being taken (e.g., talking) and *content.receiver* is the person or object being acted on. The content action and receiver are optional while the name is required. *Content.category* allows users to group content into their own categories. For example, the researcher can assign all individual "student-working" and "student-talking" (e.g., Jane talking, John working, etc) descriptions into a more general category of "student activity." This provides users with a natural mechanism for grouping coded data and should also simplify the selection of annotation subsets. The *content.comments* provides a free form space for optional user comments. The $d_j.content.comments$ associated with the descriptive objects are different from the more specific $va_i.comments$.

The descriptive object history information about when an annotation was created or last modified is optional (as denoted by the shaded arc). The spatial information provides default spatial values to relieve users from having to respecify them every time the same descriptive object is used. Each descriptive object contains a reference to a media object. A media object is the visual or auditory representation of the video annotation (e.g., a circle, arrow, talk bubble icon, etc.). Several descriptive objects can share the same media object. In this way, the users can consistently assign, for example, all "student-talking" descriptive objects to a black talk bubble icon and all "teacher-talking" descriptive objects to a red talk bubble icon. If we let $M = \{md_1, md_2, \ldots, md_p\}$ be a set of media objects, then each media object md_k (where $1 \leq k \leq p$) has the characteristics depicted in Figure 3.

Users can choose one of three kinds of media: audio, 1-D, or 2-D. (In our diagrammatic representation, connected arcs represent alternatives.) The 1-D and 2-D media types provide additional media choices. Once a media object has been created, it is stored on a palette so as to be easily accessible for re-use. This will aid users in coding the video data in a consistent manner.

Although we are currently requiring researchers to input annotations manually, we expect that previous work by others in the area of object extraction (e.g., [20]) will eventually be used to generate annotations automatically. We also expect, however, that it will be too inefficient to operate on the raw data directly. Hence, even when image analysis and object recognition algorithms have matured, it is likely that they will still be applied *upfront*, to interpret video and generate annotations much like those presented in this section, rather than during query processing.

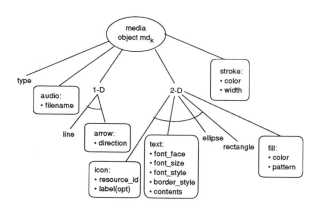

Figure 3   Characteristics of a media object.

3   OVERVIEW OF OUR APPROACH

Our overall goal is to support users in analyzing video data by providing tools for querying video annotations in search of relationships and data trends. We postulate that visually presenting the results retrieved from relative queries will facilitate this searching for trends. The query and review part of the video analysis process is similar to the process used in visual information seeking (VIS) [3]. The VIS process is a process for *browsing* database information; a process characterized by rapid filtering, progressive refinement, continuous reformulation of goals, and visual scanning to identify results. These characteristics make VIS particularly well suited for searching for trends in the video annotations. We are thus adopting this methodology as our underlying framework.

Figure 4 presents our overall approach to applying and extending VIS to the problem of video data analysis [15]. In our MultiMedia VIS (MMVIS), users first code the video data with annotations. These annotations are stored in an underlying database (also known as the Annotation Server). Users can then explore and analyze the video through iteratively specifying queries using a visual query language (VQL) and reviewing the visualization of results presented. Similar to VIS, our interface will also use *dynamic query filters* [2]. Our filters, however, will be customized to handle relative *temporal* queries. The advantage of query filters is that they allow rapid incremental adjustment of query parameters via the use of buttons and sliders. This is in contrast to text-based query languages, where query specification and modification are typically much

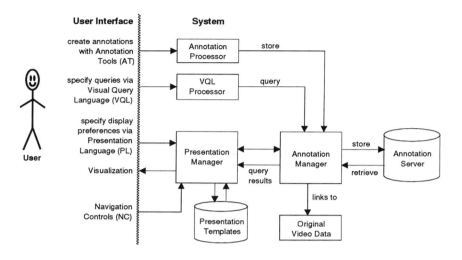

Figure 4   Framework for MultiMedia Visual Information Seeking (MMVIS).

more complicated and less intuitive. Our temporal extensions represent a novel application of the dynamic query filter technology.

The queries are interpreted by a VQL processor and then forwarded to the Annotation Manager. The retrieved results are passed to a Presentation Manager. The Presentation Manager takes the query results, along with any user-defined display preferences and updates a visualization. In this way, the visualization is updated every time users make changes to any query filter. Users can visually scan the results to look for data trends. If no trends are found, they can use the presentation language (PL) to clarify the visualization, the navigation controls to further explore query results, or the VQL to incrementally adjust the query. In addition, if users wish to test a new hypothesis or explore different characteristics of the data, they can use the VQL to do so. Thus, queries are expressed *incrementally* as users specify desired values for each query parameter. In such an environment, users can gain a sense of causality between adjusting a query filter and the corresponding changes presented in both the other query filters and the visualization.

Based on the long-term objectives outlined above, we now have tackled a subset of the issues required to build the MMVIS environment. The goals of this chapter are (1) to define a general temporal visual query language (TVQL) that can be easily integrated into a variety of applications and (2) to design a TVQL interface that is easy and intuitive to use by application (i.e., video annotation and analysis) users who typically are query language novices. Thus, the specific problem addressed in this chapter is that of the users'. need for a simple interface for specifying relative temporal queries to video data. *Relative* queries are necessary for examining *relationships* between events and thus for identifying trends. A *visual* language is desired to correspond with the graphical nature of the objects in the database and is much more suitable for the type of novice users we are targeting. Finally, a *temporal* language is required to facilitate searching for temporal data trends. While we plan to explore both spatial and temporal aspects of video analysis in the future, we have focused our initial work on only the temporal aspect.

4   SPECIFYING RELATIVE QUERIES

Before we can describe our *temporal* extensions to VIS, we must first describe how to extend VIS to handle *relative* queries. While we can use the VIS approach to identify and specify interesting *subsets* of data, we cannot use the approach to specify *relationships* between these subsets [3]. In order to better understand this problem, consider a query such as "show me all annotations where the student is working *while* the teacher is speaking." While we can use dynamic queries (DQs) to select subsets such as the "student working" and "teacher speaking" annotations, we cannot use DQs to specify a desired relationship between members of these subsets. In the case of the example, we need to be able to specify a relative condition that holds true for each (teacher-speaking, student-working) pair returned. Rather than specifying a range of *absolute* conditions, we need to specify *relative* ones.

Extending the use of DQs to handle *relative* temporal queries of video data requires binding subsets of the data to variables and specifying temporal relationships between these subsets. Two subsets can be specified through the use of two sets of standard query filters. We thus provide a query palette for specifying each subset. Parameters specified in the Subset A query palette automatically bind the subset formed to the variable A. The corresponding functionality is provided for binding the second subset to variable B.

The simple example in Figure 5 illustrates how we can use query filters in the Subset A palette to bind the subset "teacher talking" to variable A, and those in the Subset B query palette to bind the "student working" subset to variable B. The actual subset query palettes allow the user to set more parameters and parameter values (e.g., to specify annotation media types, secondary actions, etc.). The sliders at the bottom of each subset palette allow users to specify *absolute* temporal information for each subset. This is in contrast to the temporal relationship R *between* sets A and B that will be specified with *specialized temporal query filters* (see Section 5). Progressive refinement of queries will be preserved by allowing the adjustment of query filters for A, B, or R at any time and in any order.

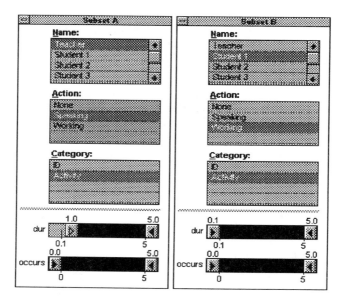

Figure 5 Simple example of potential subset query filters. The Subset A palette binds the subset "teacher talking" to variable A, and the Subset B query palette binds the "student working" subset to variable B.

Note that while value ranges for discrete predicate domains such as "Name" and "Category" are selected from lists, numerically valued ranges such as "Dur" (for duration) are selected using double-thumbed slider filters. This type of filter was introduced in [3] for specifying ranges of values. Each thumb has an arrow, pointing towards the range being specified. The thumb arrow is filled to indicate that the endpoint of a range is included, or empty to indicate that the endpoint of a range is excluded. Ranges are filled in the sliders for further clarification. The text above the slider indicates exact values. Figure 6 identifies each of these components of the double-thumbed slider.

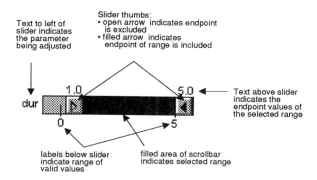

Figure 6 Description of a *double-thumbed slider* query filter.

In addition to double-thumbed sliders, Ahlberg and Shneiderman [3] introduce a number of other interfaces for different types of query filters. For example, they use a single-thumbed slider (with no arrow) for specifying a single value, or a single-thumbed slider with an arrow to indicate a range towards one of the extremes of the slider. Rather than requiring the user to change the type of slider filter for different types of ranges, we are adopting a single type of slider filter (i.e., the one illustrated in Figure 6) to handle all range query specifications. It is as powerful as the specialized type of sliders, and the uniformity should simplify the user interface.

Based on the description of the double-thumbed sliders, we now see that in the example in Figure 5, subset A includes all "teacher talking" annotations that have duration greater than 1.0 minute and less than or equal than 5 minutes. Similarly, subset B includes all "student working" annotations with duration that is greater than or equal 0.1 and less than or equal to 5.0 minutes. In both subsets, there is no restriction on when the annotations temporally occur within the 20 minute video. Again, these *absolute* temporal constraints specified in the subset palettes are different from the *relative* temporal constraints which will be specified using the temporal query palette. That is, while we can use the absolute sliders to restrict analysis to the first five minutes of the video (by setting the right thumb of the occurs filter to 5.0), we cannot use these absolute sliders to specify *relative* temporal constraints such as limiting the results to situations where A events end up to one minute before B events start. In the next section, we present our specialized relative temporal query filters which are designed to address these needs.

5   THE TVQL

This section presents a temporal visual query language (TVQL) for specifying relative temporal queries. Our TVQL is composed of temporal query filters, a disjunctive operator, and a macro operator. Our goal here is to gracefully integrate these temporal filters and operators with the standard DQ and VIS properties introduced in Section 3.

We assume that *absolute* temporal duration and position are specified with the corresponding subsets A and B (see Figure 5). *Relative* temporal duration and position can then be specified using our TVQL. Query filters for *relative* temporal duration and position are presented in Sections 5.1 and 5.2. The disjunctive operator is introduced in Section 5.2. User-created macros (i.e., the macro operator) included for improving efficiency of query specification over time are presented in Section 5.3.

5.1   The Relative Duration Query Filter

Two events A1 and B1 can be temporally related in terms of their durations. Although relative duration may sometimes be dictated by relative temporal position (e.g., if event A1 "contains" event B1, then the duration of event A1 is longer than the duration of event B1), this is not the case for all temporal position relationships (see Section 5.2). In addition, users may wish to specify relative duration queries *independent* of relative temporal position. For example, users may wish to locate all events where student S1 works on a task for a longer period of time than student S2. In this particular case, we do not care whether these two events are concurrent, partially overlapping, or positionally unrelated. To address this need, we propose a query filter for relative duration.

Given the durations of events A1 and B1 ($A1.t.duration$ and $B1.t.duration$, respectively), the basic relationship for relative duration between the events can be described as follows:

$$A1.t.duration \theta B1.t.duration$$

where $\theta \in \{ <, >, = \}$. While this relationship can be used to *qualitatively* describe the relative duration between two events, it cannot be used to specify *quantitative* information about that relative duration. For example, if we are interested in cases where event A1 has a longer duration than event B1, then we can specify the constraint $A1.t.duration > B1.t.duration$. This does not, however, specify the quantity by which A1's duration exceeds that of B1. We can address this problem by redefining the relationship in terms of differences:

$$(A1.t.duration - B1.t.duration)\theta 0$$

where $\theta \in \{ <, >, = \}$ and 0 denotes zero. If we let $\Delta dur = A1.t.duration - B1.t.duration$, then we can reduce the above specification to the following simpler expression:

$$\Delta dur\theta 0,$$

where $\theta \in \{ <, >, = \}$. Now if we are interested in cases where the duration of A1 is one or more minutes longer than the duration of B1 (e.g., student S1 spends at least one minute more on a task than student S2), then we can set $\Delta dur > 0$ and more specifically, we can set $\Delta dur \geq 1$ minute. This is in contrast to the first representation, where we would only be able to say $A1.t.duration > B1.t.duration$.

In addition to allowing us to quantify the relative duration, the Δ representation facilitates specification of values from a continuous range. This allows us to use a slider query filter for specifying relative duration (see Figure 7). Our relative duration specification is now compatible with the DQ interface we are designing for video analysis. Rather than requiring users to translate their queries into notations (e.g., Δdur) and algebraic equations, we provide full labels to the left of the filters and qualitative English text above the filters. In this way, users can "read" the query they have specified. In Figure 7, the query filter can be read as "the dur of A is more than one minute greater than the dur of B." These descriptive enhancements are described in more detail in Section 6.2.

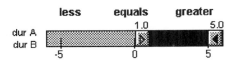

Figure 7   Query filter for specifying relative duration. Example: Student S1 works one or more minutes longer on tasks than student S2. Given a subset A bound to "student S1 working" and a subset B bound to "student S2 working," we can specify the query "Show all situations where student S1 works more than one minute longer than student S2" by setting the left thumb of the query filter to > 1 (i.e., by sliding the left thumb to position 1.0 and making sure the left thumb arrow is unfilled to exclude 1.0 in the selected range).

The type of range selection supported by DQ filters allows us to specify values at different levels of granularity (e.g., to specify a single value, a small range of values, or a larger range of values). Table 1 provides examples to illustrate this advantage for the relative duration query filter. The first example in Table 1 illustrates how to query for all (A_i, B_j) pairs such that A_i is exactly one minute longer than B_j; the second example shows how to query for all pairs such that A_i is at most one minute longer than B_j, and the final example shows how to find all pairs such that A_i is longer than B_j. While these types of queries can also be submitted using a text-based query language, the DQ-based interface allows users to easily and incrementally adjust their queries and thus easily move from a coarse-grained level of analysis to a fine-grained one and vice versa.

Table 1 Examples for using the relative temporal duration query filter to specify queries at various levels of granularity.

Example: (Find all (Ai,Bj) pairs such that:)	Query Filter
Ai is one minute longer than Bj: Ai.t.duration - Bj.t.duration = 1.0	less equals greater / 1.0 1.0 / dur A dur B / -5 0 5
Ai is at most one minute longer than Bj: Ai.t.duration - Bj.t.duration > 0 ^ Ai.t.duration - Bj.t.duration <= 1.0	less equals greater / 0.0 1.0 / dur A dur B / -5 0 5
Ai is longer than Bj: Ai.t.duration - Bj.t.duration > 0	less equals greater / 0.0 5.0 / dur A dur B / -5 0 5

5.2 Specifying Relative Temporal Position

Given two events A1 and B1, the relative temporal position between these events refers to the relationship between the temporal starting and ending points of the events. It describes information such as whether A1 starts before B1 or whether A1 and B1 finish at the same time. In order to be complete, a temporal visual query language needs to be able to specify any primitive temporal relationship [1] as well as any combination of these primitives. This section describes how our TVQL can be used to accomplish this.

Primitive Temporal Relationships

Allen [1] describes thirteen primitive temporal relationships between two events: *before, meets, during, starts, finishes, overlaps*, the symmetric counterparts to these six relationships, and the *equals* relationship (see first column of Table 2). These temporal relationships can be described in terms of the relationships between the temporal starting and ending points of each of the events. Consider two events A1 and B1, with starting and ending points a_o, a_f and b_o, b_f, respectively (i.e., where $a_o = A1.t.start\_time$, $a_f = A1.t.end\_time$, $b_o = B1.t.start\_time$, and $b_f = B1.t.end\_time$):

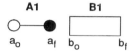

There are four pairwise endpoint relationships between these events:

$$a_o \theta b_o, a_o \theta b_f, a_f \theta b_o, \text{ and } a_f \theta b_f,$$

where $\theta \in \{<, >, =\}$. We assume that each event has duration greater than 0 so that the conditions $a_o < a_f$ and $b_o < b_f$ always hold true.

Similar to relative duration, these relationships can be redefined in terms of differences:

$$
\begin{array}{llll}
a_o - b_o \theta 0, & a_o - b_o & = & A1.t.start\_time - B1.t.start\_time; \\
a_o - b_f \theta 0, & a_o - b_f & = & A1.t.start\_time - B1.t.end\_time; \\
a_f - b_o \theta 0, & a_f - b_o & = & A1.t.end\_time - B1.t.start\_time; \\
a_f - b_f \theta 0, & a_f - b_f & = & A1.t.end\_time - B1.t.end\_time;
\end{array}
$$

where $\theta \in \{<, >, =\}$. Recall that the benefit of describing these relationships in terms of differences is that it allows us to specify quantitative and continuous ranges of values, which is a natural specification to be handled by DQ sliders. All of Allen's thirteen temporal relationships can be uniquely defined by specifying one to three of these endpoint relationships. The last four columns in Table 2 summarize the minimum endpoint relationships required to uniquely specify a corresponding primitive temporal relationship (r_t). Double-lined boxes

Table 2 Primitive Temporal Relationships. Double-line borders and bold values indicate minimum endpoint relationships required.

r_t [1]	graphical description	Freksas icons [8]	$a_o - b_f$	$a_o - b_o$	$a_f - b_f$	$a_f - b_o$
 < before	a_o a_f b_o b_f		< 0	< 0	< 0	**< 0**
m meets			< 0	< 0	< 0	**= 0**
o overlaps			< 0	**< 0**	**< 0**	> 0
fi finished by			< 0	**< 0**	**= 0**	> 0
di contains			< 0	**< 0**	**> 0**	> 0
si started by			< 0	**= 0**	**> 0**	> 0
= equals			< 0	**= 0**	**= 0**	> 0
s starts			< 0	**= 0**	**< 0**	> 0
d during			< 0	**> 0**	**< 0**	> 0
f finishes			< 0	**> 0**	**= 0**	> 0
oi overlapped by			**< 0**	**> 0**	**> 0**	> 0
mi met by			**= 0**	> 0	> 0	> 0
> after			**> 0**	> 0	> 0	> 0

indicate which relationships are required, whereas the other relationships can automatically be inferred.

Given four dynamic query filters for the four endpoint relationships, we can thus specify any *primitive* temporal relationship. Therefore, we incorporate these filters into our temporal visual query language. We do so by integrating them into a temporal query palette. Because a_o - b_o and a_f - b_f query filters can be used to uniquely define over half of the primitive temporal relationships, they are placed as the top two filters (see Figure 8).

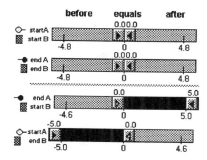

Figure 8 Query filters for specifying relative temporal position queries. Example: Given a subset A bound to "student S1 working" and a subset B bound to "student S2 working," we can specify the query "Show all situations where students S1 and S2 start and finish working at the same time" by setting the top filter startA-startB=0 and the second filter endA-endB=0.

Similar to the relative duration query filter, we provide descriptive labels to the left of the filters and qualitative labels above the filters, thereby allowing users to "read" the query filters more easily (see Section 6.2). Note that the arrows on the thumbs of the query filters in Figure 8 are always pointing inwards, thereby allowing the user to specify a *continuous* range. The significance of a continuous range is described in more detail below in the section on temporal neighborhoods.

Constraints and Interdependencies Between Filters

As in the case of other query filters (i.e., those used to specify a subset), these four temporal query filters are bound to one another so that users cannot specify invalid queries. That is, when one query filter is changed, the other three are automatically updated to exclude any invalid ranges, if necessary.

In the example in Figure 8, the user needs to set both of the top two filters. However, only one filter can be set at a time. Suppose the user first specifies the top filter (i.e., setting startA-startB to 0). As soon as this new value is set, the bottom two filters are *automatically* updated so that endA-startB > 0 and startA-endB < 0. These latter two filters are updated because these are the only valid ranges for them when startA-startB = 0 (see the last four columns of Table 2). The endA-endB filter remains unchanged, because it can have any valid value when startA-startB = 0. After the user sets endA-endB = 0, neither of the other three filters are updated because they are already set to include valid values. In this subsection, we present the strategies we have developed to automatically update the temporal query filters to maintain consistency among the temporal endpoint relationships they represent.

Table 3   Relationships between query filter ranges and temporal primitives.

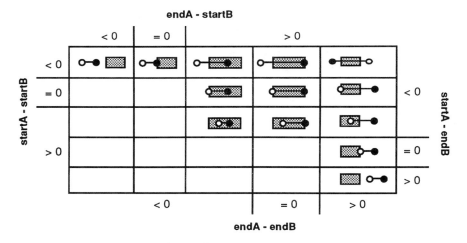

Table 3 formally presents the relationships between the temporal position query filter ranges and the corresponding temporal primitives. Based on the assumption that all A and B events have durations greater than zero, the table identifies invalid combinations and required constraints for the filters. In this way, the table provides indications of how to bind these filters to one another. For example, we can use the table to determine constraints for the previous example, where we were setting startA-startB = 0. In this situation where we are looking for all events that start at the same time, we see from the table that we are also constraining our search to find all events in which endA-startB > 0, and startA-endB < 0. There are no constraints on endA-endB because the table indicates that when startA-startB = 0, endA-endB can be $<$, $=$, or > 0. The constraints make sense, since when events start at the same time, the starting point of either event should be less than the ending point of the other.

While Table 3 is sufficient for coarse-grained constraints, it does not provide enough information for more detailed constraints. For example, if we are looking for events of type A that start one minute after events of type B start (i.e., startA-startB = 1) then we must make sure we also have a range specification for endA-startB that includes some values greater than 1. This is due to the inherent condition that all events have duration greater than zero. Table 3 indicates that when we have startA-startB = 1 (i.e., startA-startB > 0), then we must also have endA-startB > 0. However, it is does not provide detailed enough information to indicate how much endA-startB should be greater than zero.

Because we know that duration is defined as durA = endA-startA and durB = endB-startB, we can derive exact relationships between each of the query filters. For example:

$$startA\text{-}startB = (startA\text{-}endB) + (endB\text{-}startB)$$
$$= (startA\text{-}endB) + durB$$

Table 4 summarizes the filter relationships that we can derive in a similar manner and indicates the implications of these relationships for constraining the interdepencies between the filters. That is, the implications can now be used to dictate the fine-grained constraints between the filters. The table indicates that when either of the top two temporal position query filters are adjusted, both of the bottom filters must be checked to see if they should be constrained. Similarly, if the range of either of the bottom two filters are changed, all three of the other filters must be checked for possible constraints. Thus, when we add larger values to the range of the startA-startB query filter (i.e., move the right query filter thumb to the right), we must also check the range value of the endA-startB query filter to make sure it contains large enough values. Similarly, when we add smaller values to the range of the startA-startB query filter (i.e., move the left query filter thumb to the left), we must also check the range value of the startA-endB query filter to make sure it contains small enough (i.e., lesser) values.

Table 4   Algebraic Relationships Between Temporal Position Query Filters.

Query Filter (QF)	Relationships to Other QFs	Implications (given durA > 0, durB > 0)
(startA-startB)	= (endA-startB) - durA = (startA-endB) + durB	< (endA-startB) > (startA-endB)
(endA-endB)	= (endA-startB) - durB = (startA-endB) + durA	< (endA-startB) > (startA-endB)
(endA-startB)	= (startA-startB) + durA = (endA-endB) + durB = (startA-endB) + durA + durB	> (startA-startB) > (endA-endB) >> (startA-endB)
(startA-endB)	= (startA-startB) - durB = (endA-endB) - durA = (endA-startB) - durA - durB	< (startA-startB) < (endA-endB) << (endA-startB)

Combining Temporal Primitives by Neighborhood

In addition to the thirteen primitive temporal relationships, we may also need to specify a combination of these primitives. For example, we may wish to find all events where student S1 starts working at the same time that student S2 starts working (i.e., they start at the same time, but may or may not end at the same time). Because the filters allow us to specify ranges of values for the endpoint relationships, we can use them to specify such a combination of temporal relationships. That is, we can set startA-startB to 0 and endA-endB to "any" in the case of the example (see Figure 9). Note that this one query palette now specifies a disjunctive combination of related primitive temporal relationships, corresponding to the disjunction of several primitive predicates in typical textual query languages (e.g., [24]). That is, in the example, setting startA-startB = 0 and endA-endB = any is equivalent to requesting events of type A which "start", "equal", or are "started by" events of type B.

Moreover, because the filters can specify ranges and because they are bound to one another to prevent invalid combinations, we can use the filters to specify single "neighborhoods" of related temporal primitives. Freksa [8] defines two primitive temporal relationships between two events to be (*conceptual*) *neighbors* if a continuous change (e.g., shortening, lengthening, or moving of the duration of the events) to the events can be used to transform either relation to the other [without passing through an additional primitive temporal relationship]. Thus, the "overlaps" and "finished by" relations in Table 2 *are*

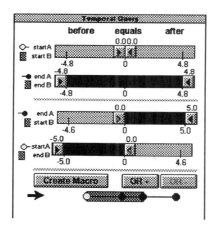

Figure 9 Using dynamic query filters to specify a temporal neighborhood. Example: Student S1 starts working at the same time that student S2 starts working. Beginning with the query specified in the previous figure (i.e., "student S1 and S2 start and finish working at the same time") and increasing the range of endA-endB to include all valid values, we can use the query filters to specify a conceptual neighborhood of (possible) temporal relationships. (Note: This figure presents the full temporal query palette. The use of the "OR+" and "OR-" buttons are described at the end of this sub-section while the "Create Macro" button is described later in this section. The temporal diagram at the bottom of the palette visually describes the query specified (see Section on Temporal Diagrams).)

neighbors, because we can move the ending point of A from the middle of B to the end of B without specifying any additional primitive relationship. On the other hand, the "overlaps" and "contains" relations are *not* neighbors. This is because we cannot move the ending point of A past the ending point of B without first passing through the "finished by" relation. A set or combination of temporal relationships between two events then forms a (*conceptual*) *neighborhood* if it consists of relations that are path-connected through conceptual neighbors. Thus, the use of continuous dynamic query filter *sliders* to specify temporal relationships allows us to capture meaningful disjunctions of the temporal primitives.

Disjunctive Operator:Combining Temporal Primitives and Neighborhoods

The disjunctive operator allows users to create a temporal query consisting of any combination of primitive and neighborhood queries. The operator consists of two buttons — an "OR+" and an "OR-" button (see Figure 9). When users click on OR+, the current state of the temporal query filters is saved in the current temporal diagram (see Section 6.1), and a copy of that diagram is added to the bottom of the palette. An arrow to the left of the diagrams indicates the current part of the OR query that is being specified or edited. If users wish to edit a previously specified part, they can simply click on its corresponding diagram, which moves the arrow to indicate that that part of the OR query is being edited. In addition, the dynamic query filters are also automatically updated to match the part of the disjunctive temporal query being edited. The OR- button can be used to remove the currently selected part of the disjunction.

Consider the example where a user wishes to find all events where student S1 and student S2 start working at the same time, but finish working at different times. This example requires a discontinuous range for the same endpoint relation (i.e., for the endA-endB filter, since we need to set endA-endB < 0 or endA-endB > 0), thus making it impossible to specify this with one set of query filters. Figure 10 illustrates the use of dynamic query filters and the disjunctive operator for this example. A user can specify the first half of the disjunction by setting startA-startB $= 0$ and endA-endB < 0 (see Figure 10a), and then clicking on the OR+ button. Once the OR+ button has been clicked, a new temporal diagram appears at the bottom of the query palette. An arrow points to this newly created temporal diagram to indicate the part of the disjunction being specified. A user can then specify the remainder of this query by setting endA-endB > 0. The new diagram is automatically updated to reflect the temporal primitives specified by the query filters (see Section 6.1 on temporal diagrams). The final state of the temporal query palette for this example disjunctive query is presented in Figure 10b. This example illustrates how the sliders and the disjunctive operator form complementary mechanisms which are sufficient to specify any disjunctive combination of temporal (position) relationships between two sets of events.

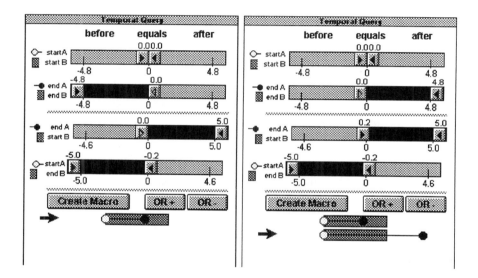

Figure 10   Using the disjunctive operator to specify a non-neighborhood. Example: Students S1 and S2 start working at the same time but finish working at different times. The user specifies this query by forming the following disjunction: "students S1 and S2 start working at the same time but student S1 finishes before student S2" OR "students S1 and S2 start working at the same time but student S1 finishes after student S2." Part (a) of the figure shows the state of the temporal query palette after the user has specified the first part of the disjunctive query. Part (b) shows the final state of the palette after the user has clicked the OR+ operator and finished specifying the second half of the disjunctive query.

5.3   User-Created Macros

Although users can easily specify temporal queries through the temporal query filters, they may have a tendency to use some settings over and over again. For this reason, we provide mechanisms for users to 1) define and save "meaningful" groups of, or macros for, temporal relationships and 2) load and re-use these macros. While it may be difficult to define and enumerate all meaningful groups of relationships, we can identify some groups that we expect to be of use. For example, we can specify an "all starts" temporal relationship to describe the case where events start at the same time. In addition, we can provide a button (i.e., operator) to allow users to create and name their own macros for specifying temporal relationships. Users can then load any macro into the temporal query palette and manipulate the query filters starting from the settings specified by the macro.

6 VISUAL ENHANCEMENTS TO TVQL

Although users can quickly adjust the query filters to specify any of the individual or any combination of the relative temporal position primitives, they may find difficulty in determining whether or not the query specified corresponds to the desired query semantics. Part of this ambiguity may be inherent in the finely-grained definitions of the primitives (e.g., three different primitives meet the specification that events "start" at the same time). In order to reduce ambiguity, we have thus incorporated two techniques for providing quick visual confirmation of the specified query — the use of temporal diagrams and descriptive labels. We consider these aids to be unique augmentations to our temporal query language, increasing the utility of our approach to novice users. Each of these is described in more detail below.

6.1 Temporal Diagrams

Figures 9 and 10 include temporal diagrams which we have added to the bottom of the temporal query palette to enhance usability. These diagrams are qualitative visual representations of the specified temporal position query. In the diagrams, the rectangle refers to B events, while the connected circles are used to designate potential relative positions of A events. The open circles represent possible starting points for set A, while filled circles represent possible ending points. Freksa [8] uses similar diagrams to describe individual relationships but then uses different icons to describe combinations of temporal relationships (see columns 2 and 3 of Table 2). While the use of Freksa's icons provides a compact visual description, it is more difficult to decipher than our temporal diagrams. This is partly due to the fact that individual endpoint relationships (e.g., differences between starting vs. ending points) are obscured. That is, temporal queries model relationships over time, and this continuous temporal dimension is not explicitly captured in Freksa's icons. In addition, Freksa did not intend to develop a query language for users, but rather to demonstrate some theoretical principles of temporal neighborhoods. Our goals thus are met by a more intuitive capture of individual temporal relations and their relationships. Table 5 presents sample comparisons between the use of Freksa's icons and the temporal diagrams we propose. These examples illustrate how our temporal diagrams not only indicate the number of primitives combined, but also that these primitives share the same starting point.

Table 5   Comparison of Freksa's Icons to Temporal Diagrams.

We have developed a transformation function to automatically generate the temporal diagrams from the relative temporal position query filters. The primitive operators of this transformation function are defined using Table 6. We introduce a half-filled circle (e.g., visual results of (11) and (12) from Table 6) to denote the overlap of starting and ending points of A.

The transformation function has twelve (vs. thirteen, the number of temporal primitives) components because it evaluates potential *endpoints* specified rather than specific primitives selected. That is, it is used to determine which of the five starting points of A are specified, which of the five ending points of A are specified, and whether there is a case where a starting and ending point of A overlap at either the starting or ending points of B. The function is complete because it tests for each possible endpoint position.

In general, the relative temporal position query filters pass values to the transformation function. Each part (i.e., line) of the function evaluates as true or false. The visual results of each valid part of the transformation function are then collapsed into one temporal diagram and a line is used to connect the endpoints. Consider the example of Figure 9: "student S1 starts working at the same time that student S2 starts working." In this example, we have startA-startB = 0, endA-endB = any, startA-endB < 0 and endA-startB > 0. Using

Table 6   Transformation function used to define temporal diagrams.

	Filter Value(s)	Visualized by
(1)	startA-startB < 0	
(2)	startA-startB = 0, endA-startB <> 0	
(3)	startA-startB > 0, startA-endB < 0	
(4)	startA-endB= 0, endA-endB <> 0	
(5)	startA-endB> 0	
(6)	endA-startB < 0	
(7)	endA-startB = 0, startA-startB <> 0,	
(8)	endA-startB > 0, endA-endB < 0	
(9)	endA-endB = 0, startA-endB<> 0	
(10)	endA-endB > 0	
(11)	startA-startB = 0, endA-startB = 0	
(12)	endA-endB = 0, startA-endB = 0	

the transformation operators depicted in Table 6, we see that the following
parts evaluate to true:

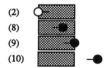

(2)
(8)
(9)
(10)

This leads to the following composite diagram:

As described in Section 5.2, query filters are linked together so as to permit the
specification of only logically feasible situations. Hence, only valid relationships
will be passed to the transformation function from the query filters. As a
consequence, it is not possible to derive an invalid diagram, such as one in
which the only starting point of A comes after one or more of its ending points.

In addition, because only continuous ranges are specified by the query filters, all valid starting and ending point combinations of the diagrams are included. A new temporal diagram is derived for each part of a query formed using the disjunctive OR+ operator (see Figure 10).

The temporal diagrams presented in this section represent a valuable aid for confirming the specified query to the users in a visually intuitive manner (e.g., see Figure 10). This should increase the speed and certainty with which users modify or construct complex queries.

6.2   Descriptive Labels: Additional Textual and Visual Aids

In order to provide further clarification of the specified temporal query, we also include textual and iconic descriptive labels (see Figures 7 to 10). The text labels to the left of the query filter identify the relationship being specified. The corresponding icons to the left of the text labels of the relative temporal position query filters provide visual cues to aid users in quickly identifying which query filter they wish to adjust. These icons are the corresponding part of the A and B visual representations which are used in the temporal diagrams. For example, *start A* is represented by an *open* circle. A short line segment is added to the right of the open circle to emphasize that it represents the *starting* point (see Figures 8 to 10).

The labels above the query filters provide *qualitative* descriptions for the corresponding underlying quantitative ranges. The relative duration query filter uses *less*, *equals*, and *greater* qualitative descriptors (see Figure 7) while the relative temporal position query filters use the *before*, *equals*, and *after* descriptors (e.g., see Figure 10). Together, the descriptive labels above and to the left of the temporal query filters allow users to formulate relative temporal queries without having to translate them into notations (e.g., a_o) and algebraic equations. In addition, if users are temporally browsing the data through (randomly) manipulating the query filters (vs. intentionally looking for a specific temporal relationship), they can use the descriptive labels to "read" the specified query once they have identified an interesting result. In Figure 10a, for example, the query palette can be read as "the start of A equals the start of B, and the end of A is before the end of B." The qualitative relationship specified can also be visually verified with the corresponding temporal diagram. In this way, the descriptive labels and temporal diagrams complement each other.

7   MAPPING TVQL TO SYSTEM QUERIES

This section describes how the VQL processor will map the temporal query specification expressed by the DQ filters into an internal system query for the Database Manager. There are three steps to this mapping:

1. Each of the temporal DQ filters corresponding to a part of a disjunctive temporal query (or simply a single set of the filters, if there is no disjunction) is mapped to a temporal predicate, using tables 7a and 7b below;

2. these predicates are AND-ed together;

3. each of the disjunctive components are OR-ed together.

Table 7a   Mapping temporal DQ filter name to corresponding system notations.

Temporal DQ Filter Name	Corresponding System Notation
startA-startB	Ai.t.start_time - Bj.t.start_time
endA-endB	Ai.t.end_time - Bj.t.end_time
startA-endB	Ai.t.start_time - Bj.t.end_time
endA-startB	Ai.t.end_time - Bj.t.start_time
durA-durB	Ai.t.duration - Bj.t.duration

In the case of the example in Figure 8 ("Students S1 and S2 start and finish working at the same time"), where there is no disjunction, the VQL Processor would first use the above table to map the startA-startB query filter to the temporal predicate Ai.t.start_time - Bj.t.start_time = 0, the endA-endB query filter to the temporal predicate Ai.t.end_time - Bj.t.end_time = 0, etc. These temporal predicates would then be ANDed together to build a temporal clause for the final query (ORing is not necessary, since the example does not include a disjunction). The resulting textual query generated for this example corresponds to:

```
range of description(Ai).content.name = "student S1"
range of description(Ai).content.action = "working"
```

Table 7b Mapping temporal DQ filter thumb settings to algebraic range specifications

DQ Thumb Settings for DQ Filter <DQ Var>	Corresponding Algebraic Range Specification
▶◀ , leftVal = rightVal	<DQ Var> = leftVal
▶ , leftVal	<DQ Var> >= leftVal
▷ , leftVal	<DQ Var> > leftVal
◀ , rightVal	<DQ Var> <= rightVal
◁ , rightVal	<DQ Var> < rightVal

```
range of description(Bj).content.name = "student S2"
range of description(Bj).content.action = "working"
retrieve into A_R_B (a=Ai.id, b=Bj.id)
where Ai.id ≠ Bj.id
when  Ai.t.start_time - Bj.t.start_time = 0
   AND Ai.t.end_time - Bj.t.end_time = 0
   AND (Ai.t.start_time - Bj.t.end_time ≥ - 300
        AND Ai.t.start_time - Bj.t.end_time < 0)
   AND (Ai.t.end_time - Bj.t.start_time > 0
        AND Ai.t.end_time -Bj.t.start_time ≤ 300)
   AND Ai.t.duration - Bj.t.duration = 0;
```

In this example, the last three lines of the temporal condition provide redundant information (e.g., if two events start and end at the same time, then they must also have the same duration). This indicates how the TVQL Processor could optimize the generated query to reduce the number of temporal constraints specified. We are currently investigating the use of special-purpose indexing structures for optimizing the TVQL Processor even further.

8   PRELIMINARY EVALUATION

The example mapping of a TVQL query to a text-based query in the previous section illustrates one of the advantages of our visual approach. By using the TVQL, users can specify temporal constraints by simply adjusting the ranges of the temporal query filters. This can be done through *direct manipulation*, without having to type predicates as for a textual query. In this way, the use of filters allows users to *browse* the database without having to remember the syntax of a text-based language. In other words, users can also use direct manipulation to *incrementally* adjust their queries. In the text-based language, they would have to retype the query over or regain and then edit the text.

On the other hand, a forms-based query interface might address some of the drawbacks of a text-based query language. We hypothesize, however, that our visual query approach will be more effective than a forms-based language for the purpose of searching for *temporal trends* in the video data. This hypothesis is supported by a study comparing the use of dynamic queries to a forms-based query language [2]. In this study, the researchers found that users performed significantly better using dynamic queries over a forms-based approach for three out of five tasks, one of which involved looking for trends in the data.

We are currently in the process of evaluating users' conceptual understanding of the TVQL interface through user testing. Preliminary results indicate that the dynamically updated temporal diagrams are strong visual aids explaining the semantics of the query to the users.

9   RELATED WORK

Research in temporal queries has focused more on the context of historical databases rather than on databases of temporal media (e.g., [25]). Historical databases, such as those used to manage medical images [5] are different from databases of temporal media in that they focus on *discrete* changes entered into the databases as an effect of changes made in the real world (e.g., John broke his leg on April 10, 1994). That is, these databases focus on discrete changes to static objects rather than changes in continuous, dynamic media (such as video).

Although other researchers are working on extensions to dynamic query filters, this work has focused on aggregation extensions to the interface [9, 11]. While this recent work can be added to our system for the purpose of forming subsets, they are not sufficient to meet the needs of video analysis described in this chapter. Our extensions to VIS and dynamic queries address these needs by 1) providing a framework for specifying *relative* queries between subsets and 2) providing specialized temporal query filters for specifying relative *tem-*

poral queries between subsets of data. The relative framework will allow us to continue to work on future relative extensions to dynamic queries, such as specialized query filters for spatial and motion analysis. Our temporal query filters are consistent with the original DQ filters in terms of interlinking the filters together and maintaining the notion of progressive refinement through continuous value range selections.

Besides the work in dynamic query filters by Ahlberg et al [2] and others (e.g., [11]), previous work in graphical or visual query languages has focused on diagrammatic, forms-based, or iconic approaches. Diagrammatic query languages allow users to specify queries by using direct manipulation of schema-type constructs to represent a set of objects and their relationships (e.g., [28, 23]). Essentially, you could build a query graphically by representing each object by a circle, attaching predicates to the circles, and using lines to denote relationships between the circles. While such an interface could be used to build temporal queries, it would lack the continuous browsing support provided by our TVQL. Similarly, while novel techniques have been used to combine forms-based queries with automated object extraction from videos (e.g., [21]), such an interface would also require users to specify temporal primitives as well as ranges of temporal values by hand, thus disrupting the ability to review the video data in a temporally continuous manner.

While some work has begun in temporal queries of continuous, dynamic media, such work has tended to focus on issues other than analysis. For example, work by [18] focuses on synchronization and multimedia playback. Work by Davis [7] focuses on repurposing video, using iconic annotations to represent objects and events in a video and collecting these icons in a parallel timeline format. While his iconic language supports temporal encodings including *relative* ones, it requires users to select icons for each type of temporal relationship individually. In addition, it is not clear whether the language is restricted to only retrieving pre-coded relationships. In contrast, our system allows users to *discover* temporal relationships through using the TVQL (which provides *continuous* ranges of temporal values) and to explore the video data in a *temporally continuous* manner.

Research in multimedia databases varies somewhat due to the interpretation of the term *multimedia*. Some researchers consider image databases (i.e., images + text databases) to be multimedia, but such databases do not deal with temporally-based media such as video or audio. On the other hand, databases which handle temporal media tend to focus on semantic or text-based queries as well as on *locating* information rather than *analyzing* it (e.g., [17, 4]). In these types of databases, media are typically images or short clips with textual captions or descriptions. Information is then located by semantic inferencing on these textual descriptions (e.g., [17]). The drawback of this type of approach is that it does not take advantage of the temporal and/or spatial characteristics inherent in the media. While some image databases allow users to search using spatial information, such approaches have either not dealt with temporal media, or have focused on object extraction (e.g., [10]). We distinguish our work from previous work in this area by using both temporal and spatial characteristics of the media, as well as by addressing needs for both retrieval and analysis.

10 CONCLUSION, CURRENT STATUS AND FUTURE WORK

In this chapter, we have presented a framework for video analysis based on applying and adapting a visual information seeking (VIS) approach [3] to spatio-temporal video data. In our extensions to VIS, we have defined a temporal visual query language (TVQL) for specifying *relative temporal* queries, including relative temporal position and duration between video annotations. The four query filters used for relative temporal position enable users to specify any *primitive* temporal relationship as well as *conceptual neighborhood* combinations of these primitives. Together, the temporal query filters provide users with a visual paradigm for *browsing* the video data through direct manipulation and in a *temporally continuous* manner. For completeness, we have provided a disjunctive operator for specifying any combination of temporal primitives and temporal neighborhoods. We also introduced the use of temporal diagrams and descriptive labels to enhance the clarity of the specified query. Lastly, we have supported the reuse of redundant query specifications through user-created macros.

The primary contributions of this work include 1) a VIS approach to video analysis, 2) the temporal visual query language (TVQL) for specifying *relative* temporal queries and for facilitating *temporal analysis* (i.e., searching for temporal trends in video data), 3) a transformation function for deriving temporal diagrams, 4) a description of the automated maintenance of interdependencies between the temporal position query filters, and 5) a formal annotation model for abstracting temporal, spatial, and content-based characteristics from video data. By analyzing an annotation layer on top of the video, we have designed an approach which can be applied to other dynamic media (e.g., animation).

Our approach is not limited to the analysis of video *data* but is one which can also be used to analyze other genres of video such as movies, sports, etc.

The work presented in this chapter is just one component of the design of an integrated environment for video analysis (see Section 3). We have implemented our TVQL in a Windows-based multimedia pc (MPC) environment and are currently conducting a usability study, comparing the effectiveness of TVQL with more traditional forms-based interfaces. We are continuing work on the TVQL processor, the temporal visualizations, and the spatial and motion analysis aspects of our MMVIS environment.

Acknowledgements

This work was supported in part by University of Michigan Rackham Fellowship, NSF NYI #R1-94-57609, equipment support from AT&T, and NSF/ARPA/ NASA digital lab grant to the University of Michigan.

REFERENCES

[1] Allen, J.F. (1983). Maintaining knowledge about temporal intervals. Communications of the ACM, 26(11), 832-843.

[2] Ahlberg, C., Williamson, C., & Shneiderman, B. (1992). Dynamic Queries for Information Exploration: An Implementation and Evaluation. *CHI'92 Conference Proceedings*, 619-626: ACM Press.

[3] Ahlberg, C., & Shneiderman, B. (1994). Visual Information Seeking: Tight Coupling of Dynamic Query Filters with Starfield Displays. *CHI'94 Conference Proceedings*, 313-317: ACM Press.

[4] Chakravarthy, A.S. (1994). Toward Semantic Retrieval of Pictures and Video. *AAAI'94 Workshop on Indexing and Reuse in Multimedia Systems*, 12-18.

[5] Chu, W.W., Ieong, I.T., Taira, R.K., & Breant, C.M. (1992). A Temporal Evolutionary Object-Oriented Data Model and Its Query Language for Medical Image Management. *Proceedings of the 18th VLDB Conference*, 53-64: Very Large Data Base Endowment.

[6] Chua, T.-S., Lim, S.-K., & Pung, H.-K. (1994). Content-Based Retrieval of Segmented Images. *ACM Multimedia'94 Proceedings*: ACM Press.

[7] Davis, M. (1994). Knowledge Representation for Video. *Proceedings of the Twelfth National Conference on Artificial Intelligence*, 120-127: AAAI Press.

[8] Freksa, C. (1992). Temporal reasoning based on semi- intervals. *Artificial Intelligence*, 54(1992), 199-227.

[9] Fishkin, K. and Stone, M.C. (1995). Enhanced Dynamic Queries via Movable Filters. *CHI'95 Conference Proceedings*, 415-420. ACM Press.

[10] Gevers, T. and Smeulders, A.W.M. (1992). Indexing of Images by Pictorial Information. *Visual Database Systems, II* (E. Knuth and L.M. Wegner, Eds.), North Holland: Amsterdam, 93-100.

[11] Goldstein, J. & Roth, S. (1994). Using Aggregation and Dynamic Queries for Exploring Large Data Sets. *CHI'94 Conference Proceedings*, 23-29. ACM Press.

[12] Hampapur, A., Weymouth, T., & Jain, R. (1994). Digital Video Segmentation. *ACM Multimedia'94 Proceedings*, 357-364: ACM Press.

[13] Harrison, B.L., Owen, R., & Baecker, R.M. (1994). Timelines: An Interactive System for the Collection of Visualization of Temporal Data. *Proceedings of Graphics Interface '94*. Canadian Information Processing Society.

[14] Hibino, S. & Rundensteiner, E. (1995a). A Visual Query Language for Identifying Temporal Trends in Video Data. To appear in *Proceedings of the First International Workship on Multimedia Database Management Systems*.

[15] Hibino, S. & Rundensteiner, E. (1995b). Interactive Visualizations for Exploration and Spatio-Temporal Analysis of Video Data. To appear in *IJCAI'95 Workshop on Intelligent Multimedia Information Retrieval*.

[16] Hibino, S. & Rundensteiner, E. (Dec 1994). A Graphical Query Language for Identifying Temporal Trends in Video Data. University of Michigan, EECS Technical Report CSE-TR-225-94.

[17] Lenat, D. & Guha, R.V. (1994). Strongly Semantic Information Retrieval. *AAAI'94 Workshop on Indexing and Reuse in Multimedia Systems*, 58-68.

[18] Little, T.D.C. & Ghafoor, A. (1993). Interval-Based Conceptual Models for Time-Dependent Multimedia Data. *IEEE Transactions on Knowledge and Data Engineering*, 5(4), 551-563.

[19] Mackay, W. E. (1989). EVA: An experimental video annotator for symbolic analysis of video data. *SIGCHI Bulletin*, 21(2), 68-71.

[20] Nagasaka, A. and Tanaka, A. (1992). Automatic Video Indexing and Full-Video Search for Object Appearances. *Visual Database Systems, II* (E. Knuth and L.M. Wegner, Eds.), 113-127. Elsevier Science Publishers.

[21] Oomoto, E. & Tanaka, K. (1993). OVID: Design and Implementation of a Video-Object Database System. *IEEE Transactions on Knowledge and Data Engineering*, 5(4), 629-643.

[22] Roschelle, J., Pea, R., & Trigg, R. (1990). VIDEONOTER: A tool for exploratory analysis (Research Rep. No. IRL90- 0021). Palo Alto, CA: Institute for Research on Learning.

[23] Santucci, G. & Sottile, P.A. (1993). Query by Diagram: a Visual Environment for Querying Databases. *Software — Practice and Experience*, 23(3), 317-340.

[24] Snodgrass, R. (1987). The Temporal Query Language TQuel. *ACM Transactions on Database Systems*, 12(2), 247-298.

[25] Snodgrass, R. (1992). Temporal Databases. *Theories and Methods of Spatio-Temporal Reasoning in Geographic Space* (A.U. Frank, I. Campari, and U. Formentini, Eds.), Springer-Verlag: New York, 22-64.

[26] Ueda, H., Miyatake, T., Sumino, S., & Nagasaka, A. (1993). Automatic Structure Visualization for Video Editing. *InterCHI'93 Proceedings*, (pp. 137-141): ACM Press.

[27] Weber, K. & Poon, A. (1994). Marquee: A Tool for Real-Time Video Logging. *CHI'94 Conference Proceedings*, 58-64: ACM Press.

[28] Whang, K., Malhotra, A., Sockut, G., Burns, L., & Coi, K-S. (1992). Two-Dimensional Specification of Universal Quantification in a Graphical Database Query Language, *IEEE Transactions on Software Engineering*, 18(3), 216-224.

6

A MULTIMEDIA QUERY SPECIFICATION LANGUAGE

Nael B. Hirzalla and Ahmed Karmouch

Multimedia Information Research Laboratory
Department of Electrical Engineering
University of Ottawa, Ottawa, Ontario
Canada K1N 6N5

ABSTRACT

Typically, multimedia applications involve thousands of hours of video, images, audio, text and graphics that need to be stored, retrieved and manipulated in a large multimedia database. There is therefore an important need for novel techniques and systems which provide an efficient retrieval facility of the voluminous information stored in the multimedia database. Such facility will consist of a query language, a data structure, and a content searching algorithm. In this chapter we propose a multimedia query specification language that can be used to describe the multimedia content portion to be retrieved from the database. Such a content portion is termed a multimedia segment which may contain information on the media as well as the temporal and spatial relationships that may exist between these media

1   MOTIVATION

There is a growing number of multimedia applications that require a retrieval facility offering detailed views of multimedia document contents. Such a facility should allow query-based retrieval activities directed towards extracting individual multimedia portions of documents. This leads to multimedia segment retrieval (in short *multisegment* retrieval) whereby attempts are made to retrieve individual excerpts of multimedia documents. Similar to text passage retrieval [1], multisegment retrieval rests on the exhaustive search of document content for the purpose of retrieving all multisegments that fulfill the specifications of a query.

There is a potential for multisegment retrieval facilities in applications such as multimedia document browsing and retrieval. Browsing multimedia documents through visual representations, such as Hypermedia, involves traversing numerous levels of tree-like structures. This task may find the user lost, especially when a detailed view of content is required. Therefore, it is more convenient in this case to use a multisegment retrieval facility that allows users to access document portions by formulating content queries.

Multimedia information retrieval has not received as much attention as single media information retrieval. Although query mechanisms have been proposed for specific types of documents (e.g., documents having only text and image content [2]), no attempt has been made to address a wide range of multimedia documents. In this chapter, we propose a multimedia content specification that can describe different multimedia documents. This specification permits retrieval of potentially relevant multisegments from a multimedia database. The user may, for instance, retrieve a multisegment(s) in which video shots of the 1995 G7 meeting are displayed, the voice of an anchorperson discussing the role of Canada is played out, and a text summarizing the G7 events is also displayed on the screen. To specify this query, the user must provide selective descriptions of the multisegment using a query language. These descriptions can be written provided that the user has previously seen the multisegment. The query is then processed by a multisegment retrieval algorithm that selects all the documents satisfying these descriptions.

The query language is intended to allow multisegment specification during query formulation. Providing a query language that permits easy descriptions, despite the large amount of data involved in multimedia documents, is a major issue. In the proposed specification language, multimedia information is described in terms of its content representation. The language takes into account the spatio-temporal specifications spatio-temporal specifications as well as the media specifications contained in a multimedia document or segment.

This chapter is organized as follows: In the following section, we briefly discuss the MQL language which is proposed in [15]. In section 3, we introduce the various information contained in a multisegment. In section 4 we explain how this information could be used in our multimedia query language to retrieve portions of documents from a database. Finally, in section 5 we give our conclusion and discuss future work.

2 RELATED WORK

Browsing is a sufficient technique for users to look for what they want in small databases. However, in large databases navigation and browsing are not effective. Thus, information retrieval (IR) through queries becomes crucial. Conventional IR systems focus on keywords based searching techniques which depend on data being tagged with descriptive words. These methods depend widely on the keywords provided automatically by the system or manually by the users for every piece of information. Very few of these methods retrieve complete or accurate information.

Many other languages are media specific query languages, i.e. they are defined to specify one medium in isolation, mainly image media type. In section 4, we will discuss few examples on existing media-specific query languages such as QBIC, [8]. However, in this section we will discuss a query language introduced by Kau and Tseng from Taiwan, MQL, [15], that is defined to support multimedia databases.

MQL specifies and manipulates various types of multimedia information. The language is divided into two parts: definition language and manipulation language. The data definition language, DDL, is a C^{++} like language which achieves extendibility and flexibility by employing an object-oriented framework for multimedia information management. The data manipulation language, DML, is an SQL-like language which retrieves multimedia elements from database in several ways. The syntax of the MQL-DML which is of more interest to us is described as follows in the BNF grammar:

$$< S >::= SELECT < A >< V > FROM < R > WHERE < C >$$

This syntax is basically a SELECT statement where $< A >$ is a list of attributes to be retrieved, $< V >$ is the result of version including historical version, $< R >$ is the domain class, and $< C >$ is a condition. The following is a query example taken from [15]:

Retrieve the previous image house which costs less than 8,000,000 and has a kindergarten around.

Its query syntax is as follows:

SELECT *image-version-class-instance* **PREVIOUS**

FROM *House-class-instance*

WHERE *price-text-instance<8000000*

    AND *Environment-video-instance* **CONTAINS** *"kindergarten"*

Kau and Tseng claim that by providing such a DML, MQL can satisfy the following multimedia database query requirements:

- Complex object query: completed by retrieving the whole components rooted at the wanted object which is indicated in $< A >$.

- Pattern matching query: Provided by specifying CONTAINS in the syntax. MQL will compare the given condition with the attributes of object to find the possible results. Thus, it can serve the pattern matching on image, voice or text.

- Version query: Provided when users specify a version name in $< V >$.

- Nested query: Users can filter results by according to "IN" between two SELECT statements.

We chose to address the problem of finding an expressive and simple query language for multimedia databases using a different approach. In our language, the *condition* on the multisegment to be retrieved is specified in a less abstract way. It explicitly describes the temporal and the layout structure of the multisegment as well as its content which is based on the media type as will be explained in the next two sections.

3 MULTIMEDIA INFORMATION CONTENT

The introduction of dynamic media, such as audio and video, increases the expressive power of traditional documents that include only static media, such as text and images. In a multisegment retrieval activity, the user formulates a query describing the multisegment of interest and the document(s) (or the entire database) from which the multisegment should be retrieved. Relevant multisegments that contain all aspects of the query are retrieved by analyzing the full content of all documents in the list. The syntax of a multisegment retrieval query is defined as follows:

FIND X **IN** *Doc-list*
WHERE *Multisegment-specification*

where X is a variable referring to the retrieved multisegment(s), Doc-list is a list of documents selected from the database, and Multisegment-specification is a description of the multisegment(s) of interest written in a multimedia specification language which is described later. The multisegment retrieval algorithm is responsible for extracting all the multisegments pertaining to Doc-list that match the specification. Consider the following multisegment description:

Begin
>   *a multimedia segment includes video shots on 1995 G7 meeting,*
>   *audio explaining the role of Canada,*
>   *and there is a text summarizing the G7 events.*
End

In a query, Multisegment-specification consists of a description of the content of the multisegment to be retrieved. This description could be written if the user has previously seen the multisegment. As a result, the process of multisegment specification can be made easier by allowing the user to formulate a description that is similar to what he/she has previously seen. For instance, one can describe the time relationship between rendering two media objects, or specify when a particular media object starts. The playback layout on the display screen may also be used to specify a document. For example the user may add to the above example the following:

>   *the video shots and the audio were played back simultaneously, and*
>   *the text window was displayed at the bottom of the screen*

Therefore, the multimedia information perceived by viewers can be decomposed into three different types:

- *Temporal information* that specifies the relationships in time between the various media objects.

- *Spatial information* which specifies the locations of the media objects in space.

- *Media information* describing the individual media elements composing the multisegment.

In addition, interactive multimedia documents may also include unpredictable time events, such as user interaction, reaching a particular program or document state, and programs with unpredictable execution time. These behaviors are usually remembered by the viewers and could be used to enrich the description of a multisegment. Therefore for such interactive documents, a new type of information exists, *External information*, that describes the user actions or program states. It follows that multimedia information will be divided into four separate types: Media information, Temporal information, Spatial information, and External information, (Figure 1).

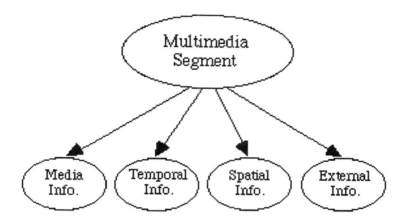

Figure 1 Information contained in a multisegment.

3.1 Media Information

Media information is the most important information in a document and is the most difficult to outline. It describes the individual Media objects in a multisegment. Different media types have different characteristics and could be described differently. For instance, an image could be described by the objects it contains and their relative positions to each other. A video clip could be described as an image with the addition of object motions or camera operations. Therefore, the Media information could also be decomposed into:

- *Media-Content* information that describes the content of the media, such as the energy spectrum of an audio, the words of a text, and the objects in an image or a video frame. Media-Content information however, may be described in various ways such as words, outlines, colors, etc.

- *Media-Spatial* information that provides the relative positions of objects within the media, such as describing a 'person' to be in front of a 'table' in an image or in a video frame, and

- *Media-Temporal* information which describes any type of change that happens over time, such as those resulting from camera operations (e.g. zoom-in) in a video clip or the average power change in an audio segment.

Obviously, it is not necessary for each media to have all these information (still images do not have Temporal information for instance). Table 1 shows the various media types and the information types they include.

	Media-Content	Media-Spatial	Media-Temporal
Text	X		
Graphics	X	X	
Moving Graphics	X	X	X
Image	X	X	
Video	X	X	X
Audio	X		X

Table 1   Information contained in different media type.

4   MULTISEGMENT SPECIFICATION LANGUAGE

In this section, we introduce a multimedia specification language based on the content model discussed above. The syntax skeleton of a query is defined as follows:

> **FIND** X **IN** *Doc-list*
> **WHERE**
> > **BEGIN**
> > *[Temporal-Specification]*   *and/or*
> > *[Spatial-Specification]*   *and/or*
> > *[Media-Content-Specification]*   *and/or*
> > *[External-Specification]*
> > **END**

Using this language, multisegment specification is performed in four steps, (Figure 2): *Media Specification, Spatial Specification, Temporal Specification,* and *External Specification.* Spatial and Temporal specifications are responsible for describing the structure of the multisegment using spatio-temporal operators. Media Specification is responsible for describing the media components using specific languages. Finally, External Specification is responsible for describing the user interactions which may contain different information for each user.

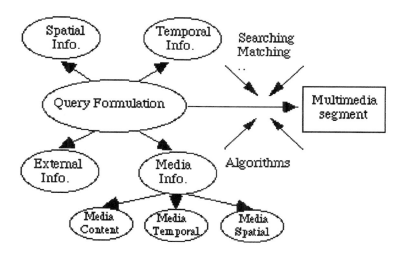

Figure 2 Query formulation.

The question raised at this point is the accuracy of the multisegment information perceived and specified back to the system by viewers. In reality, the amount and accuracy of the multisegment information specified by a user depends on the level of his/her attention during rendering and on the way these information are presented (e.g., the presentation rate and the layout). For example, the user may not be aware of the exact positions of various media objects on the screen. Therefore, most likely the information provided by the user would represent a small part of the full multisegment information. This, however, should be considered by the searching and matching algorithms which is beyond the scope of this chapter.

4.1   Temporal Specification

Using the representation of [3, 4] temporal composition can be achieved through
the reversible seven operators shown in Figure 3. These operators, *BEFORE,*
MEETS, OVERLAPS, STARTS, DURING, FINISHES, and *EQUALS,* determine how two media objects relate in time.

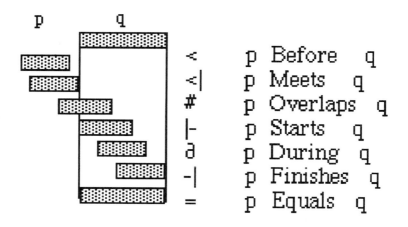

Figure 3   Graphical representation of Temporal operators.

Temporal formula, T, describes the relationships between media time intervals.
It is expressed as follows:

$$T := p; |p < O_{pt} > q; \qquad (6.1)$$

Where p and q are media objects, and O_{pt} is a temporal operator that relates
object p to object q in time. We will refer to the inverse of O_{pt} by O'_{pt}. Therefore, if $(p < O_{pt} >q)$ then $(q < O'_{pt} >p)$. For example, consider a multisegment
scenario shown in Figure 4, the associated Temporal Specification would be as
follows:

Temporal-specification
> **BEGIN**
> | *Video2* | $-|'$ | *Video1;* |
> | *Video2* | $|-'$ | *Image1;* |
> | *Video2* | $\#$ | *Audio1;* |

Video2	#	*Text1;*
Video1	#'	*Image1;*
Video1	δ	*Audio1;*
Video1	#	*Text1;*
Image1	#	*Audio1;*
Image1	#	*Text1;*
Text1	−|	*Audio1;*
END		

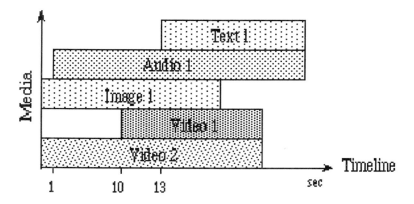

Figure 4   Timeline scenario representation.

4.2   Spatial Specification

Using spatial representations similar to that used by Bimbo et al [5], we introduce the spatial relationships shown in Figure 5 between two media objects based on their projections on one axis at a time, the x or the y-axis.

As shown in Figure 5, these operators define the relative position between two visual objects. It is clear that the spatial relationships defined by these operators are more or less the same as those used by the Temporal Specification. However it is obvious that the interpretations are different. A spatial formula considers the intervals originated by the media objects projections on an axis, x or y, is expressed as follows:

$$S := p; |p < O_{px}, O_{py} > q; \qquad (6.2)$$

Where p and q are media objects and O_{px} and O_{py} are spatial operators that relate object p projections on x and y axis, respectively, to object q projections on the same axis. We will refer to the inverse of O by O'. Therefore, if $(p < O_{px}, O_{py} > q)$ then $(q < O'_{px}, O'_{py} > p)$.

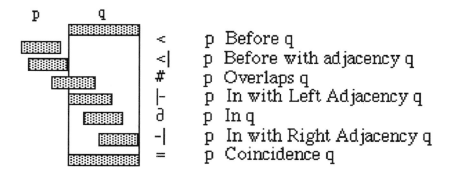

Figure 5   Spatial operators between axial projections of media objects.

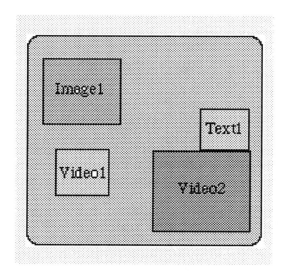

Figure 6   Spatial Layout on a display screen.

For example, the Spatial Specifications of the multisegment layout on a display screen similar to Figure 6 is shown below:

Spatial-specification
> **BEGIN**

Video2	$(<^{'},<)$	*Image1;*
Video2	$(-|^{'},<|)$	*Text1;*
Video2	$(<^{'},-|^{'})$	*Video1;*
Video1	$(\delta,<)$	*Image1;*
Video1	$(<,<|)$	*Text1;*
Image1	$(<,\#^{'})$	*Text1;*

> **END**

4.3 External Specification

The term *multimedia documents* usually refers to passive multimedia documents which play themselves back in a way specified by the document scenario. *Interactive documents* that will not only *play themselves back* but also will *change their courses* dynamically depending on user interactions received a lot of attention in the past few years. Therefore, to be able to formulate queries on interactive documents, ways to index such documents are needed to be explored. These indices will be used in a query formulation to retrieve portions of these documents.

In [16], we proposed a temporal model that is capable of representing interactive multimedia documents scenarios. The model depicts possible user action as well as their corresponding reactions, such as starting a new media, closing a current media, etc. The model has also the power to express the relationships between the various user actions in time, in spite that their time of occurrences are not known at authoring time, i.e. prior to the time they actually take place. The information corresponding to user actions that are document-specific, such as possible types of actions, activity duration, activation time, and reactions can be extracted from the model and used to index such interactive documents. User-specific indices corresponding to these actions such as, *WHO* is the user, *WHAT* was the action, *WHERE* was the user, and *WHEN* did the action take place are also considered in the query formulation and supported by the proposed query language.

The syntax of the External Specification is described later. However consider for the moment the example below:

Begin
> *Find the segment where the user named,"Dana",*
> *clicks on the left mouse button to start an anonymous image object.*

End

The syntax of this query would be:

FIND *X* **IN** DATABASE
WHERE
    EXTERNAL-BEGIN
    action1
        WHO=*"Dana"*;
        ACTION MOUSE-BUTTON-*left*;
        RESULT START *image-**;
    EXTERNAL-END

4.4 Media Specification

As described previously, Media Specification describes the media components within a multisegment. It may be decomposed into three types of information: (i) Media-Content information, (ii) Media-Spatial information, and (iii) Media-Temporal information. Not all Media have all three types of information. However, Media-Content Information may include also Media-Spatial information, as we will see later in this section.

To allow Media-Content Specification, we propose to use existing specification languages for text, image, video, and audio content types. A different content specification language is used for each media type. Furthermore, we propose a new Video-Temporal specification that will be discussed later in this section. In the following, we will give a brief overview on the common approaches used for Media-Content Specifications, focusing on Image, Video, and Audio media types.

Queryon images

There are numerous retrieval systems proposed for multimedia or image databases that use different query specifications based on images. Image media type has no temporal information. Thus, image query specification is based on the Image-Content and the Image-Spatial information. Most of the defined query specifications for images are based on one or a combination of the following approaches.

Text-based query: Most of the searching techniques in image databases are based on the use of keywords associated with the images or the video segments, [6]. Each image will have a set of attributes to describe relevant information or specific objects contained in the image. The information may include both *Image-Content* and *Image-Spatial* information. Ideally the attributes would be automatically assigned by the system during indexing process; however, current automatic methods to identify objects within an image are not sufficiently robust. Therefore, in almost all systems this is allowed to be assigned manually or semi-automatically. Queries are formulated using either standard query language, such as an extended Structured Query Language (SQL), or a free-text query, from which the system extracts the relevant terms to be used for retrieval. Attributes may be combined in a query using conjunctions (ANDs), disjunction's (ORs), and negations (NOTs). In addition, functions using synonyms, thesaurus support, and logical semantic hierarchies (e.g. Husband IS-A Man IS-A Human-being) can be built to allow the user to navigate within a set of images based on the semantic hierarchy. A simple example on the syntax which can be used for such queries is as follows:

```
Image-specification
      BEGIN
      Date = ' February 1995';
      Title = ' G7 Meeting'
      Keywords = (' France' and ' Canada') or ' USA';
      END
```

These methods are exclusively based on the initial text information associated with each image and do not directly capture the visual or image properties. As a result, there are several problems associated with these methods. (i) The search is dependent solely on the keywords, so if the current query refers to image properties that were not initially described, the search will most likely fail. (ii) Some visual properties are difficult to describe with text such as certain shapes. (iii) Even if all useful characteristics of an image are described by text, there is no common vocabulary for describing image properties or contents, so that a *thick* edge may not match a *wide* one.

Icon-based query: The pictorial objects (named objects such as *house, tree, man,* etc.) are represented by symbols or icons. These icons are used in a visual interface query language and are defined through a computer system by the user, thus the name *icon-based* query.

The image information in these systems is described in terms of image objects (i.e., *Image-Content* information) and their spatial relationships (i.e., *Image-Spatial* information). A symbolic description of a scene is a set of formulas expressing mutual relationships between pairs of objects with reference to a co-ordinate system. Two types of formulas may be considered, [5]. The first deals with the positional relationships between the objects, and the second with the directional relationships between the objects in a scene. The positional formulas take into account the relationships between the minimum enclosed parallelpiped projections of each object over an axis of the reference system (similar to the multisegment Spatial Specification described before). An example of a formula is *"object A is (completely to the left, just left, overlaps, etc.) object B"*. The directional formulas, on the other hand, consider relationships between axial planes of the objects. Two objects might be collinear, parallel, or not parallel. An example on the syntax used for such queries is as follows, where $O(x)$, $O(y)$, and $O(z)$ refer to the spatial operators being applied between the objects projections on the x, y, and z-axis, respectively.

```
Image-specification
   Content-specification
         BEGIN
         man;
         window;
         car or   truck;
         END
   Spatial-specification
         BEGIN
         object-1 [before(x), in (y),
                       overlaps (z), parallel] object-2;
         object-1 [in-with-adjacency (x), before(y),
                       after(z), not-parallel] object-3;
         object-2 [after(x), overlaps(y), coincidence(z),
                       not-collinear] object-3;
         END
```

There are some issues that should be taken into consideration for such image representations.

- The selection of the *reference coordinate system*, where two distinct approaches may be followed: using object-centered or observer-centered scene descriptions.

- The determination of scene descriptions, whether it is *automatic or manual*.

The query in this approach may be formulated using visual interface or a lower level symbolic-based query language.

Content-based query: This is the most challenging approach of all, in terms of indexing, pattern matching or searching, and its access structure. This approach allows images to be retrieved by a variety of image content descriptors (typically combining the *Image-Spatial* and the *Image-Content* information) including color, texture, and shape. These properties may describe not only the image as a whole but also the individual objects in it. It also offers virtually unlimited set of queries rather than having the system automatically classifies and organizes samples into a small number of predefined classes.

The properties of color, texture and shape are the basic image properties which most content based queries are built on. There are various ways to extract these features. One of the key aspects of content based image retrieval is shape extraction. Shape similarity has proven to be a difficult issue [7] in the content based image retrieval applications.

The query interface, for instance, may allow the user to specify color, texture, and/or shape properties visually by example. Systems, such as those described in [8] [9], provides facilities to sketch the content of an image to users. The retrieval is then performed on the reduced version of each image, [10], by comparing and selecting images that are relevant to the query.

The following query syntax can be used for such queries:

```
Image specification
        Begin
        feature-i =  feature-value;
        sketch matches  sketch-object-id;
        End;
```

Query on Video

A video stream may contain thousands of frames. The main difference between video and image media types is the presence of *motion elements* in the former. The motion is the source of the Temporal information for the video. Video-Temporal information includes information on camera breaks (*cuts*), camera operations, speed of the camera, object movements, length of the individual *shots* (a shot is a sequence of frames with no camera breaks), etc. To extract these information each video stream should be first segmented into shots by locating the cuts. A cut may be *sharp* or *gradual*. A sharp cut takes place between one frame and the next; whereas, a gradual cut takes place over a sequence of frames. Gradual cuts, such as fade-in, dissolve, and special effects, complicates the cut detection process.

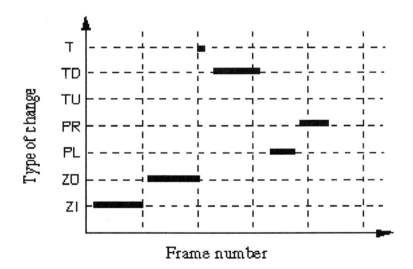

Figure 7   Detection graph.

In [11], we proposed an algorithm that detects cuts and basic camera operations such as *zoom-in, zoom-out, tilt-up, tilt-down, pan-left,* and *pan-right.* The algorithm generates a so-called *detection graph* which provides relevant information about the video. This information is used to index the video segment in order to facilitate later retrieval from the database. Figure 7, shows a sample of a detection graph where type of change is plotted versus frame number. The type of change domain is Zoom-In (ZI), Zoom-Out (ZO), Pan-Left (PL), Pan-Right (PR), Tilt-Up (TU), Tilt-Down (TD), Cut/Transition (T).

The syntax of the proposed Video-Temporal Specification is described later. The following is an example on Video-Temporal Specification associated with the video clip depicted in Figure 7.

```
Video-temporal-specification
  BEGIN
  Sequence = ( ZOOM-IN, ZOOM-OUT, CUT,
                TILT-DOWN, PAN-LEFT, PAN-RIGHT);
  Operation-1
      BEGIN
      LENGTH >  4;
      START-OFFSET > 2;
      END
  Operation-3;
      BEGIN
      LENGTH = 2;
      DISSOLVE;
      END
  Shot-2;
      BEGIN
      LENGTH >  100;
      SPEED = 30;
      Avg-Red > 100;
      MATCH  sketch-object-id;
      END
```

Each shot in a video should be represented by at leased one frame which will be used for indexing. Several techniques were proposed that are based on pixel properties, [12]. The *Average Frame* is one technique where a frame for each shot is calculated by averaging the pixels values of all the frames in the shot at every grid point. The resulting frame is called the Average frame. Then the frame that is most similar to the Average Frame is extracted from the shot to be the representative frame.

Another approach involves averaging the histograms of all the frames in a shot and selecting the frame whose histogram is the closest to the *average histogram* as the representative frame. Even though, neither of these two approaches involves semantic properties, they are sufficient for many applications.

After selecting at least one representative frame per shot, the query problem on video (i.e., *Video-Content* Specifications and *Video-Spatial* Specifications) becomes similar to that of an image.

Query on Audio

Auditory data can be grouped into categories such as music, human voice, and sounds. Audio provides a very rich information that would be used to understand the content of a video. Kageyama and Takashima, [13], proposed a method by which a user hums a tone and the system retrieves the associated melody from the database. Unfortunately, this technique cannot be applied on other types of data than a melody. Sounds of musical instruments can be specified by the spectrum pattern and the power envelope pattern. These patterns can be automatically extracted and used as indices during the storage of audio in the database. A user query may be formulated by the use of a microphone, a tape recorder, or a musical instrument. The system then matches this query with the sound-indices stored in the database and presents the results. An example on the syntax of an audio query is as follows:

```
Audio-specification
      BEGIN
      Spectrum-index =  S1;
      Power-index =  P;
      Keywords   (" Prime Minister" and " G7"
                       and (" Canada" or " Chretien"))
      Spectrum-change or Power-change
            Offset-position > 5;
            Spectrum-index >  S2;
      END
```

Speech recognition techniques deal with another type of data converting it to text. Such techniques will not be as reliable and as fast as human speech for some time, [14]. Human aided indexing, on the other hand, which includes most types of auditory data, helps in assigning keywords to each audio segment to undergo string matching during retrieval process. However, problems on keywords assignments similar to those discussed previously for text-based query on images are also valid here.

4.5   BNF Representation of the Language

We use **BNF** (Backus Naur Form) notation, where nonterminal symbols are shown in angled brackets < ... >, optional parts are shown in square brackets [...], repetitions are shown in braces {...}, and alternatives are shown in parentheses (...|...|...).

<Query-expression> ::= FIND X IN <Doc-List>
     WHERE <multisegment-specification>

<Doc-List> ::=ALL [EXCLUDE <Doc-List>] | (<doc-name>{,<doc-name>})

<multiseg-specification> ::=[NOT]<single-specification>| (<complex-specific>)

<complex-specific> ::= <multiseg-specification> <logic-op> <multiseg-specification>

<single-specification> ::=
     (TEMPORAL-BEGIN <Temporal-specification> TEMPORAL-END) |
     (SPATIAL-BEGIN <Spatial-specification> SPATIAL-END) |
     (MEDIA-BEGIN <Media-specification> MEDIA-END) |
     (EXTERNAL-BEGIN<External-Specification>EXTERNAL-END)

<Temporal-specification> ::= [{<object-id> <Spatio-Temporal-op> <object-id>}]
     [{<object-id> <Temporal-description> }]

<Temporal-description> ::={<Temporal-att> <numeric-op> <value>}

<Temporal-att> ::= LENGTH | START-OFFSET

<Spatial-specification> ::= [{<object-id> ({<Spatio-Temporal-op>}²) <object-id>}]
     [{<object-id> <Spatial-description> }]

<Spatial-description> ::= {<Spatial-att> <numeric-op> <value>}

<Spatial-att> ::= POSITION | WIDTH | LENGTH

<Spatio-Temporal-op> ::= [!] (<) | (<|) | (#) | (|-) | (δ) | (-|) | (=)

<External-specification> ::= (event-id)
     [{<attribute-name> <numeric-op> <value>}]
     [<Text-content>]
     [ACTION <action>]
     [RESULT <reaction> <object-id>]

<attribute-name> ::= WHO | WHEN | WHERE | WHAT

<action> ::= MOUSE-BUTTON- | KEYBOARD-KEY- | SCREEN-TOUCH- | OTHER

<attribute-name> ::= START | FINISH | SIMULTANEOUS-TO

<Media-specification> ::= [NOT] <Media-single> | (<Media-omplex>)

<Media-complex> ::= <Meddia-specification> <logic-op> <Media-specification>

<Media-single> ::= <object-id>
     (<Text-spec> | <Image-spec> | <Video-spec> | <Audio-spec>)

<Text-spec> ::= TEXT <Text-content> END

<Text-content> ::= INCLUDE {<Complex-Keyword> }

<Complex-Keyword> ::= (<keyword> <logic-op> <Complex-Keyword>) | <keyword>

<Image-spec> ::= IMAGE [<feature-name> <numeric-op> <value>]
     [<Text-content>]
     [MATCH <sketch-object-id>] END

<Video-spec> ::= VIDEO [<Video-Temporal-spec>] [<Shot-description>] END

<Video-Temporal-spec> ::= SEQ <ordered-camera-op>
     {[<Operation-description>][<Shot-description>]}

<ordered-camera-op> ::= (<sequence> <logic-op> <ordered-camera-op>)|<sequence>

<sequence> ::= ANYOPERATION | (<Camera-operation> {,<sequence>})

<Camera-operation> ::= [NOT] <single-operation> | (<complex-operation>)

<complex-operation> ::= <Camera-operation> <logic-op> <Camera-operation>

<single-operation> ::= ZOOM-IN | ZOOM-OUT | PAN-LEFT | PAN-RIGHT | TILT-UP
     | TILT-DOWN | BREAK

<Operation-description> ::= <operation-seq-no>
     ({<video-att> <numeric-op> <value>} | <type>)

<type> ::= FADE | WIPE | DISSOLVE | SPECIAL-EFFECT | OTHERS

<Shot-description> ::= (<shot-seq-no> | ANYONE)
     [{ <video-att> <numeric-op> <value> }] [<Image-spc>]
     [<Text-content>]

<video-att> ::= SPEED | LENGTH | START-OFFESET

<Audio-spec> ::= AUDIO [<Audio-content-spec>] [<Audio-Temporal-spec>] END

<Audio-content-spec> ::= [{<audio-att> <numerical-op> <value>}] [<Text-content>]

<audio-att> ::= SPECTRUM-INDEX | POWER-INDEX

<Audio-Temporal-spec> ::= {<change-type><change-description>}

<change-type> ::= [NOT] <single-change> | (<complex-change>)

<complex-operation> ::= <change-type> <logic-op> <change-type>

<single-change> ::= SPECTRUM-CHANGE | POWER-CHANGE

<change-description> ::= {<Change-att> <numerical-op> <value>}

<Change-att> ::= OFFSET-POSITION | DURATION | <audio-att>

<logic-op> ::= (OR | AND | XOR)

<numeric-op> ::= (=) | (<>) | (>) | (<) | (<=) | (>=)

4.6   Complete Example

The following is an example on the syntax where CITIZEN-FEB-15 refers to a
multimedia document in the database:

```
FIND X IN (CITIZEN-FEB-15)
WHERE ((TEMPORAL-BEGIN                    * Temporal specification
        Video1 (δ)       Audio1;
```

```
     Video1 (#)      Text1;                         * implicit AND
     Text1  (-|)     Audio1;
   TEMPORAL-END) AND
((SPATIAL-BEGIN                             * Spatial specification
   Video1 (<,<|)  Text1;
   SPATIAL-END) AND
(MEDIA-BEGIN                                  * Media specification
       (Text1 TEXT                           * Text specification
         INCLUDE          * Text includes the following keywords
           ("G7 1995" and ("Canada" and
           ("Events" or "Agenda")));
         END) AND
       ((Video1 VIDEO                         * Video specification
         SEQ (ZOOM-IN, ZOOM-OUT, CUT,         * Video sequence
              TILT-DOWN, PAN-LEFT, PAN-RIGHT);
         Operation-1                  * refers to ZOOM-OUT operation
           LENGTH > 4;       * units are typically in seconds
           START-OFFSET > 2;
         Operation-3;
           LENGTH = 2;
           DISSOLVE;   * DISSOLVE is a type of a gradual cut
         Shot-0;
           LENGTH > 100;
           SPEED = 30;
           IMAGE
             Avg-Red > 100;
             MATCH sketch-object-id;
             Title = "G7 1995";
             INCLUDE ("First Day" or "Anthem");
             END
       END) AND
     (Audio1 AUDIO
       SPECTRUM-INDEX = S;
       POWER-INDEX = P;
       INCLUDE  ("Prime Minister" and ("G7"and
                  ("Canada" or "Chretien")))
```

```
            SPECTRUM-CHANGE or POWER-CHANGE
                OFFSET-POSITION >5;        *when the change takes place
                SPECTRUM-INDEX > S;
            END ))
    MEDIA-END)) AND
    (EXTERNAL-BEGIN
        action1
            WHO = "Dana";
            ACTION MOUSE-BUTTON-left;
            RESULT START image-*;
    EXTERNAL-END))
```

5 SUMMARY

Multimedia databases require retrieval facilities to extract individual multi-media portions from the documents. Retrieval systems require a specification language with which the required multimedia data are described. In this chapter we proposed a multimedia query language that describes the data in terms of their spatial, temporal, and content information. A new video data specification is also proposed in which camera operations and cuts information can be described. Interactive multimedia documents are also considered to be described by the language.

On top of the proposed language, a user interface needs to be developed. In [17] we define a simple user interface that accomplishes visual interaction in a user-friendly manner. The interface is composed mainly of three windows: Temporal, Spatial, and Media Specification windows. Based on the media type users want to specify, a different media specification window is opened where they can, for instance, describe the outline of an image or the key words of a text.

Our future work will focus on developing algorithms for image indexing as well as enhancing our algorithm for video indexing, [11].

REFERENCES

[1] G. Salton, J. Allan, C. Buckly "Approaches to Passage Retrieval in Full Text Information Systems," Proc. of Sixteenth Int. ACM/SIGIR Conference on Research and Development in Information Retrieval, 1993.

[2] D. Cakmakov, D. Davcev "Experiments in Retrieval of Mineral Information," First ACM International Conference of Multimedia, Anaheim, Calif, 1993, pp. 57–64.

[3] J. Halpern and Y. Shoham, "A propositional model logic of time intervals," J. Ass. Comput. Mach., vol. 38, Oct. 1991, pp. 935–962

[4] J.F. Allen, "Maintaining Knowledge about Temporal Intervals", Comm. ACM Vol. 26, 1993, pp. 832–843.

[5] A.Bimbo, M.Campanai, P. Nesi, "Three-dimensional Iconic environment for image database querying,"IEEE trans. on Soft. Eng. Vol. 19, No 20, Oct 1993 pp. 997–1011.

[6] D. Lucarella, S. Parisotto, and A. Zanzi, "MORE: Multimedia Object Retrieval Environment," Proc. Hypertext'93, November 1993 pp. 39–50.

[7] D.Mumford, "The problem with robust shape descriptions, " First Int. Conf. On Coput. Vis. pp. 602-606, London, England, June 1987.

[8] R.Barber, W.Equitz, C.Faloutsos, M.Flickner, W. Niblack, O.Detovic, and P.Yanker, "Query by content for large on-line image collections, " Research report RJ9408 (82660) June 1993, IBM Research Division, NY.

[9] K.Hirata, Y. Hara, N.Shibata, and F.Hirabayashi, "Media-based navigation for hypermedia system," Proc. Hypertext'93, November 1993 pp. 159-173.

[10] K.Hirata and T.Kato, "Query by visual example" Advances in Database Techn. EDBT'92, Vienna, Austria, March 1992.

[11] Nael Hirzalla and Ahmed Karmouch, "Detecting cuts by Understanding Camera Operations for Video Indexing" to appear in the Journal of Visual Languages and Computing.

[12] S.Somoliar, and H.Zhang, "Content-based video indexing and retrieval," IEEE Multimedia, Summer 1994, pp. 62–72.

[13] T. Kageyama, and Y. Takashima, "Music retrieval with hummed melody," 8th Symposium on Human Interface, 1992, pp. 195–200.

[14] V.W. Zue, "From signals to symbols to meaning: On machine understanding of spoken language." Proc. of the 12th Int. Congress of Phonetic Sciences, 1991.

[15] S.C.Kau and J.Tseng, "MQL– A Query Language for Multi-media Databases," Second ACM Intenational Conference on Multimedia 1994, ACM Press, pp 511–516.

[16] N. Hirzalla, B. Falchuk, and A. Karmouch, "A Temporal Model for Interactive Multimedia scenarios," to appear in IEEE Multimedia Magazine, Fall 1995.

[17] Nael Hirzalla and Ahmed Karmouch, "A Multimedia Query User Interface," to appear in the 1995 Canadian Conferenc on Electrical and Computer Engineering, Montereal, Canada, September 1995.

7

LOAD-BALANCED DATA PLACEMENT FOR VARIABLE-RATE CONTINUOUS MEDIA RETRIEVAL

Taeck-Geun Kwon* and Sukho Lee

Department of Computer Engineering,
Seoul National University, Seoul
* also working at LG Information & Communications, Ltd.
Korea

ABSTRACT

Continuous media storage systems must provide guaranteed services and require large amount of resource consumption in terms of storage capacity and transmission bandwidth. In this chapter, we focus on a placement scheme for continuous media storage systems in a multimedia database management system to provide the load balance of disks uniformly. In particular, we consider complete control over the session presentation using VCR-like functions such as fast-forward and rewind. We propose an improved round-robin placement scheme, called *prime round-robin* (PRR), in a disk-array-based system to remove hot spots for variable-rate retrievals. In addition, we describe a disk group partitioning scheme to improve reliability and interactivity of the storage system. Since loads of the individual disks are uniformly distributed for any rate of retrieval in PRR, the service quality is superior to other placement schemes with regard to the miss ratio, the number of users admitted, and the required buffer size. Various simulation results are also presented.

1 INTRODUCTION

In spite of the success of multimedia areas, there are still many technological limitations which must be overcome before their benefits can be fully realized in multimedia database management systems (MMDBMS). The true advantage of multimedia services will only be achieved once users can retrieve and manipulate the stored multimedia data including video and audio data in the same way as users do today with VCRs [15, 19]. Multimedia data, especially con-

185

tinuous media (CM), require a constrained latency storage system with high
bandwidth [10, 16]. The storage and bandwidth requirements of continuous
media are presented in Table 1. For example, 100-minute MPEG-1 video ob-

Table 1 Bandwidth and storage requirements for various types of continuous
media

Specification	Bandwidth
Voice (8 kHz, 8 bits/sample)	64 Kbits/s
CD-quality audio (44.1 kHz, 16 bits/sample, stereo)	1.4 Mbits/s
NTSC-quality uncompressed video (512 × 480 pixels/frame, 16 bits/pixel, 30 frames/s)	118 Mbits/s
VHS-quality MPEG-1 video	$\leq$ 1.5 Mbits/s
NTSC-quality MPEG-2 video	$\simeq$ 6 Mbits/s
NTSC-quality JPEG video	$\simeq$ 15 Mbits/s
HDTV-quality uncompressed video (1248 × 960 pixels/frame, 24 bits/pixel, 30 frames/s)	863 Mbits/s

ject requires more than 1 GByte to be stored even if it is highly compressed
with the compression ratio of 1/100 [1]. Although several users would typically
be accessing the same video object at the same time, the storage system would
transmit independent streams due to the different position to display. Since
disks are mechanical devices, seek times and rotational delays have improved
very little. Comparing the required bandwidth of continuous media, especially
video data, with the current capability of secondary storage devices, the disk
drive is not expected to be enhanced satisfying in the near future, and it cannot
support hundreds of users simultaneously (see Table 2) [5]. Due to the seek

Table 2 Today's disk performance parameters

storage capacity	2 GBytes
average seek time	9.8 − 16 ms
maximum seek time	25 − 30 ms
maximum transfer rate	4.8 − 5.5 MBytes/s

time, current magnetic disk drive can transmit less than 10 MPEG-1 video
streams simultaneously according to our experiences.

In recent years, continuous media applications such as video-on-demand (VOD),
home shopping, etc. have become common. This trend of DBMS applications

push to improve storage systems regarding storage capacity and processing speed. To achieve the desired aggregated I/O performance using multiple disks, disk arrays have been proposed, and improved as redundant array of inexpensive disks (RAID) using disk striping and declustering techniques [2, 17, 20]. In RAID, objects are distributed across all the drives to achieve a high data rate with parallelism. While RAID and other parallel disk array technologies can deliver higher throughput, they are relatively expensive and not scalable. Furthermore, one cannot control the rate in RAID due to its lack of control on the placement of the data. Recently, there are a number of ongoing researches investigating techniques for parallel storage systems for multimedia data [9, 22]. The problem of is still critical in those disk-array-based storage systems because the system must transfer thousands of continuous media streams independently on time in MMDBMS. If there exist hot spots in a disk-array-based system, the system is not able to satisfy the desired quality of services due to the failure to predict access of the overloaded disk. Assuming concurrent users can access any portion of continuous media object independently and they request to retrieve continuous media at any rate, a system may fail to read continuous media due to the bandwidth limitation at hot spots. This causes significant deterioration of displaying quality and restriction of admissions for multimedia applications. In order to ensure uniform load balancing of multiple disks, continuous media storage systems must allocate segments evenly on disks for any variable-rate retrieval. In this chapter, we propose a placement scheme to prevent hot spots for VCR-like operations in a disk-array-based storage system, where various rate playbacks require to access segments uniformly. A natural solution to the problem is to strip a video object into segments and place them on disks to achieve a uniform load balance.

The storage system must support a number of concurrent users who would like to be able to browse quickly the scene of interest using VCR-like operations. In addition, multiple streams of compressed video data are transmitted independently to every user who subscribes to a multimedia service [6]. For this purpose, we have proposed a storage system with multiple disk servers and agents with buffer [11, 12]. Figure 1 shows the architectural model of the continuous media storage system. A disk server accesses its local disk and transfers segments to the agent through a high-speed network. To transmit segments, the agent first stores the prefetched segments into its local continuous media buffer and then sends the composed stream to the client when it becomes ready in the correct order. In [13], we also have investigated an efficient buffering scheme, called FFU (Far-Future-Using) buffer replacement, to remove the disk bottleneck by increasing the buffer hit ratio. This buffer replacement algorithm is suitable to apply our distributed parallel continuous media storage system. That is, the agent executes multiple queries on the same

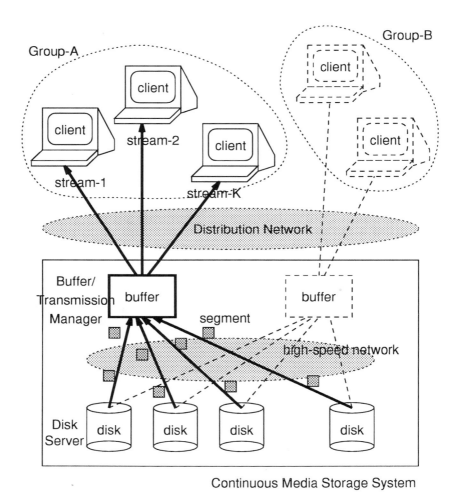

Figure 1 Architectural model of continuous media storage system

continuous media object for a group of clients to maximize the buffer utilization and the hit ratio. The FFU allows all transactions in an agent to share the buffer effectively and it replaces segments based on the access plan. In this chapter, we focus on data placement over multiple disks to remove hot spots for supporting VCR-like retrievals efficiently. Since a continuous media object is distributed on all the disks in this architecture, the problem of load balancing is very important in improving the overall performance of the storage system.

The chapter is organized as follows: In Section 2, we review related work on continuous media storage, and we briefly describe a compression technique for video data and an implementation of VCR-like operations. In Section 3, we present an architecture of storage system for continuous media which consists of multiple agents and disk servers. Section 4 describes storage and placement schemes of continuous media to support load balancing of disks for variable-rate retrievals. In addition, we present a disk group partitioning scheme to enhance the reliability and interactivity of our storage system. Section 5 evaluates the performance of our load-balanced placement scheme in comparison with conventional ones; conclusions are provided in Section 6.

2   BACKGROUND AND RELATED WORK

Video objects among continuous media are quite large. Recently, video coding technology has been standardized. Most video compression standards, such as Motion Picture Experts Group (MPEG), use inter-frame compression and store only the differences between successive frames [1, 7]. The MPEG standard uses inter-frame compression to achieve compression ratio of about 100:1 by storing only the differences between successive frames. MPEG encodes frames in the sequence of intra-frame (I-frame), predicted frames (P-frame), and interpolated or bidirectional frames (B-frame) as shown in Figure 2. Thus, it is common that client stations decode segment by segment, called group of pictures (GOP) in MPEG, instead of frame by frame for providing FF (fast-forward) and rewind. This is because GOP is the basic unit to be decoded independently in MPEG. Figure 3 illustrates how to support slow and fast retrievals in MPEG-like video data. For slow motion of video as shown in Figure 3 (a), the client station must display the same frame repeatedly, corresponding to a retrieval rate. To implement x times FF, every x-th segment must be played back as shown in Figure 3 (c) – this scheme is called *segment skipping method*. Though there are many advantages with viewpoint of a distributed network and a client station, a few frames, however, cannot be decoded successfully in the segment

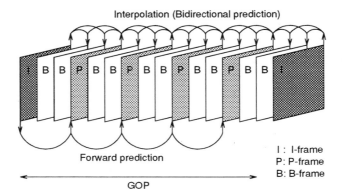

Figure 2   Frame sequence for displaying in MPEG

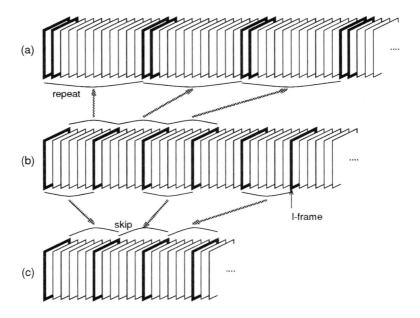

Figure 3   Implementing VCR-like operations: (a) show motion – two times slower forward (b) normal play (c) fast-forward – two times faster forward

skipping method of fast-forward and fast-backward due to the differences in presentation (storage) order and temporal (display) order of MPEG. Typically, the last several B-frames in a GOP, i.e., represented by B* in Figure 2, depend on the I-frame of a next GOP and the last P-frame of the current GOP. Moreover, several techniques have addressed recovery at the client from MPEG-like video; this research area is beyond our study. Without the sophisticated frame recovery techniques, Chen et al.[4] have observed that the segment skipping method is visually acceptable and no additional buffer in a client's hardware and transmission bandwidth is required.

Continuous media impose real-time delivery requirements that are not satisfied by conventional physical storage systems. A number of constrained block allocation schemes have been studied to reduce the seek time of disk [3, 19, 23]. In [8], a theoretical framework for storage and retrieval of time-dependent data is established. For providing effective FF/rewind services, the research on disk placement and bandwidth reservation is the primary area to implement the continuous media storage system. Recently, an outstanding contribution to continuous media placement has been introduced, called the *segment selection scheme* [4]. It consists of two alternative methods; the *segment sampling method* (SSM) and the *segment placement method* (SPM). The SSM is based on the simple round-robin placement, but shifts the data segments retrieved in hot spot disks. To achieve better quality in retrieving a continuous media object, one must reduce the number of shifts. The SPM, however, allocates segments across disks to minimize the variation on the number of segments skipped while balancing the load on the disk array for some pre-determined speeds. Another simple approach providing VCR-like functions is to store *fast-forward replica* for each object in the system and starts displaying the replica instead of the normal speed object [2]; which requires additional storage space and complex synchronization mechanism.

3 ARCHITECTURE OF CONTINUOUS MEDIA STORAGE SYSTEM

The continuous media storage system must have a capability of disk load balancing for independent transactions which require to access the stored continuous media simultaneously. The system must have the aggregated bandwidth for access to multiple disks in parallel. In addition, the system should adapt to non-uniformly distributed access patterns, called *skewed* transactions. One popular application of the storage system for video data is VOD service, in

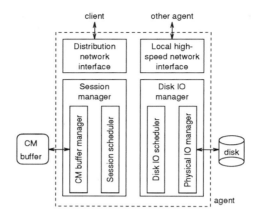

Figure 4   Logical structure of an agent and disk server

which the popular movies are required frequently, so load balancing is essential to reduce hot spot data in the system. Without delay, the storage system must allow users to change the mode of operation and the retrieval speed at any time.

One of solutions to implement continuous media storage system, especially video server, is to build on the top of Massively-Parallel-Processor (MPP). The other solution is to develop client-server based architecture on high-speed networks. We have investigated modular structure of continuous media storage system which provides the aggregated bandwidth of multiple disks. In order to provide aggregated I/O bandwidth of disk in a video server, a video object can be segmented and dispersed in a *round-robin* manner on distributed disk servers which are connected to a high-speed network. The architecture of our system is based on the disk server structure [21]. Before delivering video stream to a client station, the agent aligns video segments to reduce the functionality of clients. To overcome the disk I/O bottleneck, the scheduler calculates the actual time to access its own disk for resolving the contention of disk accesses. Our continuous media storage system, consists externally of multiple agents and disk servers which have their own local disks and buffers. In detail, an agent manages several sessions to simultaneously access the same object and it transmits independent streams to the users who view the same object with time lag. This is accomplished by a disk I/O manager and a session manager as shown in Figure 4. After receiving a user's request, the agent determines the deadline for the requested operations and the session manager in the agent sends disk I/O requests to each disk server with deadlines. One of disk servers

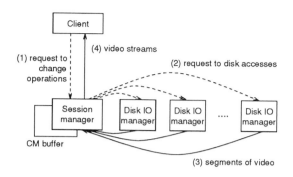

Figure 5 A scenario of control and data flow

plays the role of an agent which is the master server of other disk servers for a session and composes the distributed video segments for a client. A disk server is responsible for providing local disk accesses and handling a stream as an agent using its own video buffer simultaneously. The disk server accesses video segments according to the scheduled access plan and transfers them into the agent which is the origin of the request of disk accesses. Figure 5 illustrates the overall flow of control and data in a continuous media storage system. Since an agent manages the whole session for a user, the storage system avoids interruptions from other users' requests. When a user changes playback options, i.e., the mode of operation, direction, speed, etc., the agent reschedules for the changed operation and sends new disk I/O requests to all disk servers containing the target segments.

4 SUPPORTING VARIABLE-RATE RETRIEVAL

4.1 Resource Reservation

A fundamental problem in developing MMDBMS with capable of real-time continuous media retrieval involves how to manage storage and network resources. Recently, high-speed networks such as Asynchronous Transfer Mode (ATM), Switched Multi-mega bits Data Services (SMDS), Fiber Distributed Data Interface (FDDI), Distributed Queue Dual Bus (DQDB), etc. are able to transmit real-time data with capacity of more than 100 Mbits/s. In particular, ATM, i.e., the standard technology of B-ISDN, is allowed to deliver continuous

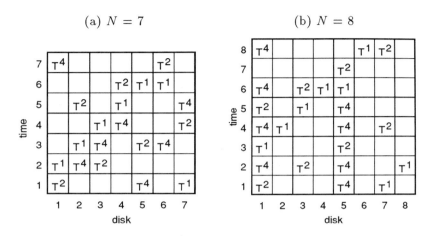

Figure 6 An example of disk accesses considering that the storage system can read one segment per time unit

media simultaneously with the desired bandwidth requirements [14, 18]. In spite of significant improvement of network performance, the storage system has relatively lack of resources available regarding disk I/O bandwidth. Since clients compete for the same resources, the storage system must have resource reservation schemes to ensure guaranteed services.

Letting N be the number of disks, Figure 6 shows two examples of disk reservation with placing segments in a round-robin manner, where T^i denotes i times FF. Thus, T^1 represents a normal play. In this example, three transactions, i.e., T^2, T^1 and T^4, are requested in which we assume they start to display segments stored on disk 1, 7 and 5 respectively. Though the duration of continuous media operation is long, the sequence of disk access is repeated as long as the mode of operation is not changed. Thus the scheduler determines N time units to reserve the disk accesses exclusively.

Here we present brief algorithms of bandwidth reservation when an agent receives a new request.

1. Find the deadlines of segments at the agent which manages the entire session.

2. In segment skipping method, the system requires the same transmission bandwidth for FF and rewind as well as normal play.

For each disk storing the segments,

(a) Find the available time to read the first segment by deadline. If there is not enough bandwidth before deadline, find possible time to read the next segment on the disk.

(b) Reserve the available time slot.

We have described the detailed disk bandwidth reservation algorithms to resolve the problem of competing disk usage in [12]. All disks are accessed uniformly for N time slots if N is a prime number as shown in Figure 6 (a). However, some retrievals such as 4-time FF require to read segments stored in partial disks, e.g., disk 1 and 5, in Figure 6 (b). Such clustered disk accesses may incur periodic failures of reading segments stored in hot spots.

4.2 Placement with Uniform Load Balancing

Let S_i^j be the j-th segment of the i-th object. The segment is a unit of independent access and the time to display each segment of continuous media is identical. For example, more than one GOP in MPEG can be a segment. Assuming that segments are stored on disks in a round-robin manner, the system should access S_i^{j+sk} on disk $D_{(i+j+sk) \bmod N}$ at k-th time unit, t_k ($k = 0, 1, \cdots$) for s-time FF, where D_i represents i-th disk in the system. Figure 7 presents an example of round-robin placement (RR) and the sequence of disk accesses at rate $s = 3$ and 4 marked as superscripts. At some rates, the disk accesses are clustered; for example, 3 times FF requires to access segments stored only on D_0, D_3, D_6. In order to measure the factor of a load balance on disks, we define a *rounding distance*, denoted by $d(s)$, which represents the time units of interval performed the same disk access for s-time FF. In Figure 7, $d(3)$ is 3 because the segments stored on the same disk are accessed in every third time units. On the contrary, $d(4)$ is 9 in this example. To achieve optimal throughput the rounding distance should be N at any rate; hence, we claim the average rounding distance is associated with load balancing of disks.

There exist *hot spot* disks if a retrieval speed is the multiple of the *divisor* of N in a round-robin (RR) scheme; $s = 3, 6, 9, 12 \cdots$ in $N = 9$ for example. All retrievals at speed $s \neq kN$ ($k = 1, 2, \cdots$) require accesses to N distinct disks for N time units, if and only if N is a prime number.

object\disk	D_0	D_1	D_2	D_3	D_4	D_5	D_6	D_7	D_8
	$0^{3,4}$	1	2	3^3	4^4	5	6^3	7	8^4
	9^3	10	11	$12^{3,4}$	13	14	15^3	16^4	17
S_0	18^3	19	20^4	21^3	22	23	$24^{3,4}$	25	26
	27^3	28^4	29	30^3	31	32^4	33^3	34	35
	$36^{3,4}$	37	38	39^3	40^4	41	42^3	43	$\cdots$
	8^4	$0^{3,4}$	1	2	3^3	4^4	5	6^3	7
	17	9^3	10	11	$12^{3,4}$	13	14	15^3	16^4
S_1	26	18^3	19	20^4	21^3	22	23	$24^{3,4}$	25
	35	27^3	28^4	29	30^3	31	32^4	33^3	34
	$\cdots$	$36^{3,4}$	37	38	39^3	40^4	41	42^3	43
$\cdots$									

Figure 7   Example of a round-robin placement and retrieval

Theorem 1 (Property of round-robin placement) *In RR, all fast retrievals at rate $s \neq kN$ ($k = 1, 2, \cdots$) as well as normal play require N distinct disk accesses for N time units, if and only if N is a prime number.*

Proof. Let T_{ij}^s be a transaction to retrieve S_i beginning from the j-th segment with the speed s; S_i^j, S_i^{j+s}, S_i^{j+2s}, $\cdots$ will be presented at t_1, t_2, t_3, $\cdots$, and are stored on $D_{(i+j) \bmod N}$, $D_{(i+j+s) \bmod N}$, $D_{(i+j+2s) \bmod N}$ $\cdots$, respectively. If S_i^j and S_i^{j+ds} are stored on the same disk $D_{(i+j) \bmod N}$, then $ds = Nx$ ($x = 1, 2, \cdots$) distinctly in a round-robin manner. If N is a prime number, the minimum value of d is equal to N because a prime number N is not divisible by s ($s \neq kN$); and if N is not a prime number, there exists an integer d in $d < N$. Consequently, $T_{ij}^{s \neq kN}$ ($k = 1, 2, \cdots$) requires accesses to the same disk in every N time units, if and only if N is prime. $\square$

To avoid wasting disk usage, we use arbitrary N disks in the prime round-robin placement (PRR). Let N_p be the biggest prime number ($N_p \leq N$). In PRR, segment S_i^j is stored on $D_{f(i,j)}$, where $[x]_y$ represents 'x mod y'.

$$f(i,j) = \begin{cases} [(N - N_p + 1)i + [j]_{N-N_p+1}]_N & \text{if } j = kN_p \\ [(N - N_p + 1)i + N - N_p + [j]_{N_p}]_N & \text{otherwise} \end{cases} \quad (7.1)$$

Figure 8 presents the example of placement based on PRR when N is 9, i.e., N_p is 7. As shown, rounding distance is at least 7 at any retrieval rate except for 7, 14, $\cdots$ times FF. It is easy to avoid the clustered disk accesses, if the

object\disk	D_0	D_1	D_2	D_3	D_4	D_5	D_6	D_7	D_8
S_0	$0^{3,4}$			1	2	3^3	4^4	5	6^3
		7		8^4	9^3	10	11	$12^{3,4}$	13
			14	15^3	16^4	17	18^3	19	20^4
	21^3			22	23	$24^{3,4}$	25	26	$\cdots$
S_1	4^4	5	6^3	$0^{3,4}$			1	2	3^3
	11	$12^{3,4}$	13		7		8^4	9^3	10
	18^3	19	20^4			14	15^3	16^4	17
	25	26	$\cdots$	21			22	23	$24^{3,4}$
$\cdots$									

Figure 8   Example of a prime round-robin placement and retrieval

system provides 8, 15, $\cdots$ times FF; we call this *speed adaptation*. If N is large enough, the impact of speed change is negligible for human perception. This can be justified when we consider the storage system of MMDBMS with hundreds of disks, which allows to transmit a number of continuous media streams simultaneously and stores a large number of multimedia objects.

Since the PRR basically uses a prime number as the number of disks storing the sequence of continuous media, disk spaces are not fully utilized. Though the disk utilization of PRR is varying between 70% and 100%, the effect of disk waste is not severe if N is large enough. Moreover, in spite of disk waste, the PRR has many advantages; at most one segment access per disk is performed for N_p time units, this means the management of disk bandwidth is simple. In addition, the PRR ensures significant performance improvement due to the absence of hot spots. The quality of services depend on the number of users, and not the number of FF/rewind requests in PRR. When a user changes the mode of operations during a session, the nature of the PRR scheme is changed.

4.3   Partitioning of Disk Group

Disk-array-based systems are highly vulnerable to disk failures [5, 17]. Though redundancy has negative aspects for management of redundant information in conventional data applications, it is one possible solution to improve reliability in continuous media storage systems. However, this approach requires large amounts of additional disk spaces. In this section, we investigate a partitioning scheme to enhance the availability when disk failure occurs. If there are N disks in a system and each continuous media is stripped into all disks, single disk failure gives impact on all services. One can isolate this effect by partitioning of disk groups; i.e., several groups of disks are allowed to store different continuous media objects. When a disk fails, only a disk group fails to read segments on the disk. In each disk group, PRR placement scheme can be employed exclusively. By increasing the number of disk groups, inter-group loads can be skewed when some users would like to view some specific video, for example, though disk loads in a group are balanced. Assume an extreme case; there are N groups and each group has one disk, in this case, only one user per group can be admitted if a disk can transmit one segment per time unit, and it is clear that the system is able to immediately support any operation for the user without the degradation of service quality. This is because there is no competition in accessing the disk. However, for example, there is no load-balancing mechanism if almost all users prefer viewing several popular movies. The partitioning scheme has performance tradeoff associated with load-balancing and interactivity. In our study, the architecture of continuous media storage system has identical disk servers and the agent has a role of resource management independently. Therefore, it is easy to employ this partitioning scheme in our system.

5   PERFORMANCE EVALUATION

5.1   Simulation Model

In this subsection, we describe a model of a user view and retrieval of continuous media in an interactive session and a storage system for real-time transactions. Basically, the behavior of user can be modeled by two-state Markov process as described in [6]. To implement full VCR functionality, we extend the user's behavioral model, as shown in Figure 9. After starting a session, the user can change the mode of operation at any time. The typical operations are as follows:

- normal play (i.e., playback)

- variable-rate forward/backward retrieval

- pause

- random jump with specifying the position

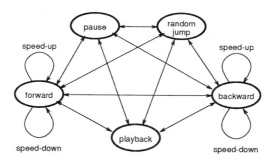

Figure 9   The behavioral model of a user

Playback operation is a major operation in continuous media applications, and it is the special case of forward retrieval at normal speed. In addition, slow motion is a kind of retrieval operations. In a segment skipping method, the bandwidth requirements of FF/rewind are the same as those of normal play in the client's viewpoint. In particular, the bandwidth requirements of disks for all FF/rewind operations as well as normal play are identical though the load balance of disks is completely achieved in PRR. Thus, at most, one segment is read from a disk during N_p time units. If a user maintains the same mode of operation, the shortest interval to read segments from the same disk is N_p time units. We assume that the client station is located in the remote site and it has limited buffers for decoding the compressed video. This situation is common in today's multimedia environment such as VOD, and it is cost effective because the buffer in an agent can be shared for users who view the same continuous media at different portions.

Though the duration of a continuous media operation is long, the system must allow a user to change the mode of operation at any time. In our simulations, we consider the following worst cases:

- One user changes his/her operation mode at a time and the others keep going on their operations. This means other transactions do not release additional resources for a new one at worst and the dynamic rescheduling is not considered.

- For continuous media operations, only FF/rewind and normal play are considered but slow motion and pause are not considered. In real-world situation, users would like to pause their retrieval operations and the system could use resources not in use by them.

5.2   Results

Load Balancing

Assume users request to retrieve continuous media at arbitrary speed for FF, rewind, etc. We define a rounding distance at rate s, as follows:

$$d(s) = \min\left(\frac{kN}{s}\right), k = 1, 2, \cdots$$

where, kN/s is an integer. Thus, $d(s)$ is equal to $d(s + kN)$. Since the number of disks is N, the rounding distance must be less than or equal to N; $d(1)$ is N in normal plays. The average rounding distance for FF/rewind ($d_{FF/rewind}$) is defined as

$$d_{FF/rewind} = \frac{1}{N-1} \sum_{s=2}^{N} d(s)$$

Assume w is the weight of normal playbacks over all retrievals, the average rounding distance for a retrieval operation including normal plays is defined as follows:

$$w d_{playback} + (1 - w) d_{FF/rewind}$$

In RR and SPM, the rounding distance of normal play, $d_{playback}$, is equal to N; $d_{playback}$ in PRR, however, equals to N_p. Since most users request normal plays of continuous media in common, the rounding distance may vary with the weight of normal plays. Figure 10 shows the average rounding distances with the varying of the number of disks (N) and the weight of normal plays (w) in various placement schemes. As shown, the load balance of disks for various speed retrievals is optimal in both RR and PRR when the number of disks is a prime number. In general, the average rounding distance in PRR is close to N; however, the distance in RR and SPM is about 70% and 50% of N, respectively. Moreover, the rounding distances in RR and SPM highly depend on the number of disks and the retrieval speed. The load balance in PRR does not depend on the weight of normal plays; however, the average rounding distances decrease according to the weight in both RR and SPM.

The storage system for MMDBMS must support user interactions on retrieval of continuous media, while it keeps serving other transactions with desired quality of services. To provide guaranteed services, the system must have a placement scheme which is not affected by the mode of operations. The PRR is well suited for variable-rate retrievals with dynamic user interactions.

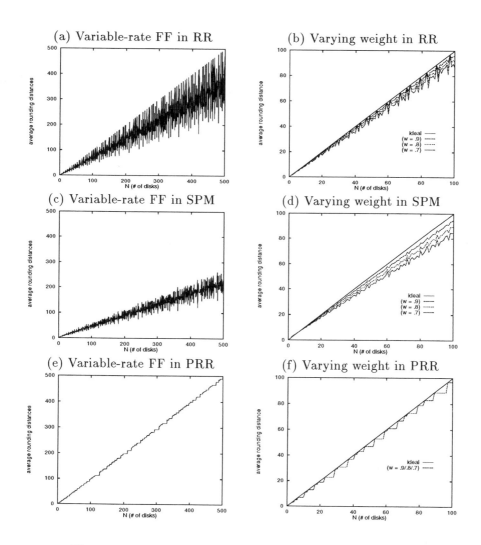

Figure 10   Rounding distances in three different placement schemes

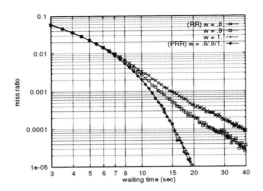

Figure 11   Average miss ratio after starting a new operation ($N = 100$, load $= 60\%$)

Miss Ratio

Since various VCR-like retrievals can be requested by users at any time, we have determined the average waiting time on different placement schemes. PRR could provide the desired quality within a few seconds after requesting any VCR-like operations regardless of the weight of normal plays; however, RR occurs *hiccups* periodically for a long time due to the hot spots as shown in Figure 11. The *miss ratio* is associated with the service quality of storage systems, and it is defined as

$$\frac{\text{\# of segments failed to be read by the deadline}}{\text{\# of segments required to be read for presentation}} \quad (7.2)$$

and the *load* of storage system is defined as

$$\frac{\text{total required bandwidth of existing transactions}}{\text{aggregated bandwidth of disks}} \quad (7.3)$$

As shown, the miss ratio decreases sharply over time after requesting operations in PRR. The simulation result shows that the weight of FF/rewind operations does not affect the miss ratio in PRR. In contrast, the failure of reading segment by deadline becomes serious with increasing the portion of FF/rewind operations in RR. Note that the miss ratio in RR is equal to the ratio in PRR only when all requests are normal plays (i.e., $w = 1$).

If the number of disks are small, the miss ratio decreases quickly in the same load. Figure 12 shows the impact of the number of disks in a system with PRR placement. As long as the loads are completely balanced over partitioned

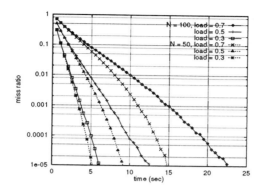

Figure 12 Miss ratio on different N

groups of the storage system, smaller group of disk partition can achieve higher performance.

Waiting Time

In continuous media retrievals, the system is allowed to support the desired service quality. The designer of MMDBMS must consider the quality such as miss ratio. In order for all users to be served successfully, the system can control the load in terms of the number of users admitted. Figure 13 (a) and (b) show average waiting time to achieve miss ratio 10^{-2} and 10^{-3} for various load. Due to stringent response time, the desired quality of services has to be guaranteed in the storage system. Thus, there is a hard limit on the number of users admitted. After changing the mode of operation, it takes 5 seconds to achieve miss ratio 10^{-3} if the load is 0.4 in PRR; however, it takes more than 25 seconds in RR. In this simulation, we assumed 20% of requests are FF operations at any rate and 80% of operations are normal plays.

Buffer Size

To read segments by deadlines, the storage system must prefetch them when disks are idle. If there are hot spots in the storage system, the segments stored in the disks must reside on the buffer until they are transmitted to the clients. That is, if the load of disks is not uniformly distributed, the storage system must have enough buffer space to reduce the segment loss by buffer overflow. Figure 14 shows the average and the maximum number of buffered segments in RR

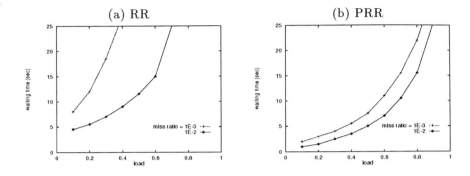

Figure 13   The waiting time to achieve a desired miss ratio ($N = 100$, $w = 0.8$)

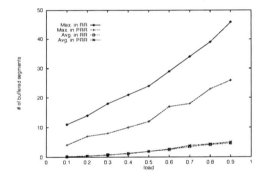

Figure 14   Number of buffered segments ($N = 100$, $w = 0.8$)

and PRR. Though the average numbers of buffered segments in RR and PRR are same, the maximum number of segments in RR is about 50% more than that of segments in PRR. Here, we assume that the storage system transmits segments to the client stations *on time*. This assumption is compatible to the current VOD environments.

6 CONCLUSIONS

This study investigates a new architecture of disk-array-based storage system to support variable-rate retrieval of continuous media. It has multiple agents which transmit independent continuous media streams whose bandwidth requirements are fixed. An agent maintains a buffer to store segments prefetched from disks in order to transmit continuous media streams through the distribution network. To improve the interactivity on users' request and the reliability on disk failures, we described a partitioning scheme in which disks are separated into smaller groups.

We presented a data placement scheme, called PRR, to achieve uniform load balance of disks for VCR-like operations. The basic idea is to introduce a rounding distance which is adapted to a prime number. The PRR scheme does not allow hot spots because the load of each disk is identical though users request FF/rewind operations at any speed. Since the bandwidth requirements of disks for FF/rewind are same as those of normal plays, no additional resources are needed when a user changes his/her operation mode and retrieval speed. By increasing the number of disks, the factor of a load balance is very close to the ideal case for any rate of retrieval. In addition, we addressed that load balancing was influenced on increasing the number of users admitted, and the waiting time to achieve desired quality decreased about 1/3 after changing the mode of operations in PRR compared with RR.

Acknowledgements

The authors would like to thank Prof. Yanghee Choi, Seoul National University, for his helpful advice and discussions.

REFERENCES

[1] Aravind, R., Cash, G.L., Duttweiler, D.L., Hang, H.M., Haskell B.G., and Puri, A., "Image and Video Coding Standards," in *AT&T Technical Journal*, pp. 67 – 89, 1993.

[2] Berson, B., Ghandeharizadeh, S., Muntz, R., and Ju, X., "Staggered Striping in Multimedia Information Systems," in *Proceedings of ACM SIGMOD*, pp. 79 – 90, 1994.

[3] Chen, H.-J. and Little, T.D.C., "Physical Storage Organazations for Time-Dependent Multimedia Data," in *Proceedings of International Conference on Foundations of Data Organization and Algorithms*, pp. 19 – 34, 1993.

[4] Chen, M.S., Kandlur, D., and Yu, P., "Support for Fully Interactive Play-out In Disk-Array-Based Video Server," in *Proceedings of ACM Multimedia*, pp. 391 – 398, 1994.

[5] Chen, P.M., Lee, E.K., Gibson, G.A., Katz, R.H., and Patterson, D.A., "RAID: High-Performance, Reliable Secondary Storage," *ACM Computing Surveys*, 26(2):145 – 186, 1994.

[6] Dey, J., Salehi, J., Kurose, J., and Towsley, D., "Providing VCR Capabilities in Large-Scale Video Servers," in *Proceedings of ACM Multimedia*, pp. 25 – 32, 1994.

[7] Le Gall, F., "MPEG: A Video Compression Standard for Multimedia Applications," *Communications of the ACM*, 34(4):45 – 68, 1991.

[8] Gemmell, D.J. and Christodoulakis, S., "Principles of Delay-Sensitive Multimedia Data Storage and Retrieval," *ACM Transactions on Information Systems*, 10(1):51 – 90, 1992.

[9] Ghandeharizadeh, S. and Ramos, L., "Continuous Retrieval of Multimedia Data Using Parallelism," *IEEE Transactions on Knowledge and Data Engineering*, 5(4):658 – 669, 1993.

[10] Ghandeharizadeh, G. and Shahbi, C., "Management of Physical Replicas in Parallel Multimedia Information Systems," in *Proceedings of International Conference on Foundations of Data Organization and Algorithms*, pp. 51 – 68, 1993.

[11] Kwon, T.-G. and Lee, S., "Scheduling of Continuous Media for Real-Time Sessions," in *Proceedings of International Conference on Distributed Multimedia Systems and Applications*, pp. 190 – 193, Honolulu, August 1994.

[12] Kwon, T.-G. and Lee, S., "Data Placement for Continuous Media in Multimedia DBMS," in *Proceedings of International Workshop on Multi-Media Database Management Systems*, Blue Mountain Lake, NY, August 1995.

[13] Kwon, T.-G. and Lee, S., "FFU: Far-Future-Using Replacement Algorithms for Continuous Media Storage System," in *Proceedings of International Computer Software and Applications Conference*, Dallas, August 1995.

[14] Little, T.D.C. and Venkatesh, D., "Prospects for Interactive Video-on-Demand," *IEEE Multimedia*, 1(3):14 – 24, 1994.

[15] Lougher, P. and Shepherd, D., "The Design of a Storage Server for Continuous Media," *The Computer Journal*, 36(1):32 – 42, 1993.

[16] Maier, D., Walpole, J., and Staehli, R., "Storage System Architectures for Continuous Media Data," in *Proceedings of International Conference on Foundations of Data Organization and Algorithms*, pp. 1 – 18, 1993.

[17] Patterson, D., Gibson, G., and Katz, R., "A Case for Redundant Array of Inexpensive Disks (RAID)," in *Proceedings of ACM SIGMOD*, pp. 109 – 116, 1988.

[18] De Prycker, M., *Asynchronous Transfer Mode: Solution for B-ISDN* Ellis Horwood, Ltd., 1991.

[19] Rangan, P.V. and Vin, H.M., "Efficient Storage Techniques for Digital Continuous Multimedia," *IEEE Transactions on Knowledge and Data Engineering*, 5(4):564 – 573, 1993.

[20] Salem, K. and Garcia-Molina, H., "Disk Striping," in *Proceedings of Data Engineering*, pp. 336 – 342, 1986.

[21] M.R. Stonebraker, "Operating System Support for Database Management," in *Communications of the ACM*, 24(7):412 – 418, 1981.

[22] Tieney, B., Johnston, W.E., Herzog, H., Hoo, G., Jin, G., Lee, J., Chen, L.T., and Rotem, D., "Distributed Parallel Data Storage Systems: A Scalable Approach to High Speed Image Servers," in *Proceedings of ACM Multimedia*, pp. 399 – 405, 1994.

[23] Yu, P.S., Chen, M.S., and Kandlur, F.F., "Grouped Sweeping Scheduling for DASD-based Multimedia Storage Management," *ACM Multimedia Systems*, 1(3):99 – 109, 1993.

8

AN OBJECT-ORIENTED MODELING OF MULTIMEDIA DATABASE OBJECTS AND APPLICATIONS
Michael Vazirgiannis

Computer Science Division,
Department of Electrical and Computer Engineering,
National Technical University of Athens, Athens, Greece

ABSTRACT

An important issue in multimedia information systems is the lack of models for integrated representation of multimedia objects and applications. Here we discuss various aspects concerning multimedia data modelling. Moreover we propose an object oriented data base model (MOAP - Multimedia Object and Application Model) that aims at representation of multimedia objects and applications. The application representation is based on composition (spatial and temporal) and scenario modelling. An important feature of the MOAP is the approach for integrated modelling of the multimedia objects as well as of the applications.

1 INTRODUCTION - ISSUES IN MULTIMEDIA DATA BASE MODELLING

The need for multimedia information systems grows rapidly in a variety of fields including business, manufacturing, education, CAD, CAE, medicine etc. Due to the diverse nature of multimedia data, systems designed to store, transport display and in general, manage such data must have considerably more functionality and capability than conventional information management systems. The main issues which multimedia database management researchers/designers need to face include [CHA94]:

- Development of sophisticated conceptual models which are rich in their semantic capabilities to represent complex multimedia objects and express their synchronisation requirements. A transformation from models to database scheme is then needed. Subsequently one also needs to specify the object retrieval algorithms.

- Designing multimedia query languages which are not only powerful enough to handle various manipulation functions for multimedia objects but also simple in handling user's interaction for these functions

- Designing powerful indexing and organisation techniques for multimedia data.

- Developing efficient storage layout models to manage real-time multimedia data.

Multimedia applications are gaining importance in the software industry due to their impact on various user communities. An important part of a multimedia application is the scenario which describes the flow of the application in spatial and temporal domains as well as handling application and system events. Current authoring systems do not provide models and tools for complete representation of complex scenario description.

In the following sections we discuss various aspects related to Multimedia Data Base and Application Modelling. A DBMS should provide certain features for storage and manipulation of certain types of data. The data that the DBMS deals with influence the data model that the DBMS is based on. A data model should determine three aspects of the data the DBMS aims to manage: the data structures, the operations defined on them and the constraints to be satisfied by the data structures and operations.

In the case of multimedia data, the data structures should support continuous data streams (e.g. audio, video) [KLA95], the behaviour characteristics should include all the functionality of multimedia objects putting emphasis on their spatial and temporal transformations.

A MM-DBMS should involve all the aspects of storage, retrieval, transformation, composition and presentation of multimedia objects and applications. The DBMS should be capable of efficient storage and retrieval of time dependent media objects (like audio and video). The media objects are rarely presented individually. Instead they are presented in interactive multimedia applications composed with other media objects, usually in a complex manner. In this case the presentation system should support synchronised presentation of sets of media objects. Also presentation constraints and spatio-temporal synchronisation requirements should be fulfilled.

In the following we discuss in more detail the aforementioned issues that are essential in designing a MM-DBMS.

2   MULTIMEDIA DATA BASE MODELLING

A number of attempts have been made to develop conceptual models for representation of multimedia objects. These models can be classified into several categories, namely[CHA94]: graphical models, Petri-Net based models, object oriented models. A brief presentation of models from the above mentioned categories follow:

Graphical models

Information in such systems represents a "page" consisting of a segment of text, graphics codes, executable programs or even audio/video data. All the pages are linked via a labelled graph, called hypergraph. The major application of this model is to specify higher level browsing features of a multimedia system. The major drawback of this approach is that there is no specific mechanism to handle temporal synchronisation among data items.

Petri Net models

The basic idea is to represent various components of multimedia objects as places and describe their inter-relationships in the form of transitions. These models have shown to be quite efficient for specifying multimedia synchronisation requirements. Timed Petri Nets have been extended to develop a model that is known as Object Composition Petri Nets [LIT90]. The particularly interesting features of this model are the ability to explicitly capture all the necessary temporal relations and to provide simulation of presentation in both the forward and reverse directions. An OCPN can represent all the thirteen possible temporal relations between two temporal intervals.

In another similar model, called Petri-NetBased-Hypertext (PNBH) [CHA94], the higher level browsing semantics can be specified. In this model, information units are treated as net places and links as net arcs. Transitions in a PNBH indicate traversal of a link or the browsing of information fragments. The segments of a PNBH can be played-out in random order, as selected by the user and restricted by the semantics of the net. The disadvantage of the Petri-net based models is that there is no mechanism to specify communication requirements and control functions for distributed composition objects.

Object oriented models

The basic idea in this approach is to represent a real world thing or concept as an object. An object usually has an identifier, attributes, methods, a pointer to data etc. One such approach is the OMEGA system [CHA94]. To facilitate the presentation of multimedia objects OMEGA uses temporal information associated with each object to calculate precedence and synchronisation between objects. In this model a multimedia object has attributes, relationships which are its value reference to other objects, components and methods.

A system based on Object Oriented Modelling techniques is Object Virtual Machine (OVM)[CHR91], a general purpose object-oriented DBMS kernel. The OVM kernel directly supports the object-oriented paradigm and provides persistency and shareability for objects. It also supports an extensive set of database features useful for data intensive applications, including queries, rules, multimedia information management and versions. OVM can be used as a multimedia object manager. OVM treats multimedia objects as first class objects. Methods and access structures for them are supported by the system. A multimedia information server has already been modelled on top of the OVM kernel.

3   STORAGE AND INDEXING ISSUES

The storage characteristics of multimedia information affects synchronised presentation of media objects that are composed in the context of a multimedia presentation. There are some features specific to multimedia information that affect the storage scheme and deviate it from traditional storage schemes for text only databases [RAN91]:

- multiple data streams in the case of multimedia presentations the media have to be separated at input (i.e. one stream for each data type) and be composed again at retrieval time. Of course there is a trade-off between storing the media together or separately (in this case synchronisation information must be maintained)

■ continous recording and retrieval of data streams The underlying DBMS must support continuous recording (storage) and playback (retrieval) of media objects. In this case the real-time aspects are important (i.e. the retrieval mechanism should provide the resources so that the playback has the same features as the recorded session).

■ large file size Image , audio and video objects generally require large storage space. For instance a collection of 500 typical color image in one of the popular formats (GIF, TIFF) require approximately 1.6GB storage space while 5min. of standard quality PAL video require 6.6 GB of storage space.

In a higher level, there are different schemes for storing the multimedia data into the data base[RAK95]:

■ External references: this approach implies that the data base contains references to external files where the real data reside.

■ Long fields: The DBMS provides structures for storage and manipulation of the multimedia information which is stored in the data base.

■ External functions: Manipulation of multimedia data is not what a traditional DML (like SQL) provides, thus it is required that the additional functionality is supported. This case is covered with external functions that are linked to the data base.

■ Object Oriented Approach: Such systems allow programmers define new data types and extend the existing functionality by adding their own programs. This applies in the case of an OODBMS.

4 MULTIMEDIA APPLICATION MODELLING

Multimedia applications can be very complex as regards the number of involved objects, transformations of the objects in the scope of an application and relationships among them. We regard a multimedia application as a container that includes scenes (aggregations of objects in a thematic domain) which in turn include objects that are transformed and interrelated for the purpose of the application. It is obvious that in a complex multimedia application it may be very difficult to describe all the possible functionality and paths the user or the application may follow. Thus an author (who is usually a non-technical person) needs tools for high level but complete description of all aspects of a multimedia application.

A key issue in the representation of multimedia applications is the description of spatial and temporal composition of objects participating in the application. Moreover the relationships (synchronisation) among objects must be represented. Therefore, one can think of a multimedia application as an event based environment in which there is a rich set of events that may occur and define the flow of application. For instance, the end of a video sequence, the spatial coincidence of two objects in the application window, the occurrence of a pattern in a media object are events that may be exploited to trigger other actions in an application. The events may further be composed in order to express richer and more complex conditions.

Spatial and Temporal Composition

The term spatio-temporal composition implies the description of the temporal and spatial relationships among the objects that participate in a multimedia application. The temporal aspects have been addressed by several research efforts [GIB91][LIT93]. On the other hand the spatial composition aspects have been underestimated.

In [LIT93] a model is presented for the representation and manipulation of relationships among temporal intervals. The model introduces the concepts of temporal instant and interval and the actions of temporal access control (start, stop, fast forward, rewind, pause, resume) and defines a set of n-ary operators for the representation of relationships among many temporal intervals. Moreover the inverse relationships are defined (binary and n-ary). Finally an algorithm for evaluation of a temporal expression is introduced for calculation of overall duration and of the temporal composition end time. This model does not address the spatial composition and scenario issues at all. Moreover this model is rather a temporal composition model rather than multimedia application representation scheme.

Another approach for representation of the temporal composition of multimedia objects is proposed in [MEY92][GIB91] where an Object Oriented model is defined. A set of classes represent multimedia objects. The temporal composition is represented using a scripting approach. Three temporal operators are defined: >>:serial execution, &: parallel execution, n*Q: repeated execution of the same object n times. The concepts of application time (World_Time) and object internal time (Object_Time) are introduced as well as temporal transformations for media objects. There are some issues though that are not addressed by this model:

- communication between objects in the same application (i.e. an event generated by an object cannot trigger an action in another object).

- does not support all the relationships among temporal intervals

Scenario - Events in the context of a multimedia application

The scenario issue is generally not addressed by most research and commercial multimedia authoring tools [AMT93] [KAL95] [MAC93]. The term scenario indicates the flow of a multimedia application in space and time and the way that the application handles the events that occur in the application context and are generated by the user, the application objects, the system.

The scenario of an application includes two constituents:

- the preorchestated ordering of actions that will take place in the multimedia application

- the response of the applications to the events that may occur in the context of the application

Events in the context of multimedia information systems widen the context of events, as used in the domain of active databases, since events convey either spatial and/or temporal information. Moreover the presentation of multimedia objects is a read-only action that has no delete or update actions to the multimedia database.

In an interactive multimedia application the various events that occur may be classified in external and internal. External events occur out of the application scope, are related to time and space and are due to changes happening independently of the application. External events may be time instances, time intervals, etc.

Internal events are raised from the application, either by objects participating in the application or by user events in the context of the application or by the system, and are functionally related to the application. Internal events are further classified into[VAZ95-2]:

- state events: these events indicate values that denote the state an object is in (e.g. object A is active)

- condition events: In the context of an application we need to represent conditions that relate to the content of a media objects. These conditions raise events that may be consumed to trigger other actions. The condition may be of the form: (pattern, obj_id) where pattern is a pattern that is detected in the media object identified by obj_id.

- transitional: such events represent continuous changes in object properties or inter-object relationships (e.g. object A goes_away_from object B, audio A1 fades_out, image A1 wipes in image A2)

- method events: Method events relate to the behaviour of entities participating in the application and correspond to the execution of a method, i.e. some user-defined operation on an object.

5   STANDARDS FOR MULTIMEDIA/HYPERMEDIA DOCUMENTS

There have been a list of efforts for providing standards for development and interchange of multimedia applications. Short descriptions for the most important of them follow:

SGML (Standard Generalized Markup Language: ISO 8879)

SGML enables the description of structured information independent of how that information is processed. It is a meta-language that provides a standard syntax for defining descriptions of classes of structured information; these descriptions are called document type definitions (DTDs). Information can be "marked up" according to a DTD, so that its structure is made explicit and accessible. The "markup" can be checked against a DTD to ensure that it is valid, and thus that the structure of the information conforms to that of the class described by the DTD. Ensuring that information is structured in a known way greatly facilitates any subsequent use of that information. DTDs define the rules to structure information but do not say how that information should be processed. Therefore, SGML and DTDs do not deal with how, say, a document should be processed for formatting on paper (eg. LaTeX), display on-line (eg. Hypercard), and mapping into a document database (eg. Oracle), but, having made the structure of the document explicit, enables all these subsequent processes to use exactly the same source document.

MHEG

Hypermedia is a very popular approach fro organising multimedia material for presentations. Conceptually a hypermedia information network consists of nodes containing multimedia information and links allowing navigation and browsing and representing the semantic relationships between the nodes. Hypermedia approach is widely used for educational applications, information points, electronic manuals, encyclopaedias etc.

MHEG has been designed as a standard for multimedia/hypermedia application representation and interchange [ISO93]. The standard objectives of MHEG are:

- MHEG as a container: MHEG is intended to act as a container for the interchange of multiple media types. The media data may be encoded according to other internationally defined standards. In order to support multimedia application interchange (as opposed to the interchange of multiple media), the standard provides structures for the composition of different media types within a single unit of interchange.

- MHEG for presentation: The standard provides structures for composition of different media types in a presentation. the composition takes the form of time sequencing, spatial positioning and logical interaction between media.

HyTime (Hypermedia/Time-Based Structuring Language)[NEW91]

HyTime is a standardised infrastructure for the representation of integrated, open hypermedia documents. It was developed principally by ANSI committee X3V1.8M, and was subsequently adopted by ISO. The HyTime standard specifies how certain concepts common to all hypermedia documents can be represented using SGML. These concepts include:

- Association of objects within documents with hyperlinks

- Placement and interrelation of objects in space and time

- Logical structure of the document

- Inclusion of non-textual data in the document

An "object" in HyTime is part of a document, and is unrestricted in form - it may be video, audio, text, a program, graphics, etc.

HTML (HyperText Markup Language)

HTML is the way in which text documents must be structured if they are to contain links to other documents. HTML is an application of SGML (Standard Generalized Markup Language). It defines a range of useful tags for indicating a node title, paragraph boundaries, headings of several different levels, highlighting, lists, etc.

The location of the anchor is the text "data model". It is a source anchor, with a target given by the URL in the HREF attribute, so the text would appear highlighted in some way in a client's window, to indicate that clicking on it would cause a hyperlink to be traversed. It is also a target anchor, with an anchor ID given by the NAME attribute.

Future Developments

HTTP and HTML are currently being extended in a backward- compatible way to add multimedia facilities. The proposed HTML+ (or HTML 3.0) contains many enhancements which are useful for multimedia support. Some of the most relevant are listed below.

"Universal Resource Numbers" are a proposed system for unique, timeless identifiers of network-accessible files presently being designed by IETF Working Groups. URNs must be distinguished from URLs, which contain information sufficient to locate the document. URNs may be allocated to nodes and may be represented in source anchors. This saves client software from retrieving a copy of something it already has - allowing sensible caching of large video clips, for instance. The disadvantage is that when something is changed and given a new URN, the source anchors of all links which point to it must be changed (and the URNs of these documents must therefore be changed, and so on). Therefore, it makes sense to allocate URNs only to very large documents which change rarely, and not to the documents which reference them. There is provision for in-line non-text data including:

- Text flow around floating figures;

- Fill out forms;

- Tables;

- Mathematical equations;

- Hypertext paths.

In the proposed definition of HTML+ there is still little support for controlling of non-textual data. Namely backdrops are not supported and buttons are supported, but in a limited way. Typically, a node is retrieved by clicking on a highlighted text phrase, or on an entry in a list. In XMosaic, bitmap images can be used as buttons. However, there is no support for different styles of button. Client software may have generic navigation buttons (eg "Back", "Next", "Home") which are always available and do not form part of a node.

Synchronisation in space is limited to the support of contextual synchronisation of images using the $< IMG >$ tag. Moreover, isochronous presentation of video and sound is not supported.

The proposed HTTP2 protocol maintains the same stateless connect, request, response, close procedure as the current HTTP protocol. Data is transferred in MIME-shaped messages, allowing all MIME data formats (including HTML) to be used. As well as the GET operation, HTTP2 has operations such as:

HEAD: Fetch attribute information about a node (including the media type and encoding).

CHECKOUT/CHECKIN/PUT/POST: These allow nodes to be checked out for updating and checked back in again, and new nodes to be created. New node data is supplied in MIME shape with the request.The request from the client can contain a list of formats which the client is prepared to accept, user identification, authorisation information (a placeholder at present), an account name to charge any costs to, and identification of the source anchor of the hyperlink through which the node was accessed.

The response from the server may contain a range of useful attributes (eg date, cost, length - but only for non-text data). The server may redirect the query, indicating a new URL to use instead. It may also refuse the request because of authorisation failure or absence of a charge account in the request.

The protocol also contains a mechanism which is designed to allow the server to make an intelligent decision about the most appropriate format in which to return data, based on information supplied in the request by the client. This may for instance allow a powerful server to store the uncompressed bitmap of an image, but to compress it on request using an appropriate encoding, according to the decoding capabilities announced by the client.

ODA (Office [Open] Document Architecture and Interchange Format)

The ODA standards support a very wide range of features and tend to be abstract in nature, hence industry experts have clarified the concept by defining Document Application Profiles (DAPs). These subsets provide support for document interchange between similar systems, which have a more restricted range of features. These DAPs will be published as ISO standards known as International Standardised Profiles (ISPs).

The current target for ODA implementors is seen as the open interchange of mixed-content 'word processor' documents. The future for ODA is not as limited as this might suggest, as a number of major suppliers are known to have products under development. However, strong support for SGML and SDIF (SGML Data Interchange Format) is lacking, reflecting the fact that few SGML suppliers are associated with OSI.

Acrobat PDF (Portable Document Format)

Adobe, Inc. has introduced a new format called Acrobat PDF, which it is putting forward as a potential de facto standard for portable document representation. Based on the Postscript page description language, Acrobat PDF is also designed to represent the printed appearance of a document (which may include graphics and images as well as text. Unlike postscript however, Acrobat PDF allows data to be extracted from the document. It is thus a revisable format. It includes support for annotations, hypertext links, bookmarks and structured documents in markup languages such as SGML. PDF files can represent both the logical and the formatting structure of the document.

Acrobat PFD thus appears to offer very similar functionality to ODA. Adobe's successful Postscript de facto standard profoundly influenced information technology. It is possible that if successful, Acrobat PDF will be almost as important.

Generally, as regards multimedia document modelling there is a lack of explicit representation of a multimedia application scenario. It is rather described as a set of object responses to specific messages rather that integrated description of a set of actions as a result of evaluation of an event expression. It would be desirable if an authoring system for multimedia applications would provide the following features:

■   complete description and manipulation of events occurring in the context of a multimedia application (classification and composition, content based events)

■   complete representation of composition (spatial and temporal) of multimedia objects

■   complete description of interactive multimedia applications based on scenaria.

6   MULTIMEDIA OBJECTS AND APPLICATION MODEL (MOAP)

The objective of the proposed model is the representation of multimedia objects and interactive multimedia applications. The modelling approach is be based on previous efforts [VAZ93][VAZ95-1] . Moreover a language is specified based on the EBNF syntax (see APPENDIX). MOAP represents:

■   multimedia objects, namely their structural features and their behaviour in terms of object oriented class hierarchies.

- interactive multimedia applications, in terms of scenaria (based on applications and system events) and composition of media objects (in spatial and temporal domains).

The fundamental unit of information in a dynamic multimedia application is the event. An event may be used to trigger actions and indicates state or transition or invocation of an object method or occurrence of a pattern (or pattern expression) in a multimedia object. MOAP supports action expressions that are triggered by event expression.

MOAP is specified as an object oriented class hierarchy as shown in Figure 1.

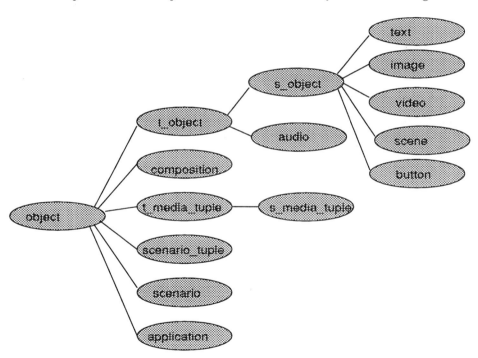

Figure 1 The inheritance hierarchy of the proposed model.

6.1 Classes for representation of multimedia objects

Multimedia objects may be classified into temporal and spatial ones. Some objects have only temporal features (i.e. sound) while all the other (image, text, video) have both temporal and spatial features. MOAP provides classes for both temporal (t_object) and spatial (s_object) multimedia objects. Both classes are abstract (i.e. they may not have instances) and define the generic functionality that is implemented in the descendant media subclasses.

Class t_object

Class t_object represents the temporal features of multimedia objects. We claim that all media types may have temporal dependencies (i.e. an image to be presented for a specific temporal interval). The description of class t_object according to the language that has been defined is:

```
class t_object subclass of OBJECT
attributes
        object_time      domain    TIME
        t_length         domain    TIME
        t_status         domain    INTEGERS
        t_scale_f        domain    FLOAT
        direction        domain    BOOLEAN
methods
        BOOLEAN          start()
        BOOLEAN          stop()
        BOOLEAN          resume()
        BOOLEAN          pause()
        BOOLEAN          go_to_beginning()
        BOOLEAN          go_to_end()
        BOOLEAN          jump(t domain TIME )
        TIME             get_object_time ()
        BOOLEAN          reverse()
        BOOLEAN          cue(ts,td)
        BOOLEAN          t_translate(time domain     TIME)
        BOOLEAN          t_scale(f domain FLOAT )
        BOOLEAN          get status()
```

```
          BOOLEAN              get duration()
          BOOLEAN              get looping()
          BOOLEAN              get direction()
          BOOLEAN              set status(st domain   INTEGERS)
          BOOLEAN              set looping(loop domain   BOOLEAN)
end
```

The default values for the class attributes are:

```
object_time   = 0
t_length = 0
t_status   =   (0:IDLE, 1:active, 2:SUSPENDED)
t_scale_f = 1.0
looping   = FALSE
direction   = TRUE
```

Class t_object is an abstraction of the features and functionality of the temporal multimedia objects (audio and video). The temporal features of a multimedia object are supported by the attribute object_time and the methods that manipulate it. It is a measurement of the internal object time that starts when the objects starts its execution, pauses when the objects pauses its execution and becomes null when the objects becomes idle. The value of the attribute object_time is proportional to the part of the object that has been processed (i.e. if 40% of a 20s video clip has been processe the object_time = 8s). The attribute t_status is the indication of the object status which can either be: active, idle or suspended. The aforementioned attributes may be used for global synchronisation in the case of multimedia presentations where many objects are involved. The attribute t_scale_f is the temporal scaling factor. Its default value is 1.

The attribute direction indicates the direction of object playback (T in the case of normal playback, F in the case of reverse playback).

The class methods manipulate the attributes of the class. The method cue (ts,td) is used for the preparation of a media segment that starts from temporal point ts and lasts for td temporal units. Method jump(ts) moves the file pointer (which points to the current objects position), so that the current temporal point moves by ts time units. This method will be used for synchronisation purposes. Temporal access control [LIT93] is supported by the methods start(), stop(), pause() and resume(). Each one of these methods changes the value of attribute status accordingly. It is important as regards synchronisation purposes that the application knows the object status and the temporal duration of each object at normal speed (t_scale_f = 1). These requirements are fulfilled by the methods get_status()and get_duration(). Finally the methods for temporal transformations are important for synchronisation procedures when there is the need for communication between the application and the object. The methods t_translate(World_time), t_scale(f), reverse() implement temporal transformations. The first translates an application time indication (World_time) into internal object time (object_time). The second changes the playback time of a temporal object according to the value of the attribute (t_scale_f). The third reverses the direction of execution and changes the value of the attribute direction accordingly.

Class s_object

The spatial objects in the proposed model are represented by the class s_object, which is an abstraction of the features and functionality of the spatial multimedia objects (text, video, image). This is an abstract class, therefore it can have no instance and its methods are redefined in the child classes. Class s_object is descendant of t_object for two reasons:

- the spatial objects in general may also have temporal features and constraints

- video has spatial and temporal features

The description of class s_object according to the aforementioned language specification is the following:

```
class s_object subclass of t_object
attributes
          m_width            domain INTEGERS
          m_height           domain INTEGERS
          transparency       domain FLOAT
          focus              domain BOOLEAN
methods
          BOOLEAN     display()
          BOOLEAN     hide()
          BOOLEAN     forward()
```

```
BOOLEAN    backward()
BOOLEAN    get_focus()
BOOLEAN    mouse_down()
BOOLEAN    mouse_enter()
BOOLEAN    mouse_leave()
BOOLEAN    mouse_move()
BOOLEAN    mouse_up()
BOOLEAN    move_by(x domain INTEGERS, y domain   INTEGERS)
BOOLEAN    move_to(x domain INTEGERS, y domain   INTEGERS)
BOOLEAN    size_by(dw domain INTEGERS, dh domain INTEGERS)
INTEGER    get_m_width()
INTEGER    get_m_height()
end
```

The attributes of the class include: the object dimensions (m_width, m_height) and the transparency factor (transparency) which is useful in the cases of overlapping spatial objects. The attribute focus indicates whether the current object has the system focus (selected etc.). The member functions of the class mainly manipulate the presentation of the object. (display()), (hide()), moving the object forward and backward in the application planes etc. (backward(),forward()). There are also methods that define the object response to system like: mouse_down(), mouse_enter(), mouse_leave(), mouse_move(), mouse_up() that define the object response to messages coming from the mouse. There are also the methods that move (relatively or absolutely) the object and moreover change the size of the object.: move_by(x,y), move_to(x,y), size_by(dw, dh).

Media classes

There is a class for each media type: text, audio, video, image. Class text represents the features and behaviour of text information as a multimedia database object. Since it has spatial features it is a descendant of class s_object. The description of class text according to the aforementioned language specification is the following:

```
class text subclass of s_object
attributes
        text_file        domain FILENAMES
        editable         domain BOOLEAN
```

```
methods
        BOOLEAN       display()
        BOOLEAN       get_editable()
        BOOLEAN       set_editable(b domain BOOLEAN)
        BOOLEAN       save(b domain BOOLEAN)
end
```

The additional fields of class text are: text_file that is the file name containing the text and editable which indicates whether the text in the presentation will be editable (TRUE) or not. Method display() redefines the corresponding from the class s_object and specialises it for text presentation. Method get_editable() returns the value of the corresponding attribute, while set_editable(b) set the value of the corresponding attribute to the value b. Finally method save() redefines the corresponding method for text. Assume that an instance of class text that corresponds to the file "/docs/file1.txt" and we want to present it in a windows sized 100x100 pixels without the possibility to modify the text. An instance of the class text is then created with the following values for the attributes:

```
        object_time    =      0
        t_length       =      0
        t_status       =      0
        t_scale_f      =      1.0
        looping        =      FALSE
        direction      =      TRUE
        m_width        =      100
        m_height       =      100
        plane          =      0
        transparency   =      0
        focus          =      FALSE
        text_file      =      "/docs/file1.txt"
        editable       =      FALSE
```

Similarly to the class text the class image is defined as follows:

```
class image subclass of s_object
attributes
        image_file     domain FILENAMES
methods
```

```
        BOOLEAN    display()
        BOOLEAN    save()
end
```

Assume that an instance of the class `image` corresponds to the image file: "/images/image1.img" and we want this object not to be transparent Then the following image class instance is created:

object_time	=	0
t_length	=	0
t_status	=	0
t_scale_f	=	1.0
looping	=	FALSE
direction	=	TRUE
m_width	=	get_m_width()
m_height	=	get_m_height()
plane	=	0
transparency	=	0
focus	=	FALSE
image_file	=	"/images/image1.img"

Class `audio` represents the data and behaviour of audio information. Since sound has only temporal feature this class is an immediate descendant of class `t_object`. The description of the class follows:

```
class audio subclass of t_object
attributes
        audio_file   domain FILENAMES
methods
        BOOLEAN            play()
        BOOLEAN            stop()
        BOOLEAN            pause()
        BOOLEAN            resume()
        BOOLEAN            go_to_beginning()
        BOOLEAN            go_to_end()
        BOOLEAN            jump(t domain TIME)
        TIME                    get_object_time ()
        BOOLEAN            reverse()
        BOOLEAN            cue(ts,td)
```

```
       BOOLEAN              t_translate(time domain WORLD_TIME)
       BOOLEAN              t_scale(f domain FLOAT)
       BOOLEAN              t_invert()
       BOOLEAN              get status()
       BOOLEAN              get duration()
end
```

The, inherited from class s_object, methods play(),stop(), pause(), resume(), go_to_beginning(), go_to_end(), jump(t), get_object_time(), reverse(),cue(ts,td), t_translate (time), t_scale(f), t_invert(), get status(), get duration() are redefined in class audio. Assume that we want to create an audio object that corresponds to the file: "/audio/sound1.wav", and we want it to be played back at normal direction at normal playback speed. Then the following instance (audio_object1) of the class audio is created.

```
       audio_file         =        "/audio/sound1.img"
       object_time        =        0
       t_length           =        get_length()
       t_status           =        0
       t_scale_f          =        1.0
       looping            =        FALSE
       direction          =        TRUE
```

Class video is defined as follows:

```
class video subclass of s_object
attributes
       video_file   domain FILENAMES
methods
       BOOLEAN  display()
       BOOLEAN  play()
       go_to(frame domain INTEGERS)
end
```

Assume that we want to create an video object that corresponds to the file: "/video/video1.mpg" and we want it to be played back at normal direction at normal playback speed. Then the following instance (video_object1) of the class audio is created.

```
       video_file      =     "/video/video1.mpg"
```

```
object_time    =    0
t_length       =    get_length()
t_status       =    0
t_scale_f      =    1.0
looping        =    FALSE
direction      =    TRUE
m_width        =    get_m_width()
m_height       =    get_m_height()
plane          =    0
transparency   =    0
focus          =    FALSE
```

6.2 Spatial & Temporal composition in Multimedia Applications

Temporal Composition

As regards the temporal composition of multimedia objects, it is important to define the time instant an the temporal interval concepts [LIT93]. The temporal intervals consist of temporal durations that are defined by two temporal instants. A temporal instant is a temporal interval of zero duration (e.g. 4:00pm). On the other hand a temporal interval is defined by two temporal instants. The temporal difference between those two instants is the duration of the interval (eg. 100ms, 8 hours). There are sample time instants and temporal interval in Figure 2.

In the temporal domain, let A be a multimedia object (sound, video). The temporal interval that corresponds to the playback duration of this object is defined as dur A. As Allen defines [ALL83] there are seven basic relationships between two temporal intervals (see Figure 3.). We define a set of temporal operators that represent the aforementioned relationships and will be used for the description of temporal composition for multimedia objects . The operators are the following:

- A-t->B: where A and B are the two temporal intervals and t is an value that indicates the temporal interval between the end of interval A and the beginning of temporal interval B. This operator covers the relation-

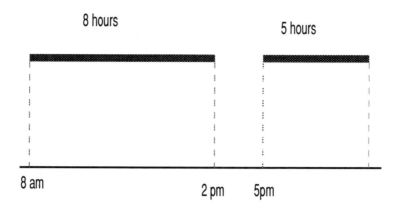

Figure 2   Time instants and temporal intervals.

ships before (for t>0), meets (for t=0), during (t<0 and |t|>
dur A and dur B >|dur A|), overlaps_with (t<0 and |t|<duration
A).

- The operators \/ and /\ cover the relationships starts and ends respectively.

- Ai (repetition) : Action A will be repeated i times.

The formal definition of the operators follow:

```
temporal operator =
  "\/"
| "/\"
| "-"t"->"
| "i*"
```

where t is a temporal interval and i is an integer value.

Spatial Composition

Another aspect of composition is the spatial one, regarding the spatial ordering
and relationship features of the objects participating in a multimedia application . There is a complete set of topological relationships describing the spatial
relationships between two objects [EGE91]. Thus two objects p, q (see fig.

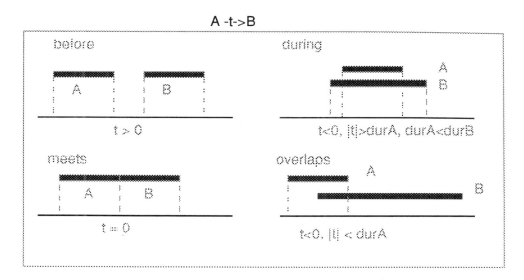

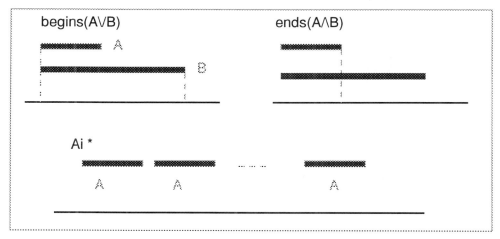

Figure 3 The temporal operators that are defined and the relationships they represent.

2.) may coincide (equal), overlap, touch_externally (meet), touch_internally (covers), be inside, lie outside, or be disjoint.

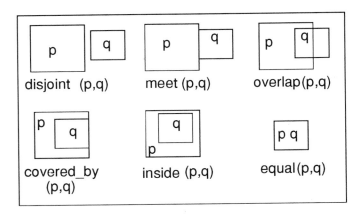

Figure 4   Topological relations between two spatial objects.

We define a set of binary operators that cover the topological relationships mentioned above

```
spatial operator=
  "disjoint"
| "meet"
| "overlap"
| "covers"
| "inside"
| "equal"
```

The semantics of these operators appear in fig. 4.

6.3   Classes for representation of interactive multimedia applications

The requirements for multimedia objects composition in the context of a multimedia application are fulfilled by set of object oriented classes that is described below. The requirements are:

■   representation of the composition of multimedia objects in space and time. Similar to a theatrical play we assume that a multimedia application is a set of scenes that may be presented according to a scenario or according to the user needs. Each scene contains a set of monomedia objects that are mixed in the spatial and temporal domain according to the application scenario.

- representation of media transformation when they participate in a complex presentation. This requirement is fulfilled by the classes t_media_tuple, s_media_tuple that represent the features and transformations of the initial media object in order to participate in a presentation. It is important to stress the fact that these classes are not time dependent thus they are not descendants of the class t_object.

- representation of the scenario that defines the flow of a multimedia application in space an time as well as the handling of messages (user interaction, system events etc.). Moreover it is necessary to stress the distinction between the classes composition and scenario. The first defines which objects will participate in a multimedia application and how (spatial and temporal parts, along with the corresponding transformations), while the second defines the flow of an application in space an time as well as the as the handling of messages (user interaction, system events etc.).

The classes that follow represent the composition of multimedia in space an time putting emphasis on the scenario of the application. The media objects must be transformed in order to participate in a multimedia presentation. The transformations regard the temporal and/or spatial domain (class composition). As regards the temporal domain the class includes a list of the transformed temporal objects (t_list). For each objects there is a tuple describing the object transformations for the participation in the current application. (class t_media_tuple). In the spatial domain there is the corresponding list of spatially transformed objects (s_media_tuple). A more detailed description of the aforementioned classes follow.

Class t_media_tuple

Class t_media_tuple represents the features and functionality of the temporal transformations of the objects that participate in a complex application. The description of the class according to the aforementioned language follows:

```
class t_media_tuple subclass of object
attributes
        m_obj           domain  object
```

```
            t_scale_f        domain  FLOAT
            t_start          domain  TIME
            t_duration       domain  TIME
            direction        domain  BOOLEAN
            effect_id        domain  INTEGERS
methods
            load()
            unload()
            prepare()
            execute()
end
```

The class t_media_tuple aims at representation of temporal objects (i.e. their temporal parts and the corresponding transformations that are included in the multimedia application. The class attributes include the identifier of the multimedia object (m_obj) that participates in the composition (i.e.) an instance of the classes text, image, audio, video), the temporal transformation factor (t_scale_f), the temporal interval start (t_start) and the duration of the interval that is used for the current composition (t_duration), the direction of playback (direction) (see Figure 5.) and the special effect that will be used (effect_id). There are methods that are related to the preparation of the transformations that are applied to the objects (load(),unload(),prepare()) and the execution of the tuple (execute()).

Let's assume for instance that we want to include in a composition the 20 seconds of the audio object (audio_object1) starting from the 5th second. The sound will be played 20% faster in inverse direction (see Figure 5). The following instance of the class t_media_tuple represents the aforementioned requirement:

```
a1        t_media_tuple
          m_obj          =     audio_object1
          t_scale_f      =     0.83
          t_start        =     5
          t_duration     =     20
          direction      =     FALSE
          effect_id      =     0
```

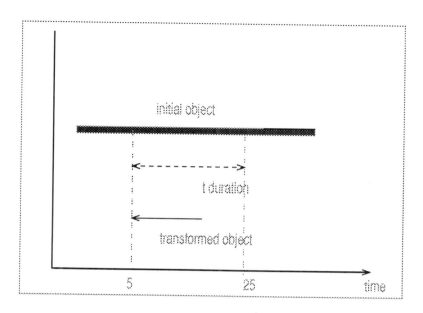

Figure 5 A temporal object and its transformations in a t_media_tuple instance.

Class s_media_tuple

Class **s_media_tuple** represents the data and behaviour of the specifications of the transformation of the spatial objects that participate in a composition. Class **s_media_tuple** is a descendant of class **t_media_tuple** in correspondence to class **s_object**, and **t_object**. The description of the class according to the aforementioned language follows:

```
class   s_media_tuple subclass of t_media_tuple
attributes
          x_coord          domain INTEGERS
          y_coord          domain INTEGERS
          a_width          domain INTEGERS
          a_height         domain INTEGERS
          effect_id        domain INTEGERS
          s_scale_f      domain FLOAT
methods
          load()
```

```
unload()
prepare()
execute()
compute_dimensions()
compute_s_scale_f()
set_dimensions(x domain INTEGERS, y domain INTEGERS,
               w domain INTEGERS, h domain INTEGERS)
```

end

The attributes of this class (apart from those inherited from class t_media_tuple) include the spatial position of the participating spatial object (x_coord, y_coord) in the application window and the dimensions (a_width, a_height) of the transformed object willl have, the spatial scaling factors one for each dimension (x_s_scale_f, y_s_scale_f) and the identifier of the special spatial effect that will be used for the presentation of the object (effect_id). The class methods refer to the preparation of the transformations that are imposed by the attribute values (load(), unload(), prepare()) that redefine the inherited from the class t_media_tuple and to the execution of the tuple (execute()). In some cases it is possible that the prerequisite is the spatial scaling factor hence the dimensions of the transformed object have to be computed (compute_dimensions()). In other cases it is possible that the prerequisite are the dimensions of the transformed hence the object spatial scaling factor has to be computed (compute_s_scale_f()). Finally the method (set_dimensions(x, y, w, h)) set the values for the position and the dimensions of the transformed object. Two indicative examples follow: Assuming that we need to include in a multimedia composition an image object (image_object1) at the position (30, 50) in a frame with dimensions 150x100 pixels. Then the following s_media_tuple instance is created :

```
im1_s   s_media_tuple
        m_obj        =    image_object1
        t_scale_f    =    1
        t_start      =    0
        t_duration   =    10
        direction    =    TRUE
        x_coord      =    30
        y_coord      =    50
        a_width      =    150
        a_height     =    100
```

```
effect_id      =      0
s_scale_f      =      im1_s.compute_s_scale_f()
```

Assuming that we need to include in a multimedia composition the first ten seconds of a video object (**video_object1**) at the position (200,50) in a frame with dimensions 100x120 pixels. The video will be played at normal speed and direction. Then the following **s_media_tuple** instance is created :

```
v1_s   s_media_tuple
          m_obj         =      video_object1
          t_scale_f     =      1
          t_start       =      0
          t_duration    =      10
          direction     =      TRUE
          x_coord       =      200
          y_coord       =      50
          a_width       =      100
          a_height      =      120
          effect_id     =      0
          s_scale_f     =      v1_s.compute_s_scale_f()
```

Class composition

This class is essentially an aggregation of the instances of classes **t_media_tuple** and **s_media_tuple** that participate in the application. The description of the class according to the aforementioned language follows:

```
class composition subclass of object
attributes
          t_list       domain LIST of   t_media_tuple
          s_list       domain LIST of   s_media_tuple
methods
          prepare()
end
```

The attribute **t_list** is the list of the **t_media_tuple** instances that participate in the current composition while the attribute **s_list** is the list with the **s_media_tuple** instances that participate in the current composition

Assume that we have a multimedia composition with the aforementioned s_media_t
and t_media_tuple instances. The following instance of the composition
class is created:

```
t_list :   <a1>
s_list :   <im1_s, v1_s>
```

Class scenario_tuple

The actions that may be executed during the execution of an application may
be simple or complex using the temporal and spatial composition operators
that have been defined earlier. According to the defined syntax the actions are
defined as follows:

```
action = CLASS_NAME.METHODNAME[parameter]
action = action {spatial_operator | temporal operator action}
action = action "i*"
```

In order to manipulate the exceptions and system interrupts it necessary to
define a structure (trigger) that detects whether a condition is fulfilled or if
an event has occurred and it will respond with a simple or composite action.
This structure is defined as follows:

```
trigger = "if"  condition|event "then" action
end

condition = class_name "."(method_name | attribute)
            conditional_operator (STRING | NUMBER)
```

It is also necessary to define formally the event concept, that may be the beginning or the end of an action (simple or complex). The definition of the event,
and event_expression follows:

```
event = class_name.method_name | TIME
event_expression = event logical_operator event
```

The most important part of an interactive multimedia application is the scenario or script concept. The flow of such an application in space and time as
well as handling the user interaction, system events, exceptions and interrupts
are modelled by the scenario class. An instance of the scenario class consists
of a set of tuples each one describing an action that will be performed when
a specific event occurs (start of end of the execution of media objects or user
action or system event).

The scenario tuples are represented by the class `scenario_tuple`. The tuple also defines the duration of the action, the synchronisation events that will be generated from the execution of this tuple, and the way that the system will handle exceptions or system interrupts during the execution of this tuple. Many of the attributes of each tuple have been introduced in programming languages for the implementation of real-time applications. The description of the class according to the aforementioned language follows:

```
class scenario_tuple subclass of object
attributes
        start_time          domain event_expression
        duration            domain event_expression
        action_list         domain LIST of actions
        synch_events        domain LIST of event
        exception_handler   domain LIST of  trigger
        interrupt_handler   domain LIST of  trigger
methods
        set_start_time(ev_expr domain event_expression )
        set_duration( ev_expr domain event_expression)
        set_action_list(actions domain LIST of actions)
        set synch_events(ev_list  domain LIST of event)
        set_exception handler(ex_h domain LIST of  trigger)
        set_interrupt_handler(in_h domain LIST of  trigger)
        get_start_time()
        get_duration()
        get_action_list()
        get synch_events()
        get_exception_handler()
        get_interrupt_handler()
        execute()
end
```

The attributes of the class have the following semantics:

start_time determines the start of execution of the actions described in the tuple. It may be of the form: **event_expression**. In this expression the starting time may depend either on absolute time or on sequence of events or on a combination of both. The sequence of events is a general logical expression of events. In this context, events are used for the ordering of actions in time domain. As already mentioned events are caused either by the start or the end of every action or by a user interaction event (e.g. selection of a button). An event may cause the execution of a simple or complex action. As we have mentioned earlier the events are caused by the beginning or the end of an action (simple or complex) or by a system message or by a user event.

Duration determines the duration of the action in the tuple. It may expressed in absolute time units or as a set of events that will cause the execution of the tuple to end. Similarly to **start_time** it has the form: (**event_expression**).

The attribute **Action_list** is the list of actions that will be performed and may refer either to an individual object (in this case actions are multimedia classes method calls e.g. play, move, display) or to a combination of objects (like overlay, overlap, resolve occlusion, scaling, cropping etc.). Moreover we can construct complex actions using elementary ones and the temporal operators defined earlier. These expressions of actions include the notion of synchronisation between the actions implicitly resulting to a more elegant design of the whole presentation. In addition, with these temporal expressions we reduce also the number of events used for explicit synchronisation with the result of a simple description of a complex multimedia application. For example, the composed action (**v1_s.execute** $\bigwedge$ **a1.execute()**) implies that the video **v1_s** and the sound a1 will start at the same time and be executed concurrently. The composite action will be terminated when both participating actions will be terminated.

The attribute **Synch_events** refers to the naming of the two special events which are generated at the start and the end point of **action_list** execution. It is an ordered pair of event names where the first name represents the event that corresponds to the beginning of the execution of the **action_list** and the other is the name of the event that corrsponds to the end point of the **action_list**. These names of the events defined in this field are used for the explicit synchronisation of the actions participating in a scenario. More precisely, we use these names in the expressions **start_time** and **duration** as we have already seen in the description of these fields above. For example, the pair (**e1,e2**) for the composed action (**v1_s.execute** $\bigwedge$ **a1.execute()**) means that when the **start_time** expression is evaluated to true then the event **e1** will be generated. At the end of this composed action the event **e2** will be also generated. If we do not care about the generation of an event we place an underscore (_) instead of its name.

The attribute **exception_handler** is a set of actions that will be executed in case of violation of the predefined time constraints or when there exists a lack of synchronisation between the participating actions. As a result, the execution of the specific action will be suspended and the **exception_handler** will take immediately priority. This action will handle the exception and will try to bring the whole system to a desirable state. One of the two events timeout or **no_synch** will have occurred showing that the exception produced from a timing constraint violation or from synchronisation problems of the action respectively.

The attribute **interrupt_handler** is an action that has to be performed immediately after a system failure or by typing special control characters (e.g. **CTRL-C**). Such failures can be produced for instance from the hardware, resource failures, environmental factors etc. and they are application independent. When a failure occurs the system receives an identifier of the interrupt which is usually a small integer and then calls this interrupt handling routine. After the execution of the handler the execution resumes at the point where it was interrupted.

The methods **set_start_time(ev_expr)**, **set_duration(ev_expr)**, **set_action_list(actions)**, **set_synch_events(ev_list)**, **set_exception_handler(ex_h)**, **set_interrupt_handler(in_h)** set the values for the corresponding attributes. The methods **get_start_time()**, **get_duration()**, **get_action_list()**, **get_synch_events()**, **get_exception_handler()**, **get_interrupt_handler()** return the values for the corresponding attributes. Finally the method **execute()** executes the current tuple.

Class scenario

An instance of this class consists of a set of tuples each of one describes the list of actions that will take place when an event expression is true.

```
class scenario subclass of LIST
attributes
        scenario_list domain LIST of scenario_tuple
methods
        start()
        stop()
        pause()
        resume()
end
```

The criterion for a set of action to be included in a scenario_tuple is the concurrent start of these actions. In general a scenario_tuple is instantiated when an action expression is triggered by an event expression.

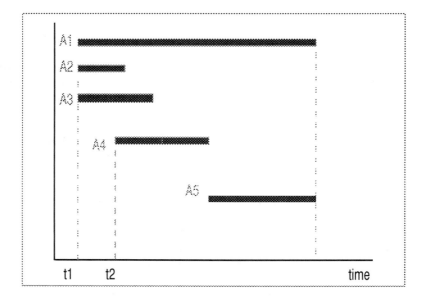

Figure 6 Temporal ordering of the objects participating in a multimedia presentation.

For instance (see Figure 6.) in a multimedia scene at the temporal point t1 image A1 is displayed, sound A2 s and video A3 also start. At the temporal point t2 narration A2 starts and when this ends music A5 starts. The end of A5 triggers the end of the scene. The scenario tuples that represent the scenario of the aforementioned scene follow:

```
TUP1 scenario_tuple
        start_time          =       t1
        duration            =       e4
        action_list         =       (A1 /\ A2 /\ A3)
        synch_events        =       (_,_)
        exception_handler   =       null
        interrupt_handler   =       null
TUP2 scenario_tuple
        start_time          =       t2
```

```
        duration          =          e4
        action_list       =          (A4-0->A5)
        synch_events      =          (_,e4)
        exception_handler =          null
        interrupt_handler =          null
```

Then the following instance of the screnario class is created.

```
sc   scenario
            scenario_list = (TUP1, TUP2)
```

Class scene

As mentioned before a multimedia application consists of a set of scenes similar to a theatrical play. The scene concept is represented by the class scene, which includes an instance (**compo**) of the composition class that describes the media that participate in the scene and their transformations. Moreover it includes an instance (**script**) of the class scenario that defines the functionality of the scene. The description of the class according to the aforementioned language follows:

```
class scene subclass of   s_object
attributes
        compo         domain        composition
        script        domain        scenario
methods
        execute()
        display()
end
```

Assuming that we have a scene (see Figure 7.) that contains the aforementioned multimedia objects. The scenario of the scene is the following: Initially the image im1_s is displayed while the music a1 starts. The music is repeated until the end of the scene. At the 10th second from the scene temporal start the video v1_s starts. The scene ends when the video ends or when the user clicks button b1.

The aforementioned scenario is represented by the following instances of the class scenario_tuple.

```
scenario_tuple t1
```

```
        start_time          =   0 or e1
        duration            =   e4 or b1.button_up()
        action_list         =   im1_s.execute() /
a1.execute()
        synch_events        =   (_,e1)
        exception_handler =     null
        interrupt_handler =     null
scenario_tuple t2
start_time          =   10
        duration            =   b1.button_up()
        action_list         =   v1_s.execute()
        synch_events        =   (_,e4)
        exception_handler =     null
        interrupt_handler =      null
```

Let the instance **sc** of the scenario class with the following attribute values

```
        scenario_list = (t1, t2)
```

The we have the instance **scene1** of the class scene with the following attribute values:

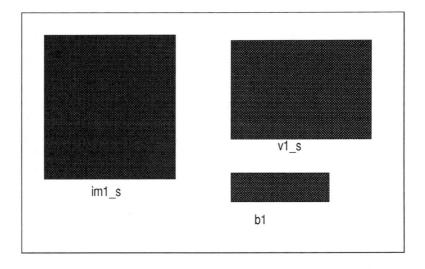

Figure 7 Scene containing sound, image and video objects.

```
compo = comp1
script = sc
```

Of course an important issue, that is not addresed here, is the evaluation of the scenario and the design of an execution mechanism.

Class application

The multimedia application is represented by the class application. This class includes a list with the identifiers of the scenes that participate in the application (`scene_list`), the scenario of the application (script instance of the scenario class) and moreover administrative information like the authors list (`author`), the date of creation/modification (`creation_date`). The application may be active, idle or suspended. This is indicated by the attribute status. The description of the class according to the aforementioned language follows:

```
class application subclass of  object
attributes
        author          domain STRINGS
        creation_date   domain DATE
        status          domain INTEGERS
        script          domain scenario
        scene_list      domain LIST of IDENTIFIERS
methods
                        start()
                        stop()
                        pause()
                        resume()
        BOOLEAN         get_status()
                        go_to_scene(sc domain scene)
end
```

The default values for the class attributes follow:

```
        author          =    " "
        creation_date   =    system date
        status          =    0 (0:IDLE, 1:active, 2:SUSPENDED)
        script          =    " "
        scene_list      =    empty list
```

Assume that an application consists of the scenes **scene1** (that was previously described)and the scenes **scene2, scene3 and scene4**. The scenario imposes that the application starts with the scene scene1 and ends after 20min time or when button b3 (in **scene3**) is pressed. The corresponding scenario follows:

```
T1 scenario_tuple
        start_time           =       t2
        duration             =       20min or b3.button_up
        action_list          =       (app.start())
        synch_events         =       (_,_)
        exception_handler    =       null
        interrupt_handler    =       null
```

and the **scenario** class instance

```
scenario_list =    (t1, t2)
```

Then the instance of the class application is created with the following values for its attributes:

```
app application
attributes
        author          =       "Author1"
        creation_date   =       "27-08-94"
        status          =       0
        script          =       sc1
        scene_list      =       (scene1, scene2, scene3, scene4)
```

7   CONCLUSIONS

We discussed various issues regarding Multimedia Data Bases. We emphasized on Modeling of multimedia objects and applications. Moreover we proposed an Object Oriented model (MOAP) for uniform representation of multimedia objects and interactive applications. The temporal & spatial features of objects and applications are covered adequately. The application representation is based on composition (spatial and temporal) modeling and scenario modeling. The scenario is described in terms of event and action expressions.

An important feature of MOAP is that there is and integrated modeling of the multimedia objects as well as of the applications that utilize them in a uniform way. Moreover the mappings between the two categories of classes are defined. The advantageous features of MOAP concentrate in the representation of interactive application scenario based on events (simple and complex). Moreover an advanced scheme for complex action description is proposed. Another advantage of MOAP is that it provides a mechanism for communication between tuples using the `synch_events` attribute of the `scenario_tuple` class.

MOAP is currently under implementation in two platforms using different approaches. The first is developing interactive editor for multimedia applications based on the model under Windows 3.11 using C++. This approach will verify the real time features of the model. The other implementation effort implements MOAP with C++ exploiting an Object Oriented storage manager (AT&T/EOS) putting emphasis to the database aspects of the model.

The model can be extended towards complete description and manipulation of events. Events are an essential primitive for modeling composition and scenario. Therefore, there is an immediate need of concrete event models, addressing issues such as classification of events, composition of events, etc.

Moreover implementation considerations must be addressed regarding the comparison to existing models like VODAK [KLA93] and commercial tools (ToolBook, Multimedia Viewer, MacroMind Director, Apple Media Tool) as well as execution models. The execution models relate to algorithms and schemes for execution of scenaria. These algorithms should address issues like scenario consistency (temporal, spatial constraints) and resource allocation and management.

REFERENCES

[1] J. F. Allen, "Maintaining Knowledge about Temporal Intervals", Communications of the ACM, vol 26, No 11, pp. 832-843, November 1983.

[2] "Apple Media Tool - Technical Reference", Apple, 1993

[3] Egenhofer, M., Franzosa R. (1991), "Point-Set Topological Spatial Relations", International Journal of Geographic Information Systems, Vol 5(2), pp. 160-174.

[4] S. Gatziu, K. Dittrich, "Detecting Composite Events in Active Database Systens Using PetriNets", Proc. of 4th Intl. Workshop on Research Issues in Data Engineering: Active database systems, Texas, February, 1994

[5] A. Ghafoor, "Multimedia Databases Coursenotes", ACM Multimedia 94 Conference.s;

[6] S. Christodoulakis, N. Ailamaki, M. Frangonikolakis, Y. Kapetanakis, L. Koveos, "An Object Oriented Architecture for Multimedia Information Systems", IEEE Data Engineering, vol. 14(3), pp. 4-15, 1991.

[7] S. Gibbs, L. Dami and D.Tsichritzis, "An Object-Oriented Framework for Multimedia Composition and Synchronisation", Object Composition, Centre Universitaire d' Informatique (Univertitaite de Geneve), pp. 133-143, 1991.

[8] ISO/IEC, "Information Technology - Coded representation of Multimedia and Hypermedia Information Objects (MHEG)", 1993.

[9] "ScriptX Technical Overview", Kaleida Labs, Inc.

[10] W. Klas, K. Aberer, E. Neuhold, "Object Oriented Modelling for Hypermedia systems Using the VODAK Model Language", NATO - ASI on OODBMSs, Springer Verlag, 1994, pp. 389-433.

[11] W. Klas, K. Aberer, "Multimedia Applications and their implications on Database Architectures", proceedings of Advances Course on Multimedia Databases in Perspective, Un. of Twente, Netherlands, 1995, pp. 19-72.

[12] Little TDC, Ghafoor A, "Synchronisation and storage models for multimedia objects", IEEE J. Selected Areas Communications 8:413-427.

[13] T.Little, A. Ghafoor, Interval-Based Conceptual Models for Time Dependent Multimedia Data", IEEE Transactions on Data and Knowledge Engineering 5(4), pp. 551-563, August 93.

[14] Macromind Director, Interactivity Manual, Macromind Inc, 1990.

[15] V. de Mey, C. Breitener, L. Dami, S. Gibbs and D. Tsichritzis (1992), Visual Composition and Multimedia, Object Frameworks, Centre Universitaire d' Informatique (Universite de Geneve), pp 243-258, 1992.

[16] S. Newcomb, N. Kipp, V. Newcomp, "THE HYTIME, Hypermedia Time based Document Structuring Language", Communications of the ACM, 34(11, November/91), pp. 67-83.

[17] T. Takow, E. Neuhold, M. Lohr, "Multimedia Database Systems - The notions and the issues", BTW, Springer Informatic Aktuell, Berlin 1995.

[18] P. V. Rangan, H. Vin, " Designing file systems for video and audio", Proc. 13th Symp, Oper. Syst. Principles, vol. 25 (10/1991, pp. 81-94.

[19] M. Vazirgiannis, M. Hatzopoulos, "A Script Based Approach for Interactive Multimedia Applications", Proceedings of the MMM (International Conference on Multi-Media Modelling) Conference, Singapore, (November 9-12, 1993).

[20] M. Vazirgiannis, M. Hatzopoulos, "Integrated Multimedia Object And Application Modelling based on events and scenarios " to appear in the proceedings of 1st International Workshop for MMDBMSs (IEEE-ACM), 8/1995, Blue Mountain Lake, NY (The Adirondacks).

[21] M. Vazirgiannis, T. Sellis, "Event And Action Representation And Composition For Multimedia Application Scenario Modelling", Technical Report, Department Of Electrical Engineering, Division Of Computer Science, National Technical University Of Athens , Greece.

APPENDIX
The EBNF definition of the laguage for MOAP specification

The following language aims at description of the model classes and its definition has been based on the EBNF notation :

```
class =
        "class"   class_name [ "subclass of"  classes]
        "attributes" atrribute_specifications
        "methods" method_specifications
        "end"
        classes            = class_name "," class_name
        class_name       = STRING
        atrribute_specifications  = attribute attribute
        attribute          = STRING  "domain" class_name
        method_specifications     = method
        method             = return_object_name  method_name "(" [parameter_lis
        return_object_name = class_name | "LIST of" class_name
        method_name       = STRING
        parameter_list    = parameter "," parameter
        parameter          = par_name "domain"class name
```

SYNCHRONIZATION AND USER INTERACTION IN DISTRIBUTED MULTIMEDIA PRESENTATION SYSTEMS

Donald A. Adjeroh and M. C. Lee

Department of Computer Science
The Chinese University of Hong Kong
Shatin N. T., HONG KONG

ABSTRACT

A typical multimedia presentation involves an integration of a variety of data types represented in different media forms such as text, graphics, audio, video, etc. Audio and video in particular impose certain temporal constraints in their presentation in order to convey the desired message. When some of the multimedia objects needed in the presentation are to be retrieved from distributed multiple sources over a network, issues such as bandwidth limitation, network delays, low quality of service, user interaction, etc. become problems that may lead to synchronization difficulties.

We present some predictive mechanisms that can be used to ensure synchronization in network-based multimedia presentations in the presence of distributed multiple sources of data, limited network bandwidth, statistical network delays, and asynchronous user interaction. The various network problems are modelled as bounded probabilistic delays. Using an interval based presentation schedule, the mechanisms predict the optimal time to initiate the request for the multimedia objects. This guarantees that the required objects will be available at the time of their presentation, regardless of network problems. Using the notion of global presentation graph, the concept of hypermedia linking, and the hierarchical modelling power of the Petri net representation, we describe how asynchronous user modification of the presentation sequence can be supported. We also provide algorithms that capture special effects based on the presentation graph.

1   INTRODUCTION

Multimedia presentation involves the integration and display of a variety of data types in the form of both static and continuous media. A multimedia presentation system thus integrates such static media objects as text, images, and graphics with data objects in the form of continuous media (video and audio) which exhibit temporal dependencies. The introduction of continuous media brings with it certain time-related constraints that must be considered at presentation time. When some or all the information making up the multimedia document is being retrieved from several remote sites over a network, the problem of meeting the temporal requirements is compounded by the limited network bandwidth and the statistical delays that may be encountered by the packets making up the multimedia data. Thus we need some synchronization mechanisms to guarantee that multimedia objects are presented at the right time and in the right sequence, and that discontinuities are not observed in the presentation. The mechanisms should provide these guarantees even in the presence of limited network bandwidth, probabilistic network delays, distributed multiple sources of data, and asynchronous user interaction.

We describe some strategies to ensure synchronization for a class of multimedia presentation systems. The major concern is presentation of *stored* multimedia data which is being retrieved from multiple remote sources, over a network with limited bandwidth and statistical delays. The approach predicts the optimal schedule for the retrieval of the required multimedia data items with minimal buffer requirements. It also accommodates asynchronous user interaction and gives the user freedom to view information in any part of the presentation. The next section traces the origins of the synchronization problem. In section 3, we present our proposed predictive mechanisms and describe how asynchronous user interaction is supported in section 4. Section 5 provides an overview of other efforts in the area of multimedia synchronization while section 6 contains our concluding remarks.

2   THE SYNCHRONIZATION PROBLEM

The problem of synchronization in a distributed multimedia presentation can be traced to various factors. Some of these are described below.

Multiplicity of Data Objects. Multimedia data by its very nature is an aggregate of data objects from different media required to be presented as a single information unit. Thus multimedia can be viewed as an integration of data from such diverse media as text, graphics, audio, video, etc. This multiplicity implies that, if the various media objects are to convey the desired information to the user, there must be a way of co-ordinating how and when they are presented, both in terms of a single media object and as a group.

Spatial Aspects of Multimedia Data Integration. Multimedia information systems are often described in terms of the sources and destinations of the multimedia data. Multimedia systems have been characterized using four data location models namely: local single source, local multiple sources, distributed single source, and distributed multiple sources[3]. The local single source model poses little synchronization problems since the intra-stream synchronization can be performed before hand, and inter-stream synchronization can easily be achieved by fetching the needed blocks at a pre-determined rate from the single source. With multiple local sources, there may be need for synchronizing the different data streams coming from the various sources. But when we have distributed, and possibly multiple sources and destinations, we also have to consider some other issues such as network delays, delay variations, scheduling of the resources, clock variations, etc.

Temporal Constraints. Most of the problems of synchronizing continuous media data can be traced to the timing constraints imposed on their presentation. Issues such as *jitter* and *skew* become problems because users expect the presentation of multimedia data to be continuous in time and thus may not accept discontinuities in their playout. The temporal requirements are only exacerbated by other issues such as the spatial location of the data, delays in the communication network, clock variations between sources and destination, etc.

Problems from the Network. In situations where the multimedia data is to be fetched over a network as in a distributed multimedia presentation system, some other problems arise. Principal among these are limited network bandwidth, end-to-end network delays, delay variations in individual media streams and skew between multiple streams of the same multimedia object. Other issues that could lead to synchronization problems in network-based multimedia presentation systems include clock variations, low quality of service (QOS), data loss, late arrival of data, and disordered delivery of data.

Asynchronous User Interaction. When the user is allowed to interact freely with the presentation, some new synchronization problems can arise. In presentations involving continuous media, there may be need for synchronization when the user requests for some special effects such as *fast-forward*, or *fast-reverse*. Also, a user may abruptly choose to view other topics in the presentation rather than just following a particular pre-defined presentation sequence. To support this kind of flexibility, synchronization mechanisms are also needed.

Although some of the problems can be reduced by using high QOS specifications and the availability of high bandwidth, these could be very costly and difficult to provide. Thus, in the near future, the general support for distributed multimedia communication may still have to be based on simple networks that may not be able to provide the needed capacity and high QOS [26, 32]. Therefore, alternative mechanisms have to be devised to guarantee synchronized distributed multimedia presentations, even with limited network bandwidth and possibly low QOS. Such mechanisms should also be able to handle synchronization problems that may arise from asynchronous user interaction.

3   PREDICTIVE SYNCHRONIZATION MECHANISMS

This section describes our approach to multimedia synchronization. We call it *predictive synchronization* since it is premised on predicting the optimal request schedule for the multimedia objects based on the desired presentation time and network characteristics. We view the problem of limited network bandwidth as having the net effect of some delays in the network and thus model it using some bounded delays in the overall transmission and presentation. The mechanisms provide ways to capture flexible and special user interaction such as allowing the user to determine what he wants to see.

3.1   Presentation Schedule

Unlike *live* multimedia data (such as live video and audio in which the presentation of the data is being made at almost the same time as it is being captured), the timing requirements of stored media streams can be known in advance. Thus, for a class of multimedia presentations involving mainly stored media, such as presentation of stored multimedia data for learning, advertising, news casting, demonstrations, etc., it is possible to specify the relative time at which each object involved is to be presented. We capture such a specification with a *presentation schedule* which indicates the duration, relative timing and relative presentation deadline for each multimedia object.

One approach that has often been adopted in modelling temporal information involves the notion of time *instants* and time *intervals* [1]. An instant is a moment on a time line, with an effective duration of zero seconds. An interval is a duration between two instants. Intervals can be specified with respect to other intervals to form temporal relations. Binary relations between intervals are represented using some abstractions such as *starts, finishes, equals, during, before, overlaps,* and *meets.* This basic model has been extended by Little and Ghafoor [19] to capture multiple and reverse temporal relations.

To represent the presentation schedule, we use multiple temporal relations [19], and the notion of *atomic data units.* For any given media stream, the atomic data unit is the smallest data item that can be presented, such as a video frame or an audio sample. Each atomic data unit has a presentation duration equivalent to an *atomic interval* (e.g. 1/30s for a video frame). The atomic interval is the same for any given media type and is the smallest interval recognised in the schedule. Thus the presentation duration of any stream can be expressed as a multiple of the atomic interval of the media type making up the stream. Figure 1 shows a presentation schedule for some different media streams.

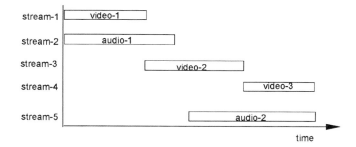

Figure 1   Time line for presentation of 5 media objects

With this interval-based representation, multiple streams can be accommodated using multiple temporal relations. The relative positioning of the time intervals then models the temporal dependencies between the multimedia streams. The time instants making up the intervals represent the relative points in time during which the particular media stream will be presented. With only the knowledge of the presentation time of the first object, the presentation times of all other objects can be calculated based on their temporal relations. This further implies that the particular time instant at which a presentation can start can easily be modified without affecting the entire schedule. This feature is central to the modelling of user interaction since we can modify the presentation interval of a given multimedia object without needing to modify the overall presentation schedule.

3.2 The Presentation Graph

Using the presentation schedule, we construct a *presentation graph* representing the multimedia objects, their intervals and their temporal relations as a timed Petri net. The Petri net representation [23, 20] is well known for its ability to model both concurrent and sequential activities. They provide facilities for modelling interprocess timing relationships and both synchronous and asynchronous events. These properties make Petri nets attractive for modelling the unique requirements of multimedia presentation [29, 18, 22].

A marked Petri net is a directed bipartite graph defined as: $N = (T, P, A, M)$, where $T = \{t_1, t_2, ..., t_m\}$ is a finite set of transitions; $P = \{p_1, p_2, ..., p_n\}$ is a finite set of places; $A : \{P \times T\} \cup \{T \times P\}$ is a set of arcs representing the flow relation; $M : P \rightarrow I, I = \{0, 1, 2, ...\}$ is a mapping from the set of places to the integers; $P \cup T = \emptyset$. The marking of the Petri net assigns a non-negative number of tokens to the places in the net. In the classical Petri net, the places are commonly used to model conditions, while the transitions model events. A place that is holding a token is interpreted as having met the truth value of the condition. The events (transitions) are also often assumed to be instantaneous. Petri net execution is then achieved by the firing of transitions. Only enabled transitions may fire, and a transition is said to be enabled if each of its input places has at least one token. When a transition fires, some token is removed from each of its input places while some token is added to each of its output places[1]. The firing of a transition thus modifies the markings in the Petri net.

In timed Petri nets, the concept of time is introduced into the classical Petri net definition by associating some time delay with the places and/or transitions in the net. This provides more modelling power to the Petri net definition and facilitates the modelling of time related processes such as scheduling, performance evaluation, etc. We use a modified form of timed Petri nets [4] to represent our presentation graph and adopt an approach similar to the Object Composition Petri Nets (OCPN) [18]. We retain the concept of instantaneous firing of transitions, but assign some non-negative time parameters to each place in the net.

---

[1] The number of tokens removed or added depends on the weights on the arcs. However, we consider only *k-bounded* Petri nets, with $k=1$. Thus each place in our Petri net can hold a maximun of one token.

The presentation graph is thus a 7-tuple, defined as follows:

$P_G = (T, P, A, D, B, R, M)$

where

$T = \{t_1, t_2, ..., t_m\}$ is a finite set of transitions

$P = \{p_1, p_2, ..., p_n\}$ is a finite set of places

$A : \{P \times T\} \cup \{T \times P\}$ is a set of arcs representing the flow relation

$M : P \rightarrow I, I = \{0, 1, 2, ...\}$ is a marking

$D : P \rightarrow R^+$ is a mapping from a set of places to the non-negative real numbers and represents the presentation intervals

$B : P \rightarrow R^+$ is a mapping form a set of places to the non-negative real numbers, representing the extent of the resources so far consumed

$R : P \rightarrow \{r_1, r_2, ..., r_j\}$ is a mapping from the set of places to a set of multimedia objects

$P \cap T = \emptyset$

Properties of the Presentation Graph

Let $I_p(t)$ = set of input places to transition t

$O_p(t)$ = set of output places to transition t

$I_t(p)$ = the input transition for place p

$O_t(p)$ = the output transition for place p

Like in the classical Petri net, the firing of a transition t removes a token from each of its input places p_i ($p_i \in I_p(t)$) and adds a token to each of its output places p_j ($p_j \in O_p(t)$). A transition fires immediately it is *enabled*. A transition t is enabled only when the tokens in each of its input places is ready to enable it. A token in a place p_i becomes ready to enable a transition when $\tau_{p_i}^b \geq \tau_{p_i}$. However, unlike in the classical Petri net, upon firing a transition t, the token deposited in its output place p_j is locked within p_j until the resource in p_j (and that in any other place p_k that shares the same output transition with p_j) is completely consumed (i.e. until $\forall p_k \in I_p(O_p(p_j)) \; \tau_{p_k}^b \geq \tau_{p_k}$). Thus before firing a transition t_i the following holds: $\forall p_i \in I_p(t_i) \; \tau_{p_i}^b \geq \tau_{p_i}$ and $\forall p_j \in O_p(t_i) \; \tau_{p_j}^b = 0$. The firing initiates the consumption of the resource represented by the output place p_j and thus advance the value of $\tau_{p_j}^b$. After the firing of a transition t_i, the following holds: $\forall p_i \in I_p(t_i) \; \tau_{p_i}^b = null$ and $\forall p_j \in O_p(t_i) \; \tau_{p_j}^b > 0$.

A resource in place p_i is said to be under consumption if $0 < \tau_{p_i}^b < \tau_{p_i}^b$. This corresponds to a multimedia object that is currently being presented or one whose presentation is paused. The token would thus be locked in the place during the time when the place is under consumption, and possibly after, depending on the relationship between the object and the other objects. Generally, given a multimedia object/resource represented by place p_i the following four situations can be identified depending on the stage of the object's consumption:

(i) $\tau_{p_i}^b = 0$: Resource consumption (presentation) not yet started.

(ii) $0 < \tau_{p_i}^b < \tau_{p_i}$: Resource currently being consumed; token locked in p_i.

(iii) $\tau_{p_i}^b \geq \tau_{p_i}$: Resource consumption completed, token not yet removed. Token in place p_i ready to enable output transition $O_t(p_i)$. If $\tau_{p_i}^b > \tau_{p_i}$, it means the resource is waiting to be synchronized with some other resource(s).

(iv) $\tau_{p_i}^b = null$: Resource already consumed and token removed.

Figure 2 shows the seven binary temporal relations [1] and their corresponding representation in our enhanced timed Petri net model, while the presentation graph equivalent for the presentation schedule of Figure 1 is shown in Figure 3. In Figure 3, the places labelled as δ_i's represent dummy delays needed to capture the temporal relations among objects, while the one labelled as just δ is needed to avoid transition-to-transition arcs thus ensuring Petri net consistency. By manipulating the consumption parameter τ_p^b, transitions can be caused to fire, thus tokens can be removed from (or deposited in) a place, and the consumption of resources can be started, stopped, speeded up, etc. Thus in addition to capturing the presentation schedule, the presentation graph also forms the basis for supporting dynamic user interaction during presentation.

3.3   Modelling Network Delays

Most synchronization problems encountered in multimedia presentations in a distributed environment can be traced to various delays in the network. The delays can be caused by different factors such as transmission time, packetization, compression and decompression, CPU speed, channel establishment schemes, scheduling algorithms at the nodes, etc. The network delays are often statistical in nature, but also can be bounded to some minimum and maximum values. For instance, Goyal *et al.* [13] have defined a class of scheduling algorithms with delay guarantee and proposed a method for determining delay bounds for heterogeneous networks with such class of scheduling schemes. Our synchronization mechanisms are based on network delays and we assume that

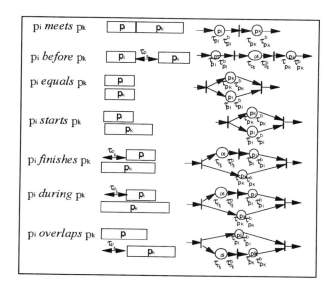

Figure 2 Timed Petri net representation for the binary temporal relations

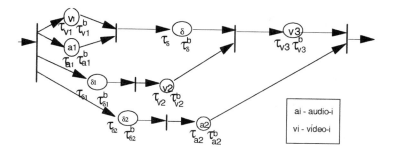

Figure 3 Petri net structure for the presentation schedule of Figure 1

the delays are statistical, but bounded, and that the bounds can be determined using some techniques, such as those proposed in [13, 5, 6, 11].

3.4   Modelling Limited Bandwidth

Multimedia data (especially continuous media) usually require large storage space and often place high demand on the network capacity in order to meet their time constraints. However current generally available networks do not meet the huge bandwidth requirements of multimedia data. This bandwidth limitation poses a major problem for synchronization in multimedia presentation. With advances in network technology providing multi-giga bit networks, and/or by use of high QOS specifications, the problem of bandwidth limitation can be significantly reduced. However, currently such high capacity networks are not the norm and the provision of high QOS is still very costly for the average user.

We make the assumption that a low capacity communication channel can be mapped into a high capacity channel and vice versa by incorporating an appropriate time delay between transmissions on the channels. Thus we view the problem of limited bandwidth as having an ultimate effect of imposing some delays on the arrival of the requested multimedia objects. Less bandwidth will lead to transmitting more packets and thus more time (and also more overheads) will be incurred before all the required data items are received at the destination. The delay introduced by the bandwidth limitation will be statistical since each packet (including the extra packets) will still experience the probabilistic network delays. However, the delay can be bounded to a given range. Thus we model the network bandwidth limitation in terms of an additional probabilistic delay which can be bounded within some predictable range.

3.5   Predicting the Request Schedule

Given the presentation schedule for the multimedia objects, the problem of synchronization reduces to ensuring that the objects are presented at their scheduled times, regardless of network delays, bandwidth limitation, and other network problems. Thus, we need to derive a *request schedule* from the presentation schedule based on network characteristics and the characteristics of the multimedia objects. The request schedule specifies the actual time at which requests for the multimedia objects must be made by the presentation system to ensure that they will be available for presentation as specified in the presentation schedule.

To determine the request schedule, we need a control time T_c, such that scheduling the retrieval request to be made at time T_c units ahead of the actual presentation time will always guarantee meeting the relative deadlines as specified in the presentation schedule. The control time also accommodates the possible delays that may be encountered by the request messages before they reach the source. To determine the optimal control time, we consider three cases viz.

1. Single data unit

2. Multiple data units in a single stream

3. Multiple data streams

Single Data Unit. Here we consider the *end-to-end delay* which is used to capture the delays experienced by the data unit, right from the source to the presentation site. It varies from live media to stored media and also from one media to the other. It is affected by such factors as coding, compression, packetization, decoding, propagation, CPU speed, etc. The delay due to bandwidth limitation is not part of this end-to-end delay since we expect that a single data unit cannot require more than the available bandwidth.

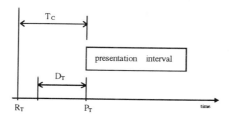

Figure 4   Control Time - As shown, to meet the presentation schedule for this single data unit, the request for the data unit must be made well in advance to compensate for both the end-to-end delay, and the time the request message will take before it reaches the source. (Henceforth, we use the term end-to-end delay to also include request message delay).

If the total delay experienced by the single data unit is D_T, then to guarantee that the data unit will be available at the presentation site by the scheduled presentation time, we must choose a control time T_c such that $T_c \geq D_T$. Thus the *request time* R_T for the single data unit will be given by: $R_T = P_T - T_c$, where P_T is the scheduled presentation time.

Single Data Stream. With multiple data units of the same stream, we can use the same approach as above to compute the control time. However, now we have to make some new considerations - specifically bandwidth limitation and delay jitter. It was assumed in the case of a single data unit that there will be no bandwidth constraint since we have only one data unit. However, it is possible for a multimedia data stream to require more bandwidth than is available. Thus for the single data stream we also consider bandwidth limitation and model it as some time delay with predictable bounds.

Delay jitter refers to the variation in delays experienced by the packets making up a multimedia stream as they travel over a network. In terms of the presentation, this translates to the variation in the amount of delay experienced by the atomic data units (video frames or audio samples) before they become available for presentation. The allowable bounds on jitter is usually determined based on the limits of human perception. Table 1 is taken from [14] and shows some characteristic values. If the jitter is more than the allowable bounds, discontinuity will be noticed in the presentation. Some jitter control mechanisms [10] and some techniques to determine delay jitter bounds [16] have been proposed. We make the following assumptions: (i) that the underlying network

QOS	Maximum delay(s)	Maximum delay jitter(ms)	Average throughput (Mbits/s)	Acceptable bit error rate	Acceptable packet error rate
Voice	0.25	10	0.064	$< 10^{-1}$	$< 10^{-1}$
Video (TV quality)	0.25	10	100	10^{-2}	$< 10^{-3}$
Compressed video	0.25	1	2-10	10^{-6}	$< 10^{-9}$
Data (file transfer)	1	-	2-100	0	0
Real-time data	0.001-1	-	< 10	0	0
Image	1	-	2-10	10^{-4}	10^{-9}

Table 1   Multimedia streams: characteristic parameter values

is reliable and order-preserving and that the network delays and packet loss can be bounded; (ii) that there exists some method for identifying the packets, their sources, and the order in which they were sent by the source - such as by just numbering them. We can then determine some appropriate delay that can be introduced to compensate for delay jitters before presentation. The notion of *diversity vector* have been used to derive the maximum delays and delay variations a packet within a data frame may experience and still be acceptable to the application [24]. The diversity vector indicates the acceptable temporal separation between the data segments making up a given multimedia object. Using the same approach, however in the context of an atomic data unit and the more usual notion of jitter bounds, it follows that, to compensate adequately for jitter, the following two conditions must hold: $\left|\frac{dD}{dt}\right|_{max} \geq \frac{2.r.J_{max}}{n(n+1)}$ and $D_{max} \leq \frac{J_{max}}{n}$, where J_{max} = maximum jitter bound, r = rate of packet generation at the source, n = number of packets per atomic data unit, D = packet delay in the channel, D_{max} = maximum acceptable packet delay.

Thus the control time for multiple data units of the same stream must account for possible bandwidth limitation and delay jitter, in addition to the end-to-end delay indicated for a single data unit. With the knowledge of the acceptable jitter bounds, we can determine the bounds on delays which can be imposed to smoothen the synchronization difficulties arising from delay jitter.

Multiple Data Streams. When we have multiple data streams - as is the case in a typical multimedia presentation, an additional concern is the *skew* between the various streams. Skew is the difference between the stream time systems of the various data streams that make up the multimedia object. Unlike jitter which refers to only a single stream, skew is mainly noticed on an aggregate of multimedia streams and thus involves inter-stream synchronization [27]. Skew can result from a number of factors, such as variation in delays experienced by different streams in the network, delays at the end systems, loss of data, clock variation between the source and destination machines, low quality of service specification, etc. Like jitter, skew is also quantified in terms of skew bounds acceptable for an application based on the limits of human perception.

Here we only consider the class of skew problems that are caused by delays or delay variations in the network. Methods for approaching the other skew problems such as data dropping, duplication, interpolation, etc. have also been proposed [24, 27]. It is obvious that if the jitter problem can be eliminated, the problem of skew between streams will be greatly reduced. Still, some delay-related skew problems cannot be accommodated adequately by only controlling the jitter. Like in delay jitter, It is also possible to determine appropriate delays to compensate for skew based on the allowable skew bounds between the multimedia streams. Thus, in requesting for the objects, we incorporate some delay to smoothen out the media streams that may have experienced some skew before reaching the presentation site.

The delays introduced above are statistical and bounded. Thus, they can vary from a minimum to a maximum value as shown below:

End-to-end delay $D_E : D_{Emin} \leq D_E \leq D_{Emax}$

Bandwidth limitation $D_B : D_{Bmin} \leq D_B \leq D_{Bmax}$

Jitter compensation $D_J : D_{Jmin} \leq D_J \leq D_{Jmax}$

Skew compensation $D_S : D_{Smin} \leq D_S \leq D_{Smax}$

Then to ensure that the needed objects are requested at a time that always guarantees smooth presentation, we determine the control time T_c, using the worst case delays. Thus, $T_c = D_{Emax} + D_{Bmax} + D_{Jmax} + D_{Smax}$. The request schedule for the presentation can then be calculated as: $\forall i, R_i = P_i - T_c$, where i is the ith multimedia object, R_i is the request time for the ith object, P_i is the actual presentation time for the ith object, computed from the presentation schedule.

3.6   Buffer Requirement

The control time computed in the previous section can be said to be pessimistic since it uses only the maximum delays. It is premised on the worst case situation and thus will guarantee that the presentation schedule is always met. However, since communication networks are not deterministic, some data units may experience less than the predicted maximum delays and thus reach the destination before their actual presentation time. Such data units will then need to be buffered until their presentation schedule is reached. Thus, the amount of buffer required at any time will depend on the number of data units that are *waiting* to be presented having arrived ahead of their presentation time.

To compute the buffer requirements, we consider two extremes - under maximum delays and in the case of minimum delays. The minimum waiting time W_{Tmin}, and thus minimum buffer requirement will occur when all the data units experience maximum delays: $W_{Tmin} = T_c - (D_{Emax} + D_{Bmax} + D_{Jmax}, + D_{Smax}) = 0$. Then there will be no need for a buffer. This is idealistic and may not really be the case in practice. Conversely, the maximum waiting time W_{Tmax}, will be experienced when all the data units arrive with minimum delays. Thus, $W_{Tmax} = T_c - (D_{Emin} + D_{Bmin} + D_{Jmin} + D_{Smin})$. Then, the maximum buffer requirement will be: $B_{Rmax} = \frac{W_{Tmax}}{T}$, where T is the atomic interval of the multimedia stream. For multiple streams, T will be the atomic interval of the stream with the smallest atomic interval.

The B_{Rmax} computed above represents the maximum amount of buffer that need to be allocated to avoid discontinuities in the presentation. We can also determine the actual dynamic buffer requirement at any time during the presentation since the data objects may experience a varying amount of delay over the network. This can be done using information on the bounds on network delay, current position in the presentation schedule, the multimedia objects that have been requested but not yet received, and the ones that have arrived, but not yet presented - i.e. those currently waiting in the buffer.

4   USER INTERACTION

In this section, we describe how user interaction is supported by the proposed mechanisms. The synchronization mechanisms provide the ability to modify the amount of consumed resources for each place in the net. This essentially modifies the effective presentation deadlines for the multimedia objects represented in the presentation graph, without changing the semantics of its Petri net structure. Transitions in the net are instantaneous, thus user interaction can only occur when the state of the Petri net execution is in a place. Whenever a request for special user interaction is encountered, the Petri net execution is paused and the state of the presentation is recorded, including the consumption parameter for the objects, τ_p^b. When normal presentation in resumed, the remaining presentation duration for the objects is updated based on the type of special user interaction. This ability to modify the amount of consumed resources is central to the support of special user interaction.

Generally, the duration of special user interaction only affects the time instants at which the subsequent multimedia objects are presented and not their time intervals. Since our presentation schedule is interval based, the duration of special user interaction does not affect the presentation schedule and we can always determine the presentation times by instantiating the new time instants as appropriate. Similarly, the modification of the presentation interval of a given object does not necessarily affect the presentation interval of the other objects, but only their presentation deadlines which can easily be calculated[2]. We partition the synchronization problems due to user interaction into two forms namely, synchronization problems due to special effects, and synchronization difficulties arising from user modification of the presentation sequence.

---

[2] Though the presentation duration of the objects in parallel relationship may be affected, the underlying presentation graph remains unchanged.

4.1   Synchronization for Special Effects

By synchronization for special effects we are concerned with the synchronization requirements when a user requests for certain special operations such as *skip, pause, resume, reverse*, etc. As was indicated earlier, the buffer required by the synchronization mechanisms is used only to compensate for data items that will experience less than the predicted maximum delays. This means that when a request for some special effect such as reverse is made, the multimedia object may have to be requested again from their remote sites. This may lead to some unnecessary delays during special effect operations. To avoid this problem, we suggest the use of local secondary storage to temporarily keep the retrieved objects after they have been presented. The availability of adequate secondary storage is only desirable and not a necessity for our mechanisms.

Pause/Resume Operation

This is the simplest of the special operations. Whenever a pause request is made, we record the state of the presentation (say in terms of the last object requested for retrieval, the current objects being presented, etc.) and then stop further retrieval requests. Then at the time a *resume* request is made, we record the amount of time that the presentation was paused, and restart the presentation from where it was stopped. Using the knowledge of the last retrieval request that was made prior to the pause operation, and the amount of time that the presentation was paused, we then readjust the presentation time of subsequent objects and thus determine a new control time for the next retrieval. The new control time is computed, this time with consideration of the presentation times of the current objects in the buffer and of the next objects that should have been retrieved. Since the buffer was not cleared, the user may not notice any discontinuities in pause/resume operations.

Fast-Reverse Operation

Upon receiving a request for a reverse operation[3], the state of the current presentation is recorded, and the current presentation is paused temporarily. As in any other special interaction, the state of the net execution is always at a place since our transitions are instantaneous. Assume the Petri net execution is at place p_c at the moment the request for reverse was issued, and that the reverse operation involves just the objects currently being presented. First, we

---

[3] We treat *reverse* and *fast-reverse* operations as being synonymous, since the difference is only a scale factor. Same applies to *forward* and *fast-forward* operations.

determine the new τ_p^b for p_c and all the objects that are in a parallel relation with it. This is done by computing a new position within the presentation intervals of the objects from where the presentation is to be re-started. Then let t_{p_c} be the input transition to p_c (i.e $t_{p_c} = I_t(p_c)$ or equivalently $p_c \in O_p(t_{p_c})$). Then for all the input places to t_{p_c}, the consumption parameter τ_p^b is set to the presentation interval τ_p. Also modifications are made to the consumption parameters of the input places to the input transition for the places that are presented together with the object represented by p_c, i.e. those with which it shares a parallel relation (*overlaps, equals, during, starts* or *finishes*). The above procedure will cause the transition t_{p_c} (and also the input transitions to the other objects in a parallel relation with p_c) to fire, and thus restart the consumption of the represented object. Upon restarting, the consumption (presentation) of objects is advanced using the new values of τ_p^b.

If the reverse operation involves objects that are further behind p_c in the presentation graph, the presentation graph is traversed in a backward fashion until the target object is reached. At the target, say p_T, the above procedure is carried out using the target object as the current place in the Petri net execution. However, for each intermediate transition between p_T and p_c, the τ_p^b for its input places are reset to zero, indicating that the object represented in such places can still be consumed.

Fast-Forward Operation

The fast-forward operation is similar to the fast-reverse operation, only that the directions are opposite. Thus our approach to fast-forward is similar to that used for fast-reverse. Again, assume the Petri net execution is at place p_c at the time the request was made and that the fast-forward operation will involve just the objects that are currently being presented. We determine the new τ_p^b for p_c and for all the objects with which it shares a parallel relation. Let t_{p_c} be the output transition for p_c (i.e. $t_{p_c} = O_t(p_c)$ or $p_c \in I_t(t_{p_c})$). For all the input places to t_{p_c}, we set τ_p^b to τ_p. Also we modify as necessary, the τ_p^b for the input places to the output transition for the places that are presented together with the object in place p_c. In addition, for all the input places to the input transitions of p_c, the τ_p^b is set to τ_p. The above steps are carried out for the input places to the input transitions for the other places that are in parallel relation with p_c. This will fire the necessary transitions, including t_{p_c}, and thus start the consumption of the object represented in the output places of the transitions. The presentation comenses using the new values of τ_p^b computed for the places concerned. For multi-skip operation involving objects far ahead of the current objects being presented, the above process is carried out at the target object by using the target object p_T as the current place in the Petri net execution. However, for each intermediate transition on the path between p_c and p_T, the τ_p^b value for its input places is set to *null*, to indicate that the represented objects have been "presented". The algorithms for fast-reverse and fast-forward operations are presented at the end of this subsection.

With the advancement of τ_p^b, the presentation deadline of some objects will be reached abruptly, and thus new requests may to be made. However, some of the objects with abruptly-reached presentation deadlines may not appear on the presentation since the deadlines may have passed by the time they arrive. The objects can still be placed temporarily in secondary storage in case of a reverse operation. Unlike the reverse operation, where the user can come back to the point where the special effect started, the forwards operation does not allow the user to come back. Presentation continues from the target object for the forward. Coming back to the initial presentation after a forward operation is treated as another special effect - reverse operation.

It may be noted that the fast-forward or fast-reverse operation can be specified in terms of a temporal skip (forward or backward skip), with the skip factor being specified by the user. This is typically the case when the user wishes to make requests of the following nature: "skip the next 5-minute of the presentation" or "go back to what was presented 4 minutes ago". The appropriate τ_p^b for the places involved in the forward or reverse operation can easily be computed based on the specified temporal skip, and the presentation for special effect may start mid-way into the presentation intervals of the multimedia objects.

Algorithms for Fast-Reverse and Fast-Forward

The basic idea behind the algorithms is that the update of the consumption parameter involves the firing of the input transitions to the places concerned. The input places to the input transitions must then be made ready to enable the transitions, and this is achieved by modifying the consumption parameters of these input places as necessary. Also, a special effect on a given object implicitly involves other objects that are in parallel relation with the object in question. Thus the consumption parameter of these objects may also need to be modified. The algorithms attempt to capture these requirements needed to ensure a smooth and synchronized presentation. The algorithms make use of the following definitions:

$I_p(t_i)$ = set of input places to transition t_i
$O_p(t_i)$ = set of output places to transition t_i

$I_t(p_i)$ = the input transition for place p_i

$O_t(p_i)$ = the output transition of place p_i

p_c = current place in the Petri net execution at the time a request for special interaction is made.

p_T = place representing the target object in a special interaction.

$P_p(p_i)$ = set of places representing objects that must be presented together with the object in place p_i ($p_i \in P_p(p_i)$).

$t_{p_i} \to t_{p_j}$ = the *reachability path* from transition t_{p_i} to t_{p_j} such that $t_{p_i} = O_p(p_i)$ and $t_{p_j} = I_p(p_j)$, where p_1 and p_j are places. The reachability path can be computed from the Petri net *reachability tree*.

$P(t_{p_i} \to t_{p_j})$ = set of places lying on the reachability path $t_{p_i} \to t_{p_j}$.

$T(t_{p_i} \to t_{p_j})$ = set of transitions lying on the reachability path $t_{p_i} \to t_{p_j}$.

T_{p_i} = point in the presentation interval of the object represented in place p_i where the presentation of the object should start ($0 \le T_{p_i} \le \tau_{p_i}$ depending on the type of relation between the objects).

Algorithm Fast-Reverse

Stop Petri net execution; record state of presentation

$p_i = p_c$

if ($p_i \ne p_T$) or ($p_T \notin P_P(p_i)$)

    { while ($p_T \notin I_p(I_t(p_i))$ and $I_p(I_t(p_i)) \ne \emptyset$)

        { $\forall p_j \in I_p(I_t(p_i))$

            $\tau_{p_j}^b = 0$

            $p_i = p_k$ such that $p_k \in I_p(I_t(p_i))$ and $p_k \in P(t_{p_T} \to t_{p_c})$ }}

if $I_p(I_t(p_i)) = \emptyset$

    { report error: begining of presentation reached

        exit   }

/* target object reached */

$\forall t_i \in T(t_{p_T} \to t_{p_c})$ and $\forall p_i \in I_p(t_i)$

    { $\tau_{p_i}^b = 0$

    $t = I_t(I_p(I_t(p_i)))$

    $\forall p_k \in I_p(t)$ $\tau_{p_k}^b = \tau_{p_k}$

    $\forall p_n \in P_p(p_i)$ $\tau_{p_n}^b = T_{p_n}$ }

$\forall p_m \in P_p(p_T)$ and $\forall p_x \in I_p(I_t(p_m))$ $\tau_{p_x}^b = \tau_{p_x}$

$\forall p_m \in P_p(p_T)$ $\tau_{p_m}^b = T_{p_m}$

Restart Petri net execution with new setings

/* end of fast-reverse algorithm */

Algorithm Fast-Forward

Stop Petri net execution; record state of presentation

$p_i = p_c$

if $(p_i \neq p_T)$ or $(p_T \notin P_P(p_i))$

    { while $(p_T \notin O_p(O_t(p_i))$ and $O_p(O_t(p_i)) \neq \emptyset)$

        { $\forall p_j \in O_p(O_t(p_i))$

            $\tau^b_{p_j} = null$

            $p_i = p_k$ such that $p_k \in O_p(O_t(p_i))$ and $p_k \in P(t_{p_c} \rightarrow t_{p_T})$ }}

if $O_p(O_t(p_i)) = \emptyset$

    { report error: end of presentation reached

       exit   }

/* target object reached */

$\forall t_i \in T(t_{p_c} \rightarrow t_{p_T})$ and $\forall p_i \in I_p(t_i)$

    { $\tau^b_{p_i} = null$

      $t = I_t(I_p(I_t(p_i)))$

      $\forall p_k \in I_p(t)$ $\tau^b_{p_k} = \tau_{p_k}$

      $\forall p_n \in P_p(p_i)$ $\tau^b_{p_n} = T_{p_n}$ }

$\forall p_m \in P_p(p_T)$ and $\forall p_x \in I_p(I_t(p_m))$ $\tau^b_{p_x} = \tau_{p_x}$

$\forall p_m \in P_p(p_T)$ $\tau^b_{p_m} = T_{p_m}$

Restart Petri net execution with new setings

/* end of fast-forward algorithm */

4.2   Modifying the Presentation Sequence

It is often the case that the user may wish to view some other presentation topics which may be related to the current presentation, but are not currently in the presentation schedule. This in effect is dynamic modification of the presentation sequence and has been a major problem in multimedia/hypermedia presentation systems. A main concern in supporting user modification of the presentation sequence has always been how to determine when the user may wish to branch out to a different presentation and how this can be captured in the presentation model. This could be very difficult to determine before hand. Our approach to the problem is based on the concept of hypermedia linking using the hierarchical modelling capability of the Petri net representation. A place in the Petri net representation of the presentation graph can be another Petri net. Thus there is a global presentation graph which is made up of subnets of smaller presentation graphs. Branching to another presentation graph is then analogous to following a *hypermedia link*. User modification of the underlying presentation sequence is then viewed as being equivalent to starting on a new presentation graph, with the retrieval time being instantiated as the current time instant. The entry point into a branch (and thus a different presentation sequence) is represented as a hypermedia node with a link to the desired presentation. Thus for the node where there is a branch, the object represented by the Petri net place at that node is just a hypermedia *button* indicating a branch to a different presentation.

A user may decide to view other presentations at any time during the multimedia presentation, but the other presentation is expected to be related to one of the objects that is currently being presented. Thus, at each point where there is a branch, we incorporate a special node which is in a parallel relation with the object that the branch presentation is related to. (A special node cannot be in an *overlaps* relation with its parent node.) Before the branch presentation is chosen (or if it is not chosen at all), the special node appears only as a hypermedia button, with a presentation interval determined by that of its related object, and the specific type of parallel relation.

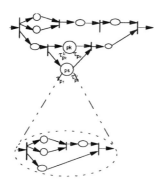

Figure 5 Replacement of a node with a subnet - This implies that if the branch is not chosen, the user may not be forced to view the presentation represented in the subnet, and that the presentation will still continue since the output transition of the special node is not inhibited from firing. The Figure shows a special node being replaced with a sub net. The special node p_s is in an *equals* relation with its parent node p_k, hence its presentation interval is the same as that of p_k. The presentation duration of the subnet is not affected by the type of relation between the special node and the parent node.

When a request for a branch into a different presentation is made, the Petri net execution on the main presentation graph is temporarily paused and a record of the current presentation state is made. Then the subnet representing the new presentation is instantiated as the current presentation graph, new presentation deadlines are computed, and the necessary multimedia objects are requested from their respective sites. When the requested objects arrive, the presentation restarts by starting the Petri net execution of the subnet and presentation continues in the usual manner as if there had been no branch. When the last resource in the subnet is consumed, the presentation reverts back to the parent net and the continues from where it was stopped. Continuation on the former presentation graph is achieved using its pre-recorded state - in a manner similar to when a pause/resume operation is made. With the above mechanisms, a subnet (different presentation) can be incorporated at any node and the level of hierarchy depends on the requirements of the presentation.

5   RELATED WORK

The problem of synchronization is central to multimedia communication and presentation, and has recently attracted some serious attention. Nicolaou [21] defined a set of synchronization properties and then proposed an architecture in the framework of a distributed computing system to provide synchronization operations based on the defined properties. Also proposed are synchronization protocols based on skew compensation between data streams [24]; regularly transmitted feedback messages to prevent buffer overruns and/or starvation beween media servers and presentation sites [25]; and methods for temporal and casual synchronization in a distributed collaborative environment based on a synchronized real time clock [31]. Generally, the protocols suggested above are at a lower level than the presented synchronization mechanisms, and most of them tend to assume the availability of adequate bandwidth. Our mechanisms can be built on top of some of them, with appropriate modifications.

There have also been efforts to provide higher level support for multimedia synchronization. Suggestions have been made for the use of programming constructs and tools for specifying synchronization using the object oriented paradigm [28, 12, 2], and for a special programming environment to support multimedia object behaviour and synchronization [15]. A method whereby the synchronization of the objects are performed partially at the sources has also been proposed [17]. However, in addition to the requirement for an accurately synchronized global clock, there is no guarantee that there will not be any synchronization loss as the objects travel over the network in distributed multiple-source environment to the presentation site. Petri net based models for synchronizing multimedia presentation have also been proposed [8, 22]. Apart from the proposals in [28, 17, 2], the others were either based on a single local source of multimedia data, or did not consider continuous media. Though the programming constructs can specify the synchronization requirements, they lack the mechanisms to ensure that such requirements are met. Thus they will still rely on the kind of predictive mechanisms that have been presented.

Predictive synchronization mechanisms that have been proposed includes the *time-advance* model [7] and the *look-ahead* model [18]. In time-advance, the required multimedia data is computed ahead of the desired presentation time based on a global clock which is set to be fast by a fixed amount of time - the time advance. For a single local source of multimedia data, this approach may work. However in a presentation environment which supports multiple distributed sources of data over a network, using a fixed time advance may be too inflexible and may not account for the dynamic requirements of the statistical network behaviours. The mechanisms presented here are more similar to the approach proposed by Little and Ghafoor[18]. However, our model of delays is different. Our request schedule accounts for delay jitter, skew, and the effect of possible network delays on the request messages, thus putting the control of the presentation at the presentation system itself. In addition, our presentation graph extended the timed Petri net model by providing it with the capability for dynamic modification of the amount of consumed resources. This capability provided our mechanisms with the ability to support dynamic and flexible user interaction - both in the provision of special effects and in allowing the user to determine which presentation topics to see. In another related work [22], timed Petri nets were equally used to support user interaction during synchronization, however, the problem of user modification of the presentation sequence during interaction was not addressed.

6 CONCLUDING REMARKS

A typical multimedia presentation incorporates both static media such as text, images, graphics, etc. and continuous media - audio and video. The calculations presented in this paper have centred primarily on continuous media data, since they enforce the greatest timing constraints on multimedia presentation. However, the mechanisms can easily be extended to accommodate data in static media. This is made easier by the fact that static multimedia data usually allow more tolerance to skew, and jitter problems may be ignored.

The predictive mechanisms can be implemented in the form of a special multimedia *synchronization manager* which will be placed at the site of the presentation. The synchronization manager will be provided with some information such as the presentation schedule, the presentation graphs, delay bounds, and the real time. The ordinary clock from the machine that is performing the presentation is all that is needed for this purpose. We thus avoid the problem of elaborate clock synchronization in distributed systems [30]. To handle special effects, there may be need for frequent retrieval requests and discards. The use of secondary storage to temporarily buffer some multimedia objects can help reduce this problem.

In addition to applications such as news casting, learning, demonstrations, advertisements, etc., with the idea of a presentation graph being a subnet of a global presentation graph, the proposed predictive synchronization mechanisms can also be applied to synchronization in automatic multimedia presentations [9]. Though major efforts in this area have concentrated on static media, with little or no user participation, this is bound to change in the near future. The predictive mechanisms described can be very useful when presentations involve stored continuous media, with the media objects being retrieved from various distributed sources, and when dynamic user participation is to be supported. They provide a request schedule that guarantees meeting of presentation deadlines with minimal resources - in the presence a statistical communication network and limited network bandwidth. Also they provide ways for handling special effects and dynamic user interaction without constraining the user to only a specific fixed presentation sequence. The mechanisms provide these without the need for clock synchronization between multiple sites.

REFERENCES

[1] Allen, J. F., "Maintaining Knowledge about Temporal Intervals," *Communications of the ACM*, 26, 11, 832-843, 1983.

[2] Blakowski, G., Hubel, J., Lanhrehr, U. and Muhlhauser, M., "Tools Support for the Synchronization and Presentation of Distributed Multimedia," *Computer Communications*, 15, 10, 611-619, 1992.

[3] Bulterman, D. C. A., "Synchronization of Multiple-Sourced Multimedia data for Heterogeneous Target Systems," *Proceedings, 3rd International Workshop on Network and Operating System Support for Digital Audio and Video*, La Jolla, California, 119-130, 1992.

[4] Coolahan, J. E. and Roussopoulos, N., "Timing Requirements for Time-Driven Systems Using Augmented Petri Nets," *IEEE Transactions on Software Engineering*, SE-9, 603-616, 1983.

[5] Cruz, R.L., "A Calculus for Network Delay, Part I: Network Elements in Isolation," *IEEE Transactions on Information Theory*, 37: 114-131, 1991.

[6] Cruz, R.L., "A Calculus for Network Delay, Part II: Network Analysis," *IEEE Transactions on Information Theory*, 37: 133-141, 1991.

[7] Danenberg R. B. and Rubine, D., 'A Comparison of Stream and Time Advance as Paradigms for Multimedia Systems," Internal Report (CMU-CS-94-124), School of Computer Science, Carnegie Mellon University, Pittsburgh, Philadelphia, 1994.

[8] Diaz, M. and Senac, P., "Time Stream Petri Nets: A Model for Multimedia Streams Synchronization," in, T-S. Chua and T. L. Kunii,(eds.) *Multimedia Modeling: Proceedings, 1st International Conference on Multi-Media Modeling*, Singapore, 257-273, 1993.

[9] Feiner, S. K., Litman, D. J., McKeown, K. R. and Passonneau, R. J., "Towards Co-ordinated Temporal Multimedia Presentations," in, M. T. Maybury, (ed.) *Intelligent Multimedia Interfaces*, AAAI Press/MIT Press, Cambridge Massachusetts, 137-147, 1993.

[10] Ferrari, D., "Delay Jitter Control Scheme for Packet-Switching Internetworking," *Computer Communications* 15, 6, 367-373, 1992.

[11] Ferarri, D. and Verma, D.C., "A Scheme for Real-Time Channel Establishment in Wide-Area Networks," *IEEE Journal on Selected Areas in Communications*, 8, 3, 368-379, 1990.

[12] Gibbs, S., Dami, L. and Tsichritzis, D., "An Object-Oriented Framework for Multimedia Composition and Synchronization," in, L. Kjelldahl, (ed.) *Multimedia: Principles, Systems and Applications*, Springer-Verlag, 101-111, 1991.

[13] Goyal P., Lam, S.S. amd Vin, H.M., "Determining End-to-End Delay Bounds in Heterogeneous Networks", *Proceedings, 5th International Workshop on Network and Operating Systems Support for Digital Audio and Video*, 287-298, 1995.

[14] Hehmann, D. B., Salmony, M. G. and Stuttgen, H. J., "Transport Services for Multimedia Applications on Broadband Networks," *Computer Communications*, 13, 4, 197-203, 1990.

[15] Horn, F. and Stefani, J.B., "On Programming and Supporting Multimedia Object Synchronization," *The Computer Journal*, 36, 1, 4-18, 1992.

[16] Lam, S.S. and Xie, G.G., "Burst Scheduling: Architecture and Algorithm for Switching Packet Video," Technical Report, TR-94-20, Department of Computer Science, The University of Texas at Austin, Texas, 1995.

[17] Li, L. Karmouch A. and Georganas, N.D., "Multimedia Teleorchestra with Independent Sources: Part 2- Synchronization Algorithms," *Multimedia Systems*, 1:154-165, 1993.

[18] Little, T. D. C. and Ghafoor, A., "Multimedia Synchronization Protocols for Broadband Integrated Services," *IEEE Journal on Selected Areas in Communications*, 9, 1368-1382, 1991.

[19] Little, T. D. C. and Ghafoor, A., "Interval-Based Conceptual Models for Time Dependent Data," *IEEE Transactions on Knowledge and Data Engineering*, 5, 4, 551-563, 1993.

[20] Murata, T., "Petri Nets: Properties, Analysis and Applications," *Proceedings of the IEEE*, 77, 4, 541-581, 1979.

[21] Nicolaou, C., "An Architecture for Real-Time Multimedia Communication Systems," *IEEE Journal on Selected Areas in Communications*, 8, 3, 391-400, 1990.

[22] Prabhakaran, B. and Raghavan, S. V., "Synchronization Models for Multimedia Presentation with User Participation," *Multimedia Systems*, 2, 53-62, 1994.

[23] Peterson, J. L., "Petri Nets," *Computer Surveys*, 9, 3, 221-252, 1977.

[24] Ravindran, K. and Bansal, V., "Delay Compensation Protocols for Synchronization of Multimedia Data Streams," *IEEE Transactions on Knowledge and Data Engineering*, 5, 4, 574-589, 1993.

[25] Ramanathan, S. and Rangan, V. P., "Feedback Techniques for Intra-Media Continuity and Inter-Media Synchronization in Distributed Multimedia Systems," *The Computer Journal*, 36, 1, 19-31, 1993.

[26] Rosenberg, J., Cruz G. and Judd, T., "Presenting Multimedia Documents Over a Digital Network," *Computer Communications*, 15, 6, 375-381, 1992.

[27] Sreenan J. C. "Synchronization Services for Digital Continuous Media," PhD Thesis, Computing Lab., University of Cambridge, London, 1992.

[28] Steinmetz, R., "Synchronization Properties in Multimedia Systems," *IEEE Journal on Selected Areas in Communications*, 8, 3, 401-412, 1990.

[29] Stotts, P. D. and Futura, R., "Petri-Net-Based Hypertext: Document Structure with Browsing Semantics," *ACM Transactions on Information Systems*, 7, 1, 3-29, 1989.

[30] Yang, Z. and Marshal, T. A., (eds.) *Global States and Time in Distributed Systems*, IEEE Computer Society Press, Los Alamitos, California, 1994.

[31] Yavatkar, R. and Lakshman, K., "Communication Support for Distributed Collaborative Applications," *Multimedia Systems,* 2, 74-88, 1994.

[32] Zafiroviz-Vukotic, M. and Niemegeers, I., "Multimedia Communication Systems: Upper Layers in The OSI Reference Model," *IEEE Journal on Selected Areas in Communications*, 10, 9, 1396-1402, 1992.

MODEL FOR INTERACTIVE RETRIEVAL OF VIDEOS AND STILL IMAGES

Brigitte Simonnot and Malika Smail

RIN/CNRS, Nancy, France

1 INTRODUCTION

Several studies have been conducted in the field of information retrieval (IR) since the beginning of the seventies. However, most of them concerned textual documents for which data models and retrieval models have been proposed. These models are usually reused and adapted to different media. Such is the case for images (pictures, photographs, postcards, drawings, etc). This issue can be analyzed under two aspects: (1) the keyword indexing model is not adapted to images, due to its poorness, but it is still largely used because richer models would compromise the indexing task feasibility; (2) the relevance feedback principle turned out to be even more powerful for image medium thanks to the snapshot nature of image perception. This principle was implemented in the Exprim process for interactive and progressive image retrieval [7].

Nowadays, there is a real explosion in production of video documents, namely movies, television news, recorded conferences or even animations to present numerical simulations in scientific research. Video is a powerful medium to share knowledge and information. This has been part of our motivation to study video documents. As it is the case for text, skimming through a video is a linear process, but not a completely ordered one. Digital coding provides random and direct access to sequences or frames. Interactivity is also made possible and all the more necessary to keep the user active since video has a hypnotic influence on a spectator.

Usually, a document index is only a short surrogate of the document itself. More than for still images yet, deep models for video indexing are difficult to handle because of the cognitive load of such documents. In any case, documents – in information retrieval context – are poorly indexed. Therefore, the search strategy is very important to ensure that the retrieval performances are good. As no single mechanism can be expected to give optimal retrieval in all cases, empirical studies conclude on the interest of providing various retrieval strategies in an information retrieval system (IRS) [10]. Driven by all these arguments, we propose a generic model for the retrieval process.

We discuss in section 2 the use of facets in multimedia documents and queries representation, and we introduce a general classification of the potentially interesting facets. Section 3 presents a parameterized model for information retrieval, defining a number of alternative achievements for the main primitives. In section 4, we propose a way of exploiting a typology of users' needs in order to define adequate instantiation of the proposed model.

2 FACET-BASED DOCUMENT MODEL

Common document description models are structured in attributes; an attribute is valued by a list of juxtaposed keywords. For instance, still images can be described with the following attributes: shot type, light, author, content, connotation... The **facet** is an additional structuring element of these models: a facet aggregates a set of attributes and has the semantics of a point of view on the document.

2.1 Facets for Multimedia Documents Indexing

A document or a query is a set of descriptors (or concepts) organized in facets, which are considered as different viewpoints on the searched documents. The facet is not a new notion since long time ago Ranganathan (1892-1972) introduced facets to organize knowledge and to improve "intellectual accessibility" in libraries [12]. Two original issues concern the use of the facets to describe multimedia documents and the impact this structuring possibility has all along the retrieval process. Actually, the faceted structure and its interpretation as expert viewpoints are particularly interesting for multimedia documents because this helps to describe different complementary aspects of such documents.

The use of facets is also intended to ease query formulation for users of IRS and to avoid ambiguity as much as possible by providing a sub-context for query terms [12]. If we consider a cinematographic database for instance, someone searching for a movie in which Clint Eastwood plays a role would formulate his need by a single keyword query: *"Clint Eastwood"*. As Clint Eastwood is also a movie director, movies he has directed would be retrieved as well as those in which he plays a role. If the name of the actor is linked to a facet *actor*, the query ambiguity disappears and movies in which he has played a role would be presented first. We will see later other possible advantages of the faceted structure.

Facets could be themselves structured in several classes, according to the kind of knowledge they express on documents:

• **general factual knowledge** facets are concerned with objective knowledge which is not inside the document but identifies production conditions and circumstances; for instance, these facets would relate, for a video, to *time, place, director*, and *copyrights*. A facet of this class expresses the viewpoint of a librarian who stores elements which identify the documents;

• **specific medium knowledge** facets describe the process followed by the author for the document creation in the chosen medium. Each medium has a proper language and some distinct characteristics. Hence, these facets express the viewpoint of authors. For both motion and still pictures, examples of such facets concern the various technical parameters like *centering, focusing*, and *lighting*;

• **specific application domain** knowledge facets would record different kinds of knowledge, related to the domain a document has been produced in (photography, TV news, cinema, historic reporting,...). A facet of this class corresponds to the viewpoint of experts in the domain. Table 1 shows some examples of such facets for still image collections;

• **content description** facets describe what can be seen in the document from the standpoint of an objective observer. Descriptors for these facets could be partly provided by pattern recognition algorithms;

• **connotation** facets gather subjective descriptions of document and express the viewpoint of a document *reader* trying to decode the message of the author. Documentalists are generally the privileged readers who decide which connotative terms will describe the documents. Connotation is important for art collections, advertising documents, photographs etc. Adjectives like *sad, tense, cheerful* would correspond to a connotation facet.

Application domain	Example(s) of facets
Medicine	Radiologist viewpoint Dentist viewpoint
Art	Artistic trend
Advertising	Trade name Text-image relationship
Satellite Imaging	Meteorologist viewpoint Volcanologist viewpoint Agronomist viewpoint

Table 1 Examples of domain specific facets for still images

The next subsection studies the particularities of the video documents and establishes the relationship with the facet-based structure.

2.2 Video Document Structure

A number of researchers are currently studying video, generally from a pattern recognition point of view, for automatic indexing purposes. The purpose of these studies is two-fold: object detection in video sequences and structuring of video documents.

Some approaches structure videos in an object-centered way. For Lee [13], a video is divided according to objects appearing in it: a sequence starts with the frame where some object appears and ends with the frame where the object disappears. In our point of view, this approach is particularly suitable for specific kinds of videos like those used in electronic catalogs of products. Indexing movies or video reportings in such a way is not very relevant. Furthermore, since several objects may appear in the same sequence, sequences are overlapping and it becomes difficult to define a database schema [15].

For Swanberg [19], structured video is a video stream with a strong order within individual frames and composed of shots, scenes and episodes. A shot is a video stream recorded by a camera in a single shooting. A scene is a set of shots with common semantics. An episode is a set of scenes characterized by a very specific sequence. An example is television news, beginning and ending with a specific title, and in which clips are interlinked with an anchor person's speech. Automatic detection of scene changes and cut shots quickly progresses.

The structure we use is a decomposition in three **granularity levels**, which can be found by a kind of reverse editing of the video document [5]. A **shot** is a set of frames shot continuously by a camera. A **sequence** gathers a succession of shots sharing a proper semantics. This structure level is the more appropriate for the presentation of documents. The **document** is a set of sequences, it is the production unit. These three granularity levels can be described by a composition hierarchy (see figure 1).

Each descriptive facet can be attached, by default, to one granularity level. For instance, at the whole document level, we assign general factual knowledge facets (like *author*, *copyrights*) and some facets specific to the application domain (like *genre* [1]); at the sequence level, we find *connotation* facet (some juxtaposition of successive shots gives a particular connotation to the sequence they form); at the shot level, facets are concerned with content description (*content* facet) and some specific medium information (like *centering* and *shot type*).

As we will see in the next section, the retrieval process homogenizes the different granularity levels: a sequence inherits the document description and takes advantage of the descriptions of the different shots which compose it. Besides, the proposed model exploits the faceted structure, for both structured and non structured documents, and benefits from it all along the retrieval process.

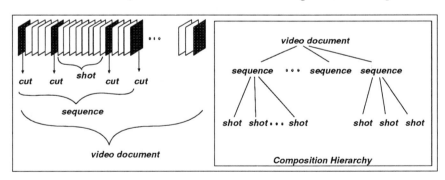

Figure 1   Video document structure

---

[1] The genre facet describes a category membership of a document, marked by a distinctive style. Examples of video genres: TV news, documentary, autobiographical film, western; examples of picture genres: landscape, still life.

3 PARAMETERIZED MODEL FOR INFORMATION RETRIEVAL PROCESS

The relevance feedback mechanism was initially proposed to support an interactive and iterative retrieval process. The goal is to improve *precision* (proportion of retrieved items actually relevant) and *recall* (proportion of relevant information actually retrieved) values by automatic query reformulation taking into account relevance assessments of users. Although not many formal experiments have been made on systems based on relevance feedback, one can say that even the best ones have a limited recall value [11]. Furthermore, there has been evidence for some time that it is very difficult to make definite unique choices for the best retrieval tactics (or strategies) during IR system design [4, 9, 11]. A general IR process supporting relevance feedback can be viewed as a set of six primitives presented in figure 2: query formulation, query modification, query interpretation, matching, visualization and choices, and query reformulation. The parameterization comes from attaching to every primitive some **strategic parameters** which express the different achievement alternatives. (Parameters names are italicized in figure 2.)

According to the facet-based document model, we analyze in the following subsections the strategic parameters we attach to each primitive.

3.1 Query Formulation

Previous interesting studies have focused on the interpretation of logical connectives (AND, OR, NOT) in everyday use [1, 3]. For instance, the interpretation of sentences containing both the AND and OR connectives has been analyzed with undergraduate students [1]. These studies have uncovered important discrepancies between people's spontaneous interpretation of sentences containing such connectives and they show that an intuitive interpretation is quite different from the formal logic one.

We believe that as long as we do not know the rules which underlie the natural use of connectives, it is preferable not to allow the user to enter a "natural expression" of the query. That is why we restricted the query model to a set of criteria (or terms) organized into facets. The facets play an important role to guide the query formulation. Actually the facet level is more significant to the user than the attribute level which can be rather technical.

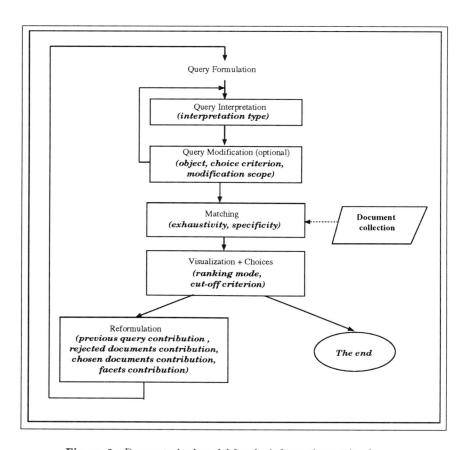

Figure 2   Parameterized model for the information retrieval process.

The user can attach a weight in the range $[-1, 1]$ to each term in the query. This weight is interpreted as follows: (i) a positive value (in $]0, 1]$) expresses the relative significance of a term presence in the descriptions of documents; (ii) a zero value expresses that a criterion is neutral towards the searched documents (zero is the default value); (iii) a negative value (in $[-1, 0[$) expresses the relative significance of a criterion absence in searched documents. Notice that allowing negative weights constitutes an original and quite natural way to express negation or exception (*unless* operator in some boolean systems).

The user can also attach a significance weight to each facet (ranging in $[0, 1]$) to express the relative importance of the corresponding viewpoints (default value is 1).

Let us examine an example of a user query:

Genre (1)	: advertisement (0.8), portrait (0.5)
Content (1)	: woman (1), perfume (1), man (-1)
Connotation (0.5)	: austere (0.5)

An intuitive interpretation of this query could be: *"retrieve an advertising image, possibly a portrait, figuring a woman and a perfume, but not a man, and diffusing an austere impression"*.

As the formulation primitive is more a matter of interaction than of strategy, no strategic parameter is attached to it.

3.2 Query Interpretation

This primitive performs a preselection of the documents likely to be relevant. The objective is to get a first subset of documents on which matching will be applied. This preselection step is unavoidable when dealing with tremendous quantities of documents.

We have justified in the previous section why we do not allow users to express their requests by boolean statements. However, we introduce at this stage a logical interpretation of the query in order to get a first subset of documents. (This mechanism is similar to what was proposed for the SIRE system [16]).

An efficient achievement of the boolean search uses inverted files. Hence, each term has an inverted list of documents (*i.e.*, set of documents indexed by this term). With the introduction of facets, we define $D_{f,t}$ as the inverted list of term t relatively to the facet f (*i.e.*, the set of documents indexed by t in the facet f). Thus, $D_{content,Nadar}$ is the image set where $Nadar$ [2] appears while $D_{author,Nadar}$ is the image set taken by Nadar. For a structured document, $D_{f,t}$ refers to the set of whole documents indexed at any granularity level by a term t in the facet f.

The strategic parameter *interpretation type* defines which boolean connectives to add between entered concepts. These connectives take into account the faceted structure of the query. We define three canonical forms for interpreta-

---

[2] Nadar is a famous French photographer of the beginning of the XXth century.

tion. A **strict** interpretation is a conjunction of the concepts in a facet and a conjunction between the facets.

For instance, due to the request:

content (1)	: woman (1), perfume (1)
connotation (0.5)	: austere (0.5)

the set of preselected documents would be $D_{content,woman} \cap D_{content,perfume} \cap D_{connotation,austere}$.

Medium interpretation is less restrictive. It corresponds to the conjunction of the disjunctions of concepts related to each facet. For the above request, the set of preselected documents would be $(D_{content,woman} \cup D_{content,perfume}) \cap D_{connotation,austere}$, *i.e.*, austere documents including woman or perfume.

Large interpretation is a disjunction between facets, and disjunction between terms inside a facet. This interpretation form is the largest one relatively to the size of preselected documents set. For the above request, the set of preselected documents would be $D_{content,woman} \cup D_{content,perfume} \cup D_{connotation,austere}$ *i.e.*, austere documents or documents including either woman or perfume (not exclusive or).

Note that query terms weighted with -1 and attached to the document level are used to cut out some documents of the selection. Weights in $]-1, 0[$ are not taken into account at this stage.

3.3   Query Modification

Whenever the result of the document preselection is unsatisfactory (too small or too large), it may be necessary to modify (expand or restrict) the query by a kind of "feedforward"[3] in order to anticipate retrieval failure. There are several alternatives to perform query expansion or restriction; if a restriction must be done, the retrieval system cannot decide it by itself but can make proposals to the user.

The first choice criterion concerns the **object** which will be modified: shall we modify the concepts or the boolean connectives linking them? If we decide to

---

[3] a term coined by Piaget

modify the concepts, then we have to choose which of them must be modified. This introduces another parameter, the **choice criterion** of the concept(s) to modify. Possible criteria may consider concept's *weight* or the *number of documents indexed* by the concept. Various helpful semantic links between descriptors may be provided by a thesaural structure. When a concept is to be expanded, we have to choose between *broader* concepts (e.g. *chimpanzee* may be expanded by *monkey*) or by *associated* concepts (e.g. *chimpanzee* may be expanded by *jungle* or *zoo*). Association linkages may be done in two distinct ways:

- *inside a facet*, by using semantic links bringing together descriptors of the same facet (e.g. *toy* and *child*);

- *between facets* (*inter facet* associations) by using links expressing heuristic rules about the medium or the application domain. For instance, such rules could be used to translate connotative needs in more objective ones like technical criteria. Actually, kinds of shots for video documents create specific atmospheres; e.g. 1) *zooming in* in a scene often emphasizes *tenseness*; hence, a failing request on *tenseness* could be modified by searching sequences with *zoom in*; 2) *anxiety* is often expressed by a sequence of contrasting shots.

This defines another parameter labeled **modification scope**.

3.4 Matching

The aim of the matching primitive is to provide a ranked set of the preselected documents. So, the matching function determines which documents are shown to the user (for a given cut-off criterion value) and which documents have large evidence to be viewed by the user. Actually, when the set of the retrieved documents is large, only the best ranked ones may be looked at. That shows the importance of the choice of the matching model.

The vector space model, which represents queries and documents as vectors in a space of descriptors is a conceptually simple way to obtain a ranked list of retrieved documents. The vector space includes an axis for each indexing term (axes are supposed to be orthogonal). Numerous matching functions have been proposed for this model [21]. The most popular is the *cosine* function which considers the cosine between a query vector and a document vector as a correlation measure between a query and a document.

We choose the vector space model to perform the matching with two major modifications. First, the vector space is no more a unique huge space including all the descriptors but a set of vector **subspaces** each of which corresponds to a facet. The size of a subspace is the number of descriptors related to the associated facet. Hence a document or a query is described by a vector in each subspace. This decomposition of the vector space constitutes a (partial) answer to the shortcomings of the model concerning the independence of descriptors.

Second, we adopt the two criteria introduced by Nie [14], **exhaustivity** and **specificity**, as two parameters. As stated by Nie, exhaustivity-based measure evaluates the inclusion level of the query in a document whereas specificity-based measure evaluates the inclusion level of a document in the query. For instance, when looking for documents about the Great Earthquake and Fire of San Francisco, someone may prefer documents which are about earthquakes, fires and San Francisco rather than documents dealing only with one or two criteria (as it is the case for documents dealing with earthquakes and fires in general) (*i.e.*, exhaustive documents are prefered). The user may also favor documents about the Earthquake of San Francisco rather than documents relating this event among other disasters (*i.e.*, specific documents are prefered); the surrogates of the two kinds of documents would contain all the descriptors of the query, but more general (or less specific) documents would have further descriptors, so the specificity measure discriminates these two kinds of documents.

We define two matching measures based on exhaustivity (respectively on specificity) to be computed in each facet subspace:

$$exh(D_{\mathcal{F}}, Q_{\mathcal{F}}) = \frac{D_{\mathcal{F}} \cdot Q_{\mathcal{F}}}{\|Q_{\mathcal{F}}\|^2} = \frac{1}{\|Q_{\mathcal{F}}\|} * (cos(Q_{\mathcal{F}}, D_{\mathcal{F}}) * \|D_{\mathcal{F}}\|)$$

$$spec(D_{\mathcal{F}}, Q_{\mathcal{F}}) = \frac{D_{\mathcal{F}} \cdot Q_{\mathcal{F}}}{\|D_{\mathcal{F}}\|^2} = \frac{1}{\|D_{\mathcal{F}}\|} * (cos(Q_{\mathcal{F}}, D_{\mathcal{F}}) * \|Q_{\mathcal{F}}\|)$$

where:

$$\begin{cases} D_{\mathcal{F}} & : \text{document vector in the subspace of facet } \mathcal{F}, \\ Q_{\mathcal{F}} & : \text{query vector in the subspace of } \mathcal{F}, \\ V \cdot W & : \text{inner product of } V \text{ and } W, \\ \|V\| & : \text{euclidian norm of } V. \end{cases}$$

We assume that $\|D_{\mathcal{F}}\| \neq 0$ and $\|Q_{\mathcal{F}}\| \neq 0$, otherwise exh and $spec$ are set to zero.

The exhaustivity (respectively specificity) measure corresponds to the norm of the orthogonal projection of $Q_{\mathcal{F}}$ (respectively $D_{\mathcal{F}}$) onto $D_{\mathcal{F}}$ (respectively $Q_{\mathcal{F}}$).

Let us examine a ranking example with these two metrics. Given the following user query:

$$q : Content\ (1) : \text{earthquake}(1),\ \text{USA}(1),\ \text{fire}(-\tfrac{1}{2})$$

Here are the description of four documents d_1 to d_4 (we restrict the descriptions to the content facet, so $\mathcal{F}$ is *content*):

d_1 : earthquake, USA, fire
d_2 : earthquake, USA, Japan
d_3 : earthquake, USA
d_4 : earthquake, volcano

This table gives the matching values [4] and the ranking corresponding to *exh* and *spec* metrics.

Document	$exh(d_i, q)$	rank / exh	$spec(d_i, q)$	rank / $spec$
d_1	$\frac{6}{9}$	2	$\frac{1}{2}$	3
d_2	$\frac{8}{9}$	1	$\frac{2}{3}$	2
d_3	$\frac{8}{9}$	1	1	1
d_4	$\frac{4}{9}$	3	$\frac{1}{2}$	3

We notice that the ranking result is intuitively understandable according to the semantics attached to each metric. Furthermore, taking into account negative criteria in the query improves the discrimination degree of the metrics: by separating d_1 from d_2 and d_3 with *exh* and separating d_1 from d_2 with *spec*.

A third measure *sim* estimates the similarity between $D_{\mathcal{F}}$ and $Q_{\mathcal{F}}$ by a function combining specificity and exhaustivity. We choose the Jaccard coefficient [20] which is a compromise between *spec* and *exh*:

$$sim\ (D_{\mathcal{F}}, Q_{\mathcal{F}}) = \frac{D_{\mathcal{F}} \cdot Q_{\mathcal{F}}}{\|Q_{\mathcal{F}}\|^2 + \|D_{\mathcal{F}}\|^2 - D_{\mathcal{F}} \cdot Q_{\mathcal{F}}}$$

---

[4] Keep in mind that zero is the default weighting value. Hence, for instance, the weight attached to *volcano* in the query is zero and the same is for the weight attached to *fire* in the document d_3.

Thus we define two strategic parameters **importance of exhaustivity criterion** and **importance of specificity criterion** which will determine the choice of one matching measure (among *sim*, *exh* and *spec*). For structured documents, the matching operates on the granularity level corresponding to each facet.

3.5   Visualization and Choices

At this stage of the retrieval process, the search results have to be presented to the user. The suitability of results presentation affects the confidence we can have in the relevance judgments that the user will do on the proposed documents.

Two main questions concern this primitive achievement: (1) if the query deals with different facets, which rankings obtained in the different subspaces or which combination of these rankings will be preferably shown to the user? (ranking mode parameter); (2) may all the retrieved documents be shown or only the most relevant? (cut-off criterion parameter).

Concerning the **ranking mode**, we have two alternatives: (i) *multi-facet ranking* which preserves the richness of the matching results by presenting the different orders obtained in the various subspaces (each subspace being attached to a particular point of view); (ii) *global ranking* synthesizing the different orders to get a unique ranking. This latter alternative requires an aggregation procedure of the different partial order criteria. For non structured documents, three aggregation functions are defined: a conjunctive function which considers facets as complementary (it takes the minimum of the partial values); a disjunctive function considers facets as competing (takes the maximum of the partial values); a compensatory function makes the average of the partial values. In the case of structured documents, the system may consider each sequence as an independant entity. In such a case, the matching measure would be an average of all the results obtained for each granularity level, weighted by the length of the segment (the length of the whole document and of the current sequence would be 1, the length of a shot would be its number of frames divided by the total number of frames of the including sequence). Another solution is to present together sequences of a same document. In this case, the similarity measure between a whole document and a query would be the weighted average of measures obtained for each lower granularity level. Sequences of a document would be proposed sequentially, but a visual clue (horizontal coloured bar for instance) may indicate the most relevant sequences.

The **cut-off criterion** is used to control the maximum number of retrieved documents the IRS should propose for visualization. It is also necessary, with video documents, to choose the parts of documents to show: large documents cannot be seen entirely at the visualization stage. Even if the user is searching for a whole movie, only short sequences would be presented. Each video sequence could be summarized by a still image, this image becoming animated on demand for a short excerpt.

Note that structure links may be used to browse through large documents by giving access to other sequences of the same movie, even if found not enough relevant by the system.

3.6   Query Reformulation

If the user is not completely satisfied by the system proposals, it is possible thanks to the relevance feedback mechanism to iterate the search after an automatic reformulation of the query by the system.

Three factors express the different alternatives for the reformulation function: **previous query contribution, chosen documents contribution**, and **rejected documents contribution** [16]. If, for instance, the previous query contribution is null then the reformulated query replaces the initial one. In other words, discovery is encouraged instead of convergence. If the chosen (respectively rejected) documents contribution is null, we recognize the "positive feedback" (respectively "negative feedback").

Like the matching primitive, reformulation applies on subspace vector representations of the queries and the documents. The above three possibilities of reformulation are particular cases of function (10.1), giving the weight of each descriptor in the new query according to three parameters: α (*previous query contribution*), β (*chosen documents contribution*) and γ (*rejected documents contribution*):

$$Q'_{\mathcal{F}} = \alpha \; Q_{\mathcal{F}} + \beta \; (\frac{1}{n_1} \sum_{D_i \in D_R} D_i) - \gamma \; (\frac{1}{n_2} \sum_{D_j \in D_{NR}} D_j) \qquad (10.1)$$

where:

$$\left\{ \begin{array}{ll} Q_{\mathcal{F}} & : \text{initial query vector} \\ Q'_{\mathcal{F}} & : \text{reformulated query vector} \\ D_R & : \text{set of proposed documents (vectors) for} \\ & \quad Q_{\mathcal{F}} \text{ and found relevant by the user} \\ D_{NR} & : \text{set of proposed documents (vectors) for} \\ & \quad Q_{\mathcal{F}} \text{ and found not relevant} \\ n_1 & : \text{number of relevant documents } (|D_R|) \\ n_2 & : \text{number of not relevant documents } (|D_{NR}|) \end{array} \right.$$

As a facet is considered as a point of view on a document, it is not always relevant to reformulate on every facet (this would lead to a divergence of the search). It is neither relevant to ignore the facets which were not in the user's query. Hence, another strategic parameter is the **contribution of each facet in the reformulation**. Thanks to this flexibility, it is possible to discover, more than new terms expressing the information need, some new viewpoints which may be interesting for the user in the sequel of the retrieval. Some inter-facet correlations may help to determine which contribution is to be chosen for each facet (section 4).

4 INSTANTIATION OF THE PARAMETERIZED MODEL

We propose in this section a conceptually simple way to use the presented model.

4.1 Criterion for the Instantiation of the Model

Even though some trends are not well identified in the information retrieval activity, we postulate that there exist different approaches corresponding to some identified retrieval situations. It has been suggested that different types of user situations, problems, goals, characteristics might require different retrieval strategies [2, 9, 10]. An objective criterion which describes quite well a search situation is the **kind of information need**. Previous studies [4, 8] have shown that it is difficult to find out reliable query characteristics that make the IRS able to predict the right choice of retrieval strategy. So we choose to base the retrieval strategies selection on this objective knowledge (nature of information need) explicitly entered by the user.

Hence, besides the generic retrieval process model, we need a well-established **typology** of potential needs that may be addressed by information retrieval systems. Needs in iconographic databases have been categorized in four types [6]: *thematic, connotative, exploratory,* and *precise*:

- **thematic** queries are motivated by a search related to a broad theme; the user wants to illustrate an article with a picture or a general idea with a video sequence. Here is an example (facets are both weighted by 1):

    Genre : TV News (1)
    Content : ecology (1), nuclear (0.5)

- **exploratory** queries occur when a user wants an overview of the database content; such queries often turn out to another kind of need. Here is an example:

    Genre : TV News (1)

- a **precise** need means that the user knows, to a large extent, which documents are needed. Here is an example:

    Genre : TV News (1)
    Content : inauguration (0.5), G7 summit (1), Paris (1)

- Connotative queries concentrate on subjective features, referring to the impression the document will give. Here is an example:

    Content : ecology (1), nuclear (0.5)
    Connotation : happy (1)

4.2 Instantiation Process

Given a typology of retrieval situations based on the chosen criterion we have to define the most adequate configurations of the retrieval process. In other words, a **retrieval strategy** will correspond to each type of need.

For each type of information need, we choose a value for every strategic parameter in the retrieval process model. Hence, a retrieval strategy refers to a particular instantiation of the parameterized model.

A well defined instantiation will carry out the discussed polymorphism in the retrieval strategy. The next subsection presents the retrieval strategies we define regarding the previously described typology (§4.1).

4.3 Four Retrieval Strategies

Strategy for exploratory needs: the interpretation type would be large. Query expansion should apply on concepts with low inverse document frequency (because search concepts are usually broad). Matching would be based on exhaustivity. At the reformulation phase, we can favor discovery of new concepts by choosing α low and β, γ high in formula 10.1, and awareness of some new points of view by reformulating on all facets.

Strategy for precise needs: the interpretation would be strict. In query modification, low user-weighted concepts would be expanded, if needed. Matching would favor specificity. As users with precise needs are generally in a hurry, the cut-off criterion will permit the user to see a lot of retrieved documents without having to resort to several steps. During the reformulation stage, previous formulation of the query is important (*i.e.*, α high) and divergence should be avoided in this case: reformulation will be limited to facets for which the user has given some keywords.

Strategy for thematic needs: a medium interpretation would be suitable. Query expansion mainly concerns the boolean connectives (by switching to large interpretation). Matching would perform a compromise between exhaustivity and specificity and ranking mode will be multi-facet. The reformulation primitive may help the user to refine his need by choosing facets related to initially entered ones; examples of related facets are (*genre, author*) and (*connotation, shot style*).

Strategy for connotative needs: inter facet associations would be favored if a modification is necessary. The initial query would be translated at the reformulation stage by preferring more objective facets. These choices are motivated by the likely conflict between the user subjectivity and the document indexers one. *Genre* is an example of objective facet which affects the "atmosphere" of an image or a video (*comedies* are often *cheerful*, *portraits* are often *solemn*).

5 CONCLUDING REMARKS

We have studied a faceted indexing model for image and structured video documents and we have shown its suitability for video retrieval. The flexible information retrieval model we propose takes advantage of the faceted structure of documents and queries. Flexibility comes from attaching to each primitive of the interactive IR process one or several strategic parameters. Finally, we have shown how this IR model can be exploited by using a typology of information needs for multi-strategy multimedia document retrieval.

A working prototype, in Smalltalk-80, implements the parameterized model and quite similar strategies for still images: an image base of photographs taken by famous French photographers at the beginning of the century. A video application is being built for TV news retrieval.

First experimentations allow us to assess the difficulty of making the right definite choices for the strategic parameters in the different IR situations. Retrieval strategies defined would be only suggested to users by the system, letting them free to modify part or the whole of them. Moreover, this observation motivates parallel investigations since we study methods for long-term adaptation of the defined retrieval strategies by using a case-based reasoning approach [18]. Another running research is considering how to give more autonomy to each stage of the retrieval process which is seen as a multi-agent cooperation [17].

REFERENCES

[1] Avrahami, J. and Kareev, Y., "What do you expect when you ask for a "cup of coffee and a muffin or a croissant"? On the interpretation of sentences containing multiple connectives", International Journal on Man-Machine studies, 1993, Vol. 38, pp. 429-434.

[2] Belkin N. and Kwasnik B.H., "Using Structural Representations of Anomalous States of Knowledge for Choosing Document Retrieval Strategies", ACM SIGIR International Conference on Research and Development in Information Retrieval, 1986, pp. 11-22.

[3] Borgman C.L., "All Users of Information Retrieval Systems are not Created Equal: an Exploration into Individual Differences", Information Processing & Management, 1989, Vol. 25(3), pp. 237-251.

[4] McCall F.M. and Willet P., "Criteria for the Selection of Search Strategies in Best-Match Document Retrieval Systems", International Journal on Man-Machine studies, 1986, Vol 25, pp. 317-326.

[5] Cherfaoui M. and Bertin C., "Two-stage Strategy for Indexing and Presenting Video", Proceedings of Storage and Retrieval for Image and Video Databases, SPIE, 1994.

[6] Cluzeau-Ciry M., "Typologie des utilisateurs et des utilisations d'une banque d'images", Le Documentaliste, 1988, Vol 25(3), pp. 115-120.

[7] Crhange M. and Halin G., "Machine Learning Techniques for Progressive Retrieval in an Image Database", Proceedings Datenbanksysteme in Buro, Tecknik und Wissenschaft, Springer-Verlag, 1989, pp. 314-322.

[8] Croft W.B., "A Comparison of the Cosine Correlation and the Modified Probabilistic Model", Information Technology, 1984, Vol 3(2) pp. 113-114.

[9] Croft W.B. and Thompson R.H., "The Use of Adaptive Mechanisms for Selection of Search Strategies in Document Retrieval Systems", Third Joint BCS-ACM symposium, 1984, Cambridge, pp. 96-110.

[10] Ford N. and Ford. R., "Towards a Cognitive Theory of Information Accessing: an Empirical Study", Information Processing and Management, 1993, Vol 29(5), pp. 569-585.

[11] Harman D., "Relevance Feedback Revisited", ACM SIGIR International Conference on Research and Development in Information Retrieval, 1992, Copenhagen, pp. 1-10.

[12] Ingwersen P. and Wormell I., "Ranganathan in the Perspective of Advanced Information Retrieval", LIBRI, 1992, Vol 42(3), pp. 184-201.

[13] Lee S.-Y. and Kao H.-M., "Video Indexing - An Approach based on Moving Object and Track", Proceedings of Storage and Retrieval for Image and Video Databases Conference, SPIE, 1993, pp. 25-36.

[14] Nie J.Y. "An Information Retrieval Model Based on Modal Logic", Information Processing and Management, 1989, Vol 25(5), pp. 477-491.

[15] Oomoto E. and Tanaka K., "OVID: Design and Implementation of a Video-Object Database System", IEEE Transactions on Knowledge and Data Engineering, 1993, Vol 5(4), pp. 629-643.

[16] Salton G. and Mac Gill M.J., "Introduction to Modern Information Retrieval", Mac Graw Hill Book Company, 1983.

[17] Simonnot B., "A Cooperation Model for Video Document Retrieval", Proceedings of Storage and Retrieval for Image and Video Databases III, IS&T/SPIE, 1995, Vol 2420, pp. 307-317.

[18] Smaïl M., "Case-Based Information Retrieval - Extended Version", Topics in Case-Based Reasoning. First European Workshop on Case-Based Reasoning, Lecture Notes in Computer Science 837, Springer-Verlag, 1994, pp. 404-413.

[19] Swanberg D., Shu C.-F., and Jain R., "Knowledge Guided Parsing in Video Databases", Proceedings of Storage and Retrieval for Image and Video Databases, SPIE, 1993, Vol 1908, pp. 13-24.

[20] van Rijsbergen. C.J., "Information Retrieval", Butterworths, 1979, London.

[21] Wang Z.W., Wong S.K., and Yao Y.Y., "An Analysis of Vector Space Models Based on Computational Geometry", ACM SIGIR International Conference on Research and Development in Information Retrieval, 1992, pp. 152-160.

11

MB⁺-TREE: AN INDEX STRUCTURE FOR CONTENT-BASED RETRIEVAL

Son Dao, Qi Yang and Asha Vellaikal

Information Sciences Lab.

Hughes Research Laboratories

Malibu, California 90265

1 INTRODUCTION

Though standard database management systems(DBMSs) dealing mainly with alphanumeric or spatial data have reached a high level of maturity, the techniques employed there cannot be effectively applied to the management of other multimedia entities such as images and video, primarily because of the differing nature of the data and the varying types of the queries posed to the system. Unlike traditional DBMSs, which normally retrieve a few records through the specification of exact queries based on the notion of "equality," the types of queries expected in an image/video DBMS are relatively vague or fuzzy and are based on the notion of "similarity". The result is that the similarity measure used can vary depending on the query posed to the system. Thus the indexing structure should be able to satisfy similarity-based queries for a wide range of similarity measures. Also, a realistic expectation of an image/video DBMS would be for it to reduce the search space by eliminating records which are completely irrelevant to the query. This "browsing" or "filtering" approach to query processing is suited to an image/video DBMS since the human visual system is quite capable of rapidly browsing through hundreds of images. In addition, the querying process in image/video DBMSs is expected to be iterative with progressively more refined queries being issued during the later stages. Thus the indexing structure should be able to efficiently support both *vague queries*(retrieving a large number of approximate matches) and "non-vague" queries(retrieving a small number of close matches).

With this in mind, we will focus our attention on indexing methods which will aid content-based retrieval in multimedia databases, that is, the searching for an entity from a database based on its intrinsic properties [9, 11]. Some work has already been done in this area, but Chiueh [4] has developed an indexing method, it addresses only one specific query (nearest-neighbor). Faloustos [6], on the other hand, utilizes indexing methods which have been developed for spatial data [2, 7, 10] and which are thereby not optimized for the queries prevalent in multimedia databases. Consequently, This paper describes the design of a new indexing structure, named the MB$^+$-tree, which takes into account more fully the characteristics of image and video DBMSs employing content-based retrieval.

2 SIMILARITY-BASED QUERIES

2.1 Similarity Measures

To retrieve an image based on its content, it is necessary to extract the features which are characteristic of the image and index the image on these features [6, 8]. Some examples of such features are histograms, shape descriptions, texture properties and so on. Typically there are a few different quantitative measures which describe the various aspects of each feature. Thus a feature can be represented as a multidimensional vector with each component denoting a different feature measure. And a feature $\mathbf{F}$ comprising n feature measures can be represented as:

$$\mathbf{F} = \begin{bmatrix} f_1 \\ f_2 \\ . \\ . \\ f_n \end{bmatrix}$$

For example, the texture attribute of an image can be modeled as a three-dimensional vector with measures of *directionality*, *contrast* and *coarseness* [9] whereas a class in a remote sensed image can be represented as a n-d vector with each component being its signature in a particular wavelength band [12]. Multidimensional indexing methods are needed to index these image features.

Feature-based indexing translates the problem of measuring image similarity into one corresponding to measuring similarity of image features. A suitable measure of similarity between an image feature vector $\mathbf{F}$ and a query vector $\mathbf{Q}$ is the weighted metric $\mathbf{W}$ which is defined as

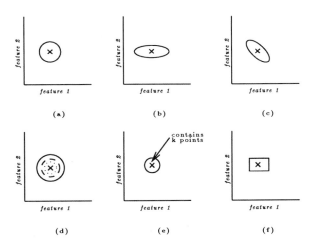

Figure 1   (a) **W** when **A**=*I* (b) **W** when **A**=*diagonal* (c) **W** when **A**=*non-diagonal and symmetric* (d) **Vague** query (e) **k Nearest-Neighbor** query (f) **Range** query

$$\mathbf{W} = (\mathbf{F} - \mathbf{Q})^{\mathbf{T}}\mathbf{A}(\mathbf{F} - \mathbf{Q})$$

Here **A** is a $n \times n$ matrix which can be used to specify suitable weighting measures such as those which take into account the correlation between various feature components or which emphasize one feature component over the other while calculating the similarity. In general, **A** is one of the following:

1. **A** = *I:* This is the case when **A** is the identity matrix such that **W** corresponds to the normal Euclidean distance. In this case, points which lie at the same distance from the query point are all equally similar. In a two-dimensional feature space, this similarity measure can be represented as a circle as shown in Figure 1(a).

2. **A** = *diagonal:* This corresponds to the weighted Euclidean distance measure where different components of the feature **F** have different weights associated with it. Note that equal similarity in this case correspond to points along an ellipsoidal contour which has its major and minor axes oriented parallel to the feature axes as shown in Figure 1(b). Such a similarity measure is useful for attributing differing importance to the various components of **F** as well as for normalizing the distance calculated for each

component of **F** by taking into account the distribution of values along that axis.

3. **A** = *non-diagonal and mainly symmetric:* This case takes into account the cross-correlation between the various components of feature *F* and can be represented as an ellipsoid which is oriented at an angle to the feature axes as shown in Figure 1(c). This is a complicated case as compared to the others and would not be considered in this paper.

Not only can all of the above three cases occur as a similarity measure in an image database but the similarity measure is "dynamic" which means that it is a function of the query which has been posed to the system and the same index file should be able to retrieve objects based on different **W**s.

2.2 Query Types

Querying in image DBMSs is envisioned to be iterative in nature with progressively sophisticated queries with relatively tighter tolerances being issued at the later stages. Queries at the earlier stages can be very "loose" such as

```
Retrieve images containing textures
similar to this sample.
```

Here the emphasis is to retrieve many images which are approximately similar to the sample image so as to allow the user to browse through them. Typically hundreds of images can be retrieved and thereby such a query can be termed as **vague**. Figure 1(d) shows a **vague** query when the similarity measure used is the Euclidean distance. The parameter here is the radius *r* of the circle surrounding the query point with a larger value for *r* resulting in more records being retrieved.

In a "tighter" query, the user specifies the number of close matches to the given query point. An example of such a query could be

```
Retrieve 10 images containing textures
directionally similar to this sample.
```

This type of query can be termed as a **k nearest-neighbor** query where the value of k is ten in the previous example. Typically the number of records returned as part of this query would be much smaller than that in a **vague** query. As shown in Figure 1(e), for a Euclidean distance measure, a circle centered around the query point is expanded till it covers the desired number of neighbors.

Another query which is common is the **range** query where an interval is given for each dimension of the feature space and all the records which fall inside this hypercube are retrieved. For the two-dimensional case shown in Figure 1(f), the **range** query reduces to retrieving all the records which lie inside a rectangle.

Thus image queries can be roughly categorized into three main groups: **vague,k nearest-neighbor** and **range** queries. Note that the first two queries can be specified using any of the similarity measures which were discussed in the previous subsection. However this paper does not deal with the case when **A** is *non-diagonal* as it is of a very high complexity. Also note that a **vague** query can be converted either to a **k nearest-neighbor** query with a large value of k or to a **range** query with a hypercube which encloses the spheroid or the hyperellipsoid. Thus this paper will consider only the latter two queries, viz. the **k nearest-neighbor** query and the **range** query.

3   THE MB$^+$-TREE

We now discuss the basic concepts behind an indexing structure which can satisfy the queries discussed in the earlier sections. We have named it the *multidimensional* B$^+$-tree or the MB$^+$-tree, as it can be considered as an extension of the standard B$^+$-tree in one-dimension to multidimensions, especially in terms of the structure and insertion and deletion algorithms. However the search methods are different as it tackles approximate or similarity queries. For the sake of easy visualization we have explained the structure and the manipulation algorithms in a two-dimensional space. Extension to higher dimensions is explained in Section 5.

3.1   Structure of MB$^+$-tree in Two Dimensions

Let R be a relation and $R.A$ an attribute of R. For any tuple r of R, the attribute $r.A$ is a pair (x, y) representing a point in a 2-dimensional space. We assume that all tuples of R have been stored on disk and $Addr(r)$ is the disk address of r. We are now trying to build an index on the attribute $R.A$. For ease of presentation, assume the background 2-dimensional space is

$$D = [X_{min}, X_{max}) \times [Y_{min}, Y_{max})$$

The space is partitioned into M vertical strips by $M - 1$ vertical lines for some M:

$$X = x_m, \quad 1 \leq m \leq M - 1.$$

Let $x_0 = X_{min}$ and $x_M = X_{max}$. The M vertical strips are

$$D_m = [x_m, x_{m+1}) \times [Y_{min}, Y_{max}) \quad 0 \leq m \leq M - 1.$$

Each vertical strip D_m is then partitioned independently into N_m regions (rectangles) by $N_m - 1$ horizontal lines

$$Y = y_{m,n}, \quad 1 \leq n \leq N_m - 1.$$

Let $y_{m,0} = Y_{min}$ and $y_{m,N_m} = Y_{max}$. The N_m regions within the vertical strip D_m are

$$D_{m,n} = [x_m, x_{m+1}) \times [y_{m,n}, y_{m,n+1}) \quad 0 \leq n \leq N_m - 1.$$

The value of N_m may be different for different vertical strips D_m, and even when $N_{m_1} = N_{m_2}$ for $m_1 \neq m_2$, the two vertical strips D_{m_1} and D_{m_2} may be partitioned by different horizontal lines. When $N_m = 1$, the vertical strip D_m is not partitioned by any horizontal line and it is considered as a region. Thus the 2-dimensional space D is partitioned into a set of disjoint regions, each of which is a rectangle. In Figure 2, the entire space is partitioned into 4 vertical strips D_m, $0 \leq m \leq 3$; both D_0 and D_2 are partitioned into 2 regions, but by different horizontal lines; D_1 is partitioned into 3 regions, and D_3 is not partitioned by any horizontal line.

Because of the way we divide the entire space, we call the horizontal dimension the first dimension and vertical dimension the second dimension. The M

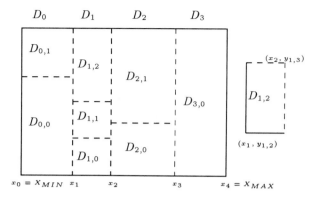

Figure 2   Dividing the 2-d space into disjoint regions

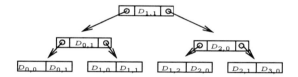

Figure 3   An example of the MB$^+$-tree

vertical strips are ordered (on the first dimension) from left to right, the N_m regions within the same vertical strip are ordered (on the second dimension) from bottom to top. This yields a linear order $\prec$ on the set of all regions. That is, a region $D_{m,n}$ precedes another region $D_{i,j}$ if and only if 1) $m < i$ or 2) $m = i$ and $n < j$. For example, the regions in Figure 2 are ordered as follows:

$$D_{0,0} \prec D_{0,1} \prec D_{1,0} \prec D_{1,1} \prec D_{1,2} \prec D_{2,0} \prec D_{2,1} \prec D_{3,0}.$$

Using the linear order $\prec$, a B$^+$-tree [5] can then be built on the set of all regions. We call the tree a 2-d MB$^+$-tree. The binary tree in Figure 3 is a possible 2-d MB$^+$-tree for the earlier example.

As in standard B$^+$-tree, each internal node of the MB$^+$-tree contains $q + 1$ pointers and q entries. Each entry represents a region $D_{m,n}$, and each pointer points at a child node, which is the root of a sub-tree of the B$^+$-tree. All leaf nodes in the 2-d MB$^+$-tree are linked together by doubly linkage. One leaf node contains one or more leaf entries, each leaf entry corresponds to a region $D_{m,n}$. Each region appears exactly once at the leaf level and all regions are ordered from left to right according to the linear order $\prec$. Notice that the last entry (right-most) in any leaf node except that in the last leaf node of the tree will appear in an internal node on the path from the root to the node. For example, the regions $D_{0,1}$, $D_{1,1}$ and $D_{2,0}$ appear in an internal node and also are the last entry of a leaf node. For more details about the structure of B$^+$-tree, see [5].

A region $D_{m,n}$ is a rectangle and is usually represented by two points, say its upper-right point $(x_{m+1}, y_{m,n+1})$ and lower-left point $(x_m, y_{m,n})$. This representation is used for $D_{m,n}$ in an internal node. At the leaf level, the entry for $D_{m,n}$ contains only its lower-left point $(x_m, y_{m,n})$. This will save space for each entry and increase the number of entries in a leaf node. We will see later how to find another point of a region at the leaf level.

For each region $D_{m,n}$, all tuples r of R with $r.A \in D_{m,n}$ form a sub-relation $R_{m,n}$. A list $L_{m,n}$ is constructed for each sub-relation $R_{m,n}$ containing pairs $(r.A, Addr(r))$ for all tuples r in $R_{m,n}$. That is,

$$\forall r \in R, \quad (r.A, Addr(r)) \in L_{m,n} \Longleftrightarrow r.A \in D_{m,n}$$

These lists are not part of the MB$^+$-tree, and are "at an extra level of indirection" [5]. Let $p_{m,n}$ be a pointer to the list $L_{m,n}$. This pointer is contained in the leaf entry for $D_{m,n}$, and all the tuples in the sub-relation $R_{m,n}$ can be retrieved from the entry through $p_{m,n}$. Thus each leaf entry of the 2-d MB$^+$-tree contains the following information (some other information can also be included):

$$< (x_m, y_{m,n}), p_{m,n} > .$$

3.2 Insertion and Deletion

To insert or delete a tuple r, the MB$^+$-tree is initially searched (as discussed later) with respect to $r.A$ to find out the leaf entry $D_{m,n}$ that contains $r.A$

and then the pair $(r.A, Addr(r))$ is inserted into or deleted from the list $L_{m,n}$ accordingly.

A split operation will be considered only when an overflow occurs to a list $L_{m,n}$. This list will be divided into two lists of about the same size. If the region to be split is a vertical strip that has not been divided by any horizontal line, it can be divided by another vertical line. We can choose a value for the minimum length of the horizontal side of the vertical strip. When vertical dividing results in a very thin vertical strip with a horizontal side smaller than the minimal value, we give up vertical dividing and do horizontal dividing. For a region resulting from horizontal dividing, we only try horizontal dividing. After a region has been divided into two smaller regions, a new entry will be inserted into the 2-d MB$^+$-tree. Using the linear order $\prec$, the insertion is a standard B$^+$-tree operation.

When a list $L_{m,n}$ becomes too small because of deletion of tuples, it may be possible to merge it with another list. Two neighboring regions within the same vertical strip can be merged, and a vertical strip not divided by a horizontal line can be merged only with another such vertical strip. After two lists merged together, one leaf entry will be deleted from the 2-d MB$^+$-tree, and it is again a standard B$^+$-tree operation.

3.3   Building 2-d MB$^+$-tree

Since the 2-d MB$^+$-tree is basically a B$^+$-tree, it can be built up by inserting one tuple at a time, as in a standard B$^+$-tree. Initially the 2-d MB$^+$-tree has only one leaf node which is also the root of the tree. The node has only one entry corresponding to the entire space, and there is only one list. Each tuple inserted is simply added to the unique list until it is full. Then splitting operation is required for the next insertion and the entire space will be divided into two vertical strips. The process continues and the space is divided into smaller vertical strips. When an already thin vertical strip is to be divided, horizontal dividing is applied within the vertical strip. For a region obtained from horizontal dividing, only horizontal dividing is applied.

In almost all spatial indexing structures, as in R-tree or R*-treetree*,a leaf entry corresponds to one disk page. We do not enforce the same limitation, but let the size of the lists at the extra level of indirection be a design parameter. The choice of this parameter should be made depending on the application and the system used. This should result in a better search performance, since the tree will have a smaller size, and for a region query or nearest-neighbor query fewer regions will be covered and the chance that the query can be answered with one region will be higher. As a trade-off, more than one page will be read in from the disk for each leaf entry. But reading a list $L_{m,n}$ of more than one page requires only one random I/O for the first page, and one sequential I/O for each of the following pages. Thus random I/Os could be replaced by sequential ones, which is much cheaper than the former. We believe that an appropriate size for the lists at the extra level of indirection will improve the performance of the MB$^+$-tree, especially on search operations.

4   SEARCH ALGORITHMS ON MB$^+$-TREE

4.1   Range Query

In a 2-d space, a range query gets transformed into a rectangle query. Given a rectangle $Rct = [x\_begin, x\_end] \times [y\_begin, y\_end]$, we want to retrieve all tuples r satisfying the condition $r.A \in Rct$. We need to find all leaf entries that represent a region overlapping with Rct, and for each such leaf entry, the corresponding list $L_{m,n}$ need to be scanned to locate all required tuples. It is straightforward to check the condition in the query and we only discuss how to find the leaf entries. The following algorithm accomplishes the task of tree searching, it calls Procedure Internal-Search with the root of the tree and the rectangle to find out all leaf nodes that have at least one leaf entry overlapping with Rct, then calls Procedure Leaf-Search for all nodes found to locate the leaf entries required.

Algorithm Tree-Search(root,Rct)
1. NODES = Internal-Search(root,Rct);
2. REGIONS = $\emptyset$;
3. for each node Node in NODES

REGIONS = REGIONS + Leaf-Search(Node,Rct)

An internal node in the MB$^+$-tree contains q entries and $q + 1$ pointer and is of the following form:

$$< P_0, rct_0, P_1, rct_1, \ldots, P_{q-1}, rct_{q-1}, P_q > .$$

Procedure Internal-Search(Node, Rct) scans the entries in Node to find all subtrees that contain at least one leaf entry overlapping with Rct. It is possible that more than one subtree may contain such an entry and all of such subtrees need to be searched recursively (step 4). But the condition to identify the first subtree (from left) is different from that to identify any other following subtree, and the procedure has two loops (step 2 and 3) to carry out the tasks separately. This is because the rectangle in an entry is not the enclosing rectangle. Since the tree is organized according to the linear order $\prec$, it is possible that only a first few entries are examined within the node (the predicate *more_subtree* in step 3).

Procedure Internal-Search(Node,Rct)
1. if Node is a leaf node return {Node};
2. for (k=0; k<q; k++)
    if ($first\_subtree(k)$)
        {nodes = {rct_k}; break;}
3. while ($more\_subtree(k)$)
    k++;
    while ($not\_next\_subtree(k)$)
        k++;
    nodes = nodes +{rct_k};
4. $S = \emptyset$;
    for all node in nodes
        $S = S\cap$ Internal-Search(node, Rct);
5. return S.

The predicate $first\_subtree(k)$ is defined as ((Rct precedes rct_k on the first dimension) or (Rct overlaps with rct_k on the first dimension and precedes or overlaps with rct_k on the second dimension)); the predicate $more\_subtree(k)$ is defined as (($k < q$) and not(Rct follows rct_k on the first dimension or (Rct overlaps with rct_k on the first dimension and follows rct_k on the second dimension))); the predicate $not\_next\_subtree(k)$ is defined as ((rct_{next} overlaps with rct_k on the first dimension) and ((rct_{next} entirely precedes Rct on the second dimension) or (rct_k follows Rct on the second dimension))) or ((rct_{next} is adjacent to rct_k on the first dimension) and (rct_{next} entirely precedes Rct on the second dimension) and (rct_k follows Rct on the second dimension)).

The basic relationship predicates (entirely) precedes, follows, overlaps and adjacent are illustrated in Figure 4.

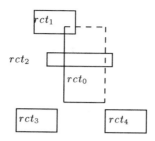

Figure 4 Rectangle rct_1 precedes and overlaps with rct_0, rct_2 precedes, over-laps and also follows rct_0, rct_3 entirely precedes rct_0, and rct_4 follows and is adjacent to rct_0 (from the right).

For R-tree and its variants such as R^+-tree and R^*-treetree*, each entry in an intermediate node is an enclosing rectangle covering all objects in a sub-tree. Then, searching such a node requires examining all entries in the node, and examining an entry requires comparing the boundary values on all dimensions. For the MB^+-tree, the searching could stop at step 6 (go to step 8 and return the set S) and some entries in the node may not need to be examined ($k < q$), and examining an entry may not require comparing on all dimensions (in step 3). The worst case time complexity of Procedure Internal-Search for the MB^+-tree is the same as for R-tree and its variants: examining all entries on all dimensions; but the procedure for MB^+-tree may give a better performance in practice, since some entries and some dimensions of some entries may not be examined. This is an advantage of using the linear order $\prec$.

A leaf node is of the following form:

$$<< rct_0, p_0 >, \ldots, < rct_{t-1}, p_{t-1} >, < rct_t, p_t >>$$

Each entry represents a region and contains only the left-bottom point

$$(x\_begin_k, y\_begin_k).$$

But to check whether it intersects the given rectangle Rct, the upper-right point is needed. As mentioned in Section 3.1, the last entry in a leaf node except that in the last leaf node of the tree will appear in an internal node on the path from the root to the leaf node. We assume that all nodes on the path are maintained in the main memory, since each path usually has at most 3 or 4 nodes. Then, the upper-right point of the last entry rct_t in the leaf node can be decided by looking up the path. For any other entry rct_k, $k < t$, the upper-right point can be found easily using the information of the next-right entry rct_{k+1}, since all leaf entries are sorted according to $\prec$. The following procedure finds all entries in a leaf node that overlap with Rct.

Procedure Leaf-Search(Node,Rct)
1. S = $\emptyset$;
2. for (k=t; k>=0; k−)
    find the upper-right point for rct_k;
    if (rct_k overlaps with Rct)
        S = S + {rct_k};
    endfor;
3. return S.

4.2   Point Query

In this query, a point (x, y) is given and the region $D_{m.n}$ that contains the point is to be found. The point query is not so important by itself, but it is used in the next query for nearest-neighbor searching. This is a special case of rectangle query, where Rct becomes a point. Since only one region contains the point, exactly one entry will be found within each internal or leaf node, and searching within a node stops after the entry is found.

Procedure Point-Search(Node,(x,y))
1. if Node is a leaf node
    return the region containing (x,y);
2. for (k=0; k<q; k++)
    if ((<(x,y), (x,y)> precedes rct_k on the first dimension)
        or (<(x,y), (x,y)> overlaps with rct_k on the first dimension and
                precedes rct_k on the second dimension))
            break;
    endfor;
3. Point-Search(P_k,(x,y)).

4.3 Nearest-Neighbor Query

Let *Dis* be a distance function defined on 2-dimensional space. Given a point (x, y) and a positive integer k, the k nearest-neighbor query finds the k nearest-neighbors of (x, y) with respect to the distance function *Dis*.

Consider the weighted Euclidean distance function:

$$Dis((x_1, y_1), (x_2, y_2)) = \sqrt{\alpha_1 \times (x_1 - x_2)^2 + \alpha_2 \times (y_1 - y_2)^2},$$

where both α_1 and α_2 are positive numbers. Note that this corresponds to the case when **A** is *diagonal* as discussed in Section 2. This function satisfies one property: if the absolute distance between P and P_1 in each dimension is at least as large as that between P and P_2, then the distance *Dis* between P and P_1 is at least as large as that between P and P_2.

One approach for the nearest-neighbor query is to transfer it to a rectangle query. In this approach, a rectangle is formed at the beginning, following which all points within the rectangle are retrieved, and the k nearest-neighbors determined. The problem with the approach is the size of the rectangle could be too small or too big. We propose another algorithm for the query on MB⁺-tree. It searches only those regions that have to be searched to determine the k nearest-neighbors.

Algorithm Nearest-neighbor-Search(k, (x,y))
1. call procedure Point-Search(root, (x,y)) to find the region $D_{m,n}$ containing the point (x,y);
2. search the list $L_{m,n}$ to find the local k nearest- neighbors of (x,y) within $D_{m,n}$;
3. determine the global k nearest-neighbors of (x,y).

Step 1 calls the procedure presented in the previous sub-section; step 2 scans the list $L_{m,n}$, computes the distance from each point of $L_{m,n}$ to (x, y), and finds the k local nearest-neighbors of (x, y). We now discuss step 3.

Let *current* be the distance between (x, y) and the k-th nearest-neighbor currently found. A region $D_{i,j}$ adjacent to $D_{m,n}$ may contain a point that has a shorter distance to (x, y) than *current*. The shortest distance to (x, y) from within such a region $D_{i,j}$ is computed and the region is searched only when necessary. The following procedure uses a list to contain those regions represented by the points that give the shortest distance to (x, y) and are sorted according to their distances to (x, y) in non-decreasing order. The search stops when the distance for the first region in the list is at least as large as *current*. When an adjacent region is searched and the set of nearest neighbors gets modified, some regions adjacent to the region may need to be searched. Such regions will be inserted into the list according to their distances to (x, y).

Procedure Global-Search(K, (x,y))
1. find the points that give the shortest distances from adjacent regions;
2. let S be a list of the points in non-decreasing order according to their distances to (x,y);
3. while S $\neq \emptyset$,
        take the first point (u,v) from S;
        if (its distance is greater than or equal to current)
           terminate;
        else
           find the region containing (u,v);
           modify the set of K nearest-neighbors and the value of current;
           insert more points into S if any adjacent region need to be searched;
    endwhile.

In 2-d space, the shortest distance from within a region and the corresponding point can be found by drawing horizontal or vertical lines. Suppose the region $D_{i,j}$ is adjacent to $D_{m,n}$ from the left as shown in Figure 5. The horizontal line passing through the point (x, y) intersects the boundary line $x = x_m$ at the point (x_m, y). This point belongs to $D_{m,n}$ according to our definition of regions (left closed and right open). So, the point within $D_{i,j}$ that gives the shortest distance to (x, y) is $(x_m - U_X, y)$, where U_X is the measure unit used on the first dimension (on the X-coordinate). The situation is similar for other regions adjacent to $D_{m,n}$. Notice that this is true for any weighted distance function Dis given at the beginning of the section.

5 HIGHER DIMENSIONAL MB⁺-TREE

The structure and algorithms of 2-d MB⁺-tree can easily be generalized into a k-dimensional space for an integer $k > 2$. We order the k dimensions in some desired way as $d_1, d_2, \ldots, d_k$, and name them the first dimension, the second dimension, and so on. The entire k-d space is partitioned into a set of disjoint regions by dividing on the first dimension first, then dividing each hypercube

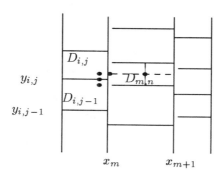

Figure 5 Determining whether adjacent regions need to be searched

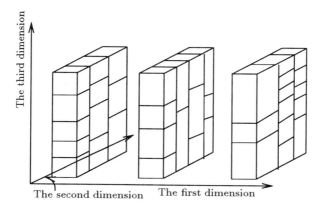

Figure 6 Division of the k-d space: here $k = 3$

on the second dimension independently, and so on. Figure 6 gives an example for the case $k = 3$.

A linear order $\prec$ can be defined on the set of all the regions by comparing the boundary values in the same order as the dimensions and a B$^+$-tree can be built using the order. The concepts of preceding, following and overlapping on any dimension can be defined the same way as for the 2-d MB$^+$-tree, and the searching algorithms for different queries can be generalized in a straightforward manner from that for 2-d MB$^+$-tree.

6   DISCUSSION

As was discussed in Section 2, queries in an image/video database can be transformed to searching in a multidimensional space. There are many methods for indexing in multidimensional space [2, 3, 4, 7, 10]. Each method partitions the space into disjoint or overlapping regions and then organizes the index file in some way. Though most of the above-mentioned methods use a tree structure akin to a B^+-tree to organize the index file, they are not based on any linear order. In contrast, our MB^+-tree exploits the major features of the B^+-tree and establishes an index structure in multidimensional space based on a linear order. This linear order gives the MB^+-tree the following advantages:

1. The space required for each entry at the leaf level is reduced by nearly half. In the 2-d space, a region is a rectangle and only one point is maintained in a leaf entry although two points are maintained in the intermediate levels as in other approaches. This will reduce the number of leaf nodes and hence the size of the MB^+-tree, which should result in better search performance.

2. The insertion and deletion operations in the MB^+-tree are very similar to those for a B^+-tree, and simpler than those in other trees such as the R-tree, R^+-tree and R^*-tree. This can be explained as follows. In other methods, entries in the intermediate levels are enclosing hypercubes(or rectangles in 2-d space) which often get modified during the insertion and deletion process. In the MB^+-tree there is no concept of an enclosing hypercube. The entries in the intermediate levels correspond to an element in the set of regions as do entries in the leaf level.

3. The MB^+-tree maintains locality to some extent and should give better performance in searching. For example, in the 2-d space, the regions within the same vertical strip are next to each other at the leaf level, and are in the same leaf node or adjacent leaf nodes; the regions in adjacent vertical strips are not far away from each other at the leaf level and have a high chance of sharing at least a portion of the paths from the root to themselves. This should decrease the number of nodes touched during a searching operation and should therefore yield better disk I/O performance than other trees since both rectangle query and nearest-neighbor query will normally retrieve points in adjacent regions on either dimension.

In all indexing structures including our MB^+-tree, a leaf entry corresponds to a set of objects (tuples). In all previous structures, the maximal size of the set was chosen to be the capacity of one disk page, i.e., the number of objects one page can contain. This is so because of the consideration of efficient disk I/O operations. We suggest that the maximal size of the set or equivalently the maximal size of each list $L_{m,n}$ be a design parameter and allowed to be more than one page. This creates an opportunity to reduce disk I/O cost by replacing random I/Os with sequential I/Os. Of course, this technique can be applied to any other index structure. Since this approach can retrieve many "similar" records at no extra surcharge, it is very useful for *browsing* capability in an image database.

As discussed in Section 2, the nearest-neighbor query is very important in multimedia databases. Some algorithms have been presented in [4, 6]. We propose a new algorithm for the k nearest-neighbor query which has the following features:

1. It optimally searches only the minimal number of regions which might contain any of the k desired records resulting in high search efficiency.

2. It works for any weighted distance function satisfying the condition in Section 4.3 and provides a flexible structure for different applications and different users. In contrast, some other algorithms, e.g., [4], work only for one predefined distance function.

Note that the second feature of our k nearest-neighbor algorithm makes it very suitable for an image database where the similarity criterion between two images or two image features is user specified. As was discussed in Section 2, this is important since the same query such as vague or nearest-neighbor, can be specified using different similarity measures.

7 CONCLUSION

Indexing structures to be used for content-based retrieval in multimedia data bases need to take into account the types of queries prevalent in such DBMSs. Accordingly, we have isolated three queries of importance in *feature-based indexing* - vague query, k nearest-neighbor query and the range query. approach. The first two are based on the notion of "similarity" and different measures of similarity can be used. These *approximate* queries can be translated to various types of searching in a multidimensional space. For such searching, we have presented an indexing structure named the MB$^+$-tree. Using the linear-order-based approach in the MB$^+$-tree gives us several useful features desirable in comparison to the standard B$^+$-tree - it

- Supports the nearest-neighbor query very efficiently.

- Supports different similarity measures.

- Requires less space for leaf level entries.

Future work will include the implementation of the proposed tree so as to compare it with other multidimensional indexing methods with respect to the queries which are of importance in content-based retrieval in an image/video database. In addition to simulated data, we will try out the method on actual image features extracted out using image processing and computer vision methods.

REFERENCES

[1] R. Agrawal, C. Faloutsos, and A. Swami, "Efficient similarity search in sequence databases," FODO Conference, Evanston, IL, Oct. 1993.

[2] N. Beckmann, H-P Kriegel, R. Schneider and B. Seeger, "The R*-tree: an efficient and robust access method for points and rectangles," ACM SIGMOD, pp.322-331,1990.

[3] J.L. Bentley, "Multidimensional binary search tree used for associative searching," CACM, 18(9), pp.509-517, 1975.

[4] T-C. Chiueh, "Content-based image indexing," the 20th VLDB, 1994, pp. 582–593.

[5] R. Elmasri and A.B. Navathe, "Fundamentals of database systems," 2nd ed., The Benjamin/Cummings Publishing Company, Inc., Redwood City, CA, 1994.

[6] C. Faloutsos, R. Barber, M. Flickner, "J. Hafner, W. Niblack, D. PetKovic, and W. Equitz, Efficient and effective querying by image content," Journal of Intelligent Information Systems, Vol. 3, 1994, pp. 1–28.

[7] A. Guttman, "R-tree: a dynamic index structure for spatial searching," ACM SIGMOD, 1984, pp. 47–57.

[8] R. Mehrotra and J.E. Gary, "Feature-based retrieval of similar shapes," Intl. Conf. Data Engineering, 1993, pp. 108-115.

[9] W. Niblack, R. Barber, W. Equitz, M. Flickner, E. Glasman, D. Petkovic, P. Yanker, C. Faloustos and G. Taubin, "The QBIC Project: querying images by content using color, texture and shape," Proc. SPIE Conf. Storage and Retrieval for Image and Video Databases, 1993, pp. 173–187.

[10] J. Nievergelt, H. Hinterberger and K.C. Sevcik, "The grid file: an adaptable, symmetric multikey file structure," ACM Trans. on Database Systems, Vol. 9, No. 1, 1984, pp. 38–71.

[11] S.W. Smoliar and H. Zhang, "Content-based video indexing and retrieval," IEEE Multimedia, Summer Iss. 1994, pp. 62–72.

[12] A. Vellaikal, C.-C. Kuo, S. Dao, "Content-based retrieval of remote sensed images with VQ," Proc. SPIE Visual Information Processing IV, 1995, Orlando, to appear.

12

PLAYOUT MANAGEMENT IN MULTIMEDIA DATABASE SYSTEMS

Heiko Thimm, Wolfgang Klas

GMD-IPSI,DolivostraBe 15,
Darmstadt, Germany

1 INTRODUCTION

The presence of multiple multimedia data streams, e.g., an audio data stream in conjunction with several video data streams within a complex advertisement show, which presentation must proceed in a mutually synchronized manner, is one of the unique features that distinguishes digital multimedia data from traditional, conventional, alphanumeric data. Sample applications in which this property of digital multimedia is especially important are electronic publishing, digital libraries, computer-based training or teaching (edutainment), advertisement, entertainment, and infotainment. Here, to form modularly structured presentations, multimedia information is "glued" together by designers (i.e., presentation authors) in a *preorchestration phase*. While some standards relevant for this phase such as SGML/HyTime [18] or MHEG [30] are more oriented towards multimedia/hypermedia documents, others such as PREMO [17] and ScriptX [47] emphasize more time-based multimedia presentations. The result of this phase is a *predefined/preorchestrated* multimedia presentation for which it is assumed that its realization is requested many times by many different (possibly simultaneous) users. Many multimedia application domains such as those mentioned before need to support a pool of such preorchestrated multimedia presentations. Support of user interactions is an important property to be provided within this context ("interactive multimedia"). It provides for users flexibility in presentation control by offering the possibility to adapt the *presentation realization phase* to the individual needs.

Playout management, in general, is the task that deals with the realization of such arbitrary preorchestrated interactive multimedia presentations. It manages the presentation realization phase by taking care of the necessary system

318

tasks and their interdependencies according to the presentation specification. These system tasks are the device management, the data stream handling, the enforcement of the synchronization constraints, and the handling of random user interactions.

Several reasons motivate the usage of a multimedia database (system) within this context. The typical database properties (e.g., data sharing, persistency, durability, consistency) provide significant ease for the management of the information, application-specific presentations are composed of. A rich data model which provides modelling constructs for the representation of multimedia presentations allows for a fine-grained and powerful modelling of multimedia information. Since the presentations are created for multiple and simultaneous usage by many different users, proper support for multi-user access can obviously be provided by a database management system.

Considering both, the fact that many multimedia applications need playout management and the benefits of the usage of a multimedia database for these applications, this chapter addresses playout management for multimedia databases. After a description of playout management from a general point of view, we discuss alternative solutions for a framework in which playout management is provided for a multimedia database. A major issue related to this is to identify the components of the entire system and their functionality needed to perform the playout management task.

Based on the evaluation of alternative approaches, we motivate that multimedia database management systems should perform the playout management by providing an integrated generic playout management service. In analogy to the provision of, e.g., physical data independency, "playout management independency" is provided too. That is, the playout management service of the multimedia database management system manages the output devices involved, handles the data streams, enforces the synchronization constraints, handles random user interactions, and (for distributed systems) even adapts the presentation parameters to the changing characteristics of the overall system environment. From our perspective, this is a natural adjustment of database management system functionality to the new requirements of multimedia applications. This allows developers to focus on the application specific problems and relieves them from the task of encoding presentation functionality or the coupling of a presentation tool. The general goal is to achieve that storage, retrieval, buffer management, transport (over a possibly high-speed network), as well as playout management are handled by a comprehensive system, the multimedia database management system, by using proper services from, e.g., operating systems and networks. Aiming at this goal, efficient solutions for the management of the dependencies among these tasks can be achieved without compromising on the functionality. Furthermore, we expect, that other database internal components can deal with multimedia data more optimally if the playout management is well integrated with them.

An example of a multimedia database system with an integrated playout management service for time-based multimedia presentations is the AMOS system (Active Media Object Stores). AMOS is a research prototype of a distributed object-oriented multimedia database management system developed at GMD-IPSI [1, 33, 42, 28]. The development of the AMOS system is driven by our experiences with real multimedia applications [32, 39, 40, 41]. Its implementation is based on the object-oriented database management system VODAK [22, 48, 2] which has also been developed at GMD-IPSI. The integrated generic playout management service is provided by respective components of the AMOS client environment. The server supports the playout management by lower-level functions, and synchronization constraints aware data delivery.

In distributed multimedia database systems multimedia presentations are based on a distributed execution of the given presentation specification. The crucial aspect here is the way in which the data to be presented is made locally available at the presentation machine considering given timing constraints. We discuss *predictable* and *non-predictable* data availability as the two alternative approaches and show why distributed multimedia database systems should be able to deal with both. The use of predictable data availability based on, e.g., operating system scheduling and bandwidth reservation techniques, respectively, has been studied previously, e.g., [4, 9, 25]. In particular, the use of dynamic quality of service control within the context of predictable data availability has been investigated by several research groups, e.g., [11, 29, 46]. However, only little experience for the use of non-predictable data availability has been made so far, e.g., [20]. Thus, our discussion of playout management in distributed multimedia database systems is focused on the problems of using non-predictable data availability. We demonstrate how a sample multimedia presentation potentially is impacted by inappropriate local data availability. Furthermore, we introduce *reactive adaptive playout management* [43, 44, 45] as a novel general concept for overcoming these problems by adapting the presentation. This includes a proposal for a concrete scheme for reactive adaptive playout management which we use to make the playout management service of the AMOS system a reactive adaptive service. This scheme provides highly flexible reactive adaptive playout management by dynamically generated *individualized schedules of corrective actions*. *Adaptation schedules* are generated for optimized adaptation of multimedia presentations. Whereas, *compensation schedules* compensate previous adaptations in an optimized way.

This chapter is structured as follows. From a general point of view, a definition of playout management is given in section 2. In section 3, different approaches for playout management in multimedia database systems are discussed. The approach taken to realize playout management as integrated service of the AMOS multimedia database management system is explained in section 4. In section 5, we discuss playout management in distributed multimedia database systems including the novel concept of reactive adaptive playout management. Our concrete scheme for reactive adaptive playout management which we want to use for the AMOS system is described in section 6. Section 7 concludes the paper.

2 PLAYOUT MANAGEMENT

In this section, we describe what we mean with playout management from a more general point of view. Note that, we are talking about the presentation of stored multimedia data which are presented according to some specification (e.g., a presentation script) defined by a presentation author in an earlier preorchestration phase. First, we give a general informal definition. Second, we provide an analysis of the tasks playout management is composed of.

2.1 Informal Definition

Let us assume that multimedia presentations are represented by some consistent scheme, for example, presentation scripts covering all aspects of an interactive presentation, i.e., identification of data sources, output devices, quality of service parameters, temporal relationships between media presentations, synchronization of data streams, opportunities for user interactions, etc.. Taking a presentation script as input, multimedia playout management controls the presentation realization phase, i.e., the period of time, from the request to realize a presentation script until the presentation has been completed. Thus, multimedia playout management can be described as the set of tasks, which is necessary for the realization of arbitrary preorchestrated multimedia presentations at runtime. It deals with the issues of the physical data and device management level, rather than the issues of the logical specification level. It has to ensure that the constraints specified in the script are satisfied. However, since the multimedia presentations are performed for humans, there are certain tolerances allowing deviations within certain boundaries. In addition to the findings reported in [37], we also have some tolerances due to the fact, that a user may not recognize every kind of deviation. For example, for a human it may not make a difference whether a video clip is presented with 25 frames/second or 23 frames/second for some limited period of time. Furthermore, playout management has to cope with user interactions. With a minimum delay, it has to adjust the state and parameters of the presentation according to what has been demanded by the user.

For the construction of the input for the multimedia playout management, e.g., a presentation script, different approaches, mostly focusing on the aspect of the temporal relationships between the media streams (intermedia synchronization), have been suggested. Examples are the petri net-based OCPN approach [24], Active Objects [15], approaches based on a common time-line [3, 8], and multimedia scripting languages such as ScriptX [47]. There are already some respective standardization efforts like, e.g., MHEG [30] and PREMO [17]. Another important issue within this context deals with quality of service specification for multimedia presentations, e.g., [35]. Multimedia as well as hypermedia documents such as SGML/HyTime documents [18] can also be regarded as pre-orchestrated multimedia presentations. However, they are not oriented towards a specification of the temporal flow of the presentation. Instead, they support the concept of a *hyperlink* which provides navigational capabilities and to some degree makes the human viewer the driving force behind the presentation. In the scope of this paper, we do not need to go into further details of the specification of interactive multimedia presentations. We just can assume that they are specified by some appropriate specification means.

2.2 Playout Management Tasks

We detail the fundamental tasks $(t_1 - t_4)$ playout management, as informally defined above, is composed of. Later on, in section 5.4, we discuss more advanced tasks relevant for playout management.

t_1 : *Device Management.* Usually, multimedia presentations involve more than just a single output device. The spectrum of possibly involved devices to be monitored and controlled ranges from pure software based presentation devices (e.g., image presentation software) to such output devices, that exploit functionality available in hardware (e.g., JPEG-chip). For some of the latter kind of devices, in particular those, that cannot be shared by several simultaneous presentations (e.g., speakers), device utilization conflicts have to be recognized and handled properly. The crucial aspect of the device management is, that it needs to know exactly how to interact and how to periodically drive the different output devices, in case of continuous data presentations.

t_2 : *Data Stream Management.* The different data to be (possibly simultaneously) presented must be fetched from their sources and passed to the output devices (respectively to their data structures) which consume, i.e. present, the data. The path from the source to the sink can span several storage hierarchies, multiple machines, and networks. Each of the actually involved units introduces some delay. For continuous data, the stream management is critical, since playout deadlines for the presentation units (e.g., a frame with respect to a video) have to be considered.

t_3 : *Synchronization Enforcement.* In general, playout management has to enforce the synchronization constraints [36, 8, 14, 24] defined within the presentation specification. *Synthetic synchronization constraints* define the coarse grained temporal relationships between the different medias of the presentation. For example, such a constraint can define that the presentations of two medias have to be performed sequentially, simultaneously, or overlap by 15 seconds. In general, the well known 13 different temporal relationships that can be defined between two time intervals are relevant within this context [16]. Between video clips and their corresponding soundtracks *natural (intermedia) synchronization constraints*, i.e. lip synchronization constraints, may be defined. Moreover, for the various continuous medias, *intramedia synchronization constraints* have to be enforced aiming toward the achievement of a constant presentation rate and a minimal delay jitter. Note that, these types of constraints cannot be enforced in an isolated fashion, since they are interdependent with each other. In fact, the simultaneous management of all these constraints at runtime is one of the most challenging tasks. For its completion, appropriate operating system support should be available.

t_4 : *Support of Interactivity.* Playout management must be able to handle user interactions with the required responsiveness at any point in time during the execution of presentation scripts. The current state of execution of the presentation must be adjusted according to the user interaction within a minimal temporal delay. For example, if the user wants to halt the complete presentation (or only the presentation of one of the component medias), the presentation must be interrupted immediately.

3   PLAYOUT MANAGEMENT FOR MULTIMEDIA DATABASES

In this section, first, we motivate playout management for multimedia databases. Second, we state some basic design and evaluation criteria. Then, in general and in terms of these criteria, we investigate alternative solutions for the provision of playout management functionality for multimedia databases.

3.1   Motivation

Typically, multimedia applications are data-intensive applications. A set of application-specific data items must be maintained (i.e., kept consistent and up-to-date) and made accessible by usually many simultaneous users. This encourages the use of database technology and respective generic tools such as a database management system.

The *data definition language* of a database management system allows to develop an adequate database which reflects the semantics of the universe of discourse at hand. The *data manipulation language* of the database management system provides an adequate means to maintain the database. For efficient querying of the database, a *query language* is provided too. The transaction management of the database management system supports concurrent access to the database by many users. In general, these services offer the well-known database properties (e.g., data sharing, persistency, durability, consistency) and relieve the developers from implementing these services by themselves. The overall system will be highly reliable, stable, and fault-tolerant as well as provide a large degree of maintainability.

Playout management is an issue of many potential multimedia application domains such as digital libraries, publication environments, assistance systems, systems for training and education, and infotaintment. As discussed above, the use of a multimedia database provides many benefits to these applications. This motivates to investigate the way playout management can be generally provided within the framework of a multimedia database which stores the data to be presented.

3.2 Design and Evaluation Criteria

From an architectural point of view, the following design and evaluation criteria $(c_1 - c_3)$ are important for the evaluation of alternative solutions for database system based multimedia applications. Emphasis is on the playout management aspect. We will use these criteria in section 3.3 to investigate and discuss several concrete solutions.

c_1 : *Location of Playout Management Execution.* A crucial point is, that playout management is a resource intensive task (consider, for example, that a single MPEG-1 video presentation requires 30 frame presentation operations per second and a data rate of about 1.5 MBit/sec.). Thus, in multi-user systems which feature playout management functionality, the following two situations have to be avoided:

- playout management cannot be performed correctly due to a lack of resources consumed by other processes,

- computations to be done for other interactive users cannot be completed within a reasonable amount of time due to a lack of resources consumed by playout management processes.

To avoid these situations, playout management processes must not compete with other processes (of other users) for the same resources. This can be achieved by introducing a client/server architecture that provides local playout management at the client site.

c_2 : *Transparency of Playout Management Execution.* The motivation behind this evaluation criteria is, that we assume, that internal components of the database management system can deal with multimedia data more optimal if the playout management execution is well integrated with them. For example, playout management can deliver important information to the buffer manager of the database management system regarding the portions of the data to be kept in memory [28]. It can also deliver, e.g., information which allows the transaction manager of the database management system to decide if a write-lock can be granted for a portion of a data item currently presented. Furthermore, the storage management can benefit from information concerning the playout management. For example, if a continuous data presentation has been interrupted, the respective asynchronously performed corresponding fetch operations can also be interrupted or cancelled.

c_3 : *Data Transportation from Database to Output Devices.* Dealing with multimedia data means dealing with high volume and usually also continuous data. Hence, copying multimedia data can be very memory-intensive and time consuming. This is critical, since it can delay the transportation of the data from a source to a sink (i.e., the data structures of the output device in our case) resulting in playout deadline violations. Therefore, for a database management system supporting multimedia applications, a direct access mechanism is advantageous. This allows for applications to fetch data directly from the database buffer, i.e., data need not be copied layer by layer into special data structures (e.g., cursor variables) in order to perform application specific computations on these data.

3.3 Alternative Solutions

In the following, we present and evaluate (in general as well as in particular with respect to the criteria $c_1 - c_3$ described above) four alternative solutions, (a) to (d), for playout management for multimedia databases. Simultaneous access by multiple users to the multimedia database is managed by the database management system. Note that, we assume a database management system that supports adequate modelling primitives allowing to store the multimedia data as database objects. Furthermore, it is assumed that accessibility to portions (e.g., a subsequence of video frames or a block of audio samples, respectively) of these elements is provided.

For a simple example, let us assume a presentation script which specifies a time-based multimedia presentation. Suppose, the presentation gives an overview of the *AMOS Multimedia Playout Manager* which is described in section 4 of this chapter. Figure 1 shows a time-line based graphical representation of the structure of this multimedia presentation. Figure 2 presents a snapshot taken at some point in time during the presentation realization phase. The presentation consists of a sound-video clip (V1 and A1) in which a speaker introduces the concept of the AMOS Multimedia Playout Manager. The general information given in the first part consists of an explanation of the integration of the MPM within the multimedia database management system AMOS and an overview of the software architecture of the Multimedia Playout Manager (MPM). For this purpose, the speaker is relating to two corresponding pictures (P1 and P2) which are presented at the respective points in time within the speech. In the second part, a further sound-less-video clip (V2) is presented which shows a demo of the MPM explained by the speaker.

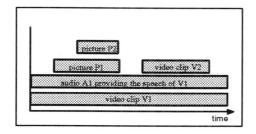

Figure 1   Structure of the AMOS MPM multimedia presentation

Figure 3 shows alternatives (a) to (d) by graphically abstracting from the client/server distribution of components. For alternatives (a) and (b), we assume that the presentation specification is externally stored, i.e., it is not part of the database. If a mapping of the specification into the modelling primitives provided by the database management system is possible, it can also be stored directly in the multimedia database. Consequently, the user is relieved from the additional task of managing the storage of the specification data. However, besides the retrieval of the data to be presented, in this case, the playout management component has also to deal with the retrieval of the specification. In alternative (c) and (d), we exactly assume such a solution.

(a) Application Based Playout Management

Description. The entire playout management functionality is realized by an application program [12, 23]. With respect to our sample presentation, playback of the continuous data streams, coarse grained as well as lip synchronization, and the handling of the user interactions is hard-wired and hand-coded individually in a proper manner. Note that, from a conceptional point of view, it makes no difference, if, as an extension, the application program provides functionality such that a particular type of specification or even arbitrary specifications are supported.

Discussion. Assuming that the database management system provides the necessary access mechanism (e.g., an appropriate application programming interface or a query interface), and supports an appropriate programming language with capabilities for implementing parallelism, the realization of the application program is still a workload-intensive and error-prone task. Especially, an efficient solution for the application's task of "connecting" the source of the data to the destination output devices is necessary. If intended as a generic

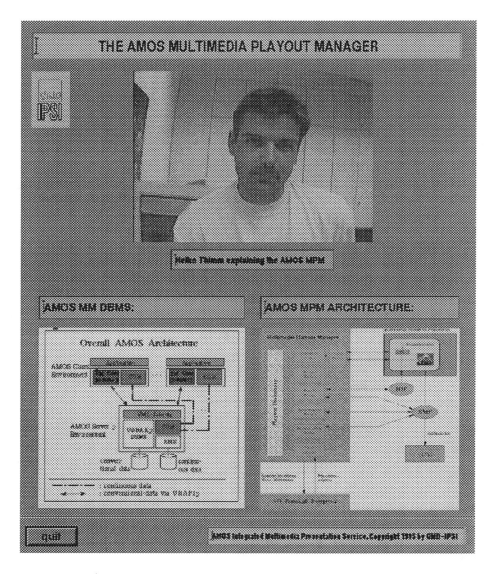

Figure 2   Snapshot of the AMOS MPM multimedia presentation

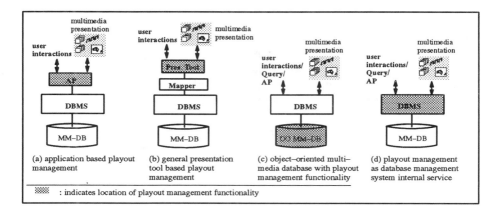

Figure 3 Alternative solutions for playout management for multimedia databases

solution for many different multimedia applications, an adequate concept needs to be worked out for how the playout management functionality can be used by other programs.

Concerning criterion c_1, the architecture of this solution can be easily mapped into a client/server-structure such that playout management is locally performed at client sides. With respect to criterion c_2, playout management remains transparent for the database management system. A judgement of this approach with respect to criterion c_3 is difficult, since the efficiency of the data transportation depends on the concrete mechanism supported by the database management system. However, there is the tendency, especially if a *direct read access* is not supported by the database management system[1], that an additional costly copy operation of the data from the database buffer into the application-specific main memory is performed.

(b) General Presentation Tool Based Playout Management

Description. In contrast to the previous approach, multimedia playout management is performed according to a more general scheme. A general presentation tool providing playout management functionality (e.g., a HyTime or MHEG

---

[1] With a direct read access, we mean the capability to allow applications to directly access a special data buffer of the database management system.

Presentation Engine) is coupled to the database management system. Differences between the interfaces of generic tools and the database management system are compensated by an *Interface Mapper*. The latter is a database application program which maps requests of the presentation tool into such a form, that they can be handled by the database management system. It also transforms answers back into a form manageable by the presentation tool. In our example, the playback of the continuous data stream, their temporal synchronization, especially the lip synchronization, between the video and its audio-soundtrack, as well as the user interactions are handled by the generic functionality of the coupled presentation tool.

Discussion. From a practical point of view, we are skeptical if such a reuse-based approach makes sense for advanced multimedia applications which demand an integrated management of multimedia information by a database management system. First of all, this approach realizes a loose coupling of the presentation environment with the database management system and its services. Coupling stand-alone general purpose presentation tools via an Interface Mapper usually leads to losses in functionality, efficiency, and flexibility. For example, most existing presentation tools are based on a filesystem interface. Thus, in order to achieve an efficient (main memory based) coupling, much effort has to be put into the realization of the Interface Mapper and maybe into the opening of some database system interfaces. Furthermore, a solution is needed to allow application programs to use the playout management services of the presentation tool.

Addressing criterion c_1, local playout management by means of a proper distributed architecture is easy to achieve. The playout management remains transparent to the database management system (criterion c_2). A general evaluation of the approach with respect to criterion c_3 is not possible, since concrete implementation approaches can vary to a large degree. However, one can expect that intermediate copy steps are introduced by the Interface Mapper.

(c) Object-Oriented Multimedia Database with Playout Management Functionality

Description. In contrast to using other types of databases, using an object-oriented database allows for encoding real world semantics of the application domain directly within the database. The entities of the universe of discourse are modelled by *database objects*. The *properties* of these objects model the structure, while the behavior is modelled by *methods*. The methods of an object can be called from outside (e.g., a query, an application program), by other database objects, or by the object itself, by sending *messages*. With respect to a multimedia application a soundtrack-less video clip can be modelled, e.g., as a database object [49]. The methods of such an object provide the typical functionality to present the video clip, possibly reflecting synchronization constraints such as the lip synchrony, and to control the presentation, e.g., *halt, restart, backward, fast-forward, go-to*. With respect to our running example, one can assume that both video clips, the audio-soundtrack, as well as the image, are available as such database objects. The presentation specification which consists of messages issued to these objects and respective control structures is modelled as a database object as well. At presentation realization time, this object invokes the specified methods of the (basic) media objects at the respective points in time.

Discussion. Using this approach, it is hard to meet the temporal requirements of multimedia presentations at runtime as well as the required responsiveness to user interactions. Playout management execution is based on the invocation of methods which is handled by components (e.g., message handler) belonging to the central database management system environment. To overcome this problem, concepts known from the area of realtime databases could be applied. Another alternative is to introduce the modelling primitive of a *schedule* as recently proposed in [1]. To achieve the required parallelism, the database management system must support *asynchronous method execution*. For the utilization of different output devices by methods, an adequate concept is required. It needs to be investigated if the devices can be modelled as objects as well [21, 38]. To relieve the users from the encoding of low-level device-specific functionality, adequate modelling primitives which encapsulate this functionality could be provided [38]. Furthermore, a solution addressing support of user interactions at presentation realization time is necessary.

Since the playout management functionality is directly implemented by means of the multimedia database objects, it is difficult to make it a client issue within a distributed system architecture (criterion c_1). Regarding criterion c_2, the provision of playout management information to other database management system components at presentation realization time is possible if one can utilize built-in datatype (e.g., audio, video) which provide basic playout operations integrated with other database management services. For example, upon execution of specific built-in methods (like *stop-a-video*) related to playout management (which semantics can be made known for the database management system), other database management system components could be notified. One advantage of this solution is that, the data to be presented (or pointers to these data) are only handled within the database management system. Thus, very efficient solutions for the data transportation are possible (criterion c_3).

(d) Playout Management as Database Management System Integrated Service

Description. In this architecture, playout management functionality is provided as integrated service of the database management system [42, 43, 44]. The latter interprets the presentation specification by mapping it into corresponding playout management actions (e.g. synchronization enforcement actions). These actions are carried out by the database management system. Furthermore, with a higher priority, the database management system handles the user interactions. In this case, the service can be integrated with other database management system services like transaction management, continuous storage management, concurrency control, etc. In our running example, the playout operations encoded in the presentation specification are interpreted and executed by the database management system itself aiming at the coarse grained synchronization of the involved continuous data streams, the enforcement of the lip synchrony, and the handling of the user interactions. This is done in close cooperation with *continuous object management* [28] for prefetching data needed.

Discussion. From the perspective of the users of the database management system, this approach certainly is preferable. The most adequate database support for multimedia applications demanding preorchestrated interactive multimedia presentations is provided. Developers can focus on the task of specifying multimedia presentations. However, a controversy discussion among database management system designers with respect to this approach can be expected. In our opinion, the key argument motivating this approach is, that playout management functionality as database management system integrated service is a quite natural extension. It provides *"playout management independency"* advantageous for many multimedia applications similar to the provision of independency from the physical data storage. Furthermore, it allows for the most useful integration with already existing database management services and further new services also required for multimedia database management systems.

An architecture realizing integrated playout management obviously should be open in the sense that the service can be adopted to specific application needs like the look-and-feel of the user interface or particular styles of presentations.

This can be achieved by providing proper standardized system interfaces which allow to "plug-in" any application-specific modules as long as these follow the interface specifications.

The issue whether or not the playout management task should be conducted by a multimedia database management system itself can be made dependent on the question if the system is intended to be used interactively or as a component within a complex program package [27]. However, in the context of interactive access to multimedia data and interactive multimedia querying of a database, playout management definitely becomes an important issue for the multimedia database management system.

Regarding criterion c_1, a client/server-architecture for the multimedia database management system such that the playout management is locally performed by clients is not difficult to achieve. Since everything is handled within the same system, efficient solutions for close cooperation of playout management components with other database management system components are possible (criterion c_2). For example, multimedia database systems have to provide continuous object management for time-dependent data between the server and a database system client. Providing integrated playout management as a database management system service covers the interfaces to the continuous object management, and, hence, frees application designers and programmers from dealing with the quite complicated interfacing of the application with the continuous object management. From our experience in developing multimedia applications, e.g., [39, 41, 40], we believe that the database management system can perform its other tasks (e.g., data retrieval from secondary storage, data buffering, network-based transport of data) in a more optimal way, due to its knowledge provided by playout management components. For the same reason, the data to be presented can be moved very efficiently from the sources to the output devices (criterion c_3) and user interactions can be handled with an excellent responsiveness. This has a direct impact on the (often quite heavy) computations performed by a multimedia database management system.

4 THE AMOS APPROACH

The objective of the AMOS project (Active Media Object Stores) at GMD-IPSI is the development of concepts needed for multimedia database management systems. As starting point, we employ the object-oriented database management system VODAK which has been developed at GMD-IPSI within the past six years [22, 2, 48]. Our concepts are integrated with the VODAK system aiming at the development of an object-oriented, and - with respect to a client/server architecture - distributed multimedia database management system. Within this development process, the AMOS system (Figure 4) is already used in prototypes and applications, e.g., [39, 41, 40]. Thus, our concepts and implementations are based on real experiences with multimedia database management system applications and they are constantly evaluated against user requirements.

In addition to the new system internal components which are realized, in our first development step, we have extended VODAK's modelling language VML [22, 48] to support multimedia datatypes. Furthermore, we also strive to extend our query language, called VQL [2], by concepts for querying multimedia data.

In this section, the AMOS approach to multimedia playout management aiming towards the realization of a respective database management system integrated service is introduced. Our approach parallels alternative (d) discussed in section 3, in general. First, we present the overall system architecture. Then, we describe the components which perform the playout management. In the last part of this section, a sample application for the education and entertainment of chess players, which was realized by using the AMOS playout management components is presented.

4.1 Architecture

In the following, we describe the architecture of the AMOS system focusing on the playout management issue.

As illustrated in Figure 4, the AMOS multimedia database management system is a distributed system based on a client/server architecture. An important aspect of the server environment is that the management of conventional data is separated from the management of the continuous data. The VODAK database management system is employed for the former, while for the latter the architecture includes a so-called *External Media Server* (XMS)[2] and a *Continuous Object Manager* (COM) [28]. The XMS deals with low level storage management issues and enables us to support high-volume continuous data - which might not fit into main memory in one portion - by allowing access to parts of the continuous data (e.g., with respect to video, access to a single video

---

[2] Our current implementation of the XMS is based on the storage management system EOS [7] which provides support for long objects.

frame or a sequence of video frames). The COM provides asynchronous buffer loading and replacement for continuous data. The COM component at the server explicitly supports the multi-user aspect by, e.g., the notion of hot spot objects, which are objects kept in the server buffer if a high access frequency is detected.

The client environment is kept "simple". Certain components of the server environment do not exist in the client environment. Clients can invoke methods stored in the VODAK database and receive their results as well as submit queries to VODAK's query interpreter and receive the query result using the *VODAK Remote Application Program Interface* (VRAPI). This allows to fetch conventional data from the VODAK database. The COM of the client environment makes continuous data stored in the XMS of the server available on demand in the client's local buffer. This is achieved by asynchronous adaptive prefetching of data (i.e., continuous data is always locally cached) and by performing proper buffer replacement strategies [28]. This allows us, to some extent, to satisfy the time continuity required for multimedia presentations and to enforce synchronization constraints. Local caching is also a means to nullify delay jitter. Furthermore, in case of presentation repetition or backward presentation, already available data units must not be retransmitted. A multimedia transport protocol is employed for the transportation of the continuous data from the server COM into the client COM. The client environment includes the playout management components which perform the playout management tasks. In section 4.2, we break down the respective box of Figure 4 and provide a comprehensive discussion of these components. The playout management components exploit the services provided by both, the COM and the VRAPI.

4.2 Multimedia Playout Management Service

Our first approach to playout management for the AMOS architecture was the *Interaction Manager* (IAM) [38]. The IAM paralleled the approach (c) described in section 3, except for the fact, that it was focused on only single media presentations. That is, the IAM was based on an implementation of methods to present and control the playback of a video or an audio. This functionality was defined as behavior of database objects. Although this was an elegant way of handling single media presentations by an object-oriented database system, it turned out, that an extension of the IAM such that it can also support multimedia presentations composed of multiple (possibly simultaneous) medias becomes very difficult. First, realizing synchronization of multiple media streams by appropriate method implementations requires the extension of the

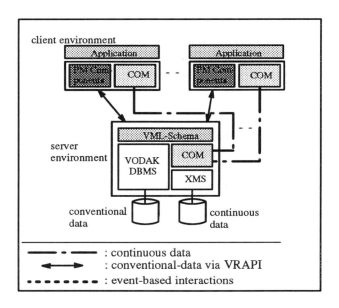

Figure 4   Overall architecture of the distributed multimedia database management system AMOS

database system by real time concepts. This is a prerequisite to provide the basic database management system primitives necessary for an implementation of the required methods. Second, efficient support of multimedia data streams requires continuous object management by the database system which requires another extension of the database management system. Based on an intensive evaluation of alternative solutions summarized in section 3.3, we decided to follow an approach in which playout management is realized as integrated service of the multimedia database management system. In this case, the synchronization aspects as well as the continuous object management can be integrated with the corresponding components of the database management system.

The AMOS playout management service realizes arbitrary time-based interactive multimedia presentations according to a given *presentation plan*. A presentation plan is not directly written by the designer of an intended presentation. Instead, it is generated dynamically at presentation realization time from a high-level specification[3]. This high-level specification[4] is made in VML

---

[3] For that reason, we use the notion of presentation plan rather then the notion of presentation script.

[4] Similar to [35], the specification includes presentation quality parameters.

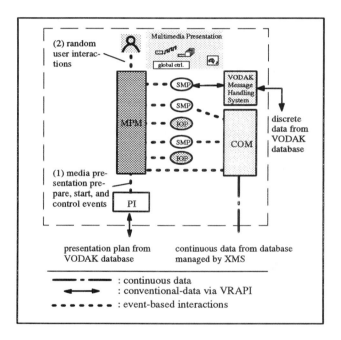

Figure 5 AMOS client environment performing a multimedia presentation

(see page 334) by support of an appropriate graphical presentation authoring environment and then stored in the VODAK database which stores conventional data. A generated plan provides a logical time axis and it contains the identifiers of the data to be presented, which are either stored in the VODAK database or the XMS. For each data object, it contains additional information about what the control interface for user interactions (e.g., stop button or slider) should look like, screen coordinates (for visual presentations) as well as requirements concerning the inter-media synchronization (i.e., quality of synchronization, e.g., lip synchrony). To gain flexibility, the high level VML-modelling can leave certain parts of the course of the presentation open to the user. For example, the actual user can be asked to decide how the presentation should proceed by selecting an alternative from a list of possible continuations (subpresentations) or available medias, respectively. These lists are dynamically generated by querying the VODAK database at presentation realization time. In the specification of the presentation, this kind of user participations, called *complex user interactions*, are explicitly reflected while *simple user interactions* (e.g., stopping a video) are neglected. At presentation realization time, the plan may only be generated up to the next complex user interaction encoded in the VML-modelling.

In the following, we first describe the different playout management components separately. Then, we show how playout management is performed by these components by means of issuing and handling events (Figure 5). We especially will detail our approach towards synchronization enforcement.

Playout Management Components

In the following, the playout management components (Figure 5) are described. The first and second component are dynamically created as temporarily (usually in multiple incarnations) existing components (threads) during a presentation. The remaining components exist all the time.

(1) SMP: Single Media Presenter. They are media- and coding-type specific execution units which present an individual data item as well as adjust (e.g., halt, start, abort, direction change, position change - depending on the concrete media) and fine tune (e.g., change of presentation speed, change of quality of service - depending on the concrete media) its presentation on demand. This involves the management of the output device. With respect to continuous data, SMPs drive the output device and the data delivery such that the intra-media synchronization constraints are enforced. SMPs presenting discrete data fetch the data from the VODAK database by using the VRAPI. For continuous

data stored in XMSs, the services of the client COM are employed. Feedback information, i.e., information regarding the actual data needs of the client, are passed during a running presentation by SMPs to the COM. Application-specific SMPs can easily be added to the standard set of predefined SMPs. This is done by providing the new SMPs as a software library which "couples" the SMPs to the MPM (will be explained later) according to the standardized interface supported by the MPM. For example, this way for a multimedia presentation of a chess game, we realized and coupled a chess-SMP which can simulate the moves of the competitors on a chessboard graphically (section 6).

(2) IOP: Interaction Object Presenter. They visualize and manage components of the user interface allowing interactive control and/or providing some information about the presentation (e.g., hot spot viewing, audio control panel). However, they do not directly handle user interactions. Instead, they pass the relevant information about user interactions to the MPM (explained below), where the actual handling takes place. The client environment supports a standard collection of IOPs, from which the control interfaces specified in the plan have to be chosen. The actual set of IOPs determines the interaction opportunities a presentation provides to the user. Similar to the support of application-specific SMPs, we also support application-specific IOPs. They are added to the standard set of IOPs by the provision of a respective software library in which the "coupling" must be encoded according to the standardized interface supported by the MPM.

(3) PI: Plan Interpreter. This component subsequently works off the actual presentation plan which is generated at the server and fetched from the VODAK database. The statements of the plan are mapped into a chronologically ordered stream of parameterized events issued to the MPM (explained next). The following types of events are distinguished:

- media presentation prepare events,

- media presentation start events,

- media presentation control events including media presentation termination.

To guarantee correct temporal triggering of the corresponding events (considering the coarse grained synchronization constraints of the plan), the PI maintains a realtime axis. Thus, the PI can be seen as the driving force of the multimedia presentations reflecting the temporal relationships between the various data streams. Upon completion of a complex user interaction notified by the MPM, the PI issues information required to continue the plan generation to the server.

(4) MPM: Multimedia Playout Manager. The MPM manages the parallelism typical for multimedia presentations and deals with the enforcement of the various constraints, especially the intermedia synchronization constraints. Furthermore, it handles the various dependencies among the different playout management tasks and reacts to random user interactions. The MPM itself is bypassed by the data to be presented and is only in charge of the overall management of a presentation. In our architecture, the MPM is the master, and the SMPs as well as IOPs are the slaves. These slaves are dynamically instantiated, controlled, coordinated, and adjusted according to the events of the PI and the user interactions.

It is reasonable to include more functionality into the MPM as it is described above. Especially, problems related to the distribution aspect (discussed in section 5) can be adequately handled by extending the functionality of the MPM. In section 6, a concrete scheme that makes the MPM capable to adapt the presentation to the changing properties of the overall environment (e.g., system load variations of server, variations of network bandwidth, variations of the local computing capacity) is discussed.

Event Driven Playout Management

In the following, we first describe the principles of the operation of all involved components realizing the playout management. Then, we detail the synchronization enforcement as one of the fundamental playout management tasks (see section 2.2).

Principles of Operation
During a presentation, (i) a discrete stream of ordered events generated by the PI and (ii) a discrete stream of random user interaction events are simultaneously received by the MPM - from the beginning until the end of a multimedia presentation (Figure 5). The patterns of both streams of events (i and ii) usually differ for each plan, user (even if same plan is used), and also presentation repetition (even if plan and user are still the same). For non-interactive presentations, i.e., if no user interactions are allowed by the plan (i.e., absence of IOPs), or if the user is strictly passive, there is no interaction events stream at all. However, if user interaction takes place, then the corresponding interaction events stream has a higher priority than the event stream issued by the PI, since the interaction events stream reflects the individual user's demands. These are

more important than the strict plan execution, and as a result of this kind of prioritization, responsiveness to user interactions is increased. The resulting merged event stream received by the MPM is mapped into corresponding playout actions such as instantiation of new SMPs or IOPs, modification of SMP states or parameters.

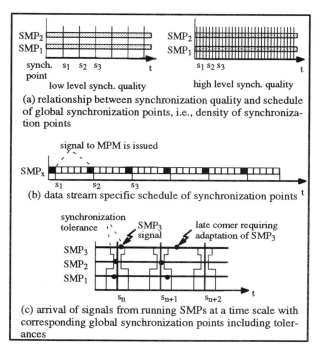

(a) relationship between synchronization quality and schedule of global synchronization points, i.e., density of synchronization points

(b) data stream specific schedule of synchronization points ^{t}

(c) arrival of signals from running SMPs at a time scale with corresponding global synchronization points including tolerances

Figure 6 Intermedia synchronization based on synchronization points and a simple signalling mechanism

Synchronization Enforcement

Asynchrony with respect to intermedia synchronization constraints can be detected via the use of *synchronization points* (lying within certain boundaries) and a simple signalling mechanism performed by the participating SMPs. This concept is similar to the concept of the *Synchronizer* [8]. Depending on the synchronization quality defined by media presentation prepare events, a formula to generate an appropriate schedule of *global* synchronization points (including lower and upper bounds for each participating data stream) is determined. A synchronization point, in general, specifies the data units that must have been presented by the participating SMPs at a specific point in time. The difference in time between two succeeding synchronization points is reciprocal to the requested synchronization quality, i.e., a high quality (e.g., lip synchrony) implies a short difference in time and vice versa (Figure 6a). The formula together with information about the involved SMPs (e.g., presentation rate, quality of service parameters) are registered in the *Global Synchronization Dictionary* which is managed by the MPM. Furthermore, in the *Private Synchronization Dictionaries* of each participating SMP, a formula to generate a data stream specific schedule of synchronization points is registered (Figure 6b). At each of these synchronization points, i.e., if the presentation of the specified data unit is completed, the corresponding SMP issues a signal to the MPM. At plan realization time (Figure 6c), the MPM can detect asynchrony for each intermedia synchronization constraint by monitoring the notification messages received from the SMPs with respect to the global synchronization points. In case of asynchrony, the MPM carries out proper corrective actions such as directing a SMP to drop or duplicate data units, restricted or non-restricted blocking, presentation rate manipulations, global presentation speed manipulations, or it (in the worst case) lets the user decide how to handle the situation by offering alternatives.

Sample Application for the Education and Entertainment of Chess Players

Our playout management approach supports a large spectrum of multimedia application domains due to its openness with respect to application-specific demands. To demonstrate this, a further concrete sample multimedia presentation is shown in this section. The presentation provides to the user comprehensive information about a chess game between the two famous chess players Kasparov and Anand. The presentation includes the pictures of both competitors and some audio explanations which describe their strategy. However, the most interesting aspect of this presentation is that it also includes a chronological animation of the competitors' moves on a chessboard. This could be achieved by implementing a generic chess-SMP which performs concrete moves according to parameterized messages issued by the MPM. This SMP was "coupled" to the MPM via the standardized interface supported by the MPM. The concrete moves are defined in the presentation plan which corresponding VML-representation is stored in the VODAK database. Based on this approach, e.g., a library which contains multimedia presentations of the most prominent games of chess history for educational or entertainment purposes can be developed very easily. On the one side, the database management system takes care of the playout management for many potentially simultaneous presentations. On the other hand, it provides also the well-known database system properties and helpful services for the user administration and maintenance of the database. Figure 7 shows a screendump of the chess presentation. At this snapshot of the presentation there are several SMPs and IOPs active: an IOP for the quit-button, six SMPs for the text fields shown, two SMPs for the presentation of the photo-images of the competitors, and the (application-specific) chess presenter which provides an animation of the game on a graphical chess board.

5 PLAYOUT MANAGEMENT IN DISTRIBUTED MULTIMEDIA DATABASE SYSTEMS

This section is devoted to playout management in distributed multimedia database systems [43, 44, 45]. First, we discuss the two alternatives for the delivery of the data to a presentation machine and motivate that, distributed multimedia database management systems should be able to deal with both of them. Next, we detail the problems one can face when a distributed execution of a multimedia presentation is based on non-predictable data availability. After that, we discuss issues relevant for the handling of these problems. This prepares the introduction of the general concept of *reactive adaptive playout management* given in the last part of this section.

5.1 Predictable and Non-Predictable Data Delivery

Driven by specific application properties, many multimedia database systems need to have a distributed architecture [5]. Typically, this means that a database must be maintained at a single or at several sites and that network-based access to the database from other sites must be supported. This support must explicitly reflect the specific requirements of dealing with multimedia data. With respect to multimedia presentations, e.g., this means that the data must be delivered from the database to the remote presentation sites such that smooth presentations which satisfy the given timing and synchronization con-straints can be performed. Since multimedia presentations usually embrace a large amount of data which in many cases would not fit into the main memory of the presentation machine as a whole, a "fetch-all-and-then-present"-strategy (such as employed in the first version of the *world wide web* [6]) cannot be used. Alternative strategies are necessary in which at the same time some

Figure 7   Screendump of chess presentation

data units are presented, the data units to be presented next are already delivered. A more comprehensive discussion of this is available, e.g., in [31]. Our focus with respect to this is that, such strategies either can be based on *predictable/guaranteed* local data availability[5] or *non-predictable/non-guaranteed* local data availability. The crucial difference between both is that only in the former it is guaranteed that the required data units (i.e., those that must be presented next) are available at the presentation machine at the required point in time. Whereas, in the latter, potentially, data units are not available in time[6]. However, our discussion is focused on the case where data units come late.

Although, the use of non-predictable data availability seems not to be very adequate, we argue that for distributed multimedia database systems in general both, non-predictable data availability and predictable data availability must be considered. This is a prerequisite to support applicability for different kinds of (1) computing environments, (2) different types of multimedia applications, and (3) different preferences of the user. Each of these three aspects is explained in the following:

1. Different kinds of computing environment should be supported since predictable data availability requires specific hardware and software (e.g., realtime operating system, communication system supporting resource reservation). When these are not available, then the use of non-predictable data availability is the only way to support multimedia presentations within a distributed multimedia database system.

2. Some multimedia applications strongly desire predictable data availability since they cannot cope with the potential negative effects of non-predictable data availability. Other applications, however, can easily cope with these negative effects. A system that only supports predictable data availability strictly forces the application designers to use predictable data availability even if the use of non-predictable data availability is more superior.

3. Predictable data availability involves a realtime framework for all components along the data delivery path from the database to the output-devices. All these components have to be reconciled with each other. This requires a deep understanding of the respective underlying technologies such as resource scheduling and bandwidth reservation. Therefore, for example,

---

[5] That is, there is an end-to-end guarantee for the entire data delivery path from the source(s) to the destination.

[6] They might not become available at all.

when this understanding is not available, some application designers would rather prefer to use non-predictable data availability.

5.2 Distributed Execution of Multimedia Presentations with Non-Predictable Data Availability

In general, when a multimedia presentation is performed within a distributed environment then (ideally) the user should not recognize the lower level system tasks. For example, the retrieval of the data from the respective source(s) and their delivery over a network to make them locally available for the playout must be transparent. If a non-predictable data availability approach is used, the availability of the data at the presentation machine at certain points in time (i.e., guaranteed data rates) is not ensured. A distributed multimedia database system must be aware of the potential problems that can result form this. In the following, we discuss these potential problems using a sample multimedia presentation together with a corresponding *required* performance profile [7]. To discuss the problem, we assume also a fictive *actual performance profile* [8]. Note that, these profiles address the performance for the delivery of the data to the user's machine.

The sample presentation could be a complex advertisement show of a car producer at a trade fair introducing the four models of its new car generation. Figure 14 shows a snapshot of such an advertisement show. Figure 8a illustrates its structure which consists of three phases. Each phase can be decomposed into several media presentations (MP). The *introduction phase* which introduces what the advertisement is all about and which provides a brief introduction of each of the new models consists of audio A1 & A2 and videos V1-V5. The *detailing phase* which provides detailed information about each of the four new models embraces audio A3, videos V6-V13, and pictures P1-P4. The *conclusion* which repeats the main features of each model and which summarizes the advertisement's main message consists of audio A4 & A5, and videos V14-V19. Note that, as typical for multimedia presentations of many application domains, there are periods of time with several simultaneous media presentations. For example, in the introduction phase and the conclusion of our sample multimedia presentation, temporarily, we even have four videos

---

[7] That is, the performance required to perform the multimedia presentation as specified.

[8] That is, the actual system capacity available at presentation realization time to perfrom the multimedia presentation.

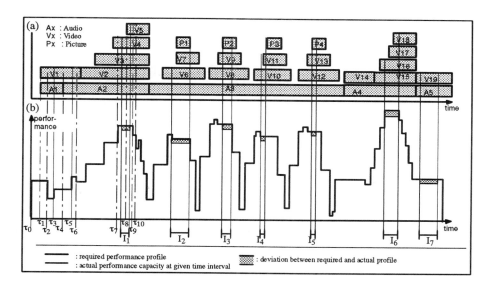

Figure 8 (a) structure of sample multimedia presentation, (b) performance profile required to achieve local data availability and periods of time with performance deviations

simultaneously presented together with an audio. With respect to, e.g., the introduction phase, we can imagine that this is done to allow for the users a better comparative visual evaluation of the four different car models.

In Figure 8b, the bold line approximates the performance profile required in order to have at any point in time[9] throughout the presentation for all component media presentations, the required data units always locally available prior to their playout such that the playout deadlines are met. For a more detailed analysis of this, we introduce the notions of *data delivery activity* and *data presentation activity* defined as follows:

- A *data delivery activity* $\alpha_{d,MP}$ makes the data required for media presentation MP available at the presentation machine such that it can be presented to the user. It retrieves the corresponding data from a multimedia database and transports the data over a network. Media type-specific nominal parameters specify the required performance of a data delivery activity.

---

[9]Note, we abstract from user interactions.

■   A *data presentation activity* $\alpha_{p,MP}$ presents the locally available data of
    media presentation MP to the user. It issues the data units to the respec-
    tive output device. Media type-specific nominal parameters specify the
    required performance of a data presentation activity.

Table 1 summarizes some points in time t_i at presentation realization time. It
explains what both the data delivery activities (column 2, 3, 4) and the data
presentation activities (column 5, 6, 7) deal with at the given points in time.
We differentiate between starting $(\alpha_{d,MP}^s/\alpha_{p,MP}^s)$, executing $(\alpha_{d,MP}/\alpha_{p,MP})$,
and terminating $(\alpha_{d,MP}^t/\alpha_{p,MP}^t)$ data delivery activities/data presentation activities.

Due to system-internal constraints (e.g., network bandwidth, CPU-time available for fetching the data from a secondary storage device), one cannot assume
that the actual performance capacity available at presentation realization time
always matches the profile of the required capacity. This is the focal point of
this problem analysis. Thus, in a simplified manner, in Figure 8b, some *critical
time intervals* I_j are considered. For the sample multimedia presentation, it is
assumed that in these time intervalls, the actual system performance is below
the required one. That is, the thin lines (i.e., lower horizontal edges of grey
boxes) show the actual (insufficient) performance at the given time intervals.
Note that, the existence of these critical time intervals is not considered in Figure 8a which shows how the presentation would look like if system performance
is always sufficient throughout the entire presentation execution. In any other
case, the presentation would look like different to that.

In table 2, with respect to each of the given critical time intervals I_j, the
potential impact on the executing activities which deliver *continuous* data is
characterized. It is shown, how the data rates of these activities could be
impacted. Instead of giving concrete values, it is described for each activity,
if its current data rate either matches the required one (column 4) or if it is
lower than the required one (column 3). For this purpose, a function denoted
by $cr(\alpha_{d,MP})$ is assumed that computes the current data rate of the given
data delivery activity and a function denoted by $rr(\alpha_{d,MP})$ which computes
the required data rate. Table 2 also reflects the fact that performance lacks do
not necessarily need to influence all executing data delivery activities. That is,
as a result of a performance lack, either all executing data delivery activities
have a lower data rate (time interval I_2, I_5, and I_7) or only some but not all
of them (time intervals I_1, I_3, I_4, I_6). Note that, the lacking performance for
the prefetching process simultaneously also impacts other properties such as
the delay jitter, or synchronization quality. The interesting fact to be pointed

τ_j	$\alpha_{d,MP}^s$	$\alpha_{d,MP}^t$	$\alpha_{d,MP}$	$\alpha_{p,MP}^s$	$\alpha_{p,MP}^t$	$\alpha_{p,MP}$
0	A1 V1		A1 V1			
1			A1 V1	A1 V1		A1 V1
2		A1	V1			A1 V1
3	A2		A2 V1			A1 V1
4			A2 V1	A2	A1	V1 A2
5	V2		A2 V1 V2			A2 V1
6		V1	A2 V2			A2 V1
7	V5		A2 V2-V5			A2 V2-V4
8			A2 V2-V5	V5		A2 V2-V5
9		V2	A2 V3-V5			A2 V2-V5
10		A2	V3-V5			A2 V2-V5

Table 1 Data delivery and presentation activities performed at some points in time. Read this table as follows: At time τ_0 the starting data delivery activities are $\alpha_{d,A1}^s$ and $\alpha_{d,V1}^s$ delivering data for component media presentation A1 and V1

out is that there is no possibility to make a reasonable prediction of what the influence on these properties will look like.

In almost all cases, if data delivery activities do not perform as required, presentation deficiencies are implied. The following deficiencies are among the most prominent ones:

I_j	$\alpha_{d,MP}$	$cr(\alpha_{d,MP}) \leq rr(\alpha_{d,MP})$	$cr(\alpha_{d,MP}) = rr(\alpha_{d,MP})$
1	A2 V2-V5	V2 V3	A2 V4 V5
2	A3 V6&V7	A3 V6 V7	
3	A3 V8&V9	A3 V8	V9
4	A3 V10&V11	A3 V11	V10
5	A3 V12&V13	A3 V12 V13	
6	A4 V15&V18	A4 V15 V16	V17 V18
7	A5 V19	A5 V19	

Table 2 Hypothetical properties at some critical time intervals with respect to data rates. Read this table as follows: In time interval I_7 the data delivery activities $\alpha_{d,A5}$ and $\alpha_{d,V19}$ are executing, i.e., delivering the data for component media presentation A5 and V19, whereas in either case the current data rate is lower than the required one.

- loss of intramedia synchrony, i.e., violation of intramedia synchronization constraints (e.g., presentation duration of the video frames is not constant such that the overall video presentation is not performed smoothly),

- loss of intermedia synchrony, i.e., violation of intermedia synchronization constraints (e.g., audio is out of synch with its corresponding video),

- loss of presentation smoothness, i.e., noticeably varying global presentation speed,

- presentation interruptions.

Usually, these deficiencies do not occur isolated from each other. The consequence of inadequate local data availability in most cases consists of a combination of these presentation deficiencies. In the worst case (assuming no reactions to that situation), for the user, the multimedia presentation can evolve to an absolutely useless, since non-coordinated, multimedia presentation.

5.3 Handling Inappropriate Local Data Availability

It has been shown that the distributed execution of multimedia presentations with non-predictable data availability is one of the issues that distributed multimedia database systems must address. The cruicial aspect of this issue is the potential occurence of *performance fluctuations* which can cause inappropriate local data availability for executing multimedia presentations. Since, due to the non-predictability, such situations cannot be avoided, a distributed multimedia database system must handle these situations. Two of the most relevant strategies to handle inappropriate local data availability are:

- *Pause and continue only when performance becomes sufficient again.* The multimedia presentation is interrupted as long as the system performance stays insufficient to make the data available as required. It is continued when the system performance recovers. The primary objective of this strategy is to enforce that the multimedia presentation is precisely executed according to a given specification. It does not allow any deviations from the specification. One drawback of this strategy is that there is no way to determine the duration of these interruptions. Thus, the user is forced to wait for an unpredictable amount of time. Another drawback is, that such interruptions might occur frequently and not as an exception when there is heavy load in the system. In general, sample scenarios adequate for this strategy are those in which emphasis is on the precise playback of multimedia presentations.

- *Overcome lacking performance by timely adaptations.* The multimedia presentation is adapted in time such that lower system performance is required and, because of that, the presentation can overcome the momentary insufficient system performance. The primary objective of this strategy is to avoid interruptions of the multimedia presentation on the expense of the precision of the presentation execution with respect to a given specification[10]. It uses deviations from a presentation specification as an

---

[10] In more concrete terms, precision with respect to presentation quality parameters included in the given specification, e.g., [35]

instrument to withstand insufficient system performance. The drawback
of this approach is that in some situations many deviations are required
such that the remaining parts of the presentation may not semantically
render a reasonable multimedia presentation anymore. In general, sample
scenarios adequate for this strategy are those in which the presentations
provide a high degree of adaptability[11]

Some of the potential scenarios are likely to be more adequate for either one
or the other strategy. However, in the end, the choice of one of the strategies
depends on the individual user and its specific requirements at the time he
wants to have the multimedia presentation (e.g., what is the purpose of the
presentation, what is his knowledge about the topic of the presentation, does
he have a limited or unlimited amount of time available for the consumption
of the presentation).

Transmitter-Active Control vs. Receiver-Active Control
The focus of our continuing discussion is on the more challenging second strategy which aims at adapting a running multimedia presentation to overcome
inappropriate local data availability. More precisely, the goal of the strategy is
to lower the required performance profile whenever it goes beyond the actual
performance capacity available. The amount of data to be retrieved from the
database and to be transported over a communication network to the receivers
is dynamically tailored. This is in contrast to static solutions based on static
and semi-static playout scheduling discussed, e.g., in [26].

Depending on the concrete instance which dynamically manages the tailoring,
we differentiate between *receiver active control* and *transmitter active control*.
When the data source, i.e., the transmitter of the data, dynamically adapts the
required performance profile considering the actual performance capacity of the
system, the underlying scheme is called a transmitter-controlled scheme[12], e.g.,
[13, 26]. In contrast to that, if the adaptation is controlled by the receiver
of the data, the underlying scheme is called a receiver-controlled scheme, e.g.,
[20]. Some concrete solutions involve feedback messages issued by the receiver
to better adapt the data delivery to the individual needs of the receiver and
the overall system properties, e.g., [34, 10].

---

[11] That is, many potential adaptations which do not change the presentation semantics are
supported.
[12] Many techniques proposed for managing congestion for multimedia streams are
transmitter-controlled.

From our point of view, receiver-active control has several inherent advantages over transmitter-active control [20]:

■ Receiver-active control reduces the computational load on the transmitter. With respect to multimedia database systems, this is an important argument since usually they have to support many simultaneously accessing users.

■ Congestions at any component of the data delivery path (i.e., congestion at the storage system, congestion at the database server and network congestion) can be detected uniformly by one mechanism at the receiver. That is, other detection mechanisms for the other components are obsolete.

■ The receiver has better and more immediate knowledge of how the data is arriving from the transmitter.

■ The receiver has more precise and comprehensive knowledge about the current state of the running multimedia presentation which is important for deciding how a running presentation can be adapted.

■ The consideration of individual user preferences with respect to how to adapt a running multimedia presentation (that may even change) is easier to achieve. In more concrete terms, information about the preferences need not to be sent to the transmitter.

5.4   Reactive Adaptive Playout Management

Reactive adaptive playout management [43, 44, 45] is a novel concept which makes a distributed multimedia database system aware of the potential problems of non-predictable data availability for performing multimedia presentations. It makes the distributed multimedia database system capable to handle the problems according to a strategy which dynamically adapts an executing multimedia presentation accordingly (see previous section). This handling is done as part of the playout management which is properly enhanced such that the problems are handled in a reactive self-adaptive way.

In the following, we show the basic features of reactive adaptive playout management by presenting an illustrative example which involves a sample multimedia presentation similar to the one discussed in section 5.2. Figure 9 illustrates the reactive adaptive behavior and its impact on the realization of the sample multimedia presentation. It shows:

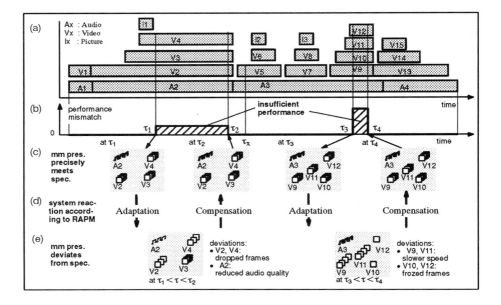

Figure 9   Realization of a sample multimedia presentation using reactive adaptive playout management

(a) a sample multimedia presentation (e.g., advertisement show of a car producer at a trade fair),

(b) two fictive mismatches between the *required* system performance and the *actual* one at presentation execution time - the result of such a mismatch is that the data is not adequately made available locally at the presentation site, i.e., the required data rates are not supported,

(c) the multimedia presentation *before* the system switches to a deviating presentation and *after* it switched back,

(d) the respective reaction of the system according to reactive adaptive playout management,

(e) how the multimedia presentation is adapted by reactive adaptive playout management.

In general, as a prerequisite for efficient reactive adaptive playout management, the system behavior must be based on a dedicated, well-elaborated scheme.

6 A HIGHLY FLEXIBLE RAPM-SCHEME

In the following, a scheme for reactive adaptive playout management (*RAPM-scheme* for short) is described which is targeted towards optimized support for executing multimedia presentations with non-predictable data availability [43]. In designing this scheme, special emphasis was put on flexibility since one crucial aspect of reactive adaptive playout management is that it must reflect the individual conditions of the overall system (e.g., avoidance of "overreactions") and the needs of the individual user in an optimized way [45, 44]. Both aspects must not be ignored, otherwise the concept of reactive adaptive playout management will not be accepted by the users.

The playout management service of the AMOS distributed multimedia database management system introduced in section 4 will be enhanced such that it behaves according to this scheme. First, we explain the goals that we wanted to achieve by developing the RAPM-scheme. Next, we describe the underlying system model to be considered. Then we detail our RAPM-scheme.

6.1 Development Goals and Underlying System Model

Our efforts to develop a concrete scheme for reactive adaptive playout management were guided by several subgoals summarized as follows:

- *Receiver-active control* as system behavior resulting from the RAPM-scheme.

- *Compensation of adaptations* when system performance becomes sufficient again. This guarantees that a multimedia presentation deviates from the original presentation specification of the presentation designer only as long as system performance is insufficient.

- *Consideration of individual system properties* such that the system reacts optimized no matter if much or only little data delivery performance is lacking.

- *Consideration of user-preferences* which allows the user to influence the way insufficient system performance is handled by the system. This allows, e.g., that the user-specific sensitivity with respect to presentation deficiencies is reflected in the system's reaction.

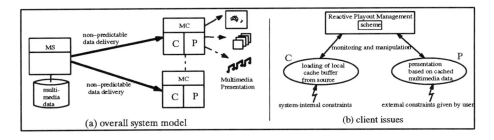

Figure 1   Illustration of underlying system model with receiver-controlled scheme for the handling of contradictory constraints

Our RAPM-scheme is tailored to client/server distributed multimedia database systems which parallel the system model portrayed in Figure 1a. The primary task of the *Media Server* (MS) is to persistently store a possibly large number of different time-based multimedia presentations (i.e., the artifacts specifying the multimedia presentation using, e.g., a scripting language as well as the involved media data) and to support multiple possibly simultaneously active *Multimedia Clients* (MC). Note that, for scaleability, the MS supports several alternative media qualities by redundantly storing the same data in different qualities (e.g., 16-bit and 8-bit audio, same video with different compression factors) or by supporting adequate transformation operations (e.g., one that transforms 24-bit color images into 8-bit grey-scale images) [19]. The data stored in the database is made accessible via non-predictable data availability.

The MCs provide generic playout management functionality for the realization of arbitrary multimedia presentations stored by the MS. In order to fulfil the temporal constraints of multimedia presentations, at presentation realization time, there are two asynchronous processes, C and P (Figure 1b). The *caching process* C manages the data needs of the MC. It prefetches the data to be presented from the MS in a timely manner. It loads proper consecutive data units or, with respect to discrete data, loads the data as a whole into the local cache. This can involve that, if performance becomes critical a lower data quality (e.g., 16-bit instead of 8-bit audio) than originally required is loaded from the MS. This also involves advanced buffer replacement strategies [28] as required due to the potentially large size of continuous data. The *presentation process* P deals with the actual presentation of the data to the user according to the presentation designer's specification. This involves the utilization of multimedia-specific presentation hardware (e.g., compression chips, speaker boxes) and software (e.g., MPEG player). Both, the loading and presentation processes themselves consist of multiple, potentially concurrent threads.

More precisely, the loading process consists of cache loading threads while the presentation process consists of presentation threads. These threads must be dynamically well coordinated with each other in order to satisfy the *external constraints* of multimedia presentations (e.g., synchronization constraints, timing constraints) considering the *system-internal constraints* (e.g., CPU-time of server, bandwidth of communication system). This is the crucial task of the reactive adaptive playout management to be performed by the MCs.

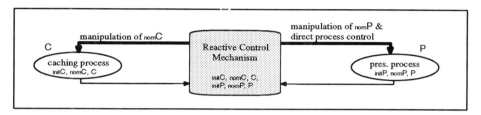

Figure 2   Adaptation model for reactive adaptive playout management

6.2   RAPM-Scheme

Our RAPM-scheme is especially tailored to dynamically bring into line the process C which makes the data available at the presentation machine and the presentation process P with the static external constraints (defined within the presentation specification) and the dynamically changing system-internal constraints. It is especially geared to handle contradictory external and system-internal constraints. These contradictions occur whenever system performance is insufficient.

The central component of our scheme is a *reactive control mechanism* which monitors, tunes and coordinates both processes C and P considering the external and internal constraints in a reactive self-regulating way. If necessary both processes are manipulated. Recall that, as explained previously, the caching process C consists of multiple possibly concurrent cache loading threads and the presentation process P consists of multiple possibly concurrent presentation threads. An abstract illustration of the reactive control mechanism is given in Figure 2 whereas Figure 3 provides a detailed illustration.

All executional units, our reactive control mechanism consists of, have access to comprehensive information about both processes and further information logged during the presentation realization phase.

Our RAPM-scheme dynamically generates and interprets *schedules of corrective actions*. This provides the required flexibility. Two types of schedules are differentiated. *Adaptation schedules* adapt the system behavior to insufficient system performance while *compensation schedules* compensate previous adaptations. Such schedules adapt the caching process and the presentation process by providing new nominal parameters ($nomC$ and $nomP$ in Figure 2). Since the generation of optimal schedules is a NP complete problem and due to the limited time available for the schedule generation, we use heuristic techniques assuming that they lead to a good approximation of the theoretical optimal schedules.

As shown in Figure 3, our RAPM-scheme can be partitioned into three consecutive phases. The first phase (1) is dedicated to the detection of parameter mismatches between nominal parameters ($nomC$ and $nomP$ in Figure 2) and actual parameters (C and P) as well as initial nominal parameters ($initC$ and $initP$) and actual nominal parameters ($nomC$ and $nomP$). The second phase (2) deals with the heuristics used to determine the adaptation strategy, i.e., the determination of new nominal parameters. The third phase (3) performs the generation and interpretation of the schedules.

In the remainder of this subsection, we first define the parameters relevant for our scheme and then detail each of the three mentioned phases.

Parameters

A stored multimedia presentation can be described more formally as a set of component media presentations as follows:

■   A stored multimedia presentation is a finite set $M \in \mathcal{M}$ of L component media presentations,

$$M = \left\{ (i, type_i, R_i, E_i) | i = 1...L, E_i = \left\{ e_i^k | e_i^k \in \mathbb{R}_0^+, k = 1...N_i \right\} \right\} \quad (12.1)$$

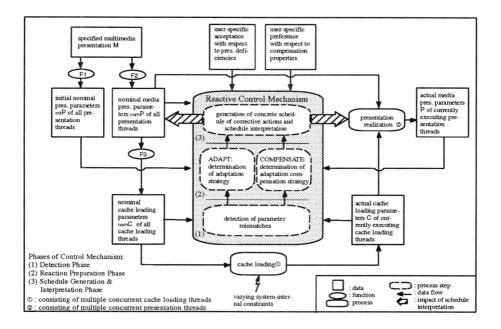

Figure 3   Proposed RAPM-scheme in details

where i .... denotes a component media presentation;

$type_i$ ... is the type of media presentation i identifying clearly the media type (e.g., *text, picture, audio, video*) and the encoding of the media data (e.g., *ASCII, GIF, M-JPEG, MPEG*, etc.) using, e.g., a look-up table;

R_i ..... a finite set of temporal relationships, such as *starts, overlaps, ends*, etc., media presentation i is participating in;

E_i ..... a finite set of media type specific explicitly defined external presentation constraints such as *data rate, data quality*, etc.;

N_i ..... denotes the number of external constraints for media type $type_i$.The number varies for different media types since some constraints are only relevant for some specific media types and irrelevant for others (e.g., color depth).

From this type of specifications, all cache loading and presentation threads to be performed at presentation realization-time can be deduced prior to the actual start of the entire multimedia presentation. This includes, for each thread, timing information (i.e., the relative point in time the thread must start and the relative point in time it must have completed its task) and relevant runtime constraints (e.g., frame rate with respect to video). Hence, we assume that for all cache loading threads, a respective set of nominal cache loading parameters and for all presentation threads a respective set of nominal presentation parameters providing these information is available prior to the presentation realization. Note that, these nominal parameters are the requirements to be managed by the caching and the presentation processes. If external and system-internal constraints do not become contradictory during the presentation realization, then these requirements are accurately satisfied. That is, the actual cache loading and presentation parameters describing how the currently active cache loading and presentation threads actually perform match the corresponding nominal parameters. However, due to the nature of our underlying system model, deviations are likely to occur. Our reactive control mechanism is a means to cope with such deviations in an optimized way. Let us now define the framework for the parameters used in our scheme (Figure 3) in detail:

■ A finite set $initP \in initP$ of *initial nominal presentation parameters* for all (i.e., L) presentation threads,

$$initP \quad = \quad \{(t_i^s, t_i^p, \ initp_{i,l}^{g_i}, \ initp_i^{g_i}, \ initp_{i,u}^{g_i})|t_i^s, t_i^p \in \mathcal{T}, \ initp_{i,l}^{g_i}, \ initp_i^{g_i},$$

$$initp_{i,u}^{g_i} \in I\!R_0^+, \ initp_{i,l}^{g_i} \leq initp_i^{g_i} \leq initp_{i,u}^{g_i}, i = 1...L,$$
$$g_i = 1...Q_i, Q_i \in I\!N\} \tag{12.2}$$

where t_i^s ..... relative point $t_i^s \in \mathcal{T}$ in time media presentation i must start;

t_i^P .... relative point $t_i^P \in \mathcal{T}$ in time media presentation i must be completed;

$initp_i^{g_i}$ initial nominal value of a presentation parameter g_i of media presentation i such as *data quality* (e.g., 16-bit or 8-bit audio), *frame rate*;

$initp_{i,l}^{g_i}$ lower bound of $initp_i^{g_i}$;

$initp_{i,u}^{g_i}$ upper bound of $initp_i^{g_i}$;

Q_i .... number of presentation parameters for media presentation i with media type $type_i$.

- A finite set $nomP \in nom\mathcal{P}$ of *nominal presentation parameters* for all (i.e., L) presentation threads,

$$nomP = \{(t_i^s, t_i^P, \ nomp_i^{g_i})|t_i^s, t_i^P \in \mathcal{T}, \ nomp_i^{g_i} \in I\!R_0^+, i = 1...L, g_i = 1...Q_i,$$
$$Q_i \in I\!N\} \tag{12.3}$$

where $(t_i^s, t_i^P, \ nomp_i^{g_i}) \in nomP$ corresponds to $(t_i^s, t_i^P, \ initp_j^{h_j})$ in $(t_i^s, t_i^P, \ initp_{i,l}^{g_i},$ $initp_i^{g_i}, \ initp_{i,u}^{g_i}) \in initP, g_i = h_j, i = j$.

- A tuple $nomC \in nom\mathcal{C}$ of *nominal cache loading parameters* for all (i.e., L) cache loading threads,

$$nomC = ((t_1^s, t_1^P, \ nomc_1^1, \ nomc_1^2, ..., \ nomc_1^{K_1}, \ nomv_1), (t_2^s, t_2^P, \ nomc_2^1,$$
$$nomc_2^2, ..., \ nomc_2^{K_2}, \ nomv_2), ..., (t_R^s, t_R^P, \ nomc_R^1, \ nomc_R^2, ...,$$
$$nomc_R^{K_R}, \ nomv_R), (t_{R+1}^s, t_{R+1}^P, \ nomc_{R+1}^1, \ nomc_{R+1}^2, ...,$$
$$nomc_{R+1}^{K_R+1}), (t_{R+2}^s, t_{R+2}^P, \ nomc_{R+2}^1, \ nomc_{R+2}^2, ..., \ nomc_{R+2}^{K_R+2}),$$
$$...(t_L^s, t_L^P, \ nomc_L^1, \ nomc_L^2, ..., \ nomc_L^{K_L})) \tag{12.4}$$

with $t_i^s, t_i^P \in \mathcal{T}$, $nomc_i^{g_i} \in I\!R_0^+$, $nomv_i \in I\!N_0, g_i = 1...K_i, K_i \in I\!N$ and for $i = 1...R, type_i$ are *continuous* media types and for $i = R+1...L, type_i$ are *discrete* media types,

where t_i^s ..... relative point $t_i^s \in \mathcal{T}$ in time the cache loading thread
for media presentation i must start;

t_i^P .... relative point $t_i^P \in \mathcal{T}$ in time the cache loading thread
for media presentation i must be completed;

$nomc_i^{g_i}$ nominal value of a specific cache loading parameter
g_i of media presentation i such as *data rate*;

$nomv_i$ nominal cache savety level for the respective component *continuous* media i specifying the amount of locally cached consecutive data units to be maintained
while component media presentation i is realized;

K_i .... number of cache loading parameters for the respective component media presentation i with type $type_i$.

- The list $nomV$ of *nominal cache savety levels* $nomv_i$, $i = 1...R$, contained
in the tuple $nomC$.

- A tuple $C \in \mathcal{C}$ of *actual cache loading parameters* which reflect the characteristics of the executing cache loading threads at a certain point in time
during the presentation realization,

$$
\begin{aligned}
C \quad = \quad &((c_1^1, c_1^2, ..., c_1^{K_1}, v_1), (c_2^1, c_2^2, ..., c_2^{K_2}, v_2), ..., (c_R^1, c_R^2, ..., c_R^{K_R}, v_R), \\
&(c_{R+1}^1, c_{R+1}^2, ..., c_{R+1}^{K_R+1}), (c_{R+2}^1, c_{R+2}^2, ..., c_{R+2}^{K_R+2}), ..., \\
&(c_L^1, c_L^2, ..., c_L^{K_L})) \quad\quad\quad\quad\quad\quad\quad\quad\quad\quad\quad\quad\quad (12.5)
\end{aligned}
$$

where each $c_i^{g_i}$ contained in C corresponds to the $nomc_j^{h_j}$ contained in
$nomC$ with $g_i = h_j$ and $i = j$, and each v_i contained in C corresponds to
$nomv_j$ contained in $nomC$ with $i = j$.

- The list V of *actual cache savety levels* v_i, $i = 1...R$, contained in the tuple
C.

- A finite set $P \in \mathcal{P}$ of actual presentation parameters which reflect the
characteristics of the executing presentation threads at a certain point in
time during the presentation realization,

$$
P \quad = \quad \{p_i^{g_i} | p_i^{g_i} \in \mathbb{R}_0^+, i = 1...L, g_i = 1...Q_i, Q_i \in \mathbb{N}\} \quad (12.6)
$$

where $p_i^{g_i} \in P$ corresponds to $nomp_j^{h_j} \in nomP$ for $g_i = h_j$ and $i = j$.

- Function $F_1 : \mathcal{M} \rightarrow \text{init}\mathcal{P}$
computes all initial nominal presentation parameter values from the information given in the specification M prior to the presentation realization.

- Function $F_2 : \mathcal{M} \rightarrow \text{nom}\mathcal{P}$
  computes all nominal presentation parameter values from the information given in the specification M prior to the presentation realization.

- Function $F_3 : \text{nom}\mathcal{P} \rightarrow \text{nom}\mathcal{C}$
  computes all nominal cache loading parameter values from the set of nominal presentation parameter values $nomP$ prior and during the presentation realization whenever $nomP$ is altered.

Note that, the concrete values of the actual media presentation parameters P are dependent on the presentation process which itself is determined by the nominal media presentation parameters $nomP$ and the actual cache loading parameters C. Especially the actual cache savety levels V play an important role. For example, if there is not enough data cached, i.e., an actual cache savety level v_i is too low, then a decrease of a respective c_i^g contained in C (e.g., *data rate*) can imply a decrease of the corresponding actual presentation parameter $p_i^g \in P$.

Examples of Parameters
In order to show how the parameters of our framework look like, we assume a sample multimedia presentation M which consists of two videos, an audio, a picture and some text. Timing information is not relevant for this purpose. Table 1 summarizes nominal presentation parameters $nomp_i^{gi}$ together with respective values. As explained in the previous section, from these parameters, the nominal cache loading parameters $nomc_i^{gi}$ are deduced. Table 2 shows some of these parameters together with respective parameter values.

Note that, each additional presentation and cache loading parameter that we will discover via intensive evaluation studies of our RAPM-scheme will be included in the respective set of potential parameters.

Detection of Mismatches

Mismatch detection in our control mechanism (indicated as (1) *Detection Phase* in Figure 3) has the overall goal to monitor the system behavior during the realization of a multimedia presentation and to trigger the execution of the subsequent second and third phase when necessary.

initP, *nomP*, and *nomC* defined in the previous section reflect external constraints expressing the performance behavior required to realize the multimedia presentation exactly as it has been defined by the presentation designer, i.e.,

media pres. i	$type_i$	$nomp_i^1$	$nomp_i^2$	$nomp_i^3$	$nomp_i^4$	$nomp_i^5$	$nomp_i^6$
1	video (M-JPEG)	frame rate: 25 frames/sec.	frame size: 160 × 120	color depth: 8 bit/pixel	max. dropped frames: 3 frames/sec.	compression fact.: 30 %	inter-media synch. qual.: medium
2	video (MPEG-1)	frame rate: 30 frames/sec.	frame size: 352 × 240	color depth: 8 bit/pixel	inter-media synch. qual.: medium		
3	audio (CD-quality)	sample size: 16 bit/sample	play-back speed: 1.0	inter-media synch. qual.: medium			
4	picture (GIF)	resolution: 300 × 200	color depth: 24 bit/pixel	max. pres. delay: 2 sec.			
5	text (ASCII)	max. pres. delay: 2 sec.					

Table 1 Presentation parameters of a concrete multimedia presentation (L=5, Q_1=6, Q_2=4, Q_3=3, Q_4=3, Q_5=1).

fulfillment of all external constraints. The parameter sets C and P characterize the system's actual performance capacity at a certain point in time which can be lower than the required one. Such contradictions between *required* and *actual* performance can be described as *cache loading parameter mismatches* which are either *critical* or *non-critical*, i.e., tolerable[1]:

---

[1] Note that, tolerable cache loading parameter mismatches can become critical ones very quickly.

media pres. i	$type_i$	$nomv_i$	$nomc_i^1$	$nomc_i^2$	$nomc_i^3$
1	video (M-JPEG)	cache savety level: 50 frames	data rate: 2.300.000 Bit/sec.	max. dropped frames: 3 frames/sec.	intermedia synch. qual.: medium
2	video (MPEG-1)	cache savety level: 60 frames	data rate: 1.500.000 Bit/sec.	intermedia synch. qual.: medium	
3	audio (CD-quality)	cache savety level: 2 seconds of audio data	data rate: 1.411.200 Bit/sec.	playback speed: 1.0	intermedia synch. qual.: medium
4	picture (GIF)		max. pres. delay: 2 sec.		
5	text (ASCII)		max. pres. delay: 2 sec.		

Table 2 Cache loading parameters of a concrete multimedia presentation (L=5, R=3, K_1=3, K_2=2, K_3=3, K_4=1, K_5=1).

- *tolerable cache loading parameter mismatch:*
  $tol\_caching\_mismatch(C,\ nomC) =$
  $\exists i, g : c_i^g \leq\ nomc_i^g \wedge \forall j : v_j \geq\ nomv_j,$
  c_i^g, v_j contained in C, $nomc_i^g$, $nomv_j$ contained in $nomC$.

  Explanation: As long as all actual cache savety levels are greater than or equal to their corresponding nominal cache savety levels, decreased actual cache loading parameters are tolerated.

- *critical cache loading parameters mismatch:*
  $crit\_caching\_mismatch(C,\ nomC) =$
  $\exists i, g : c_i^g \leq\ nomc_i^g \wedge \exists j : v_j \leq\ nomv_j,$
  c_i^g, v_j contained in C, $nomc_i^g$, $nomv_j$ contained in $nomC$.

  Explanation: If actual cache loading parameter values are lower than their nominal parameter values and there are actual cache savety levels which are too low, then there exists a critical cache loading parameters mismatch. The occurence of a critical cache loading parameter mismatch means that it can be anticipated with a high certainty that the presentation process will run out of data in case nominal parameter values are not changed.

In case of a tolerable caching mismatch, it is possible that the system recovers by itself. That is, the system regains the necessary performance behavior resolving the mismatch. Otherwise, the tolerable mismatch implies a critical caching mismatch at some later point in time. In case such a critical cache loading parameters mismatch is detected, the need for an appropriate reaction is identified. Hence, one rule for detecting the need to react to contradictory constraints is simply:

Detection Rule R_1:
If $crit\_caching\_mismatch(C, nomC)$ then ADAPT.

If at some point in time detection rule R_1 fires, according to our RAPM-scheme, a reaction intended to prevent that the presentation process runs out of data is performed[2]. As shown later on, this reaction consists of adaptations performed on the current set of nominal presentation parameters $nomP$. Adaptations cause intentional mismatches between these presentation parameters $nomP$ and the originally required (initial) set of presentation parameters $initP$. Furthermore, adaptations can lead to interrupted media presentations (i.e., interrupted presentation threads) which actually should run according to the timing information given in $nomP$. Both types of mismatches can be defined more formally as follows:

- *intentional presentation parameter mismatch:*
  $int\_pres\_parameter\_mismatch(nomP, initP) =$
  $\exists i, g : nomp_i^g \leq initp_i^g,$
  $nomp_i^g$ contained in $nomP$, $initp_i^g$ in $(initp_{i,l}^g, initp_i^g,$
  $initp_{i,u}^g) \in initP.$

  Explanation: If nominal presentation parameter values are lower than the initial nominal presentation parameters values, then there exists an intentional presentation parameters mismatch.

- *intentional presentation structure mismatch:*
  $int\_pres\_structure\_mismatch(initP, P) = \exists i, t : state\_dev(i, t),$

---

[2]Note that, due to the cache savety level, this reaction is performed in advance of the theoretical point in time at which the presentation process would run out of data.

where $state\_dev(i, t)$ is a function that evaluates if media i is interrupted at a point $t \in \mathcal{T}$ in time at which it actually should run according to the timing information given in $initP$, i.e., if the actual state deviates from the initially required one.

Explanation: If media presentations are interrupted at a certain point in time at which they actually should run, then there exists an intentional presentation structure mismatch.

In general, these types of intentional mismatches should be restricted to those periods of time in which the system does not perform sufficiently. Hence, they must be resolved when system performance becomes sufficient (again), i.e., whenever there is no longer neither a tolerated nor a critical caching mismatch. That is, the adaptations performed so far have to be adequately compensated. The rule for detecting such points in time is as follows:

Detection Rule R_2:
If $\neg tol\_caching\_mismatch(C, nomC)$ AND $\neg crit\_caching\_mismatch(C, nomC)$
AND ($int\_pres\_parameter\_mismatch(nomP, initP)$ OR
$int\_pres\_structure\_mismatch(initP, P)$) then COMPENSATE.

Note that, tolerated caching mismatches can become critical ones very quickly. Thus, in order to prevent compensations while a tolerated mismatch becomes a critical one, rule $R2$ allows compensations only when there is also no tolerated caching mismatch.

Heuristic Reaction Preparation

The goal of heuristic reaction preparation in our reactive control mechanism (indicated as (2) *Reaction Preparation Phase* in Figure 3) is to prepare a system reaction in case one of the detection rules explained above fires. More clearly, it is targeted at selecting an *adaptation or compensation strategy* which is appropriate to handle the situation the system is facing. A comprehensive analysis to heuristically identify how the system must react is performed considering all relevant parameters. Independent from the type of rule fired, the primary goals of this analysis are:

- to acquire knowledge about the quantitative level of the mismatch at hand by evaluating the relevant pairs of mismatching parameters,

- to predict the performance profile required by the running multimedia presentation for the next period of time by evaluating all nominal parameter values,

- to acquire knowledge about the sensitivity of the respective component media presentations with respect to certain manipulations (e.g., non-speech audio presentations, e.g. music, are less sensitive with respect to presentation speed manipulations than speech audio presentations) by evaluating the range of tolerance of the respective initial nominal parameter values.

Presentation Deficiency	Weight
(1) interruptions	0.0
(2) variating global pres. speed	0.0
(3) asynchrony	0.8
(4) down-scaled data quality	1.0
(5) down-scaled pres. complexity	1.0

Table 3   Declaration of user-specific acceptance with respect to presentation deficiencies. Weight is a value out of the interval [0.0, 1.0] where 0.0 means not accepted at all and 1.0 means accepted.

Compensation Property	Weight
(1) min. compensation duration	1.0
(2) min. noticeability	0.0
(3) prioritized upscaling of pres. complexity	1.0
(4) prioritized upscaling of data quality	0.0

Table 4   Declaration of user-specific preferences with respect to compensation properties. Weight is a value out of the interval [0.0, 1.0] where 0.0 means not preferred and 1.0 means highly preferred.

In addition to the result of the analysis, user-specific preferences are considered. For adaptations (i.e., rule R_1 fired), *weighted presentation deficiencies* (Table 3) expressing the user's individual level of acceptance with respect to given presentation deficiencies are considered. For compensations (i.e., rule R_2 fired), *weighted compensation properties* (Table 4) expressing the user's individual preferences with respect to given compensation properties are considered. Using a proper heuristic, based on this information, an appropriate strategy is selected. In our context, a strategy, in general, defines the requirements to be fulfilled by the *individualized adaptation or compensation schedule* to be generated in the next phase. Up to now, we are taking the following set (which needs to be extended in the future) of *schedule requirements* for both, adaptation and compensation schedules, into consideration:

- *Single-step vs. multiple-steps.* While the execution of a single-step schedule is restricted to a single point in time, a multiple-steps schedule involves multiple points in time. Single-step schedules are usually more appropriate for quantitative low-level parameter mismatches, while for large quantitative parameter mismatches schedules consisting of multiple steps are usually more appropriate. With respect to compensation, if a short compensation duration is preferred, then a single-step schedule is usually superior.

- *Unconditional vs. conditional.* These properties are only relevant for schedules consisting of multiple steps. The difference between both properties is, that only a conditional schedule involves the consideration of future values of some cache loading parameters at schedule execution time. Unconditional multiple-steps schedules are usually sufficient when significant performance deviations throughout the schedule execution are not expected. Otherwise, conditional multiple-steps schedules are more appropriate.

Generation and Interpretation of Adaptation and Compensation Schedules

In this phase of our reactive control mechanism (indicated as (3) *Schedule Generation & Interpretation Phase* in Figure 3) considering the schedule requirements determined in the preceding phase, a *heuristically* optimized adaptation [3] or compensation schedule consisting of *corrective actions* is generated and subsequently interpreted. So far, for the generation of these schedules, we are taking into account the following set of primitives:

- *Corrective actions.* It is differentiated between:

---

[3] A comprehensive discussion of how to optimize the selection of deviations from a given presentation specification to prepare the generation of an adaptation schedule is presented in [44].

- *presentation parameter alterations* which alter some data qualities and/or data rates given as values of respective presentation parameters $nomp_i^{gi}$ contained in $nomP$ considering the parameter boundaries defined in $nomP$,

- *presentation interruptions* which pause all running media presentations,

- *presentation structure downscale actions* which pause specific currently running media presentations,

- *presentation upscale actions* which have the effect that pausing media presentations continue with their execution.

- *Timers.* A timer is a primitive for the specification of multiple-steps schedules delaying the execution of the next directive in a sequential schedule for a given period of time. In other words, timers allow to control the minimal distance in time between the execution of consecutive schedule directives.

- *Statements for Conditional Branching.* These statements provide a means to make the execution of corrective actions dependent on the actual cache loading parameter values. When such a condition is interpreted, the actual values of the respective cache loading parameters are queried at that point in time.

```
begin_adaptation_schedule;
pres_parameter_alteration(pres. param. val.);
timer(integer value);
switch (cache loading param.) {
case (condition involving cache loading param.):
   pres_parameter_alteration(pres. param. val.);
case (condition involving cache loading param.):
   pres_struct_downscale(media pres.);
case (condition involving cache loading param.):
   pres_interrupt(integer value);
}
timer(integer value);
switch (...)

end_adaptation_schedule.
```
(a) schedule for an adaptation

```
begin_compensation_schedule;
pres_parameter_alteration(pres. param. val.);
timer(integer value);
pres_parameter_alteration(pres. param. val.);
timer(integer value);
pres_parameter_alteration(pres. param. val.);
end_compensation_schedule.
```

Note that, this schedule compensates previous presentation parameter adaptations in three steps. The target parameter values can be achieved by, e.g., constantly, degressively, or progressively increased parameter values.

(b) schedule for a compensation

Figure 4   Skeletons of sample schedules

Using these primitives, optimized adaptation and compensation schedules can be heuristically generated. Figure 4 shows the skeletons of two sample schedules using a syntax similar to a procedural programming language. Note that, via conditional branching, these primitives allow to integrate *feedback loops* into a concrete schedule. The advantage of this is, that the unpredictability of the changing performance capacity can be better handled since the schedule interpretation can be dynamically adapted to the potential changes in the performance capacity occurring simultaneously to schedule interpretations. This also allows to evaluate the effectiveness of previous corrective actions.

Concerning the heuristic generation of optimized schedules, the user-specific preferences (Table 3 and 4) are considered again. An adaptation schedule is considered well optimized if it influences the effects resulting from the lacking system performance such that the low accepted presentation deficiencies are minimized considering the performance profile predicted for some future periods of time. That is, the schedule makes the system putting more effort in preventing non-tolerated presentation deficiencies. A compensation schedule is considered well optimized, if it leads to a compensation of all relevant previous adaptations such that the weighted compensation properties exemplarily shown in Table 4 are accurately reflected.

7 CONCLUSION

Multimedia playout management, subsumes all those tasks necesarry to perform a multimedia presentation according to a given specification (e.g., multimedia/hypermedia document specification, presentation script). Typically, the presentations are specified/preorchestrated for replicated execution by many (possibly simultaneous) users. Many data management issues to be encountered in the development of a respective system such as the sharing of the multimedia data, data persistency, maintenance, versioning, and the user administration, can be easily solved by employing a multimedia database management system. This provides significant ease to the development task. However, it also brings up the question of how to organize the playout management within a multimedia database systems. Different approaches are possible. We propose that the playout management should be performed by the multimedia database management system by a dedicated integrated system service. That is, the system provides, in analogy to, e.g., physical data independency, "playout management independency" too. We regard this as a natural adjustment of database management system technology to the new requirements of multimedia data and application domains. The fundamental goal of this new idea is the provision of a database management system integrated playout management service which supports standards for presentation specification languages (e.g., ScriptX [47] and PREMO [17]) as well as multimedia documents (e.g., SGML/HyTime [18]). However, it must not be seen as just an extension of the database management system functionality. The necessary playout management task involving data stored in a multimedia database can be done much more efficiently. Other database management system internal components (especially further novel ones required by multimedia data such as a continuous object management service [28]) can benefit from data acquired throughout the task completion. To give an example for how the suggested integrated playout management service can be realized, we presented the AMOS multimedia database management system under development at GMD-IPSI. We especially focused on the components which realize the playout management service of AMOS and their integration with other components. Furthermore, we showed the openness of the AMOS playout management service with respect to application-specific demands.

For distributed multimedia database systems *both*, predictable data availability based on the use of realtime technologies and non-predictable data availability must be considered as data delivery means. Henceforth, a main issue of playout management in distributed multimedia database systems is to provide solutions for both types of data delivery means. In contrast to the use of predictable data availability, only little experience in using non-predictable data availability for distributed multimedia database systems is available. Reactive adaptive playout management is a contribution to overcome this gap. We introduced reactive adaptive playout management as a general concept for distributed multimedia database systems. Furthermore, we showed a concrete scheme for reactive adaptive playout management which can very flexibly handle the different system properties and user preferences by individualized adaptation and compensation schedules. We will use this scheme to make the AMOS playout management service a reactive adaptive playout management service.

To summarize, at the very beginning of research on multimedia database systems, playout management was not considered to be a crucial issue for a multimedia database management system. As more and more experience with real applications of multimedia database systems becomes available, there arises the requirement for database management system support in conjunction with a means for playout management. Motivation, issues and concrete solutions with respect to playout management in multimedia database systems and especially distributed multimedia database systems have been provided in this paper.

REFERENCES

[1] Aberer, K., Klas, W.: "Supporting Temporal Multimedia Operations in Object Oriented Database Systems'", Proc. of IEEE Multimedia Computing and Systems, Boston, USA, May 1994, pp. 352–361

[2] Aberer, K., Fischer, G.: "Semantic Query Optimization for Methods in Object Oriented Database Systems", Proc. of the 11th Int. Conf. on Data Engineering, Taipei, Taiwan, March 1995, pp. 70–79

[3] Anderson, D.P., Homsy, G.: "A Continuous Media I/O Server and Its Synchronization Mechanism", IEEE Computer, October 1991, pp. 51–57

[4] Anderson, D.P.: "Meta Scheduling for Distributed Continuous Media", Report No. UCB/CSD 90/599, Computer Science Division, University of California Berkeley, October 1990

[5] Berra, B., Chen, C.Y.R., Ghafoor, A., Lin, C.C., Little, T.D.C., Shin, D.: "Architectures for distributed multimedia database systems", computer communications, Vol. 13, No. 4, May 1990, pp. 217-231

[6] Berners-Lee, T., et al.: "World-Wide Web: The Information Universe", Electronic Networking, Vol. 2, No. 1, Spring 1992, pp. 52–58

[7] Biliris, A., Panagos, E.: "EOS: An Extensible Object Store", Proc. of the 1994 ACM SIGMOD, Minneapolis, USA, May 1994, p. 517

[8] Blakowski, G., Hübel, J., Langwehr, U.: "Tools for Specifying and Executing Synchronized Multimedia Presentations", Network and Operating System Support for Digital Audio and Video, 2nd Int. Workshop, Heidelberg, Germany, Springer, November 1991, pp. 271–281

[9] Campbell, A., Coulson, G., Garcia, F., Hutchison, D.A.: "A Continuous Media Transport and Orchestration Service", Proc. SIGCOMM '92, 1992, pp. 391–400

[10] Cen, S., Pu, C., Staehli, R., Cowan, C., Walpole, J.: "A Distributed Real-Time MPEG Video Audio Player", Proc. of the Fifth International Workshop on Network and Operating System Support of Digital Audio and Video (NOSSDAV'95), April 1995, Durham, NH, USA

[11] Chou, S. T.C., Tokuda, H.:"System Support for Dynamic QOS Control of Continuous Media Communication", Proc. of the Third Int. Workshop on Network and Operating System Support for Digital Audio and Video, La Jolla, Ca., USA, November 1992, Springer LNCS 712, pp. 363–368

[12] Christodoulakis, S., Ho, F., Theodoridou, M.: "The Multimedia Object Presentation Manager of MINOS: A Symmetric Approach", Proc. Int. Conf. on Management of Data, Washington, 1986, pp. 295–310

[13] Delgrossi, L., et al.: "Media Scaling in a Multimedia Communication System", Proc. of the First ACM Multimedia Conference, Anaheim, Ca., USA, August, 1993, pp. 99–104

[14] Ehley, L., Furht, B., Ilyas, M.: "Evaluation of Multimedia Synchronization Techniques", Proc. IEEE Int. Conf. on Multimedia Computing and Systems, Boston, May, 1994, pp. 514–519

[15] Gibbs, S.: "Composite Multimedia and Active Objects", Proc. of the ACM OOPSLA '91, Phoenix, AZ, October 1991, pp. 97–112

[16] Hamblin, C.L.: "Instants and Intervals", in J.T. Fraser, et al. (Ed), Proc. of the 1st Conf. of the Int. Society for the Study of Time, Springer Verlag 1972, pp. 324–331

[17] Herman, I., et al.: "PREMO: An ISO Standard for a Presentation Environment for Multimedia Objects", Proc. ACM Multimedia 1994, San Francisco, Ca., USA, October 1994, pp. 111–118

[18] ISO/IEC Information Processing, Hypermedia Time based Structuring Language (HyTime), International Standard 10744, 1992

[19] Käppner, T., Wolf, L.C.:"Media Scaling in Distributed Multimedia Object Services", Proc. of the Second Int. Workshop Multimedia: Advanced Teleservices and High Speed Communication Architectures, Heidelberg, Germany, September 1994, Springer LNCS 868, pp. 34–43

[20] Katseff, H.P., Robinson, B.S.: "Predictive Prefetch in the Nemesis Multimedia Information Service", Proc. of the ACM Multimedia 94, San Francisco, Ca., USA, October 1994, pp. 201–209

[21] Klas, W.:"Tailoring an Object Oriented Database System to Integrate External Multimedia Devices", Int. Workshop on Heterogeneous Databases and Semantic Interoperability, Boulder, USA, February 1992

[22] Klas, W., Aberer, K., Neuhold, E.J.: "Object Oriented Modeling for Hypermedia Systems using the VODAK Modeling Language (VML)", Object Oriented Database Management Systems, NATO ASI Series, Springer Verlag Berlin Heidelberg, August 1993

[23] Koegel, J.F., Rutledge, L.W., Rutledge, J.L., Keskin, C.:"HyOctane: A HyTime Engine for an MMIS", Proc. ACM Multimedia, August 1993, Anaheim, CA, USA, pp. 129–136

[24] Little, T.D.C., Ghafoor, A.: "Synchronization and Storage Models for Multimedia Objects", IEEE J. on Selected Areas in Comm., Vol. 8, No. 3, April 1990, pp. 413–427

[25] Little, T.D.C., Ghafoor, A.:"Scheduling of bandwidth constrained multimedia traffic", in Computer Communications, Vol. 15 No. 6, July/August 1992, Butterworth Heinemann Ltd., pp. 381–387

[26] Little, T.D.C.:"A Framework for Synchronous Delivery of Time Dependent Multimedia Data", in Multimedia Systems, Vol. 1, No. 2, 1993, pp. 87–94

[27] Meyer–Wegener, K.: "Multimedia–Databases", in German, B.G. Teubner Stuttgart, 1991

[28] Moser, F., Kraiss, A., Klas, W.: "L/MRP: A Buffer Management Strategy for Interactive Continuous Data Flows in a Multimedia Database Management System", Proc. of the VLDB '95, Zürich, Switzerland, September 1995

[29] Nakajma, T., Tezuka, H.: "A Continuous Media Application Supporting Dynamic QOS Control on Real Time Mach", Proc. of the ACM Multimedia 94, San Francisco, Ca., USA, October 1994, pp. 289–297

[30] Price, R.: "MHEG: An Introduction to the future International Standard for Hypermedia Object Interchange", Proc. ACM Multimedia 93, Ca., USA, June 1993, pp. 121–128

[31] Qazi, N., Woo M., Ghafoor, A.:"A Synchronization and Communication Model for Distributed Multimedia Objects", ACM Multimedia, August 1993, Anaheim, CA, USA, pp. 147–155

[32] Rakow, T.C., Muth, P.: "The Video Server - Managing Analog and Digital Video Clips", Proceedings ACM SIGMOD '93 Conference, Washington DC, May 1993, pp. 556–557

[33] Rakow, T., Löhr, M., Neuhold, E.J.:"Multimedia Databases The Notions and the Issues", GI Fachtagung Datenbanksysteme in Büro, Technik und Wissenschaft BTW 95, Dresden, Germany, March 1995, Springer, pp. 1–29

[34] Ramanathan, S., Rangan, P.V.: "Adaptive Feedback Techniques for Synchronized Multimedia Retrieval over Integrated Networks", IEEE/ACM Transactions on Networking, Vol. 1, No. 2, April 1993, pp. 246–260

[35] Staehli, R., Walpole, J., Maier, D.: "Quality of Service Specifications for Multimedia Presentations", to appear in Multimedia Systems , August 1995

[36] Steinmetz, R.: "Synchronization Properties in Multimedia Systems", IEEE Journal on Selected Areas in Communications, Vol.8, No. 3, April 1990, pp. 401–412

[37] Steinmetz, R., Engler, C.: "Human Perception of Media Synchronization", IBM European Networking Center, Technical Report 43.9310, 1993

[38] Thimm, H., Rakow, T.C.: "Upgrading Multimedia Data Handling Services of a Database Management System by an Interaction Manager", Arbeitspapiere der GMD No. 762, St. Augustin, July 1993

[39] Thimm, H., Rakow, T.C.: "A DBMS Based Multimedia Archiving Teleservice Incorporating Mail", Proc. of the 1st Int. Conf. on Applications of Databases, Vadstena, Sweden, June 1994, Springer LNCS 819, pp. 281–298

[40] Thimm, H.: "A Multimedia Enhanced CSCW Teleservice for Wide Area Cooperative Authoring of Multimedia Documents", ACM CSCW'94 WS on Distributed Systems, Multimedia, and Infrastructure Support in CSCW, Chapel Hill, NC, USA, October 1994, ACM SIGOIS Bulletin, December 1994, Vol. 15, No.2, pp. 49–57

[41] Thimm, H., Roehr, K., Rakow, T.C.: "A Mail Based Teleservice Architecture for Archiving and Retrieving Dynamically Composable Multimedia Documents", Proc. of the Int. COST 237 Workshop, Multimedia Transport and Teleservices, Vienna, Austria, November 1994, Springer LNCS 882, pp. 14–34

[42] Thimm, H., Klas, W.: "Playout Management - An Integrated Service of a Multimedia Database Management System", Int. WS on Multimedia Database Management Systems, Blue Mountain Lake, NY, August 1995, IEEE Computer Society Press, pp. 38–47

[43] Thimm, H., Klas, W.: "Reactive Playout Management - Adapting Multimedia Presentations to Contradictory Constraints", Arbeitspapiere der GMD No. 916, St. Augustin, May 1995

[44] Thimm, H., Klas, W.: "δ-Sets for Optimized Reactive Adaptive Playout Management in Distributed Multimedia Database Systems", Arbeitspapiere der GMD No. 924, St. Augustin, July 1995

INDEX